The Abilities and Achievements
of Orientals in North America

This is a volume in

PERSONALITY AND PSYCHOPATHOLOGY
A Series of Monographs, Texts, and Treatises

Under the Editorship of David T. Lykken

A complete list of titles in this series appears at the end of this volume.

The Abilities and Achievements of Orientals in North America

Philip E. Vernon

Department of Educational Psychology
The University of Calgary
Calgary, Alberta, Canada

1982

ACADEMIC PRESS

A Subsidiary of Harcourt Brace Jovanovich, Publishers
New York   London
Paris   San Diego   San Francisco   São Paulo   Sydney   Tokyo   Toronto

ACADEMIC PRESS, INC.
111 Fifth Avenue, New York, New York 10003

United Kingdom Edition published by
ACADEMIC PRESS, INC. (LONDON) LTD.
24/28 Oval Road, London NW1 7DX

Library of Congress Cataloging in Publication Data

Vernon, Philip Ewart.
    The abilities and achievements of Orientals in
North America.

    (Personality and psychopathology)
    Bibliography: p.
    Includes index.
    1. Chinese Americans--Ability testing. 2. Japanese
Americans--Ability testing. 3. National characteristics,
Chinese. 4. National characteristics, Japanese.
I. Title. II. Series.
BF432.C5V47   155.8'495073   82-1700
ISBN 0-12-718680-8   AACR2

PRINTED IN THE UNITED STATES OF AMERICA

82 83 84 85   9 8 7 6 5 4 3 2 1

Contents

4. Japanese Culture, Childrearing, and Personality

5. Tests of Japanese Children

6. Oriental Immigration to Hawaii

7. Tests of Children and Students in Hawaii

8. Chinese and Japanese Immigrants to Canada

15. Japanese Attitudes, Values, and Interests

16. Personality Studies of Chinese

17. Epilogue   271

Preface

The experiences of oriental immigrants in the United States and Canada—Chinese and Japanese—provide a remarkable example of adverse environment *not* affecting the development of intelligence. There is no doubt that, in the past, they were subjected to great hardships, hostility, and discrimination. They were regarded as a kind of inferior species, who could be used for unskilled labor and menial jobs, but could never be accepted as equals into the white community. And yet the Orientals survived and eventually flourished until they came to be regarded as even higher achievers, educationally and vocationally, than the white majority.

Though these facts are well established, no psychologist seems to have pulled together all the literature concerned with the abilities, achievements, and personality characteristics of oriental immigrants and their descendants. When I started to search, I found that there were far more relevant books and articles than I had expected. This book, then, aims to summarize as much as possible the published material, to relate it to the cultural background from which the immigrants came and to their checkered history in North America (including Hawaii and Canada), and to discover the implications, if any, for psychological theory. It contains no startling new conclusions, but it does help one to see some of the problems of heredity, environment, and acculturation in a fresh light. This will, I hope, account for the apparently odd juxtaposition of historical and observational chapters with fairly technical psychological chapters.

Actually, a polymath would be needed to integrate adequately the historical, cultural, sociological, linguistic, and psychological materials. I do not claim any particular expertise in disciplines other than the psychological, but I have read a considerable number of books by better qualified writers and have striven to present their conclusions as succinctly and impartially as possible. Since completing most of the work, Preiswerk and Perrot's (1978) devastating criticism of the ethnocentrism of almost all historical studies of foreign cultures came to my notice. As they point out, every writer injects his or her own values into the interpretation of other cultures. For example, one author stated that ''Japan was fifty years ahead of China, who refused to copy Western habits.'' Clearly, the implication is that oriental groups are backward if they do not accept Western technology and democracy. Yet both the Chinese and Japanese have regarded themselves as supremely civilized for centuries. Obviously I cannot escape from this type of bias, but I have made extensive psychological observations and/or carried out research in at least a dozen widely varying foreign countries, from the Arctic to the Antipodes, and from Peru to Uganda (see Vernon, 1969).

Although this book is an exploration of racial and ethnic differences, it is most certainly not ''racist'' in intent or conclusions. Occasionally I suggest that there are some biological differences—mental as well as physical—between Orientals and Occidentals, but in such cases, I also give careful consideration to possible alternative environmental causes. In most cases both genetic and environmental or cultural factors are involved. Except that the term *racial* always implies to me that there are recognizable differences in physical attributes (see the Glossary), both this term and *ethnic* (or *racial-ethnic*) overlap so much that I have used them almost interchangeably. I have been similarly loose in using *Caucasian, white, American, United States, and Westerners* as generally synonymous terms.

A great deal of psychological research in Japan is published by Japanese psychologists in English-language journals, and a more limited amount comes from Hong Kong, Taiwan, or mainland China. I have thought it relevant, therefore, to outline the current cultural situation in Japan and Hong Kong (but I have not attempted to deal with modern China). Furthermore, the present influx of oriental immigrants into North America is larger than ever before; hence, it is necessary to take some account of the countries from which they come. Unfortunately, there is very little information available regarding differences between Orientals arriving now and those who came in the past and their descendants.

Inevitably a large proportion of the book consists of brief accounts of a great many investigations. Thus it may seem to some readers like a series of entries from filing cards. In fact I have tried to extract the main features of each publication, evaluate these, and organize the findings into a fairly readable whole. I have avoided a great deal of technical detail. Indeed, other critics may complain because I have seldom quoted standard deviations or probability statistics. (However, in three of the chapters in which the details threatened to become excessive, I have relegated them to appendixes.) But I hope to have provided a guide that will help the highly qualified psychologist to consult the original publications if fuller information is needed. At the same time I have tried to keep the material sufficiently simple to attract the interest of lay Chinese and Japanese readers and those members of the general public who have dealings with them and would like to know more about them. A short glossary is appended for readers unfamiliar with psychological research. For those who feel defeated by the sections on mental tests, there are less technical summaries at the ends of Chapters 2, 5, 7, 8, 9, 11, 13, 15, and 16.

I feel that an apology is due to women readers. A great deal of the research, especially in the 1920s and 1930s, was carried out with boys or men only, and many publications that have studied both sexes have not separated their findings. In many cases I decided, with regrets, to say little about differences between boys and girls or men and women in order to simplify the presentation.

Acknowledgments

This work was carried out with the aid of a grant from The Pioneer Fund (New York). I am most grateful to the fund's president, Harry F. Weyher, for his support and encouragement.

I thank my wife Dorothy for her assistance in many aspects of this research, particularly in collecting information from the Departments of Education in California and Hawaii, and the Calgary Board of Education. My son Tony (representing the third generation of Vernon psychologists) also helped in tracking references and checking the text.

Next, I am much indebted to Arthur Jensen, who first drew my attention to this topic and encouraged me to study it. He also provided printouts of his unpublished investigations. I acknowledge with gratitude the assistance of Anita Li of the University of Calgary, who read and commented on the Chinese, Canadian, and Hong Kong chapters, and S. Guy, a native Japanese who has lived for many years in the United States and Canada, who made helpful comments on the Japanese chapters. Neither of these ladies is, of course, responsible for any faulty judgments I may have made. I have also had much help from J. W. C. Chan of the Education Department of Hong Kong.

Valuable information was provided by several staff officers of the Education Departments in the cities of Los Angeles, Honolulu, and Calgary, and by psychologists at the University of Hawaii. Others who assisted include F. Hsia, A. Sibatani, and L. Wang.

Finally I am grateful for the facilities provided by Roy Brown and Jane Vaughan of the Department of Educational Psychology at the University of Calgary, and for the excellent typing of Linda Culshaw.

Permission to reprint the following tables, granted by publishers, authors, and other proprietors of copyright, is gratefully acknowledged. Table 2.1: Graham, 1926; copyright 1926 by the American Psychological Association. Reprinted with permission of the publisher and author. Tables 2.3, A.1, A.2, A.3, and A.4: Reprinted with permission of A. R. Jensen. Table 5.3: Chan, Eysenck, & Götz, 1980; reprinted with permission of author and publisher. Table 7.5: Smith, 1942;

copyright 1942 by The Journal Press. Table 7.8: Werner, Simonian, & Smith, 1968; copyright 1968 by The Journal Press. Table 11.3: Kline and Lee, 1972; reprinted with permission of authors and publisher. Table 11.5: Tsushima & Hogan, 1975; reprinted with permission of Tsushima and Hogan and Heldref Publications. Table 12.2: Backman, 1972; copyright 1972 by the American Educational Research Association. Tables 13.1 and 13.2: McCarthy & Wolfle, 1975; copyright 1975 by the American Association for the Advancement of Science. Tables 14.3 and 14.4: Tuddenham, Brooks, & Milkovich, 1974; copyright 1974 by the American Psychological Association. Adapted by permission of the publisher and authors. Table B.2: Tanaka, 1972; reprinted with permission of the publisher.

1

The Immigration of Chinese to the United States

CHRONOLOGY

1784	Earliest trade relationships of Americans and British with China.
1815	First Chinese visited America.
1824 *et seq.*	American and European missionaries in China.
1842	Treaty of Nanking, following the opium wars, gave territorial and trading rights in five ports to foreign countries. Hong Kong ceded to Britain.
1848	First importation of Chinese laborers to California.
1849	Gold rush in California.
1850	Further Chinese laborers imported for railroad building in the West.
1850–64	Taiping uprising: warfare with Britain and France; United States neutral.
1850s–80s	Demonstrations and riots against Chinese in San Francisco. Importation of Chinese laborers to eastern states, often as strikebreakers.
1852	First immigration to Hawaii.
1858	Immigration to British Columbia, with discovery of gold.
1868	Burlingame Treaty, limiting Chinese immigration to the United States.
1882	Exclusion Act passed by Congress barring further immigration (except of limited categories); extended until 1924.
1890–95	First Sino–Japanese war weakened the Chinese Empire.
1899–1901	Boxer uprising against foreigners. Territorial rights of trading nations imposed.
1911	Sun Yat-sen's rebellion against Manchu government. Downfall of Imperial Dynasty; foundation of republic.
1915	Japan's imposition of "21 Demands," making China a protectorate.
1924	All immigration of Orientals to United States prohibited.

1931 Japanese seizure of Manchuria.
1937 Second Sino–Japanese war. Massacre of Nanking. Occupation of China; installation of a puppet government.
1941 Pearl Harbor. Improved attitudes toward Chinese in United States.
1945 British army defeated Japanese in China. War between Kuomintang and Communists.
1946 Chinese wives and children admitted to United States.
1949 Chiang Kai-shek defeated. Nationalist government removed to Taiwan.
1954 All American racial legislation abolished.
1965 Free immigration of Chinese, dependent on skills or family relations, as with other nationals.
1972 United States recognized Communist government.

SOURCES OF INFORMATION

The main sources of information on which I have relied include: W. C. Smith, *Americans in Process* (1937); F. L. K. Hsu, *Under the Ancestors' Shadow* (1948); Rose Hum Lee, *The Chinese in the United States of America* (1960); S. C. Miller, *The Unwelcome Immigrant* (1969); S. M. Lyman, *The Asian in the West* (1970); F. L. K. Hsu, *The Challenge of the American Dream* (1971); and articles by Stoessinger (1970), Fersh (1972), and Alsop & Satter (1976).

DEMOGRAPHY

Table 1.1 provides census figures for Chinese and Japanese populations in the American mainland and Hawaii from 1860 to 1970.

Note the rapid initial rise of Chinese in mainland America, but a continuous drop after 1890 when legal restrictions on entry were enforced. A slow rise occurred after 1920, and a much more rapid expansion took place after World War II, when the Immigration Act was repealed. In Hawaii, immigration started somewhat later, and the total number of Chinese on the islands stayed at 20,000–30,000 from 1890 to 1940. Thereafter, the numbers began to creep up, and are probably still doing so, though the increase may well be due as much to natural growth as to further immigration.

Table 1.2 provides 1970 census figures for all of the main ethnic minorities, with percentages of the population both in the United States as a whole, and in California and Hawaii. Clearly, Chinese and Japanese constitute much larger percentages in these two states than in the rest of the country. Just about half of

TABLE 1.1
Total Numbers of Chinese and Japanese in the United States and Hawaii

Census year	Chinese			Japanese		
	Mainland	Hawaii	Total	Mainland	Hawaii	Total
1860	34,933	NA	NA	NA	NA	NA
1870	63,199	NA	NA	NA	NA	NA
1880	105,465	NA	NA	148	NA	NA
1890	107,488	16,752	124,240	2,039	12,610	14,649
1900	89,863	25,767	115,630	24,326	61,111	85,437
1910	71,531	21,674	93,205	72,157	79,675	151,832
1920	61,639	23,507	85,146	11,010	109,274	220,284
1930	74,954	27,179	102,133	138,834	139,631	278,465
1940	77,504	28,774	106,278	126,947	157,905	241,852
1950	117,629	32,376	150,005	141,768	184,598	326,366
1960	199,095	38,197	237,292	260,877	203,455	464,332
1970	383,023	52,039	435,062	373,983	217,307	591,290

Note: NA indicates information not available.

all Chinese and three-quarters of Japanese live there. Surprisingly, the Chinese percentage in Hawaii is barely one-quarter that of Japanese, although the Chinese began to immigrate much earlier. Also there are nearly twice as many Filipinos and others as Chinese in Hawaii, though the Filipinos did not begin to enter until 1902, and their maximum growth occurred after World War II.

TABLE 1.2
1970 Census: Ethnic Distributions in United States, California, and Hawaii (United States Department of Commerce, 1973)

Ethnic group	United States		California		Hawaii	
	Total	%	Number	%	Number	%
Caucasian	177,748,975	87.47	17,761,032	89.00	298,160	38.79
Negro	22,580,289	11.11	1,400,143	7.02	7,573	0.98
Indian	792,730	0.39	91,018	0.46	1,126	0.15
Japanese	591,290	0.29	213,280	1.07	217,307	28.27
Chinese	435,062	0.21	170,131	0.85	52,039	6.77
Filipino	343,060	0.17	138,859	0.70	93,915	12.21
Others (Korean, Hawaiian, etc.)	720,520	0.35	178,671	0.90	98,441	12.81
Totals	203,211,926		19,953,134		768,561	

EARLY IMMIGRATION

Apart from a few traders and envoys, there was virtually no contact between China and the Western world until the nineteenth century. In China itself there was no knowledge of the outside world, and no desire to go abroad. The Chinese regarded themselves as the only civilized nation, and all foreigners as barbarians. In Europe and America, China was regarded as exotic and mysterious. But the stories brought back by traders and missionaries led to a very different image of ancestor worship, female infanticide, opium smoking, writing down in columns from right to left, binding women's feet, men with pigtails, and other "unnatural" habits (Stoessinger, 1970). However, the greed of opium traders led the major trading countries to enforce territorial and trading rights in the 1840s.

In the same decade a series of natural disasters and starvation led the imperial government to permit the enlistment of large numbers of agricultural workers from southeast China. These were transported to California, where there was a desperate shortage of labor for the newly discovered gold fields. The Chinese came as indentured or bondaged coolies, speaking no English, but working in gangs as virtual slaves under overseers. An even more infamous trade, largely run by Americans, involved kidnapping Chinese and sending them to South America, under conditions as inhumane as those in the African slave traffic (Ts'ai, 1976). Though the pay received by the laborers in California was meager, they were prosperous relative to conditions at home, and most of their savings were sent home to their wives and families whom they had not been able to bring with them. After they had worked out their contracts they could take up other employment, or set up small businesses or farms on their own. Most of them expected to make their fortunes in America, and then return to China, though only a small proportion succeeded.[1]

The building of railways and roads in California and the western states required still more labor, which immigrants from Europe were unwilling to undertake. By 1880 the total numbers of Chinese, mostly in California, had risen to over 100,000 (see Table 1.1), but scarcely 1000 were women. Indeed, even in 1940 there were only a quarter as many females as males, and free admission of wives and children was not granted until after World War II. Thus, most of those who had served their time gravitated to the cities and lived almost celibate lives in the Chinatown hostels. The most notorious of these ghettos was San Francisco, with its population of 26,000 Chinese in 1890, which is a density of more than 150 to the acre, as contrasted with 25 per acre in the city as a whole. But even more important reasons for the tendency of the Chinese to congregate in

---

[1]According to Strong (1934), some 14,000 Chinese entered California each year from 1869 to 1883. If this is correct, then a great many must have returned home, especially when unemployment and riots were rife in the 1870s and 1880s.

segregated areas were that it provided more security against physical and other attacks by the majority culture, and better opportunities for the Chinese to manage their own affairs. New arrivals, who knew no English, were also taken in and helped to find employment.

SINOPHOBIA

The numbers of Chinese increased, and as more of them moved away from laboring jobs to urban employment or to farming, they were placed more in competition with whites, and there was growing hostility and criticism. Irrational stereotypes and racial prejudices were prevalent, for example, the Chinese were dirty, diseased, and dishonest; opium smokers; given to gambling, prostitution, and crime; morally evil; deceitful; untrustworthy; idolatrous heathens; inscrutable; cowardly; slant-eyed, wearing outlandish costumes and pigtails; eating bizarre foods; taking away white jobs by working for low pay; and not even spending their pay locally but sending it out of the country (Sue & Kitano, 1973).

In view of the gigantic size of the population of China, there were fears that "The Yellow Peril" would soon outnumber Caucasians in the West. The fact that they all seemed to look alike to the average white, and spoke an unintelligible language, or—at best—pidgin English, magnified the tendency to think of them as a separate, almost nonhuman, species. Even the nicknames such as John Chinaman, Chinks, the Celestials, the Mongolians, or coolies, were opprobrious. The obvious political weakness and technological backwardness of the Chinese Empire, shown in the wars with Britain and Japan, further underscored American judgments of racial weakness.[2] To put it briefly, the Chinese were unAmerican and unassimilable into white culture; the racial purity of America would be threatened if they ever bred with whites.

There was an element of truth in several of these accusations. But fears of overwhelming numbers were quite unjustified; the total number of Chinese and Japanese combined in America never exceeded one percent of the population. In 1970 they constituted just one-half percent. However, the figures were substantially higher in California at some periods, and far greater in Hawaii, though there was less prejudice there than in the western states. As to size of families, they could hardly be large in view of the paucity of females. Some of the other deficiencies referred to were largely due to the insanitary conditions under which they had to live, and to restrictions in employment and place of residence, or other forms of white discrimination. When they did possess their own homes and families, the houses were kept immaculately clean.

---

[2]As late as 1941, a public park in Shanghai displayed a notice: "Dogs and Chinese not permitted." This is now preserved in the National Museum at Peking.

The greatest resentment was felt by lower-class Americans in California and by European immigrants—especially the Irish. But the middle class were not far behind in their antagonism. The press played a large part in stirring up public feeling, and this was further fostered by the labor unions and by politicians who exploited popular fears and prejudices and who were on the lookout for vote-catching issues. There were many instances of mob violence against the Chinese, even including lynching; also their shops or homes in San Francisco were attacked. This began in 1849, but was most frequent in the 1870s when there was an economic depression and widespread unemployment. The amount of discrimination against, and oppression of, the Chinese was comparable to that of Negroes (Yee, 1973, 1974). Numerous attempts were made to legislate against Chinese in California and neighboring states such as Washington and Wyoming, though several of these acts were rejected as unconstitutional by the federal government. Special taxes were imposed with the aim of harassing the Chinese. Even the removal of queues, or pigtails, was demanded in 1876. Chinese children could not attend white schools until well into the twentieth century. Adults were barred from many types of employment, and the dead could not be buried in white cemeteries. Naturalization was denied to recent immigrants, though children born in America became citizens if their Chinese citizenship was renounced. Since many Chinese had settled in rural areas and established successful farms (which undercut white farmers), the ownership of land was prohibited. Even the right to testify in California courts was denied. Miscegenation with whites was illegal in about half of the American states. By 1868, some restriction on further immigration was embodied in the Burlingame Treaty with China. But sinophobia continued to grow, and in 1882 the Chinese Exclusion Act was passed, forbidding any entries, apart from a few restricted groups such as merchants, diplomatic corps, students, and their dependents. This was renewed until the more severe Immigration Act was passed by Congress in 1924. Small numbers of Chinese continued to gain entry by the forging of papers, or by illegally crossing the border from Canada, where the Chinese immigrants were likewise subject to a great deal of hostility (Chapter 8). Nevertheless, the total Chinese population on the mainland (i.e., excluding Hawaii) dropped considerably until the late 1930s.

SUBGROUPS OF CHINESE AND THEIR EMPLOYMENT

Despite all this hostility, there were quite a number of avenues of employment open to the Chinese, who would work diligently for low wages (Lee, 1960). For example,

1. Mining. This was prohibited in 1882, but the railroads and other unpleasant outdoor jobs still required laborers.

2. Launderers and domestic service workers.
3. Services of all kinds to other Chinese—restaurants, shops, commerce, merchandising, boarding facilities; sweatshops for women and girls.
4. Restaurants, also curio and import shops for Americans. Eating Chinese food and sightseeing in Chinatown greatly gained in popularity in the twentieth century, after the threat of continued immigration disappeared.
5. Food growing, especially fruit, and its distribution; fishing.
6. Semiskilled and skilled tradesmen (these were much restricted). Small manufacturing businesses, for example, clothing.
7. Later, many became teachers and white-collar workers in banks, commerce, offices. Eventually, many completed university degrees and entered the professions. Actually, by 1960, half of all Chinese adults fell under this category (see p. 10). The mean wages and family income were very low at first, but have now become comparable to those of whites. The middle-class Chinese have largely severed any remaining links with Chinatown.

Rose Hum Lee's book, *The Chinese in the United States of America* (1960), is a mine of information on all aspects of the subject from the beginnings of immigration up to 1960. Daniels (1976) criticized this book because of some inaccuracies, but he also agrees that it is perceptive, and that its Chinese authorship greatly enhances its value. Lee points out that the Chinese in America were, and are, by no means homogeneous, and she distinguishes four major groups:

1. American Chinese, either born in America or naturalized citizens. These are the most acculturated, but, of course, with wide variations. While retaining some of their cultural traditions, they usually prefer to speak English by the third generation, and they adopt so many American social norms that there is little by which to distinguish them, apart from physical features. There has been substantial outbreeding in this group, that is, mixed marriages.
2. Chinese Americans, foreign-born and/or immigrants who have not yet acquired citizenship. These would be lower in SES than the first group. In 1960 there were some 34,000 of them in California, or 17% of all mainland Chinese. (Lee's terminology, however, is not consistently used by other authors, and I have followed common practice in referring to all long-term immigrants and their descendants as Chinese Americans, or *CA;* while *CC* refers to Chinese in China, Taiwan, or Hong Kong, or those working temporarily in the United States. Similarly, *JA* and *JJ* are used to distinguish Japanese groups.)
3. Sojourners, who stay for some time in America as businessmen or students, but who are still China-oriented and intend to return there. They are usually of superior intelligence and/or wealth, and have little to do with Groups 1 and 2. Many sojourners have come from either Taiwan, Hong Kong, or mainland China

for university work or advanced technical training, and have returned home, often to become intellectual leaders and pioneers in modernization.

4. The stranded, who were in America in 1949, and were unwilling to return to the Communist-ruled homeland. Most of these were students who later became professionals.

In addition, there are several language groups. The largest proportion come from Kwangtung or neighboring southeastern provinces, and thus speak Cantonese. But the greatest proportion in China, especially in northern provinces, speak Mandarin; and there are several other minor variants (though much less diverse than is found in India).

Since 1960, a large proportion of recent immigrants came from Hong Kong, rather than from mainland China or Taiwan, and these tend to be more educated and Westernized than the Chinatown inhabitants. The Hawaiian Chinese obviously differ in many ways from the mainland, and they are considered in Chapter 6.

It is even more confusing to refer to Chinese and their descendants as Orientals or Asians, since there are at least as many Japanese immigrants (more in Hawaii), and several other Asian groups such as (East) Indians, Indochinese, and Korean.[3] Yet these are lumped together in some census and other statistics and in some research publications. According to the *Civil Rights Digest* (Hata *et al.*, 1976), there were some 215,000 Koreans, and 130,000 Vietnamese in the United States in 1975, and the numbers have doubtlessly increased considerably since then.[4]

CLANS, ASSOCIATIONS, AND TONGS

The social structure of Chinese communities in North America naturally derives from the traditional structures in their homeland, but with modifications appropriate to living as a small minority in a hostile environment. The extended family was the basic group in China, though it was seldom found in America owing to the paucity of women and children. Now that there is greater freedom of residence, Chinese have largely adopted the American model of the nuclear family.

The next larger grouping was the clan. This term refers to all persons coming from a certain Chinese region and bearing the same family name, that is, blood

---

[3] I will use the term Orientals only when both Chinese and Japanese are involved. Some writers even include Filipinos or Pacific Islanders as Asians or Orientals (Hsia, 1980). But to reduce confusion, I will not use separate abbreviations for Chinese and Japanese Canadians, nor for Orientals in Hawaii (see Chapter 6, Footnote 1).

[4] A news report in October 1980 stated that over 50,000 "boat people" had been accepted in Canada, and 160,000 in the United States.

relatives who owe allegiance to the same ancestors. (Clan members were not permitted to intermarry.) Though they serve various social and religious functions, such as festivities, the clans have little formalized structure or influence in America.

The most powerful groups were the benevolent associations, established initially to give help to newly arrived immigrants, and to represent all their members in negotiations with white authorities. In Chinatown they provided hostels or rooming houses, acted as bankers, gave legal advice, adjudicated disputes between members, and gave jobs to many of them. In effect, there was a large measure of self-government within the communities, though this was unofficial.

At the top of the power structure in California was the amalgamation of several associations to form what was called the Six Companies. This was a quite undemocratic organization, which was run by conservative elders—usually the most wealthy. There was a good deal of conflict between the second and later generations who were adopting white mores, and the associations that stood in the way of progress. Chinese who were able to marry tended to move out of Chinatown and to be less dependent on the associations. In the nineteenth century the existence of this complex network of associations and the tongs further hampered acceptance and understanding of the Chinese by the majority culture. By now these organizations have so declined in authority that they serve little purpose other than the preservation of Chinese culture. Most of their earlier service functions have been taken over by the American social security system, the civil rights movements, and, of course, the white schools that are attended now by almost all Chinese children.

Another useful activity of the associations was fund-raising, either for local causes (not necessarily Chinese), or for causes more removed, such as providing financial support to Sun Yat-sen in his revolution against the Manchu dynasty in 1911. The organizations neither supported nor expressed hostility to the Chinese Communist regime, although Hoover of the FBI strongly suspected them of breeding Communists (an accusation that was true of some of the younger generation in the 1950s and 1960s). Though not enamored of Chiang Kai-shek either, because of the corruption in his government, they gave generous help to Taiwan after World War II and brought large numbers of students to American universities. In 1957, feeling turned against Taiwan following the anti-American riots in that country.

The tongs were secret societies; hence, not a great deal is publicly known about them. The nefarious activities with which they were credited may well have been exaggerated by sinophobes and the press, who exploited them as another reason for condemning Chinese. However, there were some 50 such societies in San Francisco, many of them with links across the American continent and even overseas. They reached their highest potency between about 1900 and 1914 (Lyman, 1976). One of the best known was the Triad Society, an offshoot of Chinese Freemasons. Initially they were founded as enforcement agencies against Chinese who failed to pay their dues or to accede to the decisions of the associations. But they also took control of vice rings such as gambling, prostitution, and drug traffic, or ran protection rackets. Thus to some extent, they resembled the Mafia and, like their Italian counterparts, the tongs often fought with other societies for control; they often led the opposition to the benevolent associations too. Eventually the federal government stepped in and deported some of the tong leaders. Though several tongs still exist and may be involved in drugs and other criminal activities, their influence has greatly declined, and they now avoid violence.

LATER DEVELOPMENTS

With the 1924 Immigration Act and cessation of further entries, the opposition to the Chinese died down, and those who were already in America won greater acceptance. Considerable numbers also left the West Coast and settled in other states, so that they attracted less notice. Thus in 1950, 42½% of Chinese lived east of the Rockies. Table 1.2 shows that in 1970, 51% of Chinese, but 73% of Japanese, still lived in California or Hawaii. By the 1950s also, the obvious educational achievements and occupational skills of the Chinese, together with their low delinquency and crime rates and small recourse to social welfare, showed that they were, or could be, valuable members of American society. True, they met with many setbacks in trying to gain entry to superior types of employment, for example, the professions, yet their patience and persistence eventually succeeded. Now a greater proportion of Chinese Americans go to college than that of any other ethnic group (except Jews). Table 1.3 indicates the occupational distribution of six main ethnic groups in 1960, and the median income of wage earners (Schmid & Nobbe, 1965). The Chinese surpassed the Japanese as well as whites in percentage of white-collar workers, whereas about one-quarter of Japanese were still engaged in farming. However, the median income of Chinese males was still somewhat lower than those of Japanese and whites. It is generally found that Orientals need educational and other qualifications superior to those of white candidates in order to get appointed to high grade jobs (cf. Yee, 1976). They are accepted as doctors, dentists, accountants, engineers, managers in business, and so on, but seldom do they reach the top posts that would involve whites working under them. Indeed, some employers are still reluctant to take on Orientals because whites may dislike working alongside them. Alternatively, they may be paid less than whites in the same job. In other words, there is still racial discrimination, though it is much less overt. Yet even in 1978, Freeman found that oriental university faculty members publish more professional articles than white colleagues, but are paid less than them.

It is also interesting to note that Chinese females obtain the highest wage figure

TABLE 1.3
Occupational Distribution and Median Wages of Ethnic Groups in 1960 (Schmid & Nobbe, 1965)

Ethnic group	Occupations			Median wages	
	White-collar	Manual, skilled, and semiskilled	Farming	Male	Female
Caucasian	38.6%	53.0%	8.3%	$4338	$1509
Japanese	41.6	32.7	25.7	4306	1967
Chinese	50.0	48.7	1.3	3239	2067
Filipino	19.6	56.6	23.8	3035	1518
Negro	12.1	75.6	12.3	2254	905
American Indian	12.7	63.8	23.5	1792	1000

Note: These figures have been recalculated so that the percentages for all three types of employment add up to 100%.

for their sex. Presumably this is because so many of them become teachers or secretaries, or obtain other well-paid posts. As many as 51% of female Chinese were working in 1970. Sue, Sue, and Sue (1975) quote median *family* incomes in 1970 as:

United States Total	$ 9,590
Chinese	10,610
Japanese	12,515

But they point out that oriental families are more apt to have two wage earners (namely 60%, versus 51% in the United States generally). Moreover, they state that the actual poverty rate among Chinese (10%) is close to that for whites (11%), though it is lower among Japanese (6%).

POSTWAR CHANGES

Following Pearl Harbor and war with Japan, so much xenophobia was directed against the Japanese, that the Chinese benefited by comparison. After World War II the numbers of Chinese immigrants began to rise again (Table 1.1), and there was some resurgence of anti-Chinese feelings. Particularly during the Korean war they were again regarded as treacherous and deceitful, and there were occasional violent outbreaks, though nowhere near as serious as those in the nineteenth century.

In view of the vicissitudes through which Chinese had lived in the western states, it is not surprising that a good deal of social disorganization occurred. The building up of a second generation was abnormally delayed. Actually, the proportion of Chinese Americans born in America reached 30% in 1920, but it was not until the entry of wives was legalized in 1946 that the majority were able to live normal family lives. Yet the Chinese were, and still are, the most law-abiding of all ethnic groups in America (except for, probably, the Japanese). To a large extent they themselves dealt with any social deviance, just as they looked after their own newcomers and the aged. They made little call even on medical assistance, and those who went to college generally worked their way through instead of seeking support from public funds. Both the mental illness rate and divorce rate are lower than the American average (Sue *et al.*, 1975).

Thus it was surprising that, in the 1950s, within Chinese communities there appeared to be growing tension and delinquency, including gang warfare, banditry, violence, and extortion. The younger generation and some new immigrants were rebelling against the Chinese establishment, and at the same time were protesting against white discrimination. On the one hand, they were turning away from traditional norms to American patterns of behavior; on the other, they identified themselves strongly with Chinese ethnicity (Lyman, 1970). Unemployment of youth was high, and there were many drop-outs from school who became alienated. This disaffection was most marked in San Francisco and New York Chinatowns, where there was gross overcrowding. In San Francisco, 45,000 were living within one square mile, and the population of Chinese in New York was some 37,000 in 1968. Yet, according to Sollenberger (1968), the New York police did not regard Chinese crime as a serious problem. However, so many Chinese were now dispersed throughout the major cities that the trouble spread to many areas. The causes were probably social in nature such as the breakdown of traditional family solidarity, and only to a minor extent were the disturbances Communist-inspired.

Naturally this gave rise to great concern throughout the Chinese American communities, and the associations were powerless to control it. However, considerable efforts were made by various social action and religious groups to cater for the needs of the alienated. Also, groups of young Chinese adults who were themselves successful did much to rehabilitate their maladjusted contemporaries.

Later, Sue *et al.* (1975) record that there is a noticeable tendency for Orientals to ally themselves with blacks, Chicanos, and other minority groups, in demanding equality of treatment by the white majority.

THE CHINESE FAMILY AND CULTURE

It is presumptuous to attempt the delineation of Chinese culture, family structure, and personality in a few pages, particularly when the author's personal acquaintanceship with Chinese people is quite limited. But it is necessary if we are to understand the background of research into the abilities, achievements, and personality traits of Chinese, carried out by American and Canadian psychologists.

According to Alsop and Satter (1976), the individual Chinese tends to think of himself as an episode in the history of his ancestors and family. Hsu's (1948) anthropological study of a small Chinese town gives an excellent picture of the domination of the society by respect for ancestors. The highly structured Chinese family has persisted over centuries, and only began to weaken and yield to western conceptions of individualism after the bitter experiences of the early immigrants that we have described, and the gradual acculturation of subsequent generations.

Naturally there have been great changes in present-day China. But there has been so much divagation between the Chinese American and Communist cultures that no attempt will be made to comment on the latter. Useful surveys of child-rearing and education and of family organization in contemporary China have been given by Walker (1976) and Vogel (1969), respectively.

Probably the traditional Chinese family can be found in its purest form in Taiwan, especially in the rural areas (Tseng & Hsu, 1969). There, the extended family or clan may encompass a whole village. Each member of such a family has his own clearly defined status in relation to others, and he is brought up to address them according to their rank. A much wider range of kin is recognized than in western families. While the elders receive the greatest respect, there are stronger bonds within the immediate family, where the father is the kingpin who makes all the decisions. He, in turn, respects his father while still alive, and reveres him when dead along with earlier ancestors. Filial piety is the greatest of virtues. Thus, a young family often lives with the husband's parents for many years after marriage, and his wife owes obedience to them. In those families in which the father emigrated to America, his wife continued to live with them, and not with her own people.

At the same time, both parents feel obligations to their children and share responsibility in their upbringing. Sollenberger's (1968) study of Chinese families in New York stresses their cohesiveness, harmony, and warmth, and the absence of family quarrels. This certainly helps to build the children's sense of security and the feeling of belonging. Likewise they are taught to share, and they carry this over to school where the absence of bickering or competitiveness among Chinese children has often been noted (see Chapter 16). The boys are not expected, like westerners, to fight back and defend themselves. Even adolescents do not show the same kind of turbulence as we expect, unless they have become considerably Americanized. Sansingkeo (1969) describes the happiness and easy compliance of Thai children (whose ancestors originally came from China). He attributes this largely to the influence of Buddhist tenets in childrearing. Reports from present-day China also mention the unnatural quietness (by Western standards) and obedience of young preschool children in day-care centers.

Infants are traditionally breast-fed, and are indulgently weaned and toilet trained. In the first few years they always sleep at nights beside an adult. They grow up to expect kindness in the family group. However, stricter discipline is imposed from about the age of 6. The children are taught their responsibilities as family members. They also are taught to inhibit aggression and indeed to avoid any public expression of strong feelings, even affection. Control and discipline are enforced more by temporary banishment from the social life of the family, or deprivation of privileges, than by ridicule, physical punishment, or rational persuasion (see also Chyou & Collard, 1972). Alsop and Satter ascribe the successful achievement of Chinese in their educational and vocational careers to the strength of family life and stern discipline. The sons, particularly the eldest, are expected to maintain the honor of the family by their hard work and devotion. Moreover, any delinquency is regarded as reflecting on the whole family.

Since the individual is subordinate to the kinship framework, the Chinese do not consider the attainment of independence as important. Sons are expected to preserve the status quo rather than to be adventurous or to show initiative, which helps to explain why we see Chinese culture as highly conservative. Moreover, the devaluation of independent initiative implies that the Chinese think of life as determined by fate or chance, not as under human control.

The same kind of family structure tends to be carried over into business and industry, though not so clearly as in Japan. For just as kinship takes precedence over personal friendships, so does loyalty to one's business associates. In contrast to cooperation within the family, there is intense competition between families for prestige. Hsu (1948) describes the elaborate and costly marriage and funeral ceremonies, and the glorification of ancestors, in which each family vies to outdo the others.

A further word is needed on the inferior position of females. Daughters are considered less important than sons because they will eventually leave the family membership. It was thought, and perhaps still is, that giving them the same education as boys would detract from their marriageability. Even in the United States, Chinese males first attended universities in 1847, and females not until 1902. Traditionally, marriages were always arranged by the parents, without regard to the young people's wishes; no contacts were approved before the ceremony. To the Chinese in America, the habits of petting and kissing in public seemed outrageous.

There were several major religions in China—Buddhism, Confucianism, and Taoism; but there was no strife between them as between American or European sects, and also no attempts to proselytize. The Chinese are quite flexible and often adopt a polytheistic religion combining all three, worshipping numerous gods and spirits. Every household had its family shrine, where offerings were laid to the ancestors and gods (Hsu, 1948).

Christian missionaries in the nineteenth century were notably unsuccessful in winning converts. A few immigrants in America and many of their descendants did join one of the several churches there, probably as much to win acceptance and gain acquaintances among whites as because of religious preference. Hsu (1971) estimated that 20% of Chinese in San Francisco were members of Christian churches in 1968. But ancestor worship was widely maintained by immigrants and their children until well into the twentieth century. In the early days in America, it was common practice to cremate the dead and send the ashes back to China for preservation in the ancestral temple. By the middle of this century the practice had largely died out.

ACCULTURATION

The Chinese who entered America were used to a highly structured social order and family system. This could scarcely be reestablished on foreign soil when there were so few families, and where any behavior that conflicted with white norms was under sttack. They managed to survive oppression largely by keeping silent, and trying to be as inconspicuous as possible. But the later generations were less rigid and more inclined to accept and imitate American ways (Fong, 1973). Inevitably, then, there were many problems and conflicts. The younger generations felt a dual allegiance. They were still proud of their race and ancestral culture, and felt guilty if they went against the wishes of their parents and elders. Yet they realized that in order to succeed, they had to adjust to American habits and values. They were leading a kind of dual life. The extended family could not operate, except to some extent within Chinatown. Married children settled away from the parents as soon as they could afford to.

Naturally, when the children went to white schools or when the adults wished to have any dealings with whites, they had to speak English. Soon, the second and later generations were refusing to speak Chinese at home, whereas many of the first generation could speak scarcely any English. By 1950, according to Lee, about one-third of the Chinese in San Francisco habitually used Chinese, one-third English, and the rest used either or both, according to the context. Arranged marriages have largely died out, though the parents are usually consulted. Despite strong parental disapproval, there are a large number of mixed marriages, that is, marriage with Caucasians or Japanese. In 1974, the rate was 25% (Sue *et al.*, 1975); but this is much less than the Japanese (47%). Curiously, the position is reversed in Hawaii, according to Lind (1967). In 1960–1964 in Hawaii, 55% of Chinese and only 20% of Japanese marriages were mixed.

There were many American traits that the Chinese used to dislike, but are by now accepting: aggressiveness, individualism, impulsiveness, the drive to autonomy and self-sufficiency, permissiveness to children, sex equality, active participation in political affairs, and resort to the law for protection or grievances. According to Alsop and Satter, Chinese children born in 1950 and later regard themselves simply as Americans, not Chinese, and they have seldom experienced any serious discrimination. But many aspects of Chinese culture still survive besides the New Year festivities and Chinese food. Chinese is often taught as a second language in schools that many Chinese children attend. Alternately, there are privately run Chinese schools operating outside ordinary school hours. But these seem to be patronized partly because the schools keep young children off the streets until their parents get home from their jobs. Hence, the attendance declines rapidly among fourth grade or older children.

It has been said that Chinese Americans are almost completely acculturated, but are not fully integrated. Their color and physical appearance obviously distinguish them and, as mentioned previously, they are still liable to subtle forms of discrimination. Naturally, there are wide family and individual differences in degree of acculturation. Those who continue to practice Chinese religions or to act as leaders in the preservation of Chinese culture are more apt to be mistrusted by whites.

Chinese people still appear to whites as being exaggeratedly humble and deferent, and as oblique or devious in their business and other communications and interactions. They are too much given to face-saving devices, in order to avoid embarrassment or discomfort either to those they are speaking to, or to themselves. In general, they are more concerned about shame (*being seen* to be wrong) than about guilt (*feeling* that one is wrong). Because they have different ways of expressing emotions from whites, they still seem to us inscrutable and reserved. Likewise, the Chinese think of whites as unduly impulsive and brash. Many whites tend to think of the Chinese as all looking alike mainly because we do not get to know them as individuals.

Sue and Kitano (1973) and Wong (1976), among others, suggest that there are several myths or stereotypes about the Chinese that still lead to misunderstandings. Because they are no longer treated as the blacks were, they have become a "model minority" who have fully accepted American values. Most whites are scarcely aware of their treatment in the past, and entirely ignore their contribution to the development of the West, for example, the railroad building (Yee, 1973). Social studies courses in schools may teach something about American Indians in the past, but nothing about the ancient or modern civilizations of China or Japan. Another overdone myth is that "they always take care of their own," when in fact there are a great many social problems that they cannot handle. Currently, there is much more poverty, overcrowding, disease, and even malnutrition than we realize, especially among the elderly who can no longer look forward to living with their sons or daughters, or perhaps returning to China (Kalisch & Moriwaki, 1973). Some observations on the mental pathology of Chinese (both CC and CA) are included in Chapter 4.

2

Tests of Chinese Children in the United States

INTRODUCTION

The first published report on the abilities of Chinese children in the United States seems to be that of Pyle (1918). Approximately 500 Chinese aged 10 to 18 years were given a number of physical and mental tests. There is no indication of their home background nor of the background of groups of white and black students with whom the Chinese were compared. But the author mentions the language difficulties that affected their understanding of the mental tests, suggesting that the children came from homes that were predominantly Chinese-speaking.

The physical measures included height, weight, lung capacity, hand grip, cephalic index, etc. The average figures tabulated for each age group of both sexes showed the Chinese to be somewhat smaller, lighter, and less physically developed than the whites.

On rote memory tests both Chinese boys and girls scored more highly than whites at most ages; but in logical memory (reproducing a story read to them in Chinese), the girls equaled the whites, but the boys scored 13.5% lower. On Substitution (Digit–Symbol test) and Verbal Analogies the Chinese were considerably lower; and on Spot Pattern (reproducing a picture of seven dots shown on a large screen) the boys' mean was 10.5% lower. In most tests the Chinese boys exceeded girls, whereas among the white students the girls were usually superior. On all the mental tests the blacks scored lower than the Chinese, despite their greater familiarity with the English language.

Yeung (1921) tested 62 Chinese boys and 47 girls, aged 5–14 years, attending English-speaking schools in San Francisco. They were American-born, but always spoke Chinese outside school. Their parents were all working class, for example, launderers and laborers. The Stanford–Binet test was given (without

Vocabulary), and the mean IQs were 93.5 for boys and 99.9 for girls. No reason can be suggested why the sex difference is in the opposite direction to that found by Pyle and several other studies.

Graham (1926) provided fuller data regarding her sample of 63 12-year-old boys in a Chinese school in San Francisco. Only one-fifth of them were born in China, but all the homes were Chinese-speaking, the fathers being mostly tradesmen or laborers. Table 2.1 shows the mean scores on 12 group or individual tests, together with those of a comparison group of 40 white boys.

Clearly, the Chinese scored lower on verbal group tests and reading comprehension, and auditory memory for sentences. Their reading score corresponds to the 9-year level, that is, 3 years backward. But on visual memory for objects and shapes, paper formboard, and Kohs Block Design they actually scored a little higher than whites. The Stanford–Binet was also given at mean age 12.5, omitting the Vocabulary items, and the average IQ was 86.6. However when scored according to the abbreviated Army version, the mean rose to 91.

In a survey of the literature by Hsiao (1929), mention is made of a M.A. thesis by A. D. Lee: *A Comparative Study of Normal Chinese and American Children* (1921). Forty-six of each race, aged 4–14 years, were tested with the Goddard–Binet test, and it is claimed that the Chinese mean IQ was almost equal to that of whites. No information is available regarding the representativeness of these rather small samples.

TABLE 2.1

Scores of Chinese and White Boys on Ability Tests (Graham, 1926)

Tests	Chinese mean	White mean	Statistical significance[a]
1. Visual memory for objects	6.03	5.7	−
2. Digit memory	5.22	6.0	+
3. Auditory memory for sentences	13.67	20.3	+ +
4. Memory for shapes	6.46	5.6	−
5. Free association (words in 1 min)	24.73	32.2	+ +
6. Problem-solving with geometrical pieces	3.60	4.14	−
7. Kohs Block Design Mental Age	13.4	12.5	−
8. Franzen's Mentimeter Group Test	62.21	98.09	+ +
Absurdities	9.98	12.44	+
Mazes	15.5	15.94	−
Paper Formboard	7.96	6.67	+
9. Thorndike–McCall Reading Comprehension	36.0	51.55	+ +
10. National Intelligence Test A1 (Verbal)	79.70	127.55	+ +
11. National Intelligence Test A2	87.83	144.11	+ +

[a] − = not significant; + = significant; + + = highly significant.

Hao (1924) tested 602 Chinese students in Grades 1–8 in San Francisco. He used only the Digit Memory test from Whipple's Manual, but gave one test visually and another auditorally, with 14 items in each test. The means for successive grades ranged from 4.6 to 8.2 for the visual, and from 4.5 to 6.5 for the auditory. No comparison was made with a white group, but Hao claims that the Chinese exceeded white norms from about 10 years on, especially on the visual test.

Louttit (1931) tested groups of 40 to 50 12-year-old boys and girls who were Caucasian, Chinese, Japanese, or Hawaiian. Four memory tests were used. On recall of a story, Caucasians scored higher than Orientals. On Auditory Digit Span, there were no differences. But on Visual Span and Memory for Letter Squares, the Japanese were first, then the Chinese, and both exceeded the Caucasians.

Luh and Wu (1931) adapted the Binet test for Chinese (CC)[1] children, and gave it with the Pintner-Paterson performance tests to some 200 children aged around 11 years. They claim mean IQs of 114 (Binet) and 105 (Pintner-Paterson). However, the sample contained a considerable proportion of children from professional class families. Even allowing for this, the results suggest, though they cannot prove, that Chinese tested in their own language score much the same as whites.

In 1926 Goodenough discussed the difficulties of immigrants who continue to use their mother tongue out of school. She believed her Draw-a-Man test to be "independent of language" (apart from the instructions). This was applied to 2547 children, mostly Grades 1–3, of very varied ethnic origin, though almost all were American-born. She tested only 25 Chinese and 42 Japanese, hence her mean figures are of little value. However, her IQs were 101.5 for whites, 104.1 for Chinese, and 101.9 for Japanese. In her later writings Goodenough admitted that her test was susceptible to cultural influences. But as the oriental children in the 1920s were considerably underprivileged, the close equality of their scores with those of whites does suggest good intelligence in nonverbal tasks.

Sowell (1978) quotes median IQs from various studies published in each decade from the 1930s to the 1970s. The total number of Chinese American children exceeded 2000. In the first three decades the median was 102, while in the 1960s and 1970s the medians were 107 and 108. However, the number of samples and their make-up are not specified nor are the tests listed. Hence, it would be unwise to accept these figures as representative.

There appears to be very little further published research on Chinese abilities until Lesser, Fifer, and Clark's elaborate study in 1965 (see also Stodolsky and Lesser, 1967). The authors compared the scores of four ethnic groups in New

---

[1]For an explanation of these abbreviations, see Chapter 1, p. 7.

York on four aptitude, or Primary Factor, tests—Verbal, Reasoning, Number, and Spatial. These were given individually to 80 first-grade children in each group—Chinese, Jewish, black, and Puerto Rican. The distributions of scores in the total sample were normalized to a mean of 50. On this scale the Chinese obtained 48, 54, 54, and 54 on the four tests. That is, they were a little below average on Verbal, but above average on the other three factors. They were the highest group on Reasoning and Space. The Jews were much superior on Verbal with a score of 59, but not much above average on the others with means of 53, 55, and 52, that is, closely comparable with Chinese. All black and Puerto Rican scores fell between 43 and 50. When the children were classified by social class, the working class in each ethnic group obtained on a similar pattern of scores to the middle class, though at a lower level.

Flaugher and Rock (1972) gave a battery of tests to some 18,000 high school juniors in Los Angeles, including 400 Orientals (of whom the majority would probably be Japanese). The tests were chosen to represent four major ability factors—Verbal (Vocabulary), Reasoning (Letter Groups), Number (Mathematics), and Spatial (Choosing a Path). Much as in Lesser, Fifer, and Clark's study, the Orientals scored above the white student average on the last three tests, and close to average on the Verbal test.

Coleman's famous report on *Equality of Educational Opportunity* (1966) compared four minority groups on a nonverbal intelligence test and a verbal achievement test. Table 2.2 shows the results at Grades 1 and 12. (The mean scores for the total population at all ages were 50.) Here, the Orientals are the highest scorers on both tests at both ages, and are superior to the total population, including whites, except on the Verbal test where they were a little below average from Grade 3 onwards.

It should be noted that all the minority children, except blacks, were in predominantly white schools, so their learning conditions were essentially the same. Probably the great majority of the Orientals were American-born.

The Coleman Report also contains correlations at sixth grade between nonverbal ability and various indexes of SES. They are mostly higher for the Orientals than for whites, which is surprising since

	White	Oriental
Reading materials in the home	.21	.45
Consumer items in the home	.26	.51
Parental education	.21	.19
Few siblings	.06	.32

other studies (e.g., Jensen, 1973, p. 25) have yielded quite low correlations between parental occupation and child achievement.

TABLE 2.2
Minority Group Mean Test Scores (Coleman *et al.* 1966)

Tests		Oriental	American Indian	Mexican	Negro
Grade 1	Nonverbal	56.6	53.0	50.1	43.4
	Verbal	51.6	47.8	46.5	45.4
Grade 12	Nonverbal	51.6	47.1	45.0	40.9
	Verbal	49.6	43.7	43.2	40.9

PIAGETIAN AND OTHER STUDIES

Three studies by Tuddenham (1970), Feldman (1971), and Jensen and Inouye (1980) compared whites, blacks, and Chinese or Orientals on some unusual tests. Tuddenham constructed a scale of tests based on Piaget's experiments, covering conservation, seriation, classification problems, etc., suitable for Grades 1–4. These were given to approximately 200 whites, 43 blacks, and 23 oriental children, all subdivided by grade and sex. The average percentages of children who had grasped each concept (i.e., surpassed the transitional stage) were white, 33%; black, 15%; and Oriental, 36%. Thus, although all the tests depend to some extent on verbal comprehension and verbal expression of answers, the Orientals tend to score most highly. On seven out of the ten tasks the Orientals did better than whites. However, the difference is unlikely to be statistically significant.

Feldman was concerned with the comprehension and drawing of maps, which would depend largely on spatial reasoning abilities. His tests were given to 30 of each of three ethnic groups, and in each Grade 5, 7, and 9, that is, a total of 270 students. His map-reading or comprehension test consisted of 25 multiple-choice items. The mean scores were

Grade	Mean	Ethnic Group	Mean
5	13.53	Chinese	16.53
7	15.63	White	15.85
9	16.63	Black	13.51

There are, of course, increases with age, but also the ethnic groups show results similar to those of Tuddenham. It would be reasonable to say that the Chinese score on average at Grade 9 level, blacks at Grade 5, and whites at Grade 7. Feldman also devised a map-drawing test, namely drawing a plan of the school as seen from above. This was scored in terms of Piagetian levels: tautological or imaginary, perceptual–associative, concrete, and formal stages. However, ethnic differences are not reported.

Jensen and Inouye (1980) carried out a cross-ethnic study of Levels I and II abilities, that is, Associative or Rote Learning, and Conceptual Learning. A large battery of group tests was given to 2898 whites, 2361 blacks, and 426 oriental children in Grades 2-6 in a California school district. Factor analysis showed that the level I and Level II tests were clearly distinct; the former being measured by Digit Memory tests, the latter by the Lorge-Thorndike Nonverbal Intelligence test. The scores in each grade were converted to a mean of zero, and standard deviation of 1.0, with the following results:

	Level I Factor	Level II Factor
White	+0.14	+0.48
Black	−0.13	−0.66
Oriental	−0.22	+0.53

The differences on Level II between the blacks and other groups were statistically significant at each grade level, but not those for Level I. Here again, the Orientals (mostly Chinese) slightly surpass whites on Level II, despite the fact that their parents were somewhat lower in SES than those of whites. However, conventional verbal intelligence tests were not used; thus it is quite likely that they would have been less successful on these than on nonverbal tests. The picture is quite different for Level I, the Chinese being the lowest by a small amount. This hardly accords with the common view that Chinese excel in rote learning, and some of the studies cited earlier did indicate a slight Chinese superiority. But they might be somewhat handicapped if the digits were read out in English. In any case, the Digit Memory test gives weak predictions of rote learning in general.

Similar results were obtained at college level by Longstreth (1978). Black and Mexican students scored lower than whites and Orientals on the Cognitive Abilities test of intelligence, but not on the Digit Memory test.

Chen and Goon (1976) raise the question whether Orientals produce a greater number of gifted children than whites, who might be missed because of their linguistic and cultural differences. Twelve sixth-grade teachers and seven guidance counselors in seven New York elementary schools were asked to nominate all the oriental children they would recommend for gifted programs. All schools contained at least 10% of Chinese. As criteria for giftedness the children should have reading ages at least 2 years higher than their chronological age, and Arithmetic at least 1½ years. Personal characteristics such as initiative, reliability, etc., were also taken into account. Nineteen percent of all Orientals in the schools were rated as gifted, whereas the expected figure for whites having IQs of 125 and over would be 4.75%.[2] Compared with gifted whites, the Orientals were equal in reading ability, and stronger in arithmetic, and they worked more

[2]The article does not contain any precise mean scores, and this 19% is an estimate made by the author of the abstract published in *Psychological Abstracts*, 1977, No. 2076. I calculated that the overall Chinese mean quotients on intelligence or achievement tests would need to be some 13 points higher than the white means to yield this percentage, and such a superiority sounds quite improbable.

diligently. Yet a large proportion came from low-income homes where the fathers were mostly semiskilled or unskilled. Indeed some were described as being unconcerned about their children's education. Chinese was still usually spoken in their homes and with neighborhood friends.

SURVEYS BY A. R. JENSEN

Two extensive and recent studies by Jensen deserve mention, though they have not been fully published. In the early 1970s, several so-called freedom schools were set up hurriedly in San Francisco Chinatown at a time when desegregated schooling was starting, and many Chinese parents wished their children to continue attending Chinese-run schools. (These schools had no connection with Chinese language schools. Indeed, Chinese as such was not taught.) The schools' buildings and materials were somewhat below par, and the object of Jensen's survey was to evaluate the level of achievement in each grade before the pupils went on to secondary schools. There were 420 children in Grades K–6 in three schools. Fifty percent of them were foreign-born, their parents mainly coming from Hong Kong. The families were somewhat below average SES, and Chinese was almost always spoken at home. The children appeared to be highly motivated and compliant. The teachers were carefully trained, but they were all English-speaking, and the test instructions were given in English. However, in kindergarten a Chinese teacher gave the directions and trial items in Cantonese.

Some background data were obtained from the parents, but as many of them understood very little English, several of the sets of answers were incomplete. Thus, in the case of kindergarten children, father's and mother's occupations were obtained only for 7 and 5 respectively, out of 36 families. The gap was much less serious for older children. Thus, in Grade 6, 66 out of 89 families were able to give parental birthplaces, and 70 their occupations.

The numbers, mean ages, and scores on ability tests are shown in Table 2.3. Ages are quite normal for grade level. There were approximately equal numbers of boys and girls, but because the groups were small, results are quoted only for combined sexes.

Three intelligence tests were used: the Colored Book Form of the Raven Matrices, the Figure-Copying test, and Lorge–Thorndike (Pictorial test in Grades K–3, Verbal and Nonverbal in Grades 4–6). The same tests had been given to representative white samples in Bakersfield, California, and the table includes these white means.

Clearly, the Chinese are considerably higher than whites on the spatial Figure-Copying test and the Lorge–Thorndike Nonverbal norms, and they are somewhat higher on the Raven Matrices. But they are considerably below whites on the pictorial Lorge–Thorndike (which involves language comprehension), and a little lower on the Verbal Form, the overall mean for Pictorial and Verbal in seven grades being 94.2. However, note that by Grade 3 the comprehension of

TABLE 2.3
Jensen's Results for Children in Chinatown Schools

Grade	N	Median age	Colored Matrices		Figure-Copying		Lorge–Thorndike IQs	
			Chinese	White	Chinese	White	Pictorial (Chinese)	
K	36	5:6	14.17	14	18.00	15.03	88.22	
1	25	6:6	20.24	18	19.12	17.55	94.29	
2	48	7:7	23.33	23	19.65	19.46	88.74	
3	57	8:7	28.32	26	23.27	20.43	97.05	
							Verbal	Nonverbal
4	85	9:10	29.89	27	24.92	22.06	98.12	109.95
5	80	10:9	31.55	29	—	—	98.18	111.76
6	89	11:9	33.05	—	—	—	95.01	111.72
	420							

English instructions by Chinese children has so much improved that their Pictorial IQ rises from 90.4 (in Grades K–2) to 97.05.

Selected tests from the Stanford Achievement battery (1964 edition) were given. The results are tabulated in Appendix A, with American percentile equivalents. Here, the Chinese are seriously retarded on verbal and linguistic tests (Word and Paragraph Reading, Word Skills, Language, etc.), averaging around the 25th percentile. But they do better in Spelling, being at or above the 50th percentile (i.e., the white norm) from Grades 4 to 6. They do best in Arithmetic Computation, but average around the 40th percentile in Arithmetic Concepts and Applications. In general, these achievement scores are poorer than those obtained by CA and JA children at white schools, such as the Orientals in Jensen and Inouye's survey (Appendix A). It is difficult to see why, since there is no reason to think that the teaching was inefficient. Yet from Grade 3 on, the pictorial and verbal IQs are little below 100, and the nonverbal about 110. It may be that the children's scholastic retardation arises from the wide usage of the Chinese language outside school, and the lack of daily contacts with white peers.

Jensen himself (Hsia, 1980) concludes that American-born oriental children are above the white averages previously mentioned even on verbal intelligence and achievement tests. But those with, say, less than 3 years' schooling in the United States are likely to be considerably handicapped.

Correlations were calculated between each achievement test and the following background variables:

Sex   Father's occupation
Birth abroad   Mother's occupation
Amount of Chinese   Father born abroad
  spoken at home   Mother born abroad

The coefficients for Sex, Mother Occupation, and Father or Mother Born Abroad were all nonsignificant. But those for the other three variables were often significant, though small, and they are listed in Appendix A, at three grade levels: 2-3, 4, and 5-6.

Child Born Abroad correlated negatively with all verbal achievement and intelligence tests at each grade; that is, this factor has a consistent, even though small, adverse effect. Chinese Spoken at Home gave similar negative coefficients, though so small as to be negligible in Grades 2-4, and significant only at Grades 5-6. Father's Occupational Level gave positive correlations with all verbal tests in Grades 2-4, though not in 5-6, and these again were very small. With the Lorge-Thorndike Nonverbal and the Arithmetic tests, almost all correlations are negligible. It is interesting that the environmental variables studied in this research are generally less influential than has commonly been found among whites, though again no plausible explanation comes to mind except that possibly the Chinatown children had had little or no experience with objective tests, so that their scores might be lower and less reliable than usual.

A little further light was thrown by applying factor analysis (Principal Components) to all variables; the results for 169 children in Grades 5-6 are shown in Table 2.4. Clearly the two factors represent (1) Verbal abilities and achievements, and (2) Nonverbal reasoning and arithmetic achievement. Three other factors were extracted and rotated, but they were wholly specific to (3) Birthplace variables, (4) Parental occupations, and (5) Sex.

TABLE 2.4

Rotated Principal Components among Chinatown Children (Jensen, unpublished observations)

Variable	Factor I	Factor II
Chronological Age	−.156	+.337
Child's sex	+.016	+.014
Birth abroad	−.294	+.247
Chinese spoken in home	−.266	+.056
Father's occupation	−.197	+.151
Mother's occupation	+.149	−.132
Father born abroad	+.002	−.011
Mother born abroad	+.160	−.001
Raven Matrices	+.203	+.708
Lorge-Thorndike Verbal	+.788	+.382
Lorge-Thorndike Nonverbal	+.193	+.836
Word Meaning	+.880	+.087
Paragraph Meaning	+.891	+.240
Spelling	+.799	+.307
Language	+.710	+.518
Arithmetic Computation	+.261	+.782
Arithmetic Concepts	+.469	+.699
Arithmetic Applications	+.545	+.660

Note that the three variables already mentioned (Child Born Abroad, Chinese in Home, and Parental Occupation) are negatively related to verbal abilities, though the loadings are quite low. The second factor combines Arithmetic (especially Computation) with nonverbal intelligence. The other two arithmetic tests have significant loadings on the verbal and nonverbal factors. But there are some anomalies in this factor, such as moderate positive loadings for Born Abroad, Chronological Age, L-T Verbal, Language, and Spelling.[3]

Finally I will quote additional results obtained by Jensen and Inouye's tests of white, black, and oriental children in elementary schools Grades K-6. Here, the average numbers per grade were 550, 400, and 72, respectively. The investigation included the Lorge-Thorndike Pictorial, Verbal and Nonverbal tests, Figure-Copying, Digit Memory, and Stanford Achievement tests.

The mean IQs on the Lorge-Thorndike were so similar throughout Grades K-3 and throughout Grades 4-6 that only the averages are shown in Table 2.5. The detailed results are given in Table A.3. Note that the school district was a superior one, with whites getting mean IQs in the 110-120 range. Blacks are below average, though less so than in the overall American population, but the Orientals are close to white standards on the Pictorial and Nonverbal tests, and five points below on the Verbal.

On the Figure-Copying test, given in Grades K-4, the overall means were white, 9.69; black, 7.57; and Oriental, 10.49.[4] The Orientals surpassed whites in four out of the five grades. On the Digit Memory test in Grades 2-6, the Orientals scored uniformly lower than whites, though higher than blacks. Another test was included, mainly to yield data on test-taking motivation—the Making X's (Jensen, 1973). The subjects are first told to write X's in a series of squares, and 90 seconds are allowed without any pressure for speed. After a short rest, the test is repeated but with instructions to work as fast as possible. The overall scores for Grades 1 through 6 were as follows:

	Whites	Blacks	Orientals
First trial	67.45	68.39	77.32
Gain at second trial	12.61	13.17	11.18

It can be seen that the blacks not only score a little higher than whites on the first trial, but also gain more when motivated to work at speed. The Orientals are much the highest on the first trial, but having already worked so hard without being pushed, they make the lowest gain (in four out of six grades) when told to speed up as much as possible.

---

[3]Graphing the first and second factor loadings shows that the factors are oblique rather than orthogonal. This usually implies that there is a substantial general, or g factor, running through all the variables, and subsidiary verbal and nonverbal factors.

[4]Though the tests were the same in the California schools as in the Chinatown schools, a different system of scoring was used; hence, the Figure-Copying results for the two investigations are not comparable.

TABLE 2.5
Mean Lorge–Thorndike IQs of Three Ethnic Groups of Children (Jensen and Inouye, 1980)

Test	Grades	Whites	Blacks	Orientals
L–T Pictorial	K–3	110.79	93.00	109.44
L–T Verbal	4–6	118.37	92.84	113.09
L–T Nonverbal	4–6	120.17	95.36	118.34

For the Stanford Achievement Tests (see Appendix A) the pattern of scores was the same in Grades 4, 5, and 6; hence, only the mean overall percentiles are shown in Table 2.6. The blacks are lowest in all tests; the Orientals are highest on Spelling and Arithmetic Computation, but a little lower than whites on all other verbal and arithmetic tests. Although the total numbers are substantial, it is unfortunate that Orientals formed such a small proportion. It was not even possible to separate off Japanese from Chinese. Obviously, much will depend on the SES and educational level of the homes of the particular group. Clearly, the white children are much superior to the norm, suggesting an unusually large proportion of high SES and well-educated families in the area. The Orientals likewise might be to some extent selected, though they would probably not differ much from those in other California cities.

NONTECHNICAL SUMMARY AND DISCUSSION

Though a considerable number of studies of the abilities and school achieve-ments of Chinese children in the United States have been cited, the samples have been quite haphazard, and very little information is available to gauge the socioeconomic class level, the education of the parents, or the extent of knowl-

TABLE 2.6
Mean Percentile Scores in Grades 4–6 for Three Ethnic Groups

Test	Mean percentile scores		
	Whites	Blacks	Orientals
Word Meaning	82	23	71
Paragraph Meaning	73	19	64
Spelling	65	33	76
Language	62	10	58
Arithmetic Computation	49	13	59
Arithmetic Concepts	76	24	69
Arithmetic Applications	69	15	61
Total numbers in Grades 4–6	1588	1282	242

edge of English. Also, of course, the quality of immigrants and their descendants may have varied over the years 1918 to 1980 during which research studies have been published. There may also be regional variations; for example, Chinese families who moved inland or to the East Coast might be more able than those who remained in the West. Nonetheless, there is a remarkable degree of consistency in the findings of these studies and, as will appear in later chapters, quite similar results have been obtained with Chinese in Hawaii, Canada, and even Hong Kong. Thus it seems probable that the test results can be generalized to children of Chinese ancestry in any country where English is spoken. But we still badly need large-scale investigations that will make possible comparisons of those with different lengths of residence, different parental socioeconomic and educational levels, and different exposure to and familiarity with English.

Right from the 1920s Chinese American children have been found somwhat lower than whites on verbal intelligence tests and on verbal types of school achievement (e.g., reading comprehension). But they have come out the equal of, or higher than, whites on nonverbal intelligence tests such as Raven Matrices, Figure-Copying, Lorge-Thorndike, or performance tests such as Kohs Blocks and Draw-a-Man. In the earlier studies the verbal deficiency was quite considerable, but the more recent ones indicate mean IQs on verbal group tests of about 97 (i.e., little below the white average), and 110 on nonverbal and spatial tests (much above average). Chinese boys generally do better than girls, especially on the nonverbal side. Chinese are also superior in mechanical arithmetic, though not in problem or applied mathematics. Both sexes are also surprisingly, though quite consistently, superior in Spelling. This might suggest that Chinese do best in subjects involving rote learning, to which they have become accustomed by attending Chinese schools, and learning to read or write the Chinese language, which, like spelling and mechanical arithmetic, stress drill and rote learning. But the same pattern persists among later-generation children who have attended nothing but American schools and have not studied Chinese language at all. Moreover, on one of the commonly used tests supposed to measure rote learning, namely Digit Memory (given in English), Chinese tend to score below average. I have pointed out that this test is of limited diagnostic value. The application of factor analysis by Jensen in Chinatown schools showed clearly that nonverbal and arithmetical abilities are linked in the same factor.

Other studies have indicated that Chinese are above average in comprehension of maps, also in conceptual development as involved in Piaget's experiments, as well as nonverbal reasoning (measured by Thurstone's PMA or Bennett's DAT tests). And in Jensen's large-scale survey of California elementary school children, tbey obtained a higher mean than whites on his Making X's test, which depends on motor skills and motivation to try hard. There has been very little testing of specialized abilities, for example, mechanical, musical, artistic, or clerical. But boys do well on the Bennett Mechanical Comprehension test as they do on spatial reasoning ability (see Chapter 8).

When a group of children shows consistently high ability and achievement, the most common explanation is that their parents are above average in SES and education. Either they are thought to pass on superior genes to their offspring, or they provide an intellectually stimulating home environment, or both. However in this instance, several researchers have stated that their Chinese families were working class or lower middle class, and that the original immigrants came of peasant stock. In one study of Chinatown children (Jensen, unpublished observations), parental SES gave very low correlations with intelligence or achievements. Conceivably, socioeconomic status is less linked with parental abilities and education among the Chinese than whites, but this is contradicted by the findings of the Coleman Report. A considerable proportion of fathers may be "underemployed" in the sense that they are successfully engaged in laundering, farming, or other jobs regarded by whites as lower class, but actually have the ability to succeed in higher-grade or more complex jobs. Obviously, this is speculative, and it could hardly be put to the test.

Another major finding is the apparently small effect of the children speaking Chinese at home. This circumstance is linked with poorer achievement in English verbal subjects, but the connection is smaller than one would expect. Actually, being born in China or Hong Kong is more strongly associated with verbal retardation, perhaps because such children have had less contact with English-speaking children than have those born in America, who attend English-medium schools only.

None of the evidence we have presented demonstrates any clear effect of discrimination or deprivation; but this could be because the Chinese were subject to the greatest hostility in the late nineteenth and early twentieth centuries, whereas testing did not begin until 1918, when the numbers of Chinese in the population had dropped considerably. True, the lowest scores were reported in 1918 to 1921, but this may have arisen because children at that time were living in almost wholly Chinese-speaking environments, mixing little if at all with English-speaking people.

Insofar as the obvious environmental factors seem to play quite a small part in Chinese children's achievements, the case for substantial genetic influence is strengthened. But of course there are other aspects of Chinese childrearing and cultural environment that have not been taken into account in the research cited in this chapter. For example, much of the literature (Chapter 1) asserts that Chinese upbringing imbues the children with stronger motivation to learn and with greater compliance to adult demands, than are commonly found in Western cultures.

APPENDIX A

Results from Jensen's Research in Chinatown Schools, and Jensen and Inouye's Survey in California Schools

In the Chinatown research, different versions of most of the tests were used at different grade levels, so that the raw score means are not comparable, though the percentiles, also shown in Table A.1, should be so. However, Grades 2 and 3 took the same forms, as also did Grades 5 and 6. It can be seen that Grade 3 means mostly show large gains over Grade 2 (although there is little alteration in percentile scores). But by the age of about 8+, the Chinese children are making good progress despite their language handicaps. Likewise, there are gains from Grade 5 to Grade 6 on all tests, though these are a good deal smaller, and there is actually a decline on all percentiles. (Conceivably, this grade contained several dull children who had been held back from going on to Grade 7.) These results can be compared with those given in Table A.4 for Jensen and Inouye's large California sample (Grades 4–6 only), and it can be seen that these Chinatown schools do score decidedly below the rather superior white and Oriental groups, though the pattern of percentiles on different tests is quite similar. As stated in the text, there are negative correlations for Born Abroad and Chinese in the Home, and mainly positive correlations for Father SES with verbal IQ and all verbal achievement tests, though only 12 out of 45 coefficients are statistically significant at the .05 or .01 level. None of the correlations with nonverbal IQ or arithmetic tests are significant, with one strange exception in Grades 5–6, namely L-T NV = +.203 with Born Abroad, which may be a freak result.

Multiple regression analysis was carried out for each achievement test as criterion, and the background variables and intelligence scores as predictors. For all criteria, Lorge-Thorndike Pictorial or Verbal, and Lorge-Thorndike Nonverbal gave substantial correlations and beta weights. Only in a few cases did Raven Matrices or Figure-Copying add appreciably to the multiple correlation, or give

TABLE A.1
Stanford Achievement Tests in Chinatown Schools: Raw Score Means and Grade Percentiles

Test	Grade 1	%ile	Grade 2	%ile	Grade 3	%ile	Grade 4	%ile	Grade 5	%ile	Grade 6	%ile
Word Reading or Word Meaning	14.60	40	10.40	20	18.07	20	13.24	24	17.89	32	20.33	22
Paragraph Reading	8.00	22	17.10	22	32.14	23	24.67	34	25.21	32	28.94	24
Vocabulary	11.96	12	—	—	—	—	—	—	—	—	—	—
Spelling	5.52	40	8.31	40	18.39	46	28.75	50	29.18	60	34.39	52
Word Study Skills	25.48	30	27.44	32	34.54	34	32.69	38	—	—	—	—
Language	—	—	29.35	28	38.70	28	63.34	28	74.91	38	78.80	26
Science or Social Studies	—	—	—	11	17.02	20	—	—	—	—	—	—
Arithmetic	30.24	50	—	—	—	—	—	—	—	—	—	—
Arithmetic Computation	—	—	20.25	50	35.67	60	18.39	46	14.98	50	19.18	36
Arithmetic Concepts	—	—	13.25	34	24.21	38	16.79	60	10.63	42	14.34	36
Arithmetic Applied	—	—	—	—	—	—	14.97	44	13.88	40	17.07	30

TABLE A.2

Chinatown Schools: Correlations of Background Factors with Intelligence and Achievement Tests in Grades 2–3, 4, and 5–6

Tests	Born abroad			Amount of Chinese			Father SES		
	2–3	4	5–6	2–3	4	5–6	2–3	4	5–6
Raven Matrices	−.038	+.005	+.069	−.041	+.013	−.093	+.063	−.033	−.079
Figure-Copying	−.030	+.194	———	+.095	+.083	———	+.074	−.044	———
L–T Pictorial or Verbal	−.133	−.209	−.165^a	−.001	−.115	−.210^b	+.186	+.228^a	−.065
L–T Nonverbal	———	+.035	+.203^b	———	+.040	+.021	———	−.037	−.016
Word Meaning	−.166	−.227^a	−.184^a	−.155	−.139	−.247^b	+.153	+.001	−.080
Paragraph Reading	−.242^a	−.214	−.184^a	−.101	−.070	−.210^b	+.198	+.016	−.039
Spelling	−.341^b	−.111	−.154^a	−.110	−.141	−.205^b	+.169	+.065	−.105
Language	−.149	−.150	−.086	−.113	−.096	−.143	+.126	+.093	−.004
Arith. Computation	−.062	+.164	+.116	−.013	+.167	−.025	−.110	−.025	+.040
Arith. Concepts	−.163	+.025	+.016	+.000	−.201	−.074	−.009	−.008	+.098
Arith. Applied	———	−.092	+.066	———	−.191	−.046	———	+.081	+.034

Note: ^{a} = significant at .05.
^{b} = significant at .01.

significant beta weights. Omitting the intelligence tests, the three background variables listed above gave multiple correlations approximating .30 or less with achievement criteria. Occasionally one or two of the other background variables or age contributed. But when the intelligence test scores were included, the other variables very seldom yielded any significant addition to the multiple correlation.

TABLE A.3

Lorge–Thorndike IQs in Large California Sample, Grades K–6 (Jensen and Inouye, 1980)

Test	Grade	Means			Standard deviations		
		White	Black	Oriental	White	Black	Oriental
Pictorial	K	109.78	92.43	110.16	15.17	14.47	12.47
	1	111.83	93.91	108.82	13.25	13.06	15.89
	2	110.35	92.22	107.42	14.57	13.05	14.08
	3	111.21	93.43	111.38	13.79	13.40	14.11
Verbal	4	118.62	94.35	115.90	16.08	13.98	15.95
	5	117.43	92.34	111.60	16.54	14.42	14.91
	6	119.06	91.82	111.78	14.46	13.17	14.95
Nonverbal	4	119.96	95.27	121.33	15.91	15.49	14.27
	5	118.90	93.70	117.73	14.35	15.49	13.65
	6	121.65	97.10	115.96	13.35	15.23	12.75

TABLE A.4
Stanford Achievement Test Raw Score Means, Sigmas, and Percentile Levels, in Grades 4–6

	Whites			Blacks			Orientals		
	Mean	Sigma	%ile	Mean	Sigma	%ile	Mean	Sigma	%ile
Grade 4		N = 532			N = 430			N = 79	
Word Meaning	25.8	8.2	80	14.2	7.3	28	24.0	7.7	72
Paragraph Meaning	37.3	12.8	72	20.3	8.8	22	36.1	12.5	68
Spelling	33.1	11.7	62	20.8	10.6	30	36.6	11.1	74
Word Study Skills	44.7	12.0	64	27.3	11.3	24	43.7	11.9	62
Language	79.9	18.8	64	54.8	17.1	14	78.6	18.4	62
Arith. Computation	20.1	8.3	56	11.7	5.5	16	21.5	8.3	62
Arith. Concepts	20.9	6.9	80	10.6	5.4	25	19.6	6.6	74
Arith. Applied	19.5	7.2	69	9.8	4.8	20	18.0	6.8	62
Grade 5		N = 497			N = 435			N = 87	
Word Meaning	30.7	9.8	84	15.0	7.6	22	27.8	8.9	74
Paragraph Meaning	39.8	13.7	74	20.1	9.9	18	36.7	11.5	65
Spelling	30.6	11.6	68	18.7	9.2	43	33.6	11.2	76
Language	90.4	18.8	68	54.8	21.5	8	86.3	19.1	60
Arith. Computation	14.7	6.5	48	8.7	4.5	13	16.8	6.1	64
Arith. Concepts	16.5	6.3	74	8.3	3.5	26	15.2	5.3	68
Arith. Applied	20.9	7.9	74	9.5	4.9	16	20.1	7.5	70
Grade 6		N = 558			N = 417			N = 76	
Word Meaning	36.6	9.1	82	18.9	9.9	18	33.1	9.5	68
Paragraph Meaning	47.1	11.2	72	25.3	11.5	16	43.0	11.9	60
Spelling	38.7	10.9	74	25.4	12.0	26	42.5	10.5	78
Language	94.2	17.2	54	63.7	18.6	8	92.6	17.3	51
Arith. Computation	21.4	8.5	44	11.3	5.8	11	22.0	9.0	50
Arith. Concepts	21.3	5.8	74	10.9	5.5	22	19.8	6.0	64
Arith. Applied	25.2	8.0	64	10.6	6.1	9	22.4	8.9	52

California Sample (Jensen and Inouye, 1980)

Tables A.3 and A.4 give the Lorge–Thorndike IQs and Stanford Achievement test means by grade and ethnicity. In Grades 4 through 6 the Orientals' Spelling score is superior to that of whites at the .01 or .05 level; and in Grade 5 the same is true for Arithmetic Computation. Though the Orientals score lower than whites on 16 out of 22 achievement means, only one of these differences is significant, namely Paragraph Meaning in Grade 6.

3

Immigration of Japanese to the United States

CHRONOLOGY

Sixteenth
and seven-
teenth centuries Portuguese traders and missionaries in Japan.
1637   Virtual isolation from outside world for over 200 years.
1603–   Japan ruled by Tokugawa Shogunate, nominally under the emperor.
1868
1854   United States, Russia, England, and Holland allowed to open diplo-
            matic and trade relations.
1868   Fall of shogunate; emperor's authority reestablished. Meiji era. Rapid
            modernization of Japan, helped by foreign nations.
1884–85   First immigration of Japanese to Hawaii, United States, and Canada.
1894–95   First war with China. Part of Manchuria ceded, and Korea made
            independent.
1904–05   Japanese war with Russia.
1907   "Gentleman's Agreement" restricted Japanese immigration to United
            States.
1913   California Land Act prohibited ownership or leasing of land to Orien-
            tals.
1924   Immigration Act barred all oriental immigration to United States
            (with few exceptions).
1915   Japanese invaded China. Imposed "21 Demands."
1931–37   Further war with China, in defiance of League of Nations. Nanking
            massacre. Puppet government installed.
1930s   Severe deterioration in Japan–United States relations. Demand by
            Japan for large navy.

1941 Pearl Harbor attacked on December 7. Declaration of war by United
      States and Britain.
1942 Evacuation inland of all West Coast Japanese Americans and Canadians.
1943 Many Japanese in relocation centers allowed to settle further east.
1945 Camps closed.
1946 New constitution imposed on Japan. Emperor's authority removed.
1954 Racial discrimination laws abolished.

SOURCES OF INFORMATION

Among the most useful books and articles are those by Kitano (1969), Strong
(1934), Benedict (1946), Gulick (1947), Grodzins (1949), Daniels (1975),
Lyman (1970), Petersen (1971), Miyamito (1973), and Lebra (eds.) (1974). For
post-war developments: Stoetzel (1955), Bennett *et al.* (1958), Caudill (1973),
Forbis (1975), and Vogel (1979).

More emphasis is given in Chapters 3 and 4 to the history and culture of Japan
than in Chapter 1 on China. This is because much more has been published, and
because the background and personalities of the Japanese had a great deal to do
with the hardships they experienced in North America, especially during World
War II, and with their later acceptance by the white society.

EARLY HISTORY

The remarkable development of Japan from a backward, feudal state to a
major world power in the short space of about 50 years is generally familiar.
There was, in fact, some contact with European traders and missionaries in the
sixteenth and seventeenth centuries, but all foreigners were expelled in 1638, and
any converts to Christianity who refused to recant were exterminated. Over 200
years of almost complete isolation from foreign influences or knowledge followed. The country was ruled by a feudal system of powerful nobles (daimyos)
and samurai, chief of whom was the shogun, acting under the nominal authority
of the emperor (Clavell, 1975). But although the emperor was worshipped, he
had no power to rule. At last, in 1854, the United States and Russia were allowed
to negotiate diplomatic and trade relations; thus some contact was reestablished
with the Western world. After considerable internal strife between the more
progressive and more xenophobic leaders, the Tokugawa shogunate was over-
thrown in 1868, and the emperor's authority was restored. During the ensuing
Meiji era, the need for modernization was accepted, and numerous foreign advisers helped to introduce Western technology and to reorganize the economy,

agriculture, education, and the army. Many students (mostly graduates) were sent for advanced training abroad. In 1870 there were 500 such students in the United States (Bennett *et al.,* 1958). Indeed the Japanese in the 1870s were fascinated with anything western. The samurai (Chapter 4) were no longer allowed to wear swords, and they became the "gentry" and the bureaucrats, who still held all the positions of power. But they amounted only to some 7% of the population. Three-quarters consisted of peasants, some quite wealthy, others living in extreme poverty. About 40% of male adults were literate; thus a large pool of labor was available for training in industry and commerce, or as public servants, skilled workers, teachers, etc. By the end of the century Japan had fought successfully with China, and in 1905, when the encroachment of Russia in eastern Asia was resented, Japan defeated her in the Russo–Japanese war with a convincing show of strength.

Astonishing technological and economic progress followed, and it became only too obvious to the United States and European nations in the 1930s that the militarists were taking over more and more control, and that their aim was completely hegemony over Asia. Also, there were strong expansionist pressures, because so much of the land in Japan is too mountainous for urban development or agriculture. By the 1930s, Japan was planning to attack not only the British Empire in the east, but also to take on the United States. So great was her military and naval might that she nearly succeeded, having destroyed most of the American Pacific navy in 1941 and subjugated British colonies and treaty ports, and many of the Pacific islands, in 1942. In alliance with Germany and Italy, world conquest appeared possible. However, the democracies had sufficient resilience to turn the tide, and eventually forced Japan to capitulate in 1945. The occupation of Japan by the American army and the imposition of a new constitution and important social reforms in 1946 are described later in this chapter.

THE BEGINNINGS OF IMMIGRATION TO THE UNITED STATES

Apart from some emissaries and students, no emigration was allowed until the 1880s, when the pressures of overpopulation and poverty led to a change of policy. First a few, and by 1900 many thousands, went to seek their fortunes as laborers in Hawaii, the western United States, or Canada. There was no mass recruitment by foreigners as had happened in China; the emigrants were volunteers. However, they did come under contract for 3 to 5 years and were treated almost as slaves in the plantations or lumber camps, working from dawn to dusk for very low wages. They were at first generally welcomed by employers (Sue & Kitano, 1973), since the 1882 Chinese Exclusion Act, which did not apply to them, was beginning to produce a shortage of labor. They were described as "loyal, hardworking, honest, stoic, patient, patriotic, selfless, and persevering"

(Kitano, 1969). Also, Japan was admired for its easy victories over China and Russia. The Japanese were more law-abiding and honest than the Chinese, were insistent on bodily cleanliness, and were not addicted to gambling. But they were also dissatisfied with their initial menial employment; and once their contracts were fulfilled, they moved into market gardening or other occupations. A great many returned to the homeland, especially when white hostility began to grow. (The first strong anti-Japanese protest occurred in San Francisco in 1900.) But more and more came to take their places. The Japanese differed from the Chinese in that many brought in wives, especially from 1907 on, so that they were able to bear children and settle down as normal families. Marriages were sometimes arranged for them in Japan, and the brides were shipped over to men whom they had never met.

There is some disagreement among commentators as to the social class and educational level of the original stock. Some say that they were poor peasants who nevertheless made their way and became upwardly mobile (e.g., Glazer, 1969). Others claim that a large proportion were middle class, with a good eduction to Grade 8 level, and that they were successful because they were above average to begin with (Strong, 1934; Sowell, 1975). Kitano (1969, 1976), and Petersen (1971) seem to believe that both are true—that the original immigrants, mainly to Hawaii, were indeed lower class, whereas many later ones, especially on the mainland, were superior both in ability and initiative and ambition. The matter is complicated also since many of the arrivals in California came there from Hawaii.

An unique feature of Japanese immigration was the clear distinction drawn between successive generations. The first generation were called *Issei,* and their children *Nisei.* Third to fifth generations were *Sansei, Yonsei,* and *Gosei,* respectively, though the two latter terms are seldom used. In addition there were the *Kibei,* that is, the sons of Issei who were sent home to receive a substantial proportion of their education in Japan between 1920 and 1940. This practice aroused the ire of white propagandists, although they amounted only to about 13% of Japanese Americans at any one time (Strong, 1934). There was little sympathy between the Kibei and Nisei.

Whether or not the original Issei were above average in ability, it would be true to say that they were mainly lower class in their outlook, and that they came from a narrowly restricted culture, whereas the Nisei rapidly propelled themselves into the American middle class after World War II.

Anti-Japanese Agitation

As the numbers of Japanese males and their families increased, particularly in California, and as they began to compete with whites for jobs, suspicion and opposition grew. Indeed the whites felt themselves more threatened by the

Japanese in the 1900s than by the Chinese in the 1870s, although there was less actual violence against them. The amount of competition was indeed small, except in the produce industry and contract gardening. In 1940, 40% of Japanese still lived and worked in the countryside; they supplied almost all the celery and strawberries in Los Angeles county. Complaints were common that all members of a family worked without wages in the fields. Probably they were more successful than whites because they were more efficient and hardworking. Some turned to the fishing industry; those who moved into urban areas ran small businesses, including restaurants, shops, and laundries, where they naturally employed other Japanese. Some boys worked in skilled trades, for example, carpentry, and some girls as domestics, or in offices or sales jobs. But the growing second generation of Nisei, who refused to remain unskilled laborers, did have very restricted job opportunities. They could not even return to Japan, since already they were speaking more English than Japanese, and were not really fluent in either language. The Issei projected their own amibitions onto their sons, and ensured that they received the best education possible, even at considerable sacrifices.

In 1907 the so-called Gentleman's Agreement was reached with Japan, whereby further immigration would be limited to nonlaborers and to wives. Yet the total numbers of immigrants continued to rise (see Table 1.1). The Issei and later immigrants were not eligible for American citizenship until 1954. But the Nisei who were born in America were accepted as citizens provided they renounced their Japanese citizenship. Unfortunately, some three-quarters failed to do so, and this was held against them as evidence that their allegiance was to Japan and its emperor, rather than to the United States (Grodzins, 1949). California legislation prohibited the attendance of Japanese children at white schools. But President Theodore Roosevelt realized how this would offend the susceptibilities of the Japanese government and revoked it. They were also barred from using white swimming pools. Next the California growers, allied with the labor unions, politicians, and press, harassed the food producers by the California Land Act in 1913, which prohibited noncitizens from owning or leasing land. They could not, however, prevent the Issei from putting the holdings in the names of their sons who were citizens.

The major blow was the 1924 Federal Immigration Act, which denied entry to Japanese as well as Chinese. The Japanese government naturally resented this as a deliberate insult, and it was partly responsible for the hatred of the United States by Japanese militarists. The immigrants were bewildered, and their case was taken up by a number of supporters such as the American Civil Liberties Union (ACLU) and the churches, on the grounds that the Japanese were valuable citizens, but their efforts were in vain.

What were the main objections, in addition to undercutting by Japanese workers? The threat of the Yellow Peril was revived. Though their actual numbers in

California were quite a small proportion—2% of the population—it was said that "They breed like rabbits." True, their birthrate around 1920 was about twice as large as that of whites, and greater than that of Chinese (hence the continued growth of mainland Japanese in the 1920s and 1930s, shown in Table 1.1). But soon the rate began to fall, and by 1940 the average family size was quite comparable to that of Caucasians. They were feared and loathed also because of the increasing power of Japan in Asia and the Pacific.

The color and physical appearance of the Japanese made them highly visible, and thus laid them open to racial discrimination (Park, 1950). Moreover, they differed from the Chinese in being more "cocky" or assertive; they did not give in passively to injustice. The strong cohesion of the Japanese family helped to give them more confidence. Many families cooperated as business partners, and this group loyalty was also denounced as "nationalistic." Compared with other immigrant groups, for example, those from Europe, the Japanese were a more homogenous and cohesive, and therefore a more threatening, culture. There were also associations formed for representing Japanese interests and for preserving the traditional culture and helping new immigrants, though these were not so highly structured or organized as those of the Chinese. In spite of discrimination in the matter of housing, the Japanese did not concentrate to the same extent in ghettos. There were some enclaves, labeled Little Tokyos, but a large proportion of them were rural residents, and others managed to find more dispersed housing in lower-class city areas.

Though the Japanese showed rapid adaptability and openness to Western ideas, they still carried the reputation for heathen practices. Indeed it was true that in Japan itself, even in the late nineteenth century, babies regarded as surplus by their parents (especially girls) might be abandoned to die of exposure. The fact that many Japanese immigrants adhered to Buddhism and Shintoism was taken as another sign of their outlandishness and devotion to Japan, which made them nonassimilable in a Western country. Actually many did join the Christian churches, partly in the hope of winning wider acceptance, but they were often rebuffed by white churchgoers. The setting up of a number of private language schools (particularly in Los Angeles) for teaching children the speech and culture of their parents and forefathers was regarded as another fault, although the same thing was quite common, for example, among Jews or ethnic minorities from Europe. The baselessness of many of these accusations was shown by the existence of much larger proportions of Japanese in Hawaii. There, too, there was considerable opposition to their socioeconomic progress, but they lived this down and became integrated into the polyglot Hawaiian culture with remarkable rapidity (see Chapter 6). Moreover, as Strong (1934) points out, the Japanese had very low delinquency and crime rates and made little recourse to social welfare.

After 1924 the opposition in the United States died down somewhat, until reactivated by the threats of war in the late 1930s. But the Japanese remained a rather isolated community, unable to make the kind of economic progress to which they aspired, because of the unwillingness of whites to accept them as co-workers. Again, the hostility was strongest in California, and the most rabid attackers were recent white immigrants, such as the Irish. Much the same kind of stereotypes were expressed about the Japanese as had previously been applied to the Chinese though in addition the Japanese were frequently called "imperialists" and "warlike nationalists." The views of the general public were much more unfavorable than the views of college students, as sampled in investigations by psychologists (e.g., Katz & Braly, 1933). These views were also much more antimale than antifemale. For all these reasons there was little progress in acculturation from 1920 to 1940 (Sue & Kitano, 1973). The following occupational distribution for Issei in 1930 (Strong, 1934) indicates their inferior status:

Agriculture	38%
Fishing	12
Service occupations	13.5
Retail	12
Professions	5.5

Smaller proportions were employed in business, skilled trades, etc.

PEARL HARBOR AND RELOCATION

By the end of 1940 there were some 127,000 Japanese in mainland America, of whom 112,000 resided in California or other Pacific Coast states; there were about 158,000 in Hawaii. Subsequent to World War II many writers have referred to the treatment of the coastal Japanese after the Pearl Harbor attack as a shameful episode in American history, not only because it caused severe and unnecessary hardships, but also because it was quite unconstitutional for the government to imprison and relocate American citizens who had committed no crime. In fact over 70,000 of the 110,000 who were evacuated inland were American-born Nisei, who were American subjects, though admittedly only a minority had actually renounced Japanese citizenship (Miyamito, 1973). The most extensive research into why, when, and by whom the decision was made, is that of Grodzins (1949). Although he gives a rather one-sided picture, he did analyze all the accessible evidence and expressed his conclusions in sober, rather than emotional, terms. A more recent report by Daniels (1975) made use of hitherto unpublished government documents and telephone conversations. But these led to much the same conclusions as those of Grodzins.

The attack on Pearl Harbor took place on December 7, 1941. There was not, in fact, any immediate panic nor public outcry for the evacuation of Japanese

Americans. Some 1200 rabid pro-Japanese nationalists were interned, but the war department did not believe that Japan would attempt any attacks on the West Coast. However, by January 1942, following still further victories by Japan in the Pacific and southeast Asia, anti-Japanese feeling was whipped up by local politicians, the press, and the unions, etc., and complete removal of all Japanese from the western states was demanded. (It was even suggested that the sexes should be separated so as to prevent the birth of additional Japanese.) The phrase was reiterated: "A Jap is a Jap anywhere," regardless of whether or not he is an American citizen. A freeze was imposed on all Japanese bank accounts. Rumors of sabotage in Hawaii and fifth-column activities on the mainland were rampant, though none were ever substantiated. Threats were raised that vigilante actions would endanger the Japanese themselves, even if entirely innocent. The federal justice department opposed evacuation, and congressmen from inland states had little sympathy with this move. But so strong was the pressure from the West that in February the government agreed to proscribe certain protected areas (i.e., of military importance) and to remove Japanese residing there inland. Finally in March, 3 months after Pearl Harbor, the war department undertook to remove all Japanese from these states, and to set up inland relocation centers. The process was completed in August 1942, when 110,000 Japanese had been moved.

It seems extraordinary that President Franklin Roosevelt agreed to sign the necessary orders without full cabinet discussion or congressional debate. But he was harassed at that time by the war in the Pacific, and he did instruct the army to "be as reasonable as you can" (Daniels, 1975). There were some protesters, but they were overridden in the name of "military necessity." No one bothered that there were many more Italians in the West than Japanese, and also Germans, yet proposals to intern them were never implemented. Nor was it noticed that in Hawaii, where the Japanese constituted a far higher proportion of the population, no action beyond internment of a few subversives was demanded or found necessary. It also seems surprising that the Japanese themselves acquiesced so tamely. They were of course bitterly resentful, but they cooperated because of their engrained respect for authority. A very few attempted court action, but eventually the Supreme Court rejected their pleas on the grounds of war-time circumstances.

Miyamito (1973) suggests that the main factors responsible for the evacuation were (1) anti-immigrant propaganda; (2) California politics and unions; (3) economic competition of Japanese with whites; (4) segregation of Japanese communities, and racial stereotypes; and (5) Japanese–American international relations. Grodzins' conclusions were similar, but he saw as the most important outcome the precedent that had been set for arbitrary government intervention, which might recur in the future.

A great many of the internees were ruined financially, having lost their homes and businesses and receiving inadequate compensation, if any. Families were often wrenched apart. Their future in the United States appeared hopeless. The centers or camps were in desert-like areas in eastern California and as far away as Arkansas. A wage of about $15 a month was paid, plus board and medical attention. However, the restrictions were gradually relaxed, and by 1944 some 30,000 younger men, that is, Nisei, had reached Chicago or other inland cities, where they made a good impression and were accepted with little discrimination. It has been said that white Americans felt guilty over the treatment of Japanese Americans, and the use of the atom bomb, and therefore turned in their favor once the war was won.

In certain ways the relocation turned out to be a blessing in disguise. Most of the original Issei were too old to provide any leadership. Their sons, usually 30 to 40 years younger, spoke English, and therefore became responsible for carrying on negotiations with the authorities. Thus the family system, including parental authoritarianism, broke down, and the Nisei were able to make a fresh start and to show initiative, independence, and competitiveness in American society (see Broom & Kitsuze's discussion of acculturation, 1955). Naturally, there were bitter conflicts within many families, but the sons now seized the opportunity to become upwardly mobile, and in a few years made their way into professional or business careers, or skilled occupations. It is somewhat ironic that the Nisei derived their tremendous motivation for educational and occupational achievement from the traditional upbringing given them by the Issei fathers.

By the 1950s the Nisei were accepted at their face value in the East, though still regarded with some suspicion in the West. They dropped the use of their ancestral language more rapidly than the Chinese, and the influence of Japanese language schools and associations declined. They were generally regarded as able, trustworthy, and very hardworking employees, though apt to be overambitious. Kitano (1969) suggests that their family upbringing and culture had produced many able organizers, entrepreneurs, and professionals, but few outstanding leaders in politics or in the creative arts. Elsewhere Kitano (1976) refers to Japanese Americans as "middlemen," since very few fell in the lower SES range, and they were hemmed in from reaching the topmost levels.

THE SANSEI

In the 1950s and 1960s, the third generation Sansei were reaching maturity. They were somewhat of a disappointment to their parents. Not having experienced the earlier hostility of whites, they adopted many of the current white behavior patterns, and were thus regarded as "too Americanized." They all expected to enter clean white-collar jobs, and some 88% of them, as compared with 57% of Nisei, received "some" college education. By 1960, Japanese of both sexes exceeded even Chinese and whites in average years of education

(Schmid & Nobbe, 1965; Levine & Montero, 1973). They were no longer concerned about acceptance by white society, and aimed more at self-determination. Although they thought of themselves as American rather than Japanese, they were proud of their Asian-American identity, and not desirous of complete integration (Maykovich, 1973).

Gehric (1976) studied young adult Sansei by intensive interviews, and reports on their frustrations and difficulties. They had been brought up to be compliant, and to avoid expressing their feelings publicly. Thus, they regarded themselves as having been too much sheltered from the outside world. Though accepted as Americans by their peers, they made few friends with whites, and seldom got invited out. Hence, they suffered from lack of social activities. At the same time they were still strongly motivated to achieve, so as not to let their families down.

While only a small percentage of Nisei had married non-Japanese, Kikimura and Kitano (1973) state that in the early 1970s, half of the marriages of Japanese in Los Angeles were with Caucasians or other ethnic groups. According to Sue *et al.* (1975) this out-marrying was far more common among Japanese girls than boys, though Tinker (1973) believes that the imbalance is disappearing. Except for the continued infusion of new immigrants from Japan, it would seem that there will eventually be no pure Japanese.

The Sansei and later generations have become the most advanced of all ethnic groups in the United States and Canada, in terms of education and income. As Kitano and Sue (1973) put it, they are the "model minority." They have the lowest unemployment rate and crime or delinquency rate. Kitano (1969) quotes the following numbers of arrests per 100,000 of the population in 1960:

United States as a whole	1,951
Whites	1,461
Negroes	5,642
Indians	13,867
Japanese	187

In particular, Japanese seldom take part in organized or gang crime. Japanese Americans also have very little recourse to social welfare agencies. But nowadays this is becoming more common. As with the Chinese, it is not true that "they always look after their own people."

Another common stereotype of them as "overachievers" is hardly justified. Though very seldom retarded at school, they do have their share of below-average pupils; personality studies, outlined in Chapter 14, show that many are poorly adjusted. Present-day Japanese still retain the emphasis on obligations and reciprocity (see Chapter 4), and on educational achievement. There are some links with the original culture, maintained by Japanese associations, special television programs, etc. Few children are sent to Japanese language schools, but there are other private Japanese schools in large centers, catering especially to the children of transient parents who are residing only a year or two in the United States or Canada, usually as students, business representatives, or diplomatic personnel. These schools aim to keep the children's education up to the standards expected in Japan. If they attended white public schools only, they would fall considerably behind in the educational rat race at home.

DEFEAT, REFORM, AND PROGRESS IN JAPAN

Though not directly relevant to our story of Japanese Americans and Canadians, it is of interest to describe what happened to the Japanese in Japan after the war, since it throws further light on the process of acculturation.

In addition to the destruction of Hiroshima and Nagasaki by atomic bombs in 1945, most large Japanese cities were severely damaged before the emperor and the government capitulated. The country was a shambles, and for several years the general standard of living was much reduced. As is well known, the American army of occupation under General Douglas MacArthur took it over and devised a new constitution, which was accepted by the Japanese government in 1946. The treatment of the vanquished by the victors was generous and humane, hence it succeeded in its main objective of orienting Japan firmly to the West, and preventing any resurgence of militarism or any attachment to communism. All the day-to-day running of the country was left to the Japanese themselves to work out; the position of the emperor was handled tactfully. Though his divinity was abolished, and he became a constitutional figurehead, his agreement to the proposed changes was crucial to their acceptance by the country as a whole.

The fighting services were abolished, though a strong police force was substituted, which in fact possesses the equipment and training of a small army. It is also known as the self-defense force. (Incidentally, this made it possible to provide more funds for social reform.) In addition, the nationalistic fervor was reduced by decentralization and reform of youth organizations and the education system. State Shintoism too was banned. Even a democratic form of government, similar to the American form, was imposed, though it turned out that the Liberal–Democrats (i.e., the conservatives) had a permanent majority, and the opposition was too factionalized to be effective. The law of primogeniture was altered so that all offspring should have equal rights of inheritance,[1] and the tenured farming system abolished. The equality of women, including voting rights, was established. Inflation was halted, and an equitable taxation system was introduced. The large business corporations, or *zaibatsu*, were disbanded, though by now they are again a prominent feature of the economy.

[1]In rural areas primogeniture is still prevalent, so that the land does not become unduly subdivided.

The docility of the Japanese in accepting these changes contrasted strongly with their bellicosity and inhumanity during the war. It has been suggested, perhaps not very convincingly, that the wartime atrocities occurred simply because the Japanese officers and troops were obeying orders from above given by misguided leaders. But I would consider that their behavior may have been a resurgence of the cruelty associated with the samurai in the seventeenth through nineteenth centuries. Indeed, they were as cruel to their own comrades as to the enemy, killing off those who were wounded rather than let them be taken prisoner. No one can say whether this could not happen again, or whether the Japanese conversion to humanitarian ideals is by now firmly entrenched (Stoetzel, 1955).

Clearly, however, the Japanese civilian leaders in 1945–46 realized that militarism had failed, and therefore set out to build a new political and social system. Their success was remarkable, probably because of the effective cooperation among government, business leaders or employers, and workers. It would be too much to expect the Japanese to abolish all their traditional values overnight, and indeed some of them are appropriate to a modern capitalistic society, for example, paternalistic management–labor relations. But in fact the process of change had been going on throughout the twentieth century. More and more Western ideas had been imported before the war, and many customs, such as primogeniture and subjugation of women, were already beginning to break down. In some respects, indeed, traditionalism was already giving way to modernism more rapidly than it did among the Japanese in the United States, Hawaii, or Canada. Yet, Park (1950) believed that, despite the phenomenal technical growth of Japan, there had been little change in basic values.

An interesting and important investigation was carried out by Stoetzel (1955) into the amount of change that had really taken place in the attitudes of the Japanese 5 years after the new constitution. Public opinion surveys, covering 2671 adults, and intensive interviews were used, and particular attention was paid to the views of young adults. The general conclusion was that there was still a good deal of ambivalence and insecurity. Even today, there are conflicts between the traditional and the progressive features of Japanese society. Stoetzel found that democratic ideas were accepted by the great majority, but also many elements of the prewar culture were operating quite widely, for example, the lower position of women in society. Though by now more women are employed (usually at much lower wages than those of men), a great many still prefer to retain their subservient position in the home.

The majority of youths were definitely pacifist and fearful of becoming involved in any Third World War. There is still strong opposition to any rearmament, although the United States is now pressing for it. The young people were also more willing to exercise responsibility and to recognize that the future depended on their own efforts.

In another study by Kato (1961), a 20-item questionnaire was given to a mixed group of high school and college students, and adults. The questionnaire asked for their views on controversial political and social issues. The informants were generally democratic in their opinions; they were against communism but were more tolerant of it than Americans, and they were more in favor of public ownership of basic industries. Larsen *et al.* (1973) compared the attitudes and goals of student activists in Japan, United States, Norway, and Finland. And, at a younger age level, Goodman (1958) interviewed 5- to 12-year-old Japanese and American children, and analyzed essays on the topic: "What I want to be when I grow up." This too showed that, despite acceptance of many American ideas, the children continued to emphasize the Meiji values of kinship, unselfishness, duties, and obligations.

Bennett *et al.* (1958) described "the search for identity" among Japanese thinkers and leaders by interviewing and assessing some 63 young adults who had studied abroad. Many became alienated on returning because they had dropped out of the conventional channels of career-building, and found that their newly acquired qualifications had little market value. They were suspected of over-Americanization if they tried to introduce fresh ideas. Women in particular, who preferred a career to getting married, had severe difficulties.

There have been many further changes since 1955. Worship at Shinto shrines continues, but the influence of all traditional religions seems to have declined. In their place a number of new religious movements have sprung up, most notable of these being the Sakagakkai. This attracts large numbers, and it has grown into a powerful political force. Repayment of obligations is still a major value, and it could hardly be legislated against. But it is becoming more flexible, and—as in America—voluntary rather than binding. Arranged marriages also could not be abolished, but there are now many more love marriages, in which the couple usually try to get parental approval.

POSTWAR ACHIEVEMENTS OF JAPAN

A detailed survey of the social, political, and economic factors that underlie the extraordinary advances in Japan since 1946 is provided by Vogel (1979), and a more popular account of modern Japan is given by Forbis (1975). Vogel believes that the major difference between Japan and western countries is that, in the former, all important decisions are based on rational planning, and are guided by extensive study of all the relevant information. Thorough discussions are held by all parties likely to be affected. (In contrast, American leaders trust their own judgment and act on their own initiative, taking very little account of opposed interests.) In addition, the morale and loyalty of all members of most Japanese firms or businesses are extremely high. They put tremendous efforts into their work. There is very little class bias or pay differential between managers and workers, such as occur in Western countries, including the United States. Consequently, strikes are very rare, and there is scarcely any unemployment. Firms fulfill on time any contracts they undertake.

Forbis coined the phrase "111 million overachievers" to describe the astonishing growth of Japan since 1946. Certainly Japan is the most Westernized of Asian countries, and the general standards of living are now approximating those of the United States and are superior to those of most Western countries. Per capita income reached three-quarters that of the United States in the mid-1970s, and is quite comparable to those of Canada and Germany. However, the cost of living is high, and housing is far less luxurious and more cramped than in the West.

Although the population of Japan is about one-half that of the United States, and the total area close to that of the state of Montana, its economy is the second largest in the world, and its industry the most efficient. This is not generally recognized in North America, partly because the Japanese are not given to boasting, and partly because Americans resent the fact that they have been overtaken and surpassed in many ways. They often try to explain away Japanese prosperity by such special factors as low wages. This may have been a major contributor before the war but is not so now; the argument is merely a rationalization. Currently though, like most "developed" countries, Japan is faced with serious economic instability.

Japan now builds more than half the world's ships, and is the biggest producer of pianos. In 1980 Japan even exceeded the United States in numbers of cars produced. According to Vogel, the rate of car production is five times that of the United Kingdom. Japan has the fastest and most punctual train service, and the quickest mail service, the lowest illiteracy rate, and the highest proportion of adolescents completing secondary school education. There are more universities and colleges in Japan than in all Western European countries combined (according to Forbis). Also, a much larger proportion of students come from relatively low-income families than in the West. The Japanese people have the longest life expectancy, and the lowest crime rate of any developed nation.

During the period from 1960 to 1973, when crime rates were increasing in the United States and Europe, the rate actually dropped in Japan, and is now fairly stable. According to Vogel, there are four times as many murders and rapes per capita in the United States as in Japan, and more than a hundred times as many robberies (see also Kumasaka, Smith, and Aiba, 1975). The major reasons would seem to be the careful upbringing of Japanese children and the strong group pressure of each local community or business firm on their members. Currently, however, there is a striking rise in juvenile delinquency and violence.

Japan is also notorious for the radicalism and violence of student groups. But this reached its peak in 1969, and has been largely brought under control by riot police, though it is by no means defunct. This phenomenon can hardly be ascribed to the war or its aftermath, but it may reflect the growing disillusionment of the young with the intensely technological civilization in which they live, with the severe pollution that it brings about, and the frequent occurrence of corruption in high places. Although pollution is a serious problem in such a small country, Japan has actually gone further than any other country in controlling it. Lebra (1974) suggests that social deviance and student anarchy have arisen because of the breakdown of moral training in the home following the war. It is relevant too that such students have lived through "the examination hell," under continual pressure from home and school to achieve. During the interwar years only some 0.3% of the population gained entry to universities, and though this expanded sixfold in the 1950s, there was still severe competition. On entering college, students lose much of the security of family life and have not yet joined the world of adult employment. When they do attain this latter stage, they are apt to settle down and join the establishment that they were previously attacking (see also Murphy, 1974).

Torrance (1980) lists 18 ways in which Japan is number one in the world. Some of these claims seem dubious. For example, wage rates are high, but not higher than American wages in relation to cost of living. Also, many would query his belief that the social climate is more favorable to creative thinking, invention, and innovation, than in any other country. This hardly accords with the amount of cramming, homework, and private coaching preceding university entrance examinations. However, he does describe remarkable maturity in motor skills and expressive movements among children in kindergarten, and a trend away from rote to discovery learning. Finally, the Japanese are the world's most avid tourists abroad, and indeed attract some resentment in North America, the United Kingdom, and Europe because of their ubiquity and clannishness, inability to speak the language of the visited country, and their spending power. But this could hardly be called the reemergence of racial prejudice against them. Indeed there is currently more international criticism of Japanese trading practices, since Japan exports better and usually less expensive cars, cameras, electronic equipment, etc., than Western nations, and thus undercuts Western manufacturers. But here too, any controversy is not apparently accompanied by racist undertones.

4

Japanese Culture, Childrearing, and Personality

INTRODUCTION

The best-known book on this topic is Ruth Benedict's *The Chrysanthemum and the Sword* (1946). It was written at a time when the defeat of Japan in World War II appeared to be imminent, and America would soon be faced with the problems of dealing with a government and people of totally different beliefs and practices from those current in the West. How could Americans best handle a sacrosanct emperor and the extreme militarists and nationalists of the armed forces, build up a new and more democratic society that would cooperate with the West, and not be liable to yield either to totalitarianism or communism?

Benedict's work has been criticized as dealing more with the traditional samurai culture than with the typical society of the 1940s; also because it was not based on firsthand observation in Japan, and it ignored individual differences by overemphasizing the concept of a ''national character,'' as though all Japanese were alike. Nevertheless, it still seems to give the most complete analysis of Japanese values by a non-oriental writer, and it does draw on a wide range of literature by Orientals, as well as knowledgeable Western authors. Probably it applies most closely to the middle and upper class Japanese in the 1930s. Naturally there have been changes in post-war Japan, and even greater changes among Japanese who have lived for two, three, or more generations in the United States, Hawaii, or Canada, though many of the features of family life, mentioned later in this chapter still seem to apply to middle-class Japanese Americans in, say, the 1950s. Johnson, Marsella, and Johnson (1974) believe that much of the norms of social behavior current in the Meiji era still persist among Japanese Americans. Hence this chapter is mostly written in the present tense, though I am well aware that some of it may be out-of-date. As mentioned in Chapter 3, Stoetzel's (1955) book was mainly devoted to showing how far the picture had changed in Japan itself since Benedict's publication (see also Inomata, 1957).

49

HIERARCHY

Benedict's key concept is that of hierarchy. As Kitano, a Japanese American, wrote in 1969: "From birth on, a Japanese was accustomed to put the interests of his family, village, kin, nation, and emperor ahead of his personal interests. His behavior was dictated by clearly defined rules and obligations." Everybody recognized the hierarchy and nobody stepped out of place. Thus, males ranked higher than females; older persons higher than younger; educated higher than less educated; and those in senior occupational positions higher than junior. Likewise, families owe allegiance to local authorities; local administrators to the higher political and military leaders; and leaders to the state and its supreme symbol, the emperor. The same applied in the international sphere. Japan could not accept the Western notion that all states have equal rights. Instead, she wished to impose a hierarchic structure, at least in the Pacific region, with herself as head.

This goes back to the pre-Meiji era when a feudal system existed under the shogun, representing the emperor. The population was categorized into six castes in the following order: the daimyos (nobles), samurai (their body guards and retainers), peasants, artisans, and merchants. At the bottom were the Eta (similar to the Untouchables in India), who were workers in skin, leather, blood; for example, butchers. They lived in segregated ghettos in villages. Intermarriage or other contacts with the Eta were unthinkable. Forbis (1975) indicates that there are still some two million of them, but that this discrimination is slowly breaking down (cf. p. 63). In a different category are the Ainu, or Caucasoid aborigines, who had been driven out by Mongolian invaders. Only some 18,000 still exist, living as hunters and fishers on a few northern Japanese islands or the Kuriles (Russian). Many of them have interbred with Japanese, and their original language and culture have been largely repressed.

Only the daimyos and samurai were allowed to have personal names and to carry swords or other weapons. They were free to kill (and often cut into small pieces) any member of the lower castes who showed them insufficient respect. Clavell's novel *Shogun* gives a vivid picture of the extraordinary inhumanity and brutality which was combined with strong aestheticism among the Japanese in the seventeenth century. Hence, Benedict's title—*The Chrysanthemum and the Sword*—the chrysanthemum being the symbol of the arts. The samurai were intensively trained in the Bushido ideal of courage, justice, politeness, sincerity, honor, self-control, and unquestioning loyalty to their masters; they unhesitatingly committed hara-kiri, or *seppuku,* if they offended their liege–lord. Although, as shown in the preceding chapter, this sytem was effectively abolished by the Meiji restoration, yet much of the traditional ideals persisted, particularly in the armed forces, and reemerged in the atrocities committed in World War II, in the kamikaze and in the refusal of Japanese troups to surrender until this was ordained by the emperor himself.

RELIGIONS

The three main religions of Japan are Shintoism, which is indigenous, Buddhism, and Confucianism, both of which were adopted from China. They differ so widely from Western religions that is hardly possible to characterize them succinctly. But they are so closely bound up with Japanese culture that an attempt must be made. Shintoism came down from pre-history; it combines a kind of primitive nature worship with nineteenth-century nationalism. It recognizes many gods and goddesses, and innumerable spirits (*kami*), including the family ancestors, and these are worshipped with traditional ceremonies and ritual at the thousands of Shinto shrines in Japan. The Sun Goddess is believed to have sent her grandson to be the first emperor, hence he and his unbroken line of descendants were regarded as divine and commanding absolute obedience from his subjects. Thus, Shinto was the state religion, which all loyal Japanese adhered to, until it was disestablished by the American Occupation in 1946.

Buddhism is more the personal religion of the masses of Japanese. Its major teaching is the impermanence of things, and the need to subdue human passions and feelings in order to reach nirvana, or the state of perfection and ultimate detachment. The Japanese version of Buddhism, known as Mahayana, included Zen with its emphasis on meditation as the means of enlightenment, together with self-abnegation, austere discipline, humility, and generosity to others. It also stresses harmonious relations between parents and children, husband and wife, other kin, and friends. Thus, Japanese family life and child upbringing are largely based on it. Buddha is regarded as a teacher, not a god; his statue is contained within many temples where offerings are made to the deities. Often, these are combined wtih Shinto shrines.

Confucianism is atheistic, but it embodies Confucius's sayings about the rules of proper conduct and social etiquette, filial piety, benevolence and sympathy to others, loyalty, and faithfulness. It underlies many of the Meiji values and ideals.

The Japanese often adhere to a flexible combination of all three, and they took them with them to North America. Very few became Christians in Japan itself, though the present number approaches one million. Many more Nisei and Sansei adopted Christianity in the United States.

THE FAMILY

Both in Japan, and among the Issei in North America, the Japanese family is a very tight structure, more like the Western nuclear than the Chinese extended family. However links are retained with a wide range of kin, sometimes referred to as "the household," and similar to the Chinese "clan." Families of younger brothers branch off from the direct line of father–eldest son and set up on their own, but continue to get advice and support from their relatives. Though the custom is now dying out, it was common for the parents to continue to live in the eldest son's home.

Within the family the father is (or at least was) dominant, and the wife self-effacing. No one dared question his word. He was always served his food first, and even nowadays he may see little of his children because of long hours of work, or indulgence in drinking or in extramarital sex (Conner, 1976) before coming home. It has been suggested that Japanese children are somewhat backward in verbal reasoning, relative to their nonverbal intelligence, because there is so little communication, discussion, or encouragement for them to think for themselves. The mother is subservient not only to her husband, but also she must submit to the authority of the father's parents. Naturally, this causes a great deal of discord. Nevertheless, when she grows up to become a mother-in-law in turn, she assumes the same role towards her daughter-in-law. The mother's place is entirely in the home, looking after the disciplining the children, and generating a pleasant social climate. She is expected to be more loquacious than the male, smoothing over any conflicts, and always deferring to her husband or to male acquaintances. Yet she has more rights than do women in Moslem or Indian countries. She generally manages the family financial affairs. In farming families she is an indispensable worker. The greater egalitarianism in most American families seemed odd to the Japanese who emigrated. Nowadays, however, quite a number of women do have jobs, though their liberation is still far behind that enjoyed by Japanese American girls and wives. Insofar as almost all marriages were arranged by the parents, there was no necessary connection between marriage and love, although this generally grew over the years. Thus to the early Japanese in America, the displays of affection in public between lovers or spouses were regarded as shocking. An interesting indication of the close-knit family group is that the Japanese prefer to sleep close to one another. Their houses are small and contain few rooms; thus sometimes three generations or relatives of unlike sex share the same rooms.

Child Socialization

All Japanese babies tend to receive more body contact with the mother than do whites (Caudill, 1973). After one month they are carried around, tied by a sash to the mother's back, and they always sleep beside an adult. Thus a great deal of warmth, dependency, and security are fostered, and this continues even into adulthood. Indeed, dependency is the norm, not something to be grown out of (Doi, 1969). The children are spoiled and treated very permissively in the early years. They were usually not weaned until another birth was due, though now the common age is about 8 months. Toilet training started early at 3–4 months, but is now much later. The beginnings of training in posture, manners, etiquette, etc., are introduced gradually even before 2 years of age. The main method of control is shaming or ridicule, or temporary banishment from the group, rather than physical punishment or psychological persuasion. They are taught very early to suppress undue displays of anger, even of affection, to conform and speak correctly, to recognize the rules of precedence in the family, and to show obedience and deference to their elders. This applies mainly to boys, and especially to the eldest son who would inherit all the family assets when the father died. The training of girls is less strict, and is devoted more to their future functions as wives and mothers, and to accepting the dominance of the male. Thus, girls were expected to bow to their elder brothers as well as to the father, though this has now died out. In both sexes much emphasis is laid on unselfishness, and sharing with siblings or with peer-group friends.

By about the age of 9, the training of boys becomes more rigid, dealing with the rules of etiquette, how to address superiors or inferiors, and how to avoid being shamed, or shaming others. The father plays little part in the socialization. He expects and gets complete and rapid obedience, but he should not be described as highly authoritarian. The need for high achievement at school is impressed very early (Lyman, 1970), but competitiveness against other children is minimized, until tests are given in grade school. Because of this protective background boys are actually somewhat ill-equipped to cope with the examination system that they meet from Grade 4 through the secondary schools and universities. Murase (1974) discusses the resulting mental health problems among adolescents. Examinations cause a great deal of strain and anxiety, and lead to cramming rather than intelligent learning. At the same time the school counseling service is quite inadequate.

Japanese boys are dominated by a lifelong fear of being ridiculed or shamed for failure. But they do not acquire the sense of guilt or the internal controls that motivate ''good'' conduct in westerners. There is (or rather was) no mixing of the sexes at middle school and no sex instruction until the 1950s. Hence the boys are apt to be gauche when first allowed to meet their prospective brides. There is also much hazing by older boys, which generates further repressed aggressiveness.

If any delinquency is committed outside the home, or failure at school, this reflects on the honor of the whole family. Besides restitution, if possible, apologies are expected before the delinquent regains his position in the family. In the Western world, parents and friends usually try to help the youth who has committed an offense against society. But in Japan his own group sides with society in condemning him.

Adult Intercommunication

Adult Japanese are very conscious of their own status, and of those of any persons with whom they are communicating. Lyman (1970) indicates that they develop a highly sensitive and circumspect perception of others. According to

Johnson *et al.* (1974; see also Johnson & Marsella, 1978), the Japanese language itself is rich in words indicative of status, and additional cues to feelings are supplied by gestures (e.g., bowing) and facial expressions. Some words also are used only by women, others only by men. The initial greetings always embody rituals that must be followed meticulously. Each speaker shows, on the surface, politeness, equanimity, and self-detachment; but in fact both are carefully analyzing the other's strengths and weaknesses. Each avoids accusing the other of any error, since it would cause shame to the other, or, if the accusation is unjustified, the accuser would be shamed. The Japanese seldom speak directly on any issue, but use a great deal of circumlocution (Caudill, 1973). Since both parties are familiar with these tactics, each is able to infer what his interlocutor really wants. But each speaker, as it were, holds the other at arm's length, and each tries to divert attention away from himself.

Americans find if difficult to observe these conventions, since their speech is much more open, direct, often breezy, and it varies little according to the relative status of the speakers. Naturally this leads to many misunderstandings when American and Japanese try to communicate. The Japanese traditionally assume self-abasement, modesty, exaggerated deference, and politeness which, to the westerner, appear ridiculous. Among Japanese males, speech is very economical, especially in public situations. They refrain from expressing their own views, unless they can do so with authority, and they avoid showing any emotion. Thus, they tend to speak in a "flat" tone, and they lower their voices if speaking to superiors (Ayabe, 1971). Another aspect of this ritual deference is that, when things go wrong, they usually accept the blame, rather than fight about it; or they dissimulate by minimizing the effects of the other person's actions so as to save his face. The free and easy display of feelings by American speakers, and their public disagreements strike the Japanese as acutely embarrassing (Berrien, 1965).

Benedict makes the interesting suggestion that when two westerners have dealings, each is seen by the other as a distinctive and stable personality, who will react in the same way to most everyday circumstances, whereas the behavior of a Japanese depends much more on the circumstances of the particular encounter. If he does possess a basic personality structure, he is careful to conceal it and to behave strictly according to the rules for such an occasion.

Obligations

When one Caucasion helps another in any way, the latter normally feels and expresses gratitude, and is more ready to do something helpful to the former, when the occasion arises. But the first person usually does not expect or exact repayment (unless some actual financial transaction is involved). The Japanese, by contrast, live in a world of reciprocal obligations, debts, and credits (Johnson,

1977). Any favor must be returned, and the return should be calculated in such a way that the donor is adequately repaid, though not so highly that the original donor will now feel indebted. If repayment is slow in coming, it should be increased, as if interest had been charged. Since there are no clear rules for estimating the worth of a favor, the system is a source of continuous worry. Yet the obligation is as strong as our own system of paying off a mortgage. Incidentally, the son who inherits his father's estates also inherits his debts and obligations that have not been repaid, otherwise his honor would be blemished. He is also obliged to look after his mother if she is alive. However, the abolition of primogeniture by the 1946 constitution led to the decline of this convention. Benedict provides a great deal of detail on different types of obligation, and how they should be met. For example, any insult or shaming should likewise be repaid by some appropriate vengeance.

Because the Japanese male is reluctant to take the initiative and make his own decisions, he tends to seek advice on any important issue from relatives and friends, and to go by the consensus of opinion. Moreover, many business firms appear to have taken over the family structure and to organize their staff in a similar manner (Lebra and Lebra, 1974). There are many more small businesses in Japan than the United States, and in these it is common for the head of the firm to adopt paternalistic attitudes towards his employees, and they reciprocate by their loyalty to him. It is thus by no means unusual for men to stay with the same firm until their retirement. A considerable proportion of the population enjoys lifelong security. This promotes social and economic stability, and minimizes disputes or class-conflict between employers and workers. Caudill (1973) states that in all firms, in government or education, etc., there is a tight vertical structure between the various grades of employees. But with other similar organizations there is fierce competition, and therefore very few ties between equals in different organizations such as are common in the Western world.

CAUDILL'S THEMES

It will help to summarize much of this chapter, and include some further details, by listing the 12 main themes which Caudill (1973) regards as basic to Japanese culture and personality.

1. Emphasis on group and community, rather than on the aspirations of individuals.
2. Sense of obligations that must be repaid; gratitude and loyalty to one's groups.
3. Sympathy and compassion for others, though not if this conflicts with the sense of duty.
4. Ethnocentrism and nationalism; pride in being Japanese as opposed to other

nationalities. This was accentuated by 200 years of isolation, and the wars with China, Russia, and the Western world allies, but has been much reduced since World War II.

5. Underlying excitability and emotionality, which are controlled by compulsive attention to details and rules. To this one might add that conduct is determined more by external sanctions than by internalized conscience.
6. Willingness to work hard, and for long hours, toward long-range goals.
7. Devotion to parents, especially to the self-sacrificing mother.
8. Emphasis on self-effacement, and on getting others to assume responsibility.
9. Deference and politeness to superiors, or to any person with whom one has some ties.
10. Understatement, and preference for nonverbal communications.
11. Fatalism, as preached by Buddhism; everyday concerns are ephemeral.
12. Pleasure in the simple things of life, such as beautiful surroundings, in eating (which is quite abstemious), in sex (which is accepted much more openly than in the West), in playing with children, and in bathing, which promotes relaxation and enjoyment as well as cleanliness.

The Japanese also have great artistic sensitivity, though mainly in some restricted areas; for example, drawing and engraving rather than oil painting; decorative arts; sculpture and statuettes, ceramics; poetry; and musical performance rather than composition (including the Suzuki method of teaching young children to play stringed instruments).

Undoubtedly a great many of the twelve characteristics described have died out, or at least have declined, among postwar Japanese Americans. However, it has been suggested that the Nisei achieved such high educational and occupational success in so short a time because their value system happened to be similar to that of western middle class; hence, acculturation was easy. Both, for example, have a strong need for achievement (but cf. p. 195). Meredith (1965) believes that it would be more true to say that the two value systems were parallel or compatible in certain respects. And there were also such basic differences that even in the 1970s, assimilation is far from complete, and the Japanese retain a strong feeling of subcultural identity.

Briggs (1954) compared 45 JA and 31 Caucasian youth in Los Angeles, with particular regard to family structure. The father was the dominant person in making family decisions, but this was also true of the Caucasians. Actually the Japanese reported more arguments within the household, and more "talking back" to the father than did the Caucasians. But there is some doubt as to the representativeness and the SES of Brigg's samples; for example, his Japanese youths may have been very highly acculturated.

JAPANESE AND CHINESE

Clearly there are many resemblances between the childrearing practices of Japanese and Chinese, and in America both groups are very similar in abilities and high occupational achievement. But there are also many cultural differences that are presumably responsible for the greater stoicism and patience of the Chinese, and the greater drive, aggressiveness, innovativeness, and adaptability of the Japanese. For example, the Japanese family is more firmly structured, the Chinese more extended. In pre-Meiji Japan one's position in the community was entirely fixed by birth, whereas the Chinese had no such caste system, and upward mobility depended more on performance at examinations (Park, 1950). The Chinese have not shown the same brutality as the samurai of old and the Japanese army during the war. But the Chinese are notorious for their use of torture and the callous disregard for human life by the war lords and revolutionary leaders in the nineteenth and twentieth centuries. The Chinese may be devious in negotiating, but their approach does not, like the Japanese, involve adherence to strict rules of etiquette. Many other cultural differences in attitudes and patterns of behavior could be cited (Marsella, Kinzie, & Gordon, 1973). Thus, although one might think that Chinese and Japanese who had experienced similar hostility in North America might have profited from collaboration, it seldom if ever occurred. This may well have been due to the longstanding enmity between China and Japan. The Chinese will not readily forget the many aggressive attacks by Japan from the 1890s to 1945, particularly the imposition of the "21 demands" by Japanese invaders in 1915, and "the rape of Nanking" in 1937.

Psychopathology

We might expect to obtain some information on Chinese and Japanese personalities from the types of mental disorders to which they are prone. But most attempts to compare mental health, or pathology, cross-culturally have been of little value. Partly this is because psychiatrists in different countries have different definitions of common disorders, and apply different standards of classification (e.g., United States psychiatrists employ the diagnosis "schizophrenia" much more frequently than do the British). And partly because it is highly likely that in different cultures people react to different kinds of stress, or may display different symptoms of the same underlying condition (Caudill & Lin, 1969; Draguns, 1973; Marsella, 1979). Even if there are universal types of mental disorder, it is probable that they would express themselves differently in different sociocultural environments. It is scarcely possible to avoid ethnocentricity, that is, applying western concepts of mental pathology, and trying to fit

Asian or African behavior abnormalities into these concepts. Ruth Benedict and others have drawn attention to the relativity of what is called normal or abnormal in different cultures. In a study by Li-Repac (1980), therapeutic interviews of five Chinese (CA) and five white clients were videotaped. These were then shown to Chinese and white therapists, and there were many differences in their interpretations, though quite good agreement in their assessments of degree of normality–abnormality. Whites saw Chinese as more depressed and inhibited and poorly adjusted socially than did Chinese therapists, who in turn saw more severe pathology among white clients than whites did.

Marsella (1979) provides a thorough survey of the whole area, and points out the different approaches to causation or explanation of disorders. Thus, from Rousseau to Freud it was popularly supposed that mental disorders are largely attributable to the vices of civilization. But it is evident now that quite primitive peoples also show serious disturbances. However, it does seem that depression occurs more frequently in Western and urbanized societies than in non-Western mainly rural environments. Also in more primitive societies the mentally ill tend to act out their anxieties ''through gross hysterical manifestations or through aggressive panics'' (Stoller, 1969).

Thayer, Arkoff, and Elkind (1964) gave a 60-item questionnaire on mental health to 74 Orientals (of mixed origin) and 44 Caucasians, including 20 clinical and counseling psychologists. When the items were factor analyzed, considerable differences in factor structure appeared between the two races. Possibly the Orientals were more influenced by an acquiescent response set (cf. p. 196). But their views were also less sophisticated since the professional mental health movement has made little progress in Asian countries. For example, a large proportion of Orientals accepted the view that mental health can be improved by exercising one's willpower and avoiding unpleasant thoughts.

There have been many attempts to survey the incidence of various disorders in different societies. But often the published figures depend on the numbers of mental hospitals or other facilities for treatment that are available. Since there are few such hospitals in Asian or African countries, those who are seen by psychiatrists may differ considerably from the mentally ill in the total population. Then, too, there are usually considerable variations in different age groups, and between the sexes, so that any single figure for the incidence of, say, schizophrenia or depression, may be meaningless.

Psychoses in Oriental Countries

Kitano (1970) analyzed hospital records and interviewed the families of some 1800 schizophrenic Japanese in four areas: Los Angeles, Hawaii, Tokyo, and Okinawa. In all places the main symptoms appeared to be withdrawal, bizarre behavior, delusions and hallucinations, and difficulties in school or at work.

Okinawa, having the most rural environment, differed from the other three in several respects, such as a low rate of voluntary commitment but a high rate of commitment by the family. The reactions of relatives differed also, since mental illness is often seen as a stigma on the family. Hence those who are admitted as patients may become quite isolated from relations and friends. However, in Tokyo relatives do visit the patients more frequently, and in Los Angeles very little. Terashima (1969) discusses the tendency for Japanese families to react by denial, isolation, and rejection of the mentally ill. They usually regard the condition as hereditary; hence, it signifies weakness in the family. Alternatively, in more backward areas, they attribute the illness to evil spirits.

Kitano (1969) also reports low admission rates of Japanese Americans to Hawaiian mental hospitals, but states that this may be due largely to the reluctance of families to report cases of insanity. Berk and Hirata (1973) discuss the incidence of psychosis among Chinese Americans in California, criticizing the common view that the strength of the Chinese family system protects the Chinese from the strains and anxieties of modern life. With the growth of acculturation, the Chinese are less apt to conceal cases of mental illness. Thus, nowadays the incidences of schizophrenia and affective psychoses are quite similar to those of whites.

Returning to Asian figures, Lin (1953) carried out a survey in Taiwan and reported unusually small numbers of psychotics, namely 3.8 per thousand. He compares this with several other surveys where the incidences range from 3.8 per thousand in part of Germany to 10.9 in Denmark and 14.3 in Norway. He quotes 6.5 per thousand for the United States (1936–38) and 8.0 in Japan. In a follow-up survey 15 years later (Lin, Rin, Yeh *et al.,* 1969) the number of psychoses remained almost the same, though mental defectives and psychoneurotics had increased greatly.

Tseng and Hsu (1969) also write on psychoses in Taiwan, suggesting that the rate is low probably because of the warmth and security provided by the Chinese family in early childhood. There is more neurasthenia, hypochondria, and psychosomatic disorder than depression. Indeed, the Chinese do not have a word that corresponds exactly to "depression," and the people seldom express feelings of loneliness or sadness as do Westerners.

The Japanese, however, have a term "*yuutsu*" that is regarded as equivalent to depression. Tanaka-Matsumi and Marsella (1976) compared free associations to the word depression given by Japanese American and Caucasian students, and associations to *yuutsu* given by Japanese (JJ) students. The great bulk of the JA and Caucasian associations described mood states, for example, sad, lonely, down, blues. But few of these were given by Japanese, and their associations referred more to external events—rain, clouds, murky; also to worries and examinations. The authors conclude that Americans (including JA) are more inwardly-directed, the Japanese more outer-directed. To the former the self is an individualized conception; in the latter it always depends on social relationships to others.

Marsella, Kinzie, and Gordon (1973) further discuss ethnic variations in depression. In an attempt to demonstrate them, they applied Zung's Depression Scale to 500 college students in Hawaii, of whom 196 obtained high depression scores. Factor analyses of item responses were carried out with 130 Japanese, 36 Chinese, and 30 Caucasians, and somewhat different factors were obtained in the three groups. The items tended to group into similar, but sometimes distinctive, clusters. Though the results are interesting, they were obtained from essentially normal students, and therefore have little bearing on psychotic adults.

In another study, Marsella, Murray, and Golden (1974) explored the connotative meaning of "shame" among 97 Caucasian students, 102 CA, and 125 JA. They were given eight concepts (including shame), and were asked to rate them on 20 Semantic Differential scales.[1] Factor analyses of the scales in each of the groups did result in similar evaluation factors, though there were more differences on other factors. Shame was seen as aversive by all groups, but was more clearly distinguished from other emotions by the oriental groups. The differences in interpretation of shame show that a psychotherapist who is treating non-Caucasian clients needs to be aware of these varying connotations of the same concept.

A more direct comparison between Chinese and Japanese psychiatric patients was published by Rin, Schooler, & Caudill (1973; see also Caudill & Schooler, 1969). Samples of over 800 were collected in Taipei and Tokyo. The patients' doctors filled in a checklist of symptoms, and a factor analysis of these items yielded patterns quite similar to those found in other countries. The Chinese more frequently displayed hostility, break with reality, and hypochondria; the Japanese were more given to obsessionality, phobias, depression, psychosomatic disturbances, hebephrenia, or apathy. In 1969, Caudill and Schooler reported Japanese schizophrenics as being more violent and emotionally impulsive than American patients. Part of the differences between Japanese and Chinese might arise from the much greater technological advancement in Japan than Taiwan. But the authors conclude that the Japanese tend more to inward-oriented disorders (or turning against oneself); the Chinese are more outward-oriented (turning against others). This description of the Japanese seems directly contradictory to Tanaka-Matsumi and Marsella's finding (cf. p. 59).

The most extensive cross-cultural study of psychosis was carried out by the World Health Organization (1979; also Sartorius, Jablensky, & Shapiro, 1978). The major aim was to develop standard diagnostic procedures and schedules that could be used uniformly by a team of psychiatrists in nine different countries: 5

---

[1]The Semantic Differential and its application are described in Chap. 15, p. 217f.

Western, 1 African, 1 South American, and Agra and Taiwan in Asia. Also, a computerized program was constructed for categorizing patients on the basis of the schedule of symptoms. Of 1202 patients seen in 1968–69, two-thirds were diagnosed as schizophrenics, and 909, or 75%, were traced and reassessed 2 years later. Thirty-seven percent of the schizophrenics were still classified as psychotic, but a great many who showed similar initial symptoms diverged quite considerably at follow-up. The numbers of patients who were substantially improved were much higher in the underdeveloped countries (South America, Africa, and India) than those in the Western countries. Over all the centers, 23% still showed substantial social impairment, but the figures for Western countries approximated 30%, Taipei 20%, and underdeveloped countries 15%. A great deal of data was collected on predicting course and outcome from initial symptoms and background factors. Multiple regression analysis showed that 24–30% of the variance in outcome could be predicted in Western countries, but only 13–21% in the underdeveloped countries because of the greater instability of their symptoms. As one might expect, the most predictive variables differed considerably for different countries. No special characteristics of the Chinese are discussed, but Taiwan was usually intermediate between the Western and underdeveloped countries.

Two other major studies are of more methodological than substantive interest, insofar as they try to meet the difficulties in making cross-cultural comparisons. Seifert, Draguns, and Caudill (1971) collected detailed schedules of the symptoms of 412 psychiatric patients admitted to Tokyo hospitals in 1958. The majority were diagnosed as neurotic or schizophrenic, and smaller numbers as manics or character disorders. There were marked differences in the symptoms and modes of expression of these disorders. Compared with similar data collected in the United States, the overall "styles" of mental pathology were similar in Japan, though there were ethnic differences in specific features. This meant that the same diagnosis (e.g., schizophrenia) might differ considerably in meaning in the two countries. The Japanese neurotics and manics were inclined to turn against others, whereas the schizophrenics were more apt to turn against the self.

Lorr and Klett (1969) have done a great deal of work on classification of pathological symptoms by factor analysis. Two hundred patients in each of seven countries—United States, England, France, Germany, Italy, Sweden, and Japan—were assessed on a list of 75 symptoms by their psychiatrists. The data in each country were factorized, and 10 Principal Components representing different clusters of symptoms were obtained. These components or dimensions could be closely matched across countries. The most consistent ones, which were quite similar throughout, were labeled Excitement, Perceptual Distortion, Grandiosity, Anxious Depression, Retardation, and Disorientation. The profiles of scores of the countries on the 10 components are given, though the authors admit that direct comparisons across countries are dubious, partly because the samples were not all selected in the same way, and partly because the psychiatrists' training might affect their understanding of the symptoms. The main importance of this study is that checking of specific symptoms is much more objective than trying to classify patients under a few conventional, but ambiguous, categories such as schizophrenia, depression, etc. It was noticeable that the Japanese patients frequently manifested Perceptual Distortion and a Paranoid Projective syndrome, though they were not outstandingly higher or lower than the other countries on any syndromes.

Lynn (1971) has collected numerous statistics on mental disorders in 18 countries, and quotes the death rate from duodenal ulcers as 11.9 per 100,000 among Japanese, which is the highest in the world. The United Kingdom was next at 10.2; France and Norway were the lowest with 3.2 and 3.0, respectively. This condition is often attributed to the anxiety syndrome, or high neurotic drive. However in hypertension the Japanese were close to the mean for all countries. Further work by Lynn on anxiety is summarized in Chapter 14.

Suicide in Japan. One of the most objective and easily recorded symptoms of mental pathology is the suicide rate. While there are always uncertainties about unsuccessful attempts, the death rate certainly represents serious mental disturbance in all developed countries. The most common modes of self-destruction vary; and there are differences in acceptability and willingness to resort to suicide in different countries. For example, predominantly Catholic countries (where suicide is a mortal sin) have lower rates than Protestant countries and some non-Christian countries. In Japan, suicide was officially sanctioned and approved for many centuries, and this may still be partly responsible for the high rates commonly reported. The incidence also differs at different ages, usually being highest among 15- to 24-year-olds, next at 60 years and over. But it is reasonable to regard the figure for youths and young men as reflecting the degree of mental stress experienced at this period, and therefore the overall amount of strain and frustration in any society (Sato & Sonohara, 1957).

Though the figures given for different dates by different authors vary, they all agree in putting Japan at or near the top. Lynn (1971) tabulates the numbers per 100,000 of the population in 1960 as follows:

Highest				*Lowest*	
Austria	23.1			Norway	6.5
Japan	21.6			Italy	6.3
Finland	20.5	United Kingdom	10.6	Holland	6.1
Denmark	20.3	United States	10.6	Ireland	3.0

Iga (1971), Naka (1965), and Ishii (1972, 1973, 1977) have all published extensive reports on suicide at Kyoto and its university. The university rates have been exceptionally high, exceeding those of most other Japanese institutions, as well as those in the United Kingdom, United States, and most of Europe. Iga points out that Kyoto is one of the most prestigious universities, with the highest academic standards, and it is a notorious center for student radicalism (though Ishii mentions that student activists are not themselves particularly prone to suicide). On the basis of case studies of completed suicides, unsuccessful suicides, and controls, Iga believes that there is a great deal of emotional insecurity in this age group; and also that there are still many conflicts in the intelligent young between traditional and modern values. Other causes relate to the family situation and failure in academic work.

Naka (1965) studied 419 cases of completed suicide in the general population of Kyoto, including university students. Some cases were as young as 8 years. Unlike Ishii, he found suicide more frequent among working youths than in school and college students. In 1955 in the 15–19-year-old age group, for males there were 37.6 suicides per 100,000 and for females, 26.4. But in the 20–24-year-old group there were 84.8 and 47.2, respectively. The highest rate of 128.5 males and 61.7 females occurred among unemployed young adults. He lists as the most common causes: examination failure, overwork, unemployment, somatic illness, family troubles, disappointments in sex life, anxiety about the future, and weariness with life.

Ishii (1972, 1973, 1977) collected statistics at Kyoto university from 1965 to 1975. There were 46.5 per 100,000 suicides in the 1960s, but the rate declined in the 1970s, that is, at the time when student activism became most rampant. Indeed Vogel (1979) believes that the rate in recent years is quite similar to that in Western countries. Most of Ishii's data were obtained from interviewing the families of 79 suicides. He lists similar causes to Naka, adding lack of friends, little extracurricular activity, and tendency to show mental disturbance and depressive states. Suicide is not a sudden decision; it usually has a long history, including a great deal of worry while at high school. One-third of completed suicides had made one or more unsuccessful previous attempts. However, it is difficult to know at what point psychiatric help is needed. Two-thirds had not given any advance warning, and one-fifth were actually under treatment when they killed themselves. Note that all three authors put part of the blame on academic pressures, but it is by no means the chief or only cause. Indeed, in the majority of cases the major motivation could not be determined.

The Buraku

An interesting deviant group, studied by DeVos and Wagatsuma (1969) are the descendants of the Etas, known as Buraku. Though no longer outcasts, they are regarded by most Japanese as mentally and morally inferior, and there is still considerable discrimination, which is partly attributable to their own hostility to the majority culture. They tend to segregate themselves in slum areas, and have joined up with left-wing political groups. Though the children are not notably

TABLE 4.1
Delinquency Rates in a Large Japanese City for Buraku, Koreans, and Japanese

Population group	Total population	Number of delinquents	Rate per 10,000
Japanese majority area	1,098,541	493	4.49
Buraku area	47,023	71	15.10
Koreans	22,365	63	28.17
Other non-Japanese	10,468	6	5.70

backward scholastically, there is a lot of truancy, delinquency, and crime. They are particularly given to intimidation and extortion. DeVos and Wagatsuma obtained records of delinquency among 633 14- to 19-year-old boys living in a city of over one million inhabitants in 1957–63. It may be seen from Table 4.1 that Koreans living in Japan have the highest delinquency rate, but the figure for Buraku is more than three times that for the Japanese generally. Quite like the blacks in the United States, they are reacting aggressively against the conventional norms.

5

Tests of Japanese Children[1]

INTRODUCTION

Much more research involving intelligence tests has been carried out by Japanese psychologists in Japan than by Chinese in China,[2] since psychology has been taught in Japanese universities from early in the twentieth century. Both translations of Western tests and tests constructed by Japanese psychologists on Western models have been used. It is difficult to provide a comprehensive survey since doubtless more has been published in Japanese than in American journals, and this literature was inaccessible to me. However, Osaka (1961) provided a useful survey of intelligence and achievement tests in Japan from 1908 to 1958, including 93 references.

As early as 1922, Kubo translated, adapted, and standardized the Binet–Simon scale in Japanese. In order to reduce its verbal emphasis, several new performance items were introduced. How far it was possible to find Japanese equivalents for English (or French) words and sentences is not stated. The test was given to 1200 children in Tokyo, aged 2 to 15 years, and items were reassigned to their appropriate Mental Age levels. The IQs of 536 6 to 9-year-olds gave a median of 98, and a range from 65 to 125. No comparisons with Western test results were attempted.

In 1934, we find an account of the development of a nonverbal group test for fourth to sixth grade Japanese children by Tanaka. This contained 10 subtests, and it was standardized on over 3000 children. No normative data are given.

[1] Additional studies of Japanese abilities are surveyed in the later chapters on Hawaii and Canada, and on adult oriental students.

[2] There are psychologists in China, though few publish in English-medium journals. The Chinese Psychological Association was formed in 1937, and grew to over a thousand members by 1965. All psychological activities were then banned by the Cultural Revolution and the Gang of Four. But the association was resuscitated in 1977 (Ching, 1980).

WECHSLER INTELLIGENCE SCALES IN JAPAN

Let us now jump to the Wechsler scales, all three of which have been adapted and standardized for Japanese adults and children. These studies are usefully summarized by Lynn (1977b).

The Wechsler Intelligence Scale for Children (WISC) was adapted in 1951, and standardized on 1970 5- to 50-year-olds. All the verbal subtests except Digit Span were necessarily very diferent from the American originals, hence their results cannot be compared with American norms. But the performance subtests (with the exception of Picture Completion) were kept identical. Thus the mean scaled scores on Digits and performance tests, and Performance IQs, are comparable with American white norms. As against the American mean scaled score of 10 for all subtests, the Japanese scored 11.5 on Picture Arrangement and Coding, 10.6 on Block Design, 9.8 on Mazes, 8.9 on Object Assembly, and 8.4 on Digit Span. The mean Performance IQ for all Japanese age groups was 103.1 (which is significantly higher than 100 at the .05 level). But the superiority was much more marked in 5- to 7-year-olds than at later ages.

The Wechsler Adult Intelligence Scale (WAIS) was translated and restandardized on 1682 adults in the mid-1950s, but only the Digit Span, Coding, and Block Design subtests were identical, or nearly so, for comparisons to be made with American scores. The mean IQs for 35- to 44-year-old Japanese on these three tests were 100.0, 105.4, and 106.4, respectively, by American norms (which, incidentally, were based on the total United States population, not whites only). Thus the average superiority is much the same as on WISC.

The Wechsler Preschool and Primary Scale (WPPSI) was restandardized in the 1960s on 600 Japanese ages 4 to 6 years, and the five main performance tests were all unchanged. Japanese scores were considerably superior to American, and the mean Performance IQ works out at 111.7—a highly significant difference.

The average figure for all three tests in 106.6, but note that this is based almost entirely on performance tests, and no information is available on Verbal IQs. Also Lynn admits that we cannot tell just how representative the samples were of the Japanese population. However, the three studies do point to some superiority over American norms in mean IQ, which is most marked among younger children. As Lynn points out, this contradicts such commonly stated beliefs as that American tests are biased in favor of white middle class and high SES children. Despite Japan's rapid economic growth after World War II, the calorie consumption and per capita income were far lower than in America. One possible factor that Lynn does not take into account is that American test performances have also risen markedly in the last 20 years or so. Thus Thorndike (1972) found Terman–Merrill IQs some 10 points too high from 2.0 to 5.0 years, though dropping to two points by 10 years, and then increasing again to IQ 107 by 16 years. These figures rather closely paralled the superiorities noted by Lynn. The newly standardized WISC–R in 1974 was likewise found to be giving IQs about four points lower than those registered on the old WISC (Doppelt & Kaufmann, 1977). But in a study by Schwarting (1976) of 58 children who took WISC and WISC–R (in random order) the Full Scale IQs on WISC were even larger, namely by 7½ points. Comparisons of norms are dubious also because some American standardization samples have included black and other minority groups, others not. However, Lynn claims that exclusion of these groups would raise the norm only about 1½ points higher than when they are included.

In a later publication, Lynn and Dziobon (1980) developed an interesting technique for comparing IQs in two ethnic groups that have taken different verbal intelligence tests, by giving both tests to a third group, which acts as a bridge. The Kyoto NX 9–15 test is well standardized in Japan. Seven of the subtests (including Abstract Reasoning, Spatial Ability, and Numerical Ability) could be adequately translated into English, and these were given to 97 boys and 115 girls in Coleraine, Northern Ireland; their mean age was 10.3. The same group took the Primary Mental Abilities (PMA) test, which is well standardized in America. It was thus possible to convert the Japanese test scores into equivalent PMA IQs from the Irish data. The mean Japanese PMA IQ by this method was 110.26, which suggests an even greater superiority in intelligence than the studies of Wechsler tests. Note also that my suggested explanation in terms of out-of-date IQ norms does not hold, since Thorndike's Binet IQs and Japanese WISC norms showed very little change at 10 years. A possible flaw, however, is that Lynn's Irish children might be more handicapped on subtests translated from the Japanese than on PMA tests.

I would conclude, then, that Lynn's case for the superiority of the intelligence of Japanese to American children is not proven, though it seems to be better substantiated among younger than older children. Other studies, summarized in the following sections, do give stronger evidence of the superior abilities of JJ and JA older children and adults. Meanwhile, we can accept that intellectual development in the preschool years is more rapid among the Japanese. There seems to be a remarkable wealth of Japanese games and books available to parents of young children, to stimulate their minds. Some of these materials are quite similar in content to some of the WPPSI and WISC subtests.

OTHER INTELLIGENCE TEST STUDIES IN JAPAN

Kuroda (1959) gave the Suzuki version of the Binet (standardized in Japan), together with the Goodenough Draw-a-Man test and the Raven Colored Progressive Matrices, to 80 kindergarten children, aged 4½ to 6½ years. He admits that the sample was mostly middle and upper class. Comparisons were not made with

American or British norms, but Matrices mean scores are quoted for 50 children taking the individual Board Form, and 30 taking the group Book Form.

	Boys	Girls	Raven Norms
Board	20.1	19.7	12
Book	13.9	15.4	14

Raven's published median scores for 5½-year-olds are added in this table. The results are puzzling: Japanese children are much the same as Scottish on the Book Form, but far superior on the Board. The above-average SES of the Japanese sample could not account for this. Possibly the Board test was given in some easier way. Or it may be that Raven's norms at the bottom end of the age scale are unreliable. Indeed it is odd that Raven himself found lower scores on the individually administered Board Form than on the Book group version.

Another study of Japanese children was carried out by Prichard, Bashaw, and Anderson (1972). An 18-item rating scale was devised for assessing academic, emotional, and interpersonal maturity (Kim, Anderson, & Bashaw, 1968). One hundred Grade 2 Japanese children were rated by their teachers on this scale. The school grades and scores on a Japanese version of the Otis Quick-scoring test were also available. The authors agree that a scale developed in Japan would have been preferable. But on factorizing the item-ratings for Japanese children, they were found to load on the same dimensions as in the United States, that is, six items to each maturity factor. High congruence coefficients with American factors were obtained, showing that the scale was measuring much the same variables across cultures. No comparisons seem to have been made between Japanese and American maturity scores. But the authors found higher correlations between such scores and overall school achievement (.76, .54, and .61, respectively) than between Otis and achievement (.48). This is hardly surprising since the teachers who made the ratings were presumably aware of the children's scholastic abilities. Also the Otis Group test could hardly be very reliable at this age.

COMPARISONS OF SCHOLASTIC ACHIEVEMENTS

A large amount of cross-cultural data has been collected by Husén (1967) and his colleagues in their International Educational Achievement (IEA) Project. This has covered several school subjects, including Mathematics and Science (Comber & Keeves, 1973).[3] Objective achievement tests, based on analyses of

[3]Reading and Literary Comprehension have also been studied, but these tests were not given in Japan.

the curricula in different countries, were constructed at several educational levels by an international committee, and these, when suitably translated, were applied to large samples, representative of their age groups, in some 10 to 20 countries. Husén warns us not to think of the results as a kind of competitive race between the countries; he is more concerned with the effects on scores of school organization, teacher qualities, home factors, etc. However, it is worth extracting some results for a few countries, including Japan, which educates a larger proportion of its population to advanced secondary level than any other countries except America and Canada. England and Finland are included as examples of countries that are highly selective, since only about one-quarter of the population get education from 16 years up. Mean scores are shown in Table 5.1, and the percentages staying on at school at 16 years appear in the second column. Note that different tests were given to each age group, hence comparisons should not be made across rows, but only down columns.

The figures given in columns 1a, 1, and 2 are based on representative samples of the population of each country. Japanese students achieve much the highest scores in Mathematics and Science. In columns 3a and 4, the United States students are weak in Mathematics, compared with Finland and England; but all three countries are fairly similar in Science in column 2.

The final-year students in Mathematics (Sample 3a) score highest in England, but they represent only the top 22% or so of the population, as compared with Japan's 60%. And the United States figure is much the lowest, largely because it continues to educate 86% at high school. In view of this circumstance, the Japanese score of 31.4 for Mathematics in Sample 3a represents a higher level of achievement at this age than the English 35.2. There is no doubt that the mathe-

TABLE 5.1

Mean Scores in Mathematics and Science of Japanese, American, and Other Samples

Country	Percentage at school at 16+	Mathematics		Science		
		Samples		Samples		
		1a[a]	3a[b]	1[c]	2[d]	4[e]
United States	86%	16.2	13.8	17.7	21.6	13.7
England	22%	19.3	35.2	15.7	21.3	23.1
Japan	60%	31.2	31.4	21.7	31.2	Missing
Finland	31%	24.1	25.3	17.5	20.5	19.8

[a] All 13-year-olds
[b] Final year in high school
[c] All 10-year-olds
[d] All 14-year-olds
[e] Final year in high school

matics curriculum in Japan is more advanced than in the United States or United Kingdom. The final-year Japanese did not take the Science test.

Gensley (1975) also comments on the high educational achievements of Japanese students in science and mathematics, attributing them partly to good schooling, but suggesting that the students work harder because of their high educational aspirations and family pressures to do well. These two subjects are not the only highly developed ones. English is taught in all Japanese secondary schools, and examinations in English are required for university entrance. Cummings (1974) describes the changes in education in Japan since World War II. Before and during the war, great stress was laid on loyalty to the emperor, and the need to work for the nation rather than for self-advancement. Now, of course, the pendulum has swung too far, and Japanese education has become notorious for its rat-race competitiveness, and the pressures on students (see Chapter 4 on suicide).

JAPANESE-AMERICAN CHILDREN

As early as 1923, Fukuda tested 43 Japanese American children with the Stanford–Binet scale in English. Some highly verbal items were omitted or substitutes were found. The children ranged from 3 to 12 years, with median 6 years. The median IQs were boys, 92; girls, 97; and combined, 95. However, the children were probably of above average ability, since one-third of the parents were professional or upper business, and less than one-third semiskilled or unskilled. Considering their linguistic difficulties it is unlikely that a representative sample of Japanese Americans would have averaged more than IQ 90 on verbal tests in the 1920s.

In 1926, Goodenough reported some results on the Draw-a-Man test (see p. 19). Also Darsie (1926) gave several tests, including Stanford–Binet, to 686 Japanese students in California, aged 10 to 16 years. Omitting 186 from rural areas, the remainder were said to be more used to speaking English than Japanese. The mean IQ was 91, but it was mainly on linguistic items that the students were weak. The Army Beta nonverbal test was given, and here the means were much the same as those of American whites; indeed on some subtests at 12 years, the Japanese were superior. Darsie concludes that there are only slight differences in mental capacity between Japanese and Caucasians, though the Japanese are lower in memory and reasoning tasks involving English comprehension; they are equal in memory and thinking tasks based on visually presented or concrete materials, and are superior in tasks involving visual perception and recall, and tenacity of attention.[4]

---

[4]I have not had access to the original monograph, hence I cannot describe what test of "tenacity of attention" was used. It could be merely Digit Span.

Teachers' gradings showed the Japanese to be much below the white average in reading and language; a little lower in informational subjects; approximately equal in spelling and arithmetic; and superior in penmanship, drawing, and painting. There was some tendency for school grades to drop with age, but Darsie suggests that this occurs because duller white students tend to drop out of high school, whereas almost all Japanese are pressured by their families to stay on and complete twelfth year. Personality ratings indicated that the Japanese were more emotionally stable, more sensitive to approval, and responsive to beauty, though lower in self-confidence. It might be that, with the omission of rural families, the sample would be above average. But apparently they mostly lived in the poorer areas of the cities. Their performance is all the more striking when (according to Kitano, 1969) Japanese was almost always used at home, even in the 1930s.

E. K. Strong, who worked at Stanford University from 1923, published a major work on *The Second Generation Japanese Problem* in 1934. He reported only slight differences in abilities between whites, Chinese, and Japanese. The latter were somewhat retarded in linguistic subjects, though superior in mathematics and spelling. Their average age–grade placement was 4½ months below the white norm. Although those in school were now second-generation Nisei, their English speech was reported to be poor both in California and Hawaii. They retained Japanese accents and tended to follow Japanese sentence structures. In contrast, the middle and upper class Chinese were speaking perfect English. Yet the Nisei preferred using English, although their Issei parents spoke Japanese almost exclusively. Some students were attending Japanese language schools at this period, but seldom achieved much fluency in their native tongue. On the other hand, such attendance did not seem to affect their English adversely.

Strong mentions that, although the average height and weight of Japanese were lower than those of whites, there were no differences in reaction time or coordination. Thus they should be capable of any manual skill. They showed good recognition of perspective and color, and visual memory for form, but lacked originality in their drawings. None of those at college were specializing in art. (This topic is expanded later in the chapter.) Occupational interests at the high school age were similar to those of whites, though with some differences (Chapters 13 and 15).

Garth and Foote (1939) tried to find ways in which Japanese verbal thinking differed from that of whites. Although, by this date, there was very little difference in ability test scores, the content and range of associations of ideas might differ. They followed a technique developed by Jastrow in 1896. Eighty-four Japanese American boys and girls and 156 whites in Grades 10–12 were asked to write any words that came into their minds for a 5-minute period. The words were classified under 26 categories, and a comparison made between the frequencies of the categories in the two groups. The correlation between Japanese and whites was .92, indicating rather little difference in category usage, and high community of ideas. There were larger differences between the two sexes ($r = .79$), and the greatest discrepancy was between Japanese males and white females. The Japanese gave more adjectives than whites, and named wearing apparel more frequently. But in general, neither content nor parts of speech yielded much that was psychologically meaningful.

Similarly, Moran (1973) and Moran and Huang (1974) classified the free word associations of Japanese, Chinese (Taiwan), and white children aged 4 to 6 years, under Bruner's categories: *enactive, iconic,* and *symbolic,* or *logical.* Most of the oriental children's responses to a standard set of words were enactive (e.g., stool–sit, table–eat). Another group of Japanese adults had predominantly iconic associations (e.g., crow-black, black–hair). But American children's associations were more logical (e.g., crow–bird, black–white). However, the applicability of Bruner's stages to word associations is doubtful and apt to be subjective. Thus the results, as in Garth's study, seem to tell us little of interest about Chinese and Japanese children's mental processes (see also Chiu, 1972).

Evacuation in World War II

In the 1930s Japanese at school were often referred to as "ideal students" (Kitano, 1962). Indeed by the early 1940s the average number of years of education completed was 12.2 among Nisei, as compared with 10.1 for California whites (Maloney, 1968). Then in 1942 came the relocation of all Japanese living near the Pacific Coast, which of course completely upset their education. Nevertheless in most of the inland camps, arrangements were made for elementary and secondary classes, even if only with half-day attendance. Facilities, equipment, and books were inadequate, and there were very few white teachers. But later there was some relaxation, allowing Japanese to attend local schools, and some families to settle further inland. Pusey (1945) was able to test 484 Japanese junior high school students (and a few at higher grades) in a relocation center. All were American-born children of Japanese parents. They had missed three full months' schooling during the evacuation, and another 3 to 4 months when, later in 1942, there was a riot in the camp. Pusey was mainly concerned with Japanese performance in different aspects of arithmetic. He gave the Metropolitan Tests of Arithmetic Fundamentals and Arithmetical Reasoning (problem solving). On the first test, seventh and eighth grade students reached the United States norm, though ninth graders scored 5 months below the norm. In Problem Solving the means were 4, 5, and 9 months below white norms in the respective grades, and the 10th and 11th grade groups showed no tendency to catch up. This suggests that they were somewhat lower in problem than fundamental arithmetic, though if allowance was made for missing half a year's schooling, there would have been very little difference from the norms, and the younger groups at least would have exceeded white standards. I would suggest that the 9th and later grades may have done rather less well because they were naturally more rebellious against relocation and the current conditions of living, less interested in education, and more anxious about their future.

Portenier (1947) likewise compared Japanese born in America and attending high school in Cody, Wyoming, with the general norms for Wyoming students. The mean score for 226 students on the Ohio State University Psychological Test was 48.16, which is significantly lower than the 52.90 obtained from a Wyoming sample of 2000. On the Henmon–Nelson intelligence test, the mean IQ for 22 seniors was 97.6, which falls at the 22nd percentile. And on the Iowa Silent Reading Test the mean fell at the 38th percentile. These, of course, are all verbal tests. The author states that Japanese language was largely used in the homes and in out-of-school activities. This presumably meant that they did not mix much with their white peers. Also, their parents mostly came from rural occupations or fishing.

The drop in educational achievement among Sansei after the war was mentioned in Chapter 3. Presumably this was because they had been brought up in homes that were highly acculturated, and they were able to mix more freely with white peers. Thus they tended to approximate more closely to whites in scholastic motivation and achievement. Kitano (1962) quotes a report by Bell (1935) showing that the proportions of *A* and *B* grades among Japanese high school students was 62% in 1927. Kitano found that the level had risen to 91% by 1941, but then dropped in 1952 and 1955 to 81 and 70%. Likewise the mean grade point average (GPA) dropped from 8.27 to 7.50 between 1941 and 1959, although the mean Japanese IQ among students remained close to 102. But Kitano points out that one cannot guarantee that grading standards remained uniform over this period. Simultaneously the Sansei were showing an increase in social participation. The numbers who were members of three or more high school clubs were 13% in 1941, and 7% in 1952, but reached 24 and 26% in 1955 and 1960.

The Present Time

Some contemporary information was collected in Los Angeles in 1979, where the Japanese are more numerous than in any other North American city. Test scores are no longer tabulated by race, though sometimes whites, blacks, Spanish, and Asian (Japanese and Chinese) are distinguished. A Los Angeles press report (November 9) stated that over all grades, Los Angeles students score some 10% lower on achievement tests than the national norm. But students fluent in Japanese or Chinese as well as English, consistently score the highest, whereas those speaking other foreign languages besides English (e.g., Spanish) are the lowest.

A survey by Schwartz (1970, 1971) of 2200 Japanese students in Los Angeles schools also confirmed that academically they were the most successful minority. Schwartz points out that this could not be explained by the acculturation of

Japanese to white norms. Rather, it derives from the traditional values of the Japanese themselves.

In 1980 an inquiry (unpublished) was carried out by the Los Angeles School Board into the numbers of children with limited English, for whom special provision was to be made. In a district with a school population of 106,000, only 510 of those with limited English were Japanese, some being children of recent immigrants, others of temporary sojourners. A small sample of Japanese in two downtown schools, Grades 3 and 5, was taken, and their mean percentiles on tests of reading and mathematics were compared with those for the whole city; see Table 5.2. Despite the inclusion of some limited-English Japanese, their median percentiles in both tests are well above the national norm. Indeed their scores would be roughly equivalent to an Educational Quotient of approximately

TABLE 5.2
Reading and Mathematics Percentiles for Total School Population and Japanese in Los Angeles

Grade	No. of Japanese	No. with limited English	Total School Population		Japanese	
			Reading %ile	Mathematics %ile	Reading %ile	Mathematics %ile
3	87	(21)	71	86	38	43
5	83	(12)	66	84	36	42

111. Compared with the Los Angeles students, the superiority is still more marked. Note also that though the math results are better than the reading, the Japanese have caught up considerably and are no longer average or below in verbal subjects, superior only in mathematical. It was not possible to estimate the SES level of the Japanese families. But it seems highly probable that they were drawn from the poorer sections of the population, and that middle- or upper-class Japanese would mainly reside outside the downtown core. No information was available on the numbers of Japanese designated as gifted or mentally handicapped.

The 1978 Report of the California Assessment Program likewise concluded that bilingual oriental students who are already fluent in English get substantially higher English marks than the white norm, whereas those with limited English are below the norm in verbal achievement, though still above the norm in mathematics.

Physical Development

With increasing adoption by Japanese of American food habits, health care, and outdoor life, their physique has also improved. Ito (1942) found that

Japanese females born and reared in California reached menarche 20 months earlier than Japanese in Japan. Likewise in stature, Nisei exceeded Kibei (i.e., born in America but educated in Japan), who in turn exceeded native Japanese. Sitting height showed the same trend; but in body proportions and head circumference, the Japanese Americans were much the same as native Japanese. Curiously, weight showed a slight (not significant) opposite trend, the means for Nisei, Kibei, and Japanese women being 50.5, 50.9, and 51.7 kg, respectively.

Greulich (1957) did a similar study of physical dimensions with some 900 Japanese in California, aged 4½ to 18½ years, comparing them with native Japanese norms. The Japanese Americans had greater standing and sitting height and weight at all ages, being nearer to the Caucasian than to the Japanese means. They were approximately 1 year behind whites in physical development, whereas native Japanese were 2½ years behind. The X-ray skeletal ages for boys and girls were ahead of those of whites from 10 to 11 upwards, whereas native Japanese were 1½ years behind. Though in Japan there has been an increase in physical dimensions since 1953, a much larger increase has occurred among Japanese Americans, which has probably now reached its limits (Asayama, 1975). Tanner (1962) adds that Chinese Americans are behind Japanese in age of menarche.

Artistic Abilities

The art of Japan undoubtedly has a high reputation, and it was anticipated that immigrants to Western countries would display artistic sensitivity and skills, though as we have seen, this was queried by Strong (1934).

Wayne Dennis (1966) applied the Goodenough Draw-a-Man test to sizable samples of 6-year-olds in a large number of ethnic groups, and he found that children from Kyoto and from Japanese coastal villages obtained the highest Goodenough IQs (124 to 115). They were followed by American Indian tribes, then whites, Arabs, Indians, Negroes, and primitive Shilluck tribes in Sudan the lowest (IQ 53). He did not use the test as one of intelligence, but regarded these differences as due to familiarity with, and practice in, representational art.

Fukada, Vahar, & Holowinsky (1965) also state that Japanese children are superior at the Draw-a-Man test, but they were mainly concerned with qualitative features in the drawings that differentiated the Japanese and American cultures. Hilger, Klett, & Watson (1977) used Harris' revision of the Goodenough, and tested 30 Japanese 6-year-olds and 22 Ainu children. (The latter come from a relatively primitive tribe, though few are likely to be purebred; see Chapter 4.) Both groups scored well above Harris's norms, with mean scores of 33.3 and 30.0. Six-year-olds in the United States range between 18 and 23.

One might guess that the artistic skills involved in learning and drawing ideographs would overlap with the skills needed in drawing the human figure.

Iwao and Child (1966) selected 21 pairs of black and white photos of art objects, which were unlikely to be affected by cultural idiosyncrasies. In each pair, a group of American art experts had decided which was the best artistically. When applied to several hundred high school students in New Haven, Connecticut, their average percentage agreement with the experts was 47%; (note that 50% would be obtained by pure chance). However, Yale University students averaged 64%. The test was given to 60 potters in three regions of Japan. These were artists, not just copyists, though they naturally worked within their own tradition and had had very little exposure to Western art. Their score was 63%, suggesting that different ethnic groups have some communality in recognition of aesthetic merit. In another test of pictures of abstract paintings, the agreement with American judgments was 57%. Iwawaki and Clement (1972) similarly found that Japanese, American, and Brazilian students (aged 9 to 21) agreed quite closely in their judgments of patterns of dots as being "well-formed" or "ill-formed."

Iwao, Child, & Garcia (1969) gave another test consisting of 51 pairs of photos and 24 colored postcards of abstracts to American experts and to 31 Japanese adults in Tokyo, who were practicing traditional Japanese art. The mean scores for the Japanese on the two tests were 58½ and 51½%. Thus, there was rather low agreement between their judgments and the American views. Indeed, it was lower than that obtained by uneducated potters. But when the tests were given to 40 working class Puerto Ricans in Hawaii, the scores were only 43 and 45½%, respectively.

Similar investigations have been published by Eysenck and Iwawaki (1971, 1975), using 131 designs and 135 polygons. These were rated on a 5-point scale for aesthetic appeal (i.e., not as contrasted pairs). The average ratings given by 179 British and 115 Japanese students intercorrelated .82 for the polygons, and .60 for the designs. These resemblances between ethnic groups were higher than those between males and females in the same group, indicating therefore quite high cross-cultural agreement.

The second study, based on 206 male and female Japanese students, made use of the same designs and the same British group. All intercorrelations between ethnic and sex groups fell between .54 and .83.

All the items were intercorrelated in each group and submitted to factor analysis. Quite similar dimensions or types of design were found in the two groups, which is remarkable considering the lack of familiarity of either group with the artistic traditions of the other, and the abstract nature of the designs. Seven main factors, or types, are illustrated in Eysenck (1971) and Eysenck and Iwawaki (1975), namely:

1. Rectangular, straight line, and symmetrical designs
2. Ditto, circular
3. Star-shaped

4. Interlacing designs
5. Designs with shading
6. Three-dimensional appearance
7. Very simple designs

The 15 designs most liked and 15 least popular are illustrated, and the corresponding results for British students appear in Eysenck (1971). There was considerable overlap between Japanese and English choices.

Harris, DeLissovoy, & Enami (1975) worked with children rather than adults in both Japan and the United States. They prepared 60 pairs of color slides of art objects, chosen to be of some interest to children. These were judged for aesthetic merit by art experts. The subjects were 337 Japanese in Grades 1, 4, 7, and 10, who came mostly from above average SES backgrounds. The Americans consisted of 249 with similar background, who were matched for age, grade, and sex.

The total scores were United States 31, and Japan 31.5 (the chance score being 30 out of 60). Girls scored a little higher than boys in both countries. The closest agreement with the judges was in first grade, where the means were 34.5 to 42.0 for the different sex and ethnic groups. By Grade 7, the scores dropped to 21.9–29.0, indicating that children preferred the pictures that the artists regarded as of lower merit. There was a small rise at tenth grade. Japanese children were lower than whites at Grade 1, a little lower at Grade 4, but superior at Grades 7 and 10. These results do not bear out the belief that Japanese children have a highly developed artistic sense, though it may be more true at some age levels than others. Six of the pairs of objects were of Japanese origin, and on these the Japanese children scored close to 45, which is much higher than the American figure. This suggests that there is a considerable cultural factor in the type of art preferred.

Quite high agreement between Japanese and American choices was found at all ages. The pictures had also been rated by artists for "brightness," "form," and "theme." Though these qualities did not differentiate the Grade 1 preferences, they did have some influence by Grade 10. The main basis of choice seemed to be realism and familiarity.

Note that in all these studies, judgments by Western artists were the criterion against which Japanese children's and adults' choices were evaluated. It would be interesting to construct a test using Japanese artists' judgments, and see how Americans performed on this.

A new Visual Aesthetic Sensitivity Test (VAST) is described by Götz, Lynn, Borisy, and Eysenck (1979), Iwawaki et al. (1979), and Chan et al. (1980). It consists of 42 pairs of nonrepresentational shapes; in each pair, one shape has been accepted as superior to the other aesthetically. Results for English, German, Japanese, and Hong Kong children and adults are shown in Table 5.3.

The test is easier, and probably more discriminating than tests described pre-

TABLE 5.3
Mean Scores of Several Groups of Children and Adults on the VAST Test (Chan *et al.* 1980)

Group	Ages	N	Means
English boys	11–14	204 ⎫	
			30.40
English girls	11–14	165 ⎭	
English male students	Adult	38	35.79
English female students	Adult	73	34.68
German gymnasium girls	11–18	200	37 to 40
Japanese boys	11–14	171	33.07
Japanese girls	11–14	156	33.91
Japanese males	Adult	145	31.72
Japanese females	Adult	163	32.38
Hong Kong boys	7–14	287 ⎫	
			25 to 29
Hong Kong girls	7–14	252 ⎭	
Hong Kong males	Adult	58 ⎱	30
Hong Kong females	Adult	144 ⎰	

viously, since the mean scores represent about 75% correct, whereas with earlier tests the means were sometimes lower than 50%.

Clearly, the Japanese children score distinctly higher than the English, and the Hong Kong Chinese are lower still, particularly the young children (aged 7). A rather older group of German girls got the highest mean, but they would probably be of superior intelligence and SES. Curiously the Japanese adults are a little lower than the children, and the Chinese are much the same as the older children. But English adults do score higher than English children. Possibly the views on artistic merit among adult oriental adults differ more widely from those of Western adults than do the less sophisticated views of children.

The orders of item difficulty were correlated between different groups, and mostly ranged between .70 and .87 (but Hong Kong boys with English adults dropped to .58). Thus, there is considerable consistency of aesthetic preferences across ethnic groups as well as between sexes, and different age groups. Since the artistic experiences and teaching must differ widely between the different groups, Iwawaki *et al.* (1979) seem justified in claiming that the test largely measures an innate ability common to all cultures.

These studies raise the interesting question as to the relative artistic gifts and aesthetic sensitivity of Chinese and Japanese. Chinese jade and ivory carvings, and porcelain vases, going back for some 3000 years seem to be more generally appreciated in the Western world than Japanese artistic productions. The results given in Table 5.3 clearly indicate lower scores in this type of aesthetic judgment among the Hong Kong Chinese than the Japanese. But it is possible that the samples are not comparable; for example, the Hong Kong groups cover a lower age range. Also the adult means are much closer together. But generalizations about aesthetic tastes and talents obviously would not be justified on the basis of scores on a somewhat artificial kind of test (albeit superior to other tests that have been used). There is no doubt that both ethnic groups have shown great sensitivity to art throughout their long histories.

One relevant study by Adams and Osgood (1973) used the Semantic Differential for assessing the affective meaning of seven common colors among 23 ethnic goups. This test yielded a figure for sensitivity to the affective differences between colors. The highest differentiation occurred among Thai (2.9), Finnish (2.5), Japanese (2.4), and Hong Kong Chinese (1.9) versus American (1.6) and Afghan (0.9).

SUMMARY

A great deal of work on the abilities of Japanese children has been carried out by Japanese psychologists and published in English. As with the Chinese, the earlier studies of Japanese Americans showed below average scores on verbal tests of reasoning and memory. But they were equal to, or sometimes higher than, whites on nonverbal tests such as the Army Beta examination, and tests of visual perception and recall (Darsie, 1926). Since the children's homes were mainly Japanese-speaking in the 1920s and 1930s, they were naturally handicapped in reading and language, but were already equal in arithmetic and spelling, and superior in drawing and painting. According to Strong (1934) their English speech was also inferior at a time when Chinese children were speaking fluent English.

Because of their strong motivation to learn, and willingness to comply with teachers' instructions, they were often referred to as "ideal students." By 1940 a larger proportion of Japanese than whites in California were completing 12th grade schooling. But with wartime relocation in 1942, schooling was seriously disrupted, particularly at secondary level. In one survey, Japanese students fell below United States norms on verbal intelligence and reading and mathematical problems, though still comparable on arithmetic fundamentals. Following the war, the Nisei (second-generation students) became outstanding achievers educationally, and mostly moved into much higher grade jobs than their Issei parents. However, their children, the Sansei, showed some decline in educational standards, though close to average IQ. But it was noticeable that they participated more in school clubs and social activities than had their fathers; in other words they were much better acculturated.

There is little exact information on current JA abilities and achievements, but it has been found in Los Angeles that Japanese who are fluent in English are considerably above the general norm in English, as well as in mathematical, achievement. Those with limited English speech—mostly recent immigrants— are lower in verbal subjects though still good in mathematics. In Japan itself, the efficiency of the education system is well known; indeed the pressures of competitive examinations on adolescents are notorious. The International Educational Achievement Project showed Japanese achievement in mathematics and science at elementary and secondary levels to be superior to those in any other country, except some European nations where only a small and select proportion of the population stays on at school beyond 16 years. The secondary school curriculum includes a lot of English, in addition to Japanese and other subjects.

Some more direct comparisons of Japanese and North American intelligence are provided by the restandardization in Japan of the Wechsler individual intelligence scales (WPPSI, WISC, and WAIS). Only a few of the performance subtests and Digit Span are strictly comparable between the United States and Japan, since their test items did not have to be translated. According to American norms, the mean IQs of representative Japanese groups were 111.7 (4–6 yr), 103.1 (5–15 yr), and 103.9 (35–44 yr), an overall average of 106.6. However, there are certain weaknesses in these figures, though it seems highly probable that at least the younger children are more advanced intellectually than their American counterparts. Another attempt by Lynn and Dziobon (1980) to compare national standards on group intelligence tests gave a mean Japanese IQ of 110.26 on United States standards, but this too is open to question.

Considerable increases in the height and physical dimensions of Japanese have occurred over the past 50 years. But Japanese Americans have increased more rapidly, and were reported in 1957 to be nearer to whites in physical dimensions than to JJ. Also JA girls reach menarche at an earlier age than JJ.

In the artistic area, JJ children score considerably higher than United States whites on the Draw-a-Man test. Tests designed to measure aesthetic sensitivity (mainly based on western artistic objects and on western artists' judgments of aesthetic merit) give somewhat inconsistent results, with no clear superiority for Japanese. The most recent test by Eysenck and Götz did show Japanese 11- to 14-year-old children to score higher than English, but adult student scores were lower. Though there are cultural differences between Japan and the West in artistic preferences, there is also considerable agreement across cultures among both adults and children.

6

Oriental Immigration to Hawaii

CHRONOLOGY

c. 750   Polynesian settlement.
1778   Discovery of Sandwich Islands by Captain Cook.
1804   All Hawaiian islands ruled by King Kamehameha I.
1820 *et seq.*   Settlement of traders and missionaries. Hawaiian native population declined from over 300,000 to 40,000 by 1896 due to disease, etc.
1852   First importation of Chinese labor.
         Main periods of immigration:

Chinese	1870–1920
Portuguese	1878–1913
Japanese	1886–1920
Puerto Ricans	1901
Koreans	1903–1905
Spanish	1907–1913
Filipinos	1907–1931, and from 1946 on
Samoans	Currently

1879   Pineapple-growing introduced.
1893   The last queen of Hawaii, Queen Liliuokalani, forced to abdicate. Provisional government formed.
1898   Annexation by United States.
1920 *et seq.*   Large build-up of military and naval bases.
1924   Oriental Immigration Exclusion Act.
1941   Pearl Harbor attack.
1959   Admission of Hawaii to statehood of the United States.

SOURCES OF INFORMATION

Though not intended as a history of Hawaiian society, James Michener's *Hawaii* (1959) provides a fascinating picture of the origins of the numerous racial-ethnic groups that contributed to its growth, and how they interacted and built up a common culture. Porteus and Babcock's *Temperament and Race* (1926), W. C. Smith's *Americans in Process* (1937), and R. Adams' *Interracial Marriage in Hawaii* (1937), provide some early cross sections; and A. W. Lind's *Hawaii's People* (1955, 3rd ed., 1967) is a mine of mainly demographic information.

Social scientists have, of course, been interested in Hawaii as an unique example of rapid acculturation. Their work stimulated the setting up of the East-West Center at the University of Hawaii for cross-cultural studies. Also, from quite early days the University Deparments of Education and Psychology have attracted teachers and researchers of high repute such as P. M. Symonds, S. D. Porteus, K. Murdoch, G. M. Meredith, E. E. Werner, A. J. Marsella, and others.

DEMOGRAPHY

The bases of classification by race differed to some extent over the years. Thus "Others" in 1970 included Koreans, Puerto Ricans, Hawaiians, part-Hawaiians, and Indians, etc. (Lind, 1967). In Lind's own table (Table 6.1), the percentages for 1910 and 1930 add up to more than 100%. This is because he included "Portuguese" and "Other Caucasian" as separate entries, as well as "Caucasians." I have omitted the first two of these figures, and the numbers and percentages now do add up correctly. By 1950, the census had ceased making this subdivision. Actually Portuguese (22,301) exceeded Other Caucasians

TABLE 6.1
Census Statistics of Hawaiian Population, 1910–1970 (Lind, 1967)

Racial-ethnic group	1910 Number	1910 %	1930 Number	1930 %	1950 Number	1950 %	1970 Number	1970 %
Caucasian	39,158	20.4	73,702	20.0	114,793	23.0	298,160	38.3
Japanese	79,675	41.5	139,631	37.9	184,598	36.9	217,307	28.3
Chinese	21,674	11.3	27,179	7.4	32,376	6.5	52,039	6.8
Korean	4,533	2.4	6,461	1.8	7,030	1.4	——	—
Filipino	2,361	1.2	63,052	17.1	61,062	12.2	93,915	12.2
Negro	695	0.4	563	0.2	2,651	0.5	7,573	1.0
Puerto Rican	4,890	2.5	6,671	1.8	9,551	1.9 ⎫		
Hawaiian	26,041	13.6	22,636	6.1	12,245	2.5 ⎬	99,567	13.0
Part-Hawaiian	12,506	6.5	28,224	7.7	73,845	14.8 ⎪		
Others	376	0.2	217	0.1	1,618	0.3 ⎭		
Totals	191,909		368,336		499,769		768,561	

(14,867) in 1910, but the Other Caucasians (44,895) drew ahead of the Portuguese (27,588) in 1930.

Note the big jump in Caucasians since 1950. It is this that has caused the Japanese percentage (but not the total number) to drop. The continuous decline in numbers and percentages of Hawaiians and the rise of part-Hawaiians are obvious, but the 1970 census did not list them separately.

INTRODUCTION

Hawaii is justly reputed for the diversity of its ethnic stocks, for the harmony of its interracial relations, and the absence of rivalries and discrimination, compared with other multiethnic countries. Especially noticeable, also, is the trend toward cross-ethnic marriages, which are gradually turning almost the whole population into a single hybrid culture. Lind (1967) draws attention to a number of favorable circumstances that have contributed to this phenomenon: (1) the remarkable fertility of a semitropical land; (2) the friendliness and adaptability of the indigenous Hawaiian natives and their rulers; (3) the considerable distance of the islands from other major population centers (over 2000 miles from California), and (4) the drive and farsightedness of the early white traders, missionaries, and plantation owners who, while feathering their own nests, did keep in mind the prosperity of the territories as a whole, and sought to avoid overdomination by any single group of immigrants. I would be inclined myself to add the relatively small number of low SES whites in the population who, in California and British Columbia, were the most biased against oriental immigrants. The very multiplicity of racial–ethnic groups and hybrids led to less conflict between groups, and the diversity of economic growth provided opportunities for people of very diverse background and qualities to participate in the country's progress. Moreover, as early as 1900, compulsory education for all children was introduced, and this was carried out in the English medium, with the customary American emphasis on Americanization and democratic ideals. It therefore helped to break down interethnic barriers. Hawaiians, Caucasians, Orientals, and other children were all treated as equals in the schools. Oriental boys, also, are good athletes, and this increased their popularity among their peers.

EARLY IMMIGRATION

When the islands were first discovered by westerners in 1778, the Polynesian inhabitants were living virtually in a Stone Age culture. They had no metal and no private ownership—even of wives. Apart from some frightening religious observances (such as human sacrifices to the gods), and oppression by the small group of nobles and the priests, they seem to have been an easygoing and happy people. They could exist largely on taro, or poi, fruit, and fishing. But although hospitable to the whalers, traders, and even to the missionaries who set out to break down their traditional culture and to convert them from their heathen beliefs, they saw no point in the white man's economic system, based on hard work and thrift, and the acquisition of occupational skills and wealth. What they did take over from the visitors and settlers were numerous infectious diseases. As a result of these, of drunkenness, and sheer malnutrition from neglecting their staple crops, the total Hawaiian population dropped from over 300,000 in 1780 to 124,000 in 1830, and to less than 40,000 by the end of the century. Thereafter, with better health care, there was some improvement in the birth and survival rate. Nevertheless, the missionaries' efforts did bear some fruit, since the Hawaiians were quite intelligent and learned English readily. Thus, they became able to take part in the tremendous economic growth of the later nineteenth and twentieth centuries.

The settlers and their descendants soon began to realize the potential of the islands for growing sugarcane, and, later, pineapple. Because of the decline in population, and the unwillingness of the natives to work as plantation laborers, the growers sought immigrants from other countries. From the later 1850s and 1860s, large numbers of Chinese peasants (particularly the hardy and intelligent Hakkas) were imported under contract. Some 46,000 had arrived by 1900, though about half of these either returned home or went on to mainland America. As in the United States there were very few Chinese women, but many men married Hawaiian girls, and their offspring seemed to combine the good qualities of both racial-ethnic groups. However, the employers intentionally cut down on further immigration from China after 1900, and organized the series of waves of other nationalities, as listed in the chronological summary at the beginning of the chapter.

Lind estimated that between 1850 and 1950 a total of approximately 400,000 immigrants arrived, in addition to American whites. They were distributed as follows:

Japanese	180,000	Spaniards	8,000
Filipinos	125,000	Puerto Ricans	6,000
Chinese	46,000	Other Pacific	
Portuguese	17,500	Islanders	2,500
Koreans	8,000	Russians	2,000
		Germans	1,300

THE JAPANESE

The largest single group in Hawaii was the Japanese, who were regarded as better workers than the Chinese. Immigration from Japan started in the late

1860s, but much larger numbers arrived in the 1880s on. A proportion of them brought wives or imported them; thus they became the most stable community. By 1930 they reached 38% of the population, though they dropped to 28% by 1970 (see Table 6.1). One could not expect the same rapid acculturation among Orientals as among European immigrants, if only because of their distinctive physical features and use of a totally different language. Nevertheless, the Japanese did adapt quite quickly, while also retaining much of their family structure and values. Thus, for a long period they kept more to themselves than did the other groups, and although the two sexes and all races intermingled at school—in a manner disapproved of by the parents—there were very few exogamous marriages with non-Japanese spouses until well into the twentieth century, that is, the Sansei generation. As recorded in preceding chapters, the Japanese were not persecuted or evacuated after Pearl Harbor (apart from a few notorious nationalists who were interned). Nearly 12,000 volunteered to serve in the armed forces, and the exploits of the Hawaiian Japanese regiment in Europe have become legendary.[1]

CHANGE IN STATUS OF THE ORIENTAL GROUPS

From about 1920, the relative proportions of different ethnic groups in Hawaii, and of further immigrants, became fairly stable (Adams, 1937). As happened in California, the Chinese and Japanese were seldom content to remain as laborers after their contracts had expired; they ensured that their children got as good an education as possible in order to achieve superior socioeconomic status. Many of the Japanese did acquire and farm their own land, thus preserving a greater degree of family solidarity than among those who moved to urban areas. But by 1930, 71% of all Chinese were living in Honolulu and were becoming a powerful force in business and politics. Many oriental boys trained for skilled trades or business; girls for hairdressing (almost a Japanese monopoly), office workers, teachers, and nurses. Also by the 1930s more Orientals graduated from high school than did Caucasians. Indeed in 1950, 94% of them versus approximately 80% of all other groups stayed on at school at 16–17 years.

Boyd (1971) shows that there is much more occupational mobility among Chinese in Hawaii than in New York or California. For example, 18% of them are in professional work versus 5% in the other two regions. But there are only 28% in trade and 4% in personal services, as compared with about 51% and 20% on the mainland. Further information on the academic and occupational achievements of Hawaiian Orientals appears in Chapters 12 and 13.

---

[1]It is easy to confuse an ethnic group that resides in Hawaii with the offspring of mixed marriages. I have therefore referred to the former as, for example, Hawaiian Japanese or Hawaiian Chinese, and to the latter as Japanese Hawaiian or Chinese Hawaiian.

ETHNIC AND SOCIAL DIFFERENTIATION

In a great many ways, both Chinese and Japanese residents of Hawaii are more assimilated and accepted by the rest of the community than in California. They obtained voting rights earlier, and their rate of intermarriage with other groups increased more rapidly. Large numbers gave up oriental religions and joined the Christian churches. The crime rate among Chinese was lower than on the mainland, and they did not set up tongs like those in California. When Hawaiian Orientals visit the mainland they tend to find the social climate more tense, less comfortable than on the islands (W. C. Smith, 1937). However, there are still some remnants of discrimination against Orientals. Very commonly they receive lower incomes than whites doing the same jobs, and they often have to achieve higher qualifications to be accepted into higher professional or business occupations.

At one time there was a Chinatown ghetto in central Honolulu, but this was burnt down in 1900, and now there is very little segregation by ethnicity, apart from some choice suburban areas that are almost exclusively white. It would seem that there is more differentiation by SES and wealth than by color or ethnic origin. Although white Caucasians constitute the largest single group (39% by 1970), they are a minority and are referred to by the Hawaiian term *haole,* which originally meant all foreigners or strangers. It now applies mainly to American visitors or to rich American residents who, of course, still regard themselves as superior to any non-Caucasians. One way the white Caucasians try to preserve their status is by sending their children to private schools or mainland universities. In addition, such students are likely to find better professional opportunities on the mainland.

A major change in the Caucasian section of the population occurred from 1920 on, when large military and naval bases were developed at Pearl Harbor. Many servicemen in the 1920s and 1930s married Hawaiian or Japanese brides. Nowadays the numbers of whites who are descendants of the original planters and businessmen are fewer than the service and government personnel, new business entrepreneurs, and retired mainland Americans.

It is interesting that in the early decades of this century there was more cooperation between Chinese and Japanese in pursuing their rights than ever happened on the mainland. For example, they had to struggle to get their sons into the more prestigious secondary schools, hitherto reserved for whites. In the same period the Japanese so greatly outnumbered the Chinese that they soon became the dominant group in politics. However, it did not occur—as had been feared—that voters chose their representatives on a racial–ethnic basis.

Currently one can observe some degree of differentiation between the Caucasians, Japanese, Chinese, Koreans, that is, the high-achieving groups, or "the haves," and the Portuguese, Filipino, Puerto Rican, and Hawaiian or part-

Hawaiian, that is, "the have-nots." The Puerto Ricans are probably the least well adapted. The following statistics were reported by Adams (1937) on the numbers of cases of juvenile delinquency per year in 1929–30, per 100,000 of the population:

Japanese	341	Filipino	1664
Chinese	812	Hawaiian and part-	
White	1250	Hawaiian	1701
Korean	1391	Puerto Rican	2810

It is probable that similar ratios persist to the present, that is, that the Orientals are the least inclined to crime, the "have-nots" the most.

The crime figure have grown alarmingly in recent years (as in all parts of the United States), but there seem to be more attacks on and thefts from *haoles* by part-Hawaiians and other disadvantaged groups, than in the past. Partly because the great majority of school teachers in Hawaii are Japanese or Caucasian, minority group students tend to find them unsympathetic, and many drop out and become delinquent (Boggs & Gallimore, 1974). On the other hand, the remarkable advancement of Hawaii is illustrated by the decline in infant mortality from 119 to 21 per thousand between 1924 and 1960.

As visitors to the island are well aware, each of the five main islands has a different social atmosphere, as well as different scenery and natural attractions. At the time of the 1970 census, 82% of the population lived on Oahu, half of them in Honolulu. Apart from some large seaside resorts, most of the rest of the territory is agricultural or mountainous. The primary industries of sugarcane and pineapple cultivation reached their peak by 1930, but Lind shows that they are still the most efficient of their kind in the world and pay the highest wages. Tourism has become the largest money-earner; it increased from approximately one million visitors in 1970 to nearly four million in 1980. This growth owes much to the huge popularity of the islands among Japanese tourists, and it is accompanied by large investments from Japan in hotels, real estate, etc.

Problems of Language

Naturally, every immigrant group has experienced problems of language, until the second or later generations successfully learned English at school. At the time of the arrival of the Chinese, a pidgin English, very similar to that used between white traders and natives in many Asian ports, was adopted. Some Hawaiian words, and later Portuguese, Japanese, Filipino, and other elements became incorporated. This bastard dialect was widely known and used by children of all races; though it helped intercommunication among them, it also interfered with the acquisition of correct English. It is still something of a problem (Ciborowski and Choy, 1974), particularly among the children of low SES groups.

Problems of Intermarriage

Unlike the mainland, there have never been any laws against miscegenation in Hawaii, and no social stigma applies to mixed marriages. According to Lind, 11.5% of marriages were interracial in 1912, 22.8% in 1930-40, and 37.6% in 1960-64. As already mentioned, the figures have always been lower for Japanese, especially Japanese men, presumably because they still expect their women to accept an inferior status. However, the statistics for Orientals do not reveal that many of these cross-marriages gave rise to serious conflicts between the participants and their families. Their children often became ''marginal'' people, who were rejected by the purer families of either or both groups.

CONCLUSIONS

What happened to the indigenous Hawaiians? Probably by now there are less than 8000, or 1% of the population, who could claim to be pure Hawaiian, and they would be living chiefly in more remote rural areas. On the other hand, apart from recent immigrants, there must be few residents whose ancestry does not involve some Hawaiian genes. The Hawaiian population might well have died out altogether but for the vigor of part-Hawaiian descendants. Thus they have survived, but in a much diluted form. It is often supposed that life in Hawaii is somewhat more relaxed and tolerant than on the mainland, generally on account of the temperamental qualities inherited from the original natives. But even if this description is justified, no one could prove that it is not due to the cultural and linguistic influences the Hawaiians have had on the immigrants, or simply the effects of a pleasant climate and the reputation of the islands for enjoyable and restful holidays.

In the early part of this century, there were two major hybrid groups, the Caucasian Hawaiian and the Chinese Hawaiian (Adams, 1937). But by 1945 there were so many mixtures that few could be certain of their ancestry; the education department ceased trying to classify school students by race. However, even in 1970 the census recorded racial groups on the basis of each householder's own claims (Table 6.1), and the third largest group, after the Caucasian and Japanese, was the 12.8% of ''mixed race.'' Obviously, it is to everybody's advantage (except perhaps social scientists) to cease taking any account of race. If one can draw any general conclusion from Michener's book, it would seem to be that although there *were* genetic differences between the various racial–ethnic immigrant groups, the outcome of their intermixing has depended more on the cultural characteristics and values that they brought with them, and the chance factors of physical environment and of historical circumstances that they had to cope with.

7

Tests of Children and Students in Hawaii

As early as 1924, P. M. Symonds applied a number of group tests to 513 Chinese children in Grades 4 to 8. He does not describe their background, SES, or linguistic status, though by that date the majority would be second or third generation, and born in Hawaii. The mean quotients were

Pinter Non-language test	99.3
Thorndike–McCall Reading	88.3
Thorndike Word Knowledge	95.4
Kelley–Trabue Completion	85.2
Charters Diagnostic Language test	90.9

For the four verbal tests, the mean quotient is 90 versus 99 for the nonverbal. This is very much the same pattern as found in studies of Chinese Americans around the same date. In other words, the Chinese are already up to white standards on nonverbal intelligence. Note that the two lowest quotients were obtained on tests that call for understanding of complex passages in English.

THE WORK OF S. D. PORTEUS

Porteus and Babcock's *Temperament and Race* (1926) was something of a landmark in the development of cross-cultural psychology. It deserves wider recognition than it receives after 50 years, though some of Porteus's theories of racial differences in temperament would be rejected by most social scientists at the present time. He starts by criticizing the misapplication of intelligence tests for screening out "undesirable" immigrants to the United States, including Orientals. After describing the main ethnic groups—Hawaiian, Chinese, Portuguese, Japanese, Filipinos, and Puerto Ricans—he tried to arrive at an assessment of their social value to the community. Twenty-five persons with long experience in the islands rated each group on some eight traits including Planning Capacity, Impulsiveness, Emotional Stability, Dependability, Social Tact, etc. These were arbitrarily chosen as basic traits of temperament, which would be more important than intelligence in producing social adjustment. However, Porteus admits that they might be modified slowly by environmental or cultural changes.

The overall medians for Social Efficiency are listed in Table 7.1, together with the crime rates and numbers of retardates, which closely parallel the indices in reverse. Juvenile delinquincy statistics show the same trend. There were interesting differences on different traits. For instance, Japanese were very high in Planning, high in Resolution and Stability, lower in Self-Determination and Dependability, and very low in Tact. Chinese were moderately high in Planning, high in Stability and Dependability, and moderate in Self-Determination and Tact. The numbers of children per thousand referred to the psychological clinic for mental retardation differ only in the unexpectedly high incidence among Portuguese.

Turning to education, school grades were collected for the groups mentioned and some additional mixed breeds. The rank order of achievement was

Caucasian	Chinese Hawaiian	Pure Hawaiian
Pure Korean	White Hawaiian	Filipino
Pure Chinese	Mixed Hawaiian	Puerto Rican
Pure Japanese	Pure Portuguese	

Clearly, length of time over which immigration had occurred is important. Thus whites and Chinese were the first immigrants, and Puerto Ricans the most recent. All of these groups except whites were considerably handicapped by language, but Hawaiians would have had more experience with English than the others.

Porteus was a strong believer in the significance of brain size, though admit-

TABLE 7.1

Social Efficiency Ratings, Crime Rate, and Mental Retardation in Hawaiian Ethnic Groups (Porteus of Babcock, 1926)

Ethnic group	Social efficiency	Jail inmates per 1000	Mental retardates per 1000
Japanese	85.5	0.59	0.64
Chinese	82.6	1.58	1.9
Portuguese	60.0	1.53	6.6
Hawaiian	51.4	3.57	2.0
Filipino	33.0	7.08	5.0
Puerto Rican	33.3	9.32	16.6

ting that it bears little relation to Stanford–Binet or other linguistically loaded tests. On the basis of large samples of children of three ethnic groups, he gave the following ranking for head size in boys: Caucasian, Japanese, and Chinese. Girls are all smaller in head size, but follow the same order.

The Stanford–Binet was given to samples numbering 30 to 60 of each sex, at ages 9, 12, and 14. Several items were omitted as being too culture-biased (e.g., Vocabulary), and Porteus extracted scores on the 18 most suitable items, which gave the mean IQs for boys shown in Table 7.2. It is surprising to find the Hawaiians scoring as high as Japanese and Chinese at age 9, but of course they had been used to speaking a good deal of English for several generations. The figures also suggest that Hawaiians start off well, but then drop in relative intelligence level in secondary school. The Educational Ratios (i.e., Grade Age over Chronological Age) are also shown, and they are quite similar to the Binet IQs except that all four groups seem to fall off at 12 years on.

Porteus's objections to the Stanford–Binet in this context were well founded, and he put more trust in his own Mazes test, which is said to measure planning ability, reflectiveness, and learning from mistakes, and is not dependent on knowledge of English. Among mental defectives, it consistently correlated more highly with observed social adaptability than did the Binet. The Maze IQs shown in Table 7.3 were obtained for quite large samples of six ethnic groups. The American sample was a mainland group, not Hawaiian. Note that the Japanese score a little more highly than whites, but Porteus states that Japanese boys aged 13 and over dropped behind whites. The Chinese are somewhat lower and are surpassed by the Hawaiians. Many of the part-Hawaiian children were the off-spring of mixed marriages between Hawaiians and Chinese. They had shown themselves to be more adaptable than their parents, combining the Hawaiian outgoingness with Chinese industriousness and persistence. However, their scores and those of Hawaiians tend to decline with age. As with many perfor-mance tests, girls score significantly lower than boys. Porteus's final conclusion was that the Japanese have the greatest endowments of ability and temperament,

TABLE 7.2
Mean IQs and Educational Ratios for Four Ethnic Groups of Boys (Porteus & Babcock, 1926)

Ethnic group	Binet IQs			Educational ratios		
	9 yr.	12 yr.	14 yr.	9 yr.	12 yr.	14 yr.
Japanese	92.5	93	93	93.3	87.4	85.0
Chinese	92	95	94	91.8	89.3	85.3
Portuguese	88	89	88	88.4	86.5	84.2
Hawaiian	92	85.8	88	91.4	85.0	82.9

TABLE 7.3
Porteus Maze IQs of Hawaiian Ethnic Groups (Porteus & Babcock, 1926)

Ethnic group	N	Mean IQ	Ethnic group	N	Mean IQ
Japanese boys	208	101.9	Chinese boys	200	95.3
Hawaiian or			Portuguese boys	97	91.5
part-Hawaiian	95	100.1	Japanese girls	198	96.8
American boys	182	99.2	Chinese girls	188	88.9
Filipino boys	156	97.7			

and were likely to become the leading group in the community. His prediction was later fulfilled.

In another publication (1939) Porteus found Chinese children exceeding Japanese on Stanford–Binet, and on Digit Memory. But the Japanese were superior on all performance tests. He claims that "real" differences exist in abilities, not just environmental or cultural differences, but that they vary with the particular kind of ability. There is no overall superiority of one racial–ethnic group to the others.

THE WORK OF K. MURDOCH

K. Murdoch (1925) carried out similar studies to those of Porteus, working chiefly with 12-year-olds in Honolulu (though supplemented by some rural schools). She included white children, but pointed out that these would be downwardly selected, since many of the brighter ones would probably attend private schools. The mean scores on the National Intelligence Test (verbal) and the Army Beta (nonverbal) are shown in Table 7.4. Mean indices of socioeconomic status are also shown.

It may be seen that all the immigrant groups and mixed bloods score much below whites on the National Intelligence Test, but to a lesser extent on the Army Beta, where urban Japanese and Koreans are not much below the whites and surpass the Chinese. As before, the most recent immigrants are lowest; also the pure Hawaiians at age 12 are decidedly below the mixed bloods. Note though that the Chinese (by 1925) were higher in SES than other nonwhite groups, whereas Japanese were still on a par with Koreans and Portuguese, and many were still engaged in farming.

Murdoch found also that the Chinese surpassed the Japanese in school grades, as they did in the National, but not the Beta, test.

Certain music tests were also given, including the Seashore Pitch Discrimination. Mean scores are not provided, but the rank order of most of the groups on teachers' ratings was

Chinese Hawaiian	Portuguese
Pure Hawaiian	Japanese (rural)
Caucasian Hawaiian	Korean
Japanese (urban)	Chinese

In Pitch Discrimination, all three Hawaiian groups were at the top. These results confirm the common view that Hawaiians are a particularly musical ethnic group.

The personality characteristics of Murdoch's groups were rated (as in Porteus's work) on six social adjustment traits by school teachers and university faculty members. These traits were Ambition, Perseverance, Trustworthiness, Self-Assertion, Sensitiveness to Public Opinion, and Control of Emotions. The overall rank order was as follows:

Chinese	Chinese Hawaiian
Japanese (urban)	Japanese (rural)
Korean	White-Hawaiian
White American	Portuguese

The Chinese obtained higher means than whites on all traits except Self-Assertion. The Japanese were generally above average, but at or below the average on Self-Assertion and Trustworthiness. Another interesting point was that the Chinese Hawaiian were rated higher than white-Hawaiian mixed bloods, although lower on test scores. The latter were clearly not highly regarded by the community.

TABLE 7.4
Scores on Verbal and Nonverbal Intelligence Tests of Ethnic Groups in Hawaii (Murdoch, 1925)

Ethnic group	N	SES	National Intelligence Test	Army Beta
White Americans	57	3.84	229.8	66.4
Caucasian Hawaiian	59	2.96	158.2	53.1
Chinese	58	3.15	166.5	56.1
Japanese (urban)	61	2.68	159.4	61.4
Portuguese	57	2.62	140.8	44.2
Korean	33	2.56	160.2	59.0
Chinese Hawaiian	33	2.62	141.1	50.6
Hawaiian	38	2.24	128.8	43.3
Japanese (rural)	56	1.68	107.6	39.7
Puerto Rican	23	1.85	111.7	38.4
Filipino	23	1.50	81.1	30.3

Note: Standard deviations are not quoted, but they average 50 on the National Test, and 16 on the Army Beta. Thus any differences between two groups (where $N = 50$), amounting to 26 points on the National or 8 points on Army Beta, would be significant at .01.

THE WORKS OF S. SMITH AND R. G. LEITER

Obviously one cannot infer from test scores or behavior ratings in the mid-1920s to more recent times. However, S. Smith (1942) compared large groups of 10- to 14-year-old students, tested in 1924, with similar groups tested in 1938. The sizes of groups ranged all the way from 2799 Japanese (in 1924) to 43 Japanese Hawaiians (in 1938). The tests consisted of comprehension of oral and printed English, and nonverbal intelligence. The means on the two tests are shown in terms of sigma scores (i.e., range +3.0 to −3.0) in Table 7.5.

The 1924 ethnic figures are quite similar to those of other investigators (except that more mixed-blood groups are included). The gains on the English test from 1924 to 1938 are mostly small, the largest being +0.55 for whites and +0.51 for Filipinos. But Chinese (+0.33) and Japanese (+0.39) gains are also substantial.

The large gains in almost every group on the nonverbal test are surprising, and one wonders if the identical test was used on the two occasions. Or possibly all children had become more familiarized with nonverbal tests by 1938. The biggest rises are the Puerto Rican (+.98), Japanese (+.93), white (+.92), and Chinese (+.86); the lowest gain is Hawaiian (+.59). Smith comments that in 1924 the Puerto Ricans just did not understand what to do; hence their low scores and large nonverbal gain. Note that the Japanese have shot ahead of Chinese in

TABLE 7.5

Mean Scores of Ethnic Groups on English and Nonverbal Tests in 1924 and 1938 (S. Smith, 1942)

	1924		1938	
Ethnic group	Printed English	Nonverbal	Printed English	Nonverbal
Whites in Seattle	+1.55	+0.81	NA^a	NA^a
Whites in Hawaii	+0.63	+0.15	+1.18	+1.07
White Hawaiian	+0.36	−0.15	+0.46	+0.58
White Portuguese	+0.19	−0.33	+0.19	+0.44
Japanese	−0.04	+0.19	+0.35	+1.12
Chinese	+0.30	+0.11	+0.63	+0.97
Chinese Hawaiian	+0.14	−0.22	+0.23	+0.50
Korean	+0.60	+0.34	+0.76	+1.08
Portuguese	−0.35	−0.65	−0.13	+0.07
Portuguese Hawaiian	−0.23	−0.50	+0.04	+0.24
Japanese Hawaiian	NA^a	NA^a	+0.04	+0.30
Pure Hawaiian	−0.52	−0.49	−0.38	+0.10
Puerto Rican	−0.65	−1.25	−0.62	−0.27
Filipino	−0.35	−0.18	+0.16	+0.46
Filipino Hawaiian	NA^a	NA^a	−0.04	+0.23

^{a} NA = not available.

nonverbal ability, though they are still below them in English. The correlations between the rank orders for English in 1924 and 1938 is .95, and that for nonverbal even higher: .98. Thus there was very little change in abilities between the groups resulting from cultural developments over that period.

One can also see that, by 1938, it was difficult to classify by racial–ethnic origin, since there had been so many mixed marriages. Naturally this cross-mating would go on increasing with lapse of time.

A somewhat contradictory result was obtained by Leiter (1969) when he standardized his International Performance Scale in 1938 on Hawaiian Chinese and Japanese. On applying it to mainland whites he found that their Performance IQs averaged some 15 points higher than the oriental norm. Considering that the test is based entirely on performance and pictorial items, and requires scarcely any verbal instruction, one would certainly expect the Orientals at that date to get slightly higher means than Caucasians. The only explanation that comes to mind is that Leiter's samples may have been insufficiently representative.

STUDIES OF HIGH SCHOOL SENIORS IN HAWAII

Several studies have been carried out with Hawaiian high school seniors. Livesay (1942) obtained the test scores of 2139 students on the American Council Psychological Examination in 1935. The mean raw scores (not IQs) for the combined sexes, are shown in Table 7.6.

Livesay points out that his findings would not be true for the racial–ethnic groups in general, since differential selection has certainly operated in the immigration of the various groups, and in their completion of secondary education. We have no evidence on relative numbers of drop-outs in the different groups. Obviously the Japanese, who supply the largest numbers, constitute a greater

TABLE 7.6
Mean Intelligence Test Scores and Sigmas for Hawaiian Ethnic Groups in High School (Livesay, 1942)

Ethnic group	N	Mean	Sigma
Caucasian	233	179.94	54.87
Caucasian Hawaiian	133	125.72	42.79
Chinese	350	124.36	50.07
Korean	85	116.35	44.79
Japanese	1155	112.78	44.54
Oriental Hawaiian	77	112.65	39.44
Portuguese	81	107.18	44.07
Filipino	25	92.60	—

proportion of their island population than do the others, and this would result in a lowering of their mean score. On the other hand, the Caucasians are relatively so few that it is highly probable that most whites went to private schools, and this group may contain a preponderance of rather duller students. Nevertheless, the rank order of the groups is quite similar to that published by Murdoch (Table 7.4). Another possible reason for the unexpectedly low Japanese scores is that they maintained the use of their own language longer than other groups, even into the 1930s (M. E. Smith, p. 147). In most of Livesay's groups the males scored higher than the females; for example, Caucasians, 187.34 and 172.35; Chinese, 127.30 and 122.90; Japanese, 115.30 and 108.59. But among the Portuguese the girls surpassed the boys. The Filipinos provided the smallest and lowest-scoring group. But this would probably be because even the few who went to secondary schools in the 1930s were too handicapped by language to perform well.

Dixon *et al.* (1968) also worked with Hawaiian high school students, but compared only Japanese with all other groups combined. Their school achievements were assessed by three methods: (1) the School and College Aptitude Test (SCAT); (2) the Grade Point Averages (GPA); and (3) teachers' ratings. The Japanese were significantly higher than the cosmopolitans on all of these—an interesting change since Livesay's survey some 30 years previously. In addition, in both groups the females scored higher than the males on GPA and ratings, though not on SCAT. No actual scores or numbers of cases are quoted, but further data on personality differences will be described later.

Stewart, Dole, and Harris (1967) compared the scores of 815 high school students of mixed race on the School and College Aptitude Tests—verbal and quantitative (plus some further mathematics tests). These were given in Grade 10 in 1960, and again in Grade 12, 2½ years later. Table 7.7 shows the mean scores on the two occasions for boys and girls combined. (Two small groups of Mixed or Other Ethnic origin are omitted.) It will be seen that the Japanese and Chinese surpass the Caucasians on both occasions, particularly on the Quantitative test, much less so on the Verbal. All groups show considerable gains over the 2½ years, but this too is most marked in the two oriental groups, and the gain among Hawaiians is not significant. Thus, there is a tendency for racial–ethnic differences to increase with age. Females scored somewhat higher than males on the Verbal test, but not the Quantitative. This was specially noticeable for Japanese girls, whose parents encourage secondary education of girls as leading to the job of teacher. Thus, the relative performance of the ethnic groups has changed considerably since the 1920s and 1930s. But the representativeness of the sample is in some doubt. No explanation is given for the number of Japanese greatly exceeding the total numbers of all the other groups. Also we cannot allow for uneven drop-out rates, the tendency of Caucasians to patronize private schools, and other biasing factors.

TABLE 7.7
Mean SCAT Verbal and Quantitative Scores of Hawaiian High School Students
(Stewart *et al.*, 1967)

| Ethnic group | *N* | 1960 | | 1963 | |
		Verbal	Quantitative	Verbal	Quantitative
Japanese	480	25.9	31.3	34.9	36.2
Chinese	64	26.3	30.6	34.9	35.0
Caucasian	88	24.4	24.8	31.3	29.0
Filipino	79	17.8	21.6	23.2	24.4
Hawaiian	26	15.8	17.8	19.6	19.2

WERNER'S WORK IN KAUAI

During the 1950s and 1960s extensive investigations were carried out on the island of Kauai by Werner and her collaborators (1966, 1968, 1971). In the mid-1950s the population of the island numbered 28,000, most of them employed in sugar or pineapple growing, retail trades, construction and tourist industries, and government service. The infant mortality rate was very low, and there was an excellent health service.

Over 3000 pregnancies were recorded in 1954–55, and some 615 to 1000 children were followed up for 10 years. The median years of education among the parents of this group were six years for fathers, and eight years for mothers. Thus, the total sample of parents was only average in schooling or below. A thorough pediatric and psychological examination occurred at 2 years, and additional testing and interviewing at 10 years. Some 34% of the sample were Japanese, 24% Hawaiian (full or part), 18% Filipino, 6% Portuguese, 8% white, and smaller numbers of Chinese, Koreans, and Puerto Ricans. Some of the main results of psychological interest are given in Table 7.8.

The Cattell Infant Scale showed only small differences, but this mainly reflects perceptual, motor, and linguistic skills, rather than intellectual ability. The Vineland scale was filled in on the basis of home interviews. Clearly its norms are quite outdated, possibly because of the generally higher level of parental knowledge about childrearing nowadays. The Japanese are slightly the highest, but the differences are not significant. The differences beginning to show at 2 years are larger at 10 years. Although the Primary Mental Abilities test requires a certain amount of reading, the Japanese obtain IQs almost as high as those of whites. Much the same ethnic rank order was obtained on the Verbal, Reasoning, and Spatial factor subtests, but the Japanese were lower than whites on Verbal, and highest on the Number factor. The Bender–Gestalt perceptual test appears to

TABLE 7.8
Abilities and Other Qualities of Kauai Children of Different Ethnic Groups (Werner *et al.*, 1968)

Tests, etc.	Japanese	Hawaiian	Filipino	Portuguese	Caucasian	Total group
Cattell Infant Scale at 2 years: Mean IQ	103	96	95	99	98	99
Vineland Social Maturity Quotient	118	115	115	116	115	117
Primary Mental Abilities IQ at 10 years	109	99	101	96	112	103
Percent with Educational Problems	26.9	49.4	47.1	41.3	22.2	—
Percent errors on Bender– Gestalt test	8.7	13.3	14.5	13.0	16.7	—
Percent with Emotional Problems	18.6	27.8	28.3	34.8	27.8	—

be done best by Japanese, and worst by Caucasians; however again, the differences are doubtfully significant. Substantial differences occurred in educational achievement (especially Reading) as shown by teachers' ratings. Caucasians and Japanese average only about half as many problems as do Hawaiians, Filipinos, and Portuguese. The Japanese have a clear superiority also in the percentages with emotional problems, the Portuguese having the largest proportion. These figures were based on parent and teacher ratings and were checked by clinicians.

Home environments were assessed through interviews at 2 years and 10 years, and use was made of Dave's and Wolf's schedules of intellectual stimulation in the home (Bloom, 1964). The highest amount of stimulation occurred among Caucasians, then Japanese; emotional support was rated similarly. The Japanese particularly emphasized discipline and the value of educational and intellectual pursuits, even when the parents themselves were poorly educated. The Portuguese were generally at the bottom; they were mostly peasant or working class, and had very little upward mobility. Also they often speak their own language or pidgin English at home. However, all groups in Kauai are quite highly acculturated, though they retain many differences in the way they rear their children. Hawaiians continue to follow the extended family system, whereas Japanese as well as Caucasians follow the nuclear system.

The book by Werner *et al.* (1971), *The Children of Kauai,* is largely concerned with health factors in infancy and their later influences. Low birth weight, pre- and perinatal complications, and physical handicap were all predictive of slow mental development, though there were no marked ethnic or SES differences in the incidence of these symptoms. Low birth weight was associated with high infant mortality, but the survivors were mentally normal. Of those with perinatal handicaps, 21.4% showed low Cattell IQs versus 8.6% of those with no handicap. Corresponding figures for Vineland Social Maturity were 39 and 10%.

Again, 36.1% of those with severe perinatal stress (versus 22.6% of normals) showed mental functioning problems later; 16.7% (versus 1%) were in institutions or in classes for the retarded; and 30.6% (versus 9.7%) had PMA IQs below 85. Nevertheless, the authors conclude that environmental handicap is at least as harmful as reproductive casualty in its effects on mental growth. Thus, no children with favorable environment and no perinatal stress had any school achievement problems at 10 years, and all their PMA IQs were average or superior. But 33.3% of those with learning problems (versus 9.8% of normals) came from homes where there was lack of educational stimulation.

In conclusion it is interesting to note that several of Porteus's findings 30 years earlier still hold, although Kauai presents an unusually high degree of environmental homogeneity.

One other recent, technically sophisticated investigation deserves mention—that of Morton, Stout, & Fischer (1976). The ability and achievement test scores of all children in 153 elementary schools were obtained from the Hawaiian Education Department. The mean ability scores of children in the different schools were found to be associated with high teacher salaries and experience. However, there was no significant association with small classes nor with advanced teacher training. The schools were grouped according to census tracts (or areas), and the racial composition of each tract was determined. It was found that Caucasian and Oriental tracts obtained high ability test scores, whereas Hawaiian and Filipino areas tended to show low scores. However, when the mean SES levels of the tracts were held constant, the school performance differences largely disappeared, suggesting that such differences are partly cultural and social rather than genetic in origin. The findings generally duplicate those of earlier studies, and confirm Stewart, Dole, and Harris in placing the Japanese and Chinese as highest achievers.

SUMMARY OF CHAPTERS 6 AND 7

The history of Hawaii and its successive waves of immigrants is traced briefly. The racial–ethnic heterogeneity of the population is unique, as is also the relative harmony of interactions between the many ethnic groups. Though there is still considerable differentiation by social class and ethnicity, so much intermarriage has taken place that distinctions based on racial origins have become almost meaningless.

The multiethnic characteristics of the population have attracted an unusually large amount of psychological and sociological research. From 1924 on, there are data showing significant variations between the different groups, and considerable changes have occurred as each group progressed in its acculturation. Most striking has been the rise of Chinese and Japanese from their initial status as sugarcane and pineapple workers to their present predominance in educational achievement, business, politics, and the professions. The Japanese now constitute the largest percentage of the population (after the Caucasians), and in some recent studies they surpass the whites in mean educational achievement. However, comparisons are dubious because we cannot tell how many of the more able white children are sent to private schools, or how many white college students go to mainland universities. Some investigations have shown the familiar mainland United States pattern of Orientals falling well below whites on verbal intelligence and achievement tests, but equaling or exceeding them on nonverbal tests. However, this has been found less consistently in Hawaii, partly because of differences in the linguistic situation. Around the 1930s it seemed that the Japanese were persisting more than other groups in using their native language outside school. But soon English was adopted as the main language in all groups, except the most recent immigrants. Again, some studies have shown native Hawaiians and part-Hawaiians as scoring little below whites on verbal intelligence tests, but then they and their ancestors over several generations would have become more exposed to English than the Oriental and other immigrant groups. Interestingly, though, it was the younger Hawaiians (those under 12 years of age) who did best. In adolescence they appear to fall behind in intellectual and educational development.

One of the earliest and most extensive surveys was carried out by Porteus and Babcock in 1926. On the basis of scores on his Mazes test, head size, and ratings of the temperamental qualities of the major ethnic groups (but *not* verbal or Binet IQs), they ranked the social efficiency and potential value to the community of these groups as follows: Japanese, Chinese, Portuguese, Hawaiian and part-Hawaiians, Filipinos, and Puerto Ricans. This order was also the inverse of crime and delinquency rates. Caucasians were not assessed, but were highest in head size, and second on Mazes. Shortly after, Murdoch obtained virtually the same rank order on the basis of Army Beta scores of fairly small groups of 12-year-olds. On the verbal National Intelligence Test, Chinese exceeded the Japanese. Caucasians were highest on both tests.

A large-scale study by S. Smith of verbal and nonverbal test performance of 15 distinguishable ethnic groups or hybrids showed a remarkable consistency in the rank order of ethnic means between 1924 and 1938, though almost all the groups showed considerable improvements in scores (especially on the nonverbal test), presumably attributable to greater acculturation, knowledge of English, and sophistication in doing tests at the later occasion.

The work of Werner and her colleagues from 1954–71 on the island of Kauai is of particular value in going beyond the testing of doubtfully representative samples of racial–ethnic groups and concentrating on the pre- and perinatal factors and influences in upbringing that contribute to intellectual growth from birth to age 10 in all groups. Nevertheless, it is striking that, at 10 years, 49% of the

Hawaiian and 47% of Filipino children versus 22% of Caucasians and 27% of the Japanese were showing some educational problems at school. Most of these problem cases had undergone perinatal stress and/or lack of intellectual stimulus in their home upbringing.

8

Chinese and Japanese Immigrants to Canada

INTRODUCTION

The history of Chinese and Japanese immigrants in Canada was very similar to that in the United States, though with some important differences. The best that can be said about it is that there was much less physical violence carried out against the Orientals in Canada. The worst is that the treatment of Japanese in World War II was more shameful in that it was part of a deliberate scheme to reduce their numbers, particularly in British Columbia. In other words, evacuation cannot be attributed (as in the United States) largely to muddle in making arrangements and the weakness of the American government in giving in to the racial prejudices of the West Coast states.

SOURCES OF INFORMATION

The best source of information on the history of Chinese in Canada is Morton's *In the Sea of the Sterile Mountains* (1974), while for the Japanese, Adachi's *The Enemy that Never Was* (1976) is indispensable. The experiences of Japanese in the war-time evacuation are described by Takashima in *A Child in Prison Camp* (1971) and Broadfoot's *Years of Sorrow, Years of Shame* (1979). Sunahara's (1977) thesis covers the political background of this evacuation. Palmer's *Land of the Second Chance* (1972) traces the history of Chinese and Japanese, mainly in Alberta (see also Palmer, 1980; Dawson, 1975). However, there have been very few publications by Canadian psychologists.

THE CHINESE

The first Chinese laborers arrived in British Columbia in 1858, 10 years later than in California, but for the same reason—namely, the discovery of gold in the Fraser River valley. Some came directly from California or Hawaii; others were imported, mainly from Hong Kong. Many of them soon turned to domestic work or laundries, small shops and businesses, and fishing or farming. By 1871, 2000 were brought in to work in the coal mines at Nanaimo, and from 1874 many were employed in road-building gangs. By 1880 the total numbers in British Columbia had reached 6000. Of these only 200 were women, and very few men were able to bring in wives or families. Vicious attacks were launched by politicians, the press, merchants, and white immigrants, as in California, on the grounds that there were far too many of them in Victoria and Vancouver. It was claimed that they were living under insanitary conditions and were undercutting white employment, although in fàct most of their jobs were ones that whites regarded as too menial. On the other hand, many employers considered them as an invaluable source of cheap labor and domestic servants—reliable, sober, and law-abiding, despite their barbarous habits and inability to speak English. The same stereotypes and abusive epithets were applied to them as in the United States. (Even in 1909, *The Calgary Herald* newspaper objected to "the nests of Celestials and their rabbit warrens of opium smokers.") Continual attempts were made by the British Columbian government to restrict their entry and employment, though most of these were disallowed by the federal government. But they could not, for example, be employed by any branch of the provincial public service nor enter professions or school teaching.

In the 1870s, British Columbians still regarded themselves as a British Colony, and the eastern provinces of Ontario and Quebec as a foreign country. But eventually Canadian federation was agreed to, provided a railroad crossing the continent was constructed. This began in 1880 and was completed by 1885. Though many whites were employed, the contractors insisted that they had to have large numbers of Chinese laborers to undertake the difficult and dangerous work through the Rocky Mountains. These men worked in gangs under bosses or foremen for very low pay and inadequate food, and many died in accidents. No recognition of their role was given when "The Last Spike" was driven, and even today Canadians dislike to be reminded that the Canadian Pacific Railway line could not have been built without the Chinese.

A rapid further influx of Chinese immigrants followed, reaching a peak of 8000 in the single year 1882. However, a great many did return to China. Others were smuggled into the United States, and there was some gradual dispersal into other provinces. For example, the first Chinese settlers in Calgary, Alberta, arrived in 1886 (Dawson, 1975). Thus by the end of the century there were some

TABLE 8.1

Census: Numbers and Percentages of Chinese and Japanese in Canada and Parts of United States

		Chinese		Japanese	
Location	Total population	Number	Percentage	Number	Percentage
Canada, Total	21,568,310	118,815	0.55	37,260	0.17
Provinces					
Maritime	2,057,055	2,145	0.11	160	0.01
Quebec	6,027,765	11,905	0.19	1,745	0.03
Ontario	7,703,105	39,325	0.51	15,600	0.20
Manitoba, Saskatchewan	1,914,495	8,035	0.42	1,650	0.09
Alberta	1,627,875	12,905	0.78	4,460	0.27
British Columbia	2,184,620	44,315	2.00	13,585	0.62
Selected cities					
Montreal	1,214,375	7,240	0.61	705	0.06
Toronto–York	1,499,610	21,765	1.45	7,265	0.48
Winnipeg	246,270	1,690	0.69	600	0.24
Edmonton	438,425	4,940	1.13	610	0.14
Calgary	403,330	4,630	1.15	935	0.23
Vancouver–Burnaby	551,925	32,686	5.92	5,695	1.03
United States, Total	203,211,926	435,062	0.21	591,290	0.29
California	19,953,134	170,131	0.85	213,280	1.07
Hawaii	768,561	52,039	6.77	217,307	28.27

17,000 living in British Columbia, and only a few thousand in other provinces. The great majority were urban dwellers in ghettos or Chinatowns, where drugs, gambling, and prostitution flourished. As in the United States there were family associations and secret societies that helped to protect their members. But such societies dd not engage in illegal activities or gang warfare like the tongs.[1] A vigorous boycott was launched in Vancouver in 1886 against the employment of Chinese by whites; in 1903 a poll tax of $500 for each new immigrants was imposed. This reduced immigration in 1904–06 to almost nil, but the numbers soon crept up again to 3445 during the year 1910. By this time the British Columbians were becoming more concerned about Japanese immigration, but both groups continued to multiply until World War I.

During World War I, the Oriental Canadians were more acceptable because of the shortages of white labor. Also, Japan was an ally of Great Britain, and her navy provided a useful defense of the west coast of Canada against possible German submarine attacks. But after the war, with the return of the veterans, the

---

[1]Nevertheless, the term *tong* is used in Canada to refer to family or other associations, without implying any secrecy or crime.

opposition became more strident. Finally in 1923, the federal government gave in to the pressures from British Columbia and passed an immigration act against any further admission of Chinese, apart from consuls, some merchants, and students. After the passage of this act, hostility diminished, and the Chinese were able to settle down and consolidate their position. By now their children were attending white schools, and organized labor accepted them into the unions. Indeed the unions and the Cooperative Commonwealth Federation (C.C.F. party) supported their demands for enfranchisement, that is, voting rights for citizens, though this demand was not actually granted until 1949.

Palmer (1980) shows that during the Depression the Chinese suffered severely because of unemployment. In Calgary, for instance, in 1937, the Chinese had to stage sit-down protests in order to be granted relief payments of $2.12 a week, which was much less than white unemployed were getting.

In World War II, many Chinese served in the army. Wives and children were admitted freely in 1947, but Chinese immigration was not put on the same footing as that of other nations until 1967. The total Chinese population of 35,000 in 1941 had increased to 119,000 in 1971, and it has grown substantially since then. Most of the recent immigrants came from Hong Kong, with a few from Taiwan. The numbers living in various provinces and large cities in 1971 are given in Table 8.1.

THE JAPANESE

The Japanese reached Canada much later than the Chinese, first arriving in Victoria in 1886. But the numbers increased rapidly, many coming from Hawaii as well as from Japan. By 1901 over 15,000 had entered, though a large proportion were transients, and the total number of residents at this date was 4738, of whom 97% lived in British Columbia. Like the Chinese they were almost entirely males, and they worked mainly in gangs on the railways and roads, or in mining or lumber, and later in farming or fishing. Strongly racist opinions were voiced by the politicians and the press; by 1907 the agitation against the "Yellow Horde" reached its peak, and a violent riot occurred in Vancouver against Chinese and Japanese. But the Japanese fought back and repelled the mobsters. Fortunately no lives were lost. Since Britain had a trade treaty with Japan, the Canadian government had to send apologies to the emperor. The Japanese government protested against any attempt to limit the immigration of its peoples. Thus, Canada could not disregard the rights of Japanese Canadians as readily as they had those of the Chinese. However a Gentleman's Agreement with Japan in 1908 did reduce the influx to a few hundred each year. But after 1907 wives and children, if any, could be admitted; hence a large proportion of Japanese settled down to normal family life. As the birthrate was high, the total Japanese population in Canada reached 9,000, 16,000, and 23,000 in 1911, 1921, and 1931, respectively. The Chinese Immigration Act of 1923 did not apply to them, despite the efforts of the British Columbia government, but there was no further increase between 1931 and 1941.

The Japanese were even more hated than the Chinese, because they were more aggressive, clannish, independent, enterprising, and efficient. They had a higher standard of living than the Chinese, were more clean, and were equally hardworking. Indeed, they regarded themselves as much superior to the Chinese, and there was never any cooperation between them to counter white attacks. The fact that Japan had shown herself to be a major power in the Pacific increased the threat to white supremacy, and it was feared that she would eventually try to take over the province. They were now entering jobs where they were competitive with whites—shops, businesses, skilled manual, etc. They built up most of the fishing industry on the British Columbia West Coast. They bought property inland, and they were highly successful in the market gardening industry, as they had been in California. Though less densely concentrated than the Chinese, a large proportion did live in an area of Vancouver nicknamed "Little Tokyo."

By 1931, there were some 22,000 in British Columbia, and only about 1000 in all other provinces combined. Thus, most of Canada had no understanding of the problems of living with large ethnic minorities. The Japanese were accused by whites of retaining allegiance to the emperor, although the majority had become naturalized citizens, or, being born in Canada, were Canadian citizens. But there were 59 Japanese language schools in Vancouver for out-of-school instruction in the language and culture of Japan. Actually these were regarded by the pupils as boring and an opportunity for disorderly behavior. But their existence fostered the whites' distrust of Japanese loyalty. It was conveniently forgotten that, in World War I, some 200 Japanese Canadians had enlisted and fought in Europe, though they had to wear British, not Canadian uniforms!

In the 1930s a serious generation gap began to grow between the original Issei and their Nisei offspring, despite the traditional solidarity of the Japanese family. The Nisei spoke mostly English, and desired to participate in Canadian culture. They rejected unquestioning obedience to the parents, the intolerable system of mutual obligations, arranged marriages, and particularly the ban on mixing of the sexes and dancing. Though there was scarcely any delinquency or crime, the Nisei showed considerable maladjustment, introversion, and resentful defeatism by 1941. They were not really acculturated, though they had adopted many of the superficialities of white culture.

Evacuation of Japanese

In the 1920s and 1930s Japan was demanding a navy nearly as large as those of the United States or Britain; it seemed almost certain that war with America would occur sooner or later. The demands of British Columbians for complete repatriation of all Japanese became more clamant, and after the outbreak of war between Britain and Germany, all Japanese were required to register. From government documents that were secret at the time, it is clear that Mackenzie King, the premier, already had plans ready in 1938 to solve the racial unrest in British Columbia by deporting many of the Japanese and dispersing the rest in small numbers around the inland and eastern provinces. However, as Sunahara (1977) shows, there was a great deal of indecision in the government's policy over evacuation, partly because it was so preoccupied with the controversy over conscription. In general, its measures followed those already taken by the United States. The Japanese acquiesced with little resistance, partly because of their traditional conformity to authority, and partly because they were scattered over urban and rural areas, and had no central organization to press their case.

Soon after the Pearl Harbor attack in December 1941, all Japanese fishing boats and gear were confiscated. The Japanese had to register with the Royal Canadian Mounted Police as enemy aliens, though no similar indignity was imposed on German and Italian immigrants and their families. In fact, three-quarters of all Japanese Canadians were citizens by naturalization or by birth. Mass dismissals from employment took place; bank balances were frozen; and children turned out of schools. Sensational rumors of sabotage in Hawaii and California spread around, none of which was ever verified. Though the army stated that it did not regard the Japanese in British Columbia as a menace, Mackenzie King gave in to British Columbian pressures and, in January 1942, proclaimed that all 18- to 45-year old males were to be moved from the West Coast to 100 miles inland. Thus, they were separated from their families and sent to lumber or road-building gangs. Those who protested, along with some of the older Issei who had shown strong allegiance to Japan, were interned in an army prisoner-of-war camp in Angler, Ontario. But the white Canadians were still not satisfied, and the evacuation of all Japanese was announced in February. Their houses, cars, and other property (apart from 150 pounds that each adult could take with them) were impounded and sold by auction without their consent and often at ridiculous prices. Much of it also was looted. They were herded into large, foul-smelling cattle barns used as assembly centers in Hastings Park, Vancouver, and then were transported inland. By October 1942, some 12,000 were located in refurbished ghost towns in inner British Columbia; 4000 in Alberta sugar beet farms; 1000 in British Columbia road camps; 700 interned in Ontario; and some 3000 employed elsewhere in British Columbia, making a total of 21,000. According to Adachi, these sites had been singled out for the purpose even before war with Japan was declared. Palmer (1980) states that 2600 were sent to Alberta, despite strong protests from the provincial government and the press. It was feared that, like the Hutterites, they would sequester large areas of farmland, and undercut white farms because of their frugality and efficiency.

Those families living in the ghost towns and detention camps were terribly overcrowded, and quite inadequate heating was available in winter. The only good point was that most of the adult males could rejoin their families. Various jobs were provided, but the pay amounted only to 20 to 40 cents an hour, from which deductions were made for board, etc. At first there was no schooling for the children, but in most centers Grades 1 through 8 were organized with quite inadequate facilities, and were largely run by untrained volunteer teachers. However, considerable assistance was given by the churches. Nevertheless, after the war it has been stated that the great majority of students were able to reenter public schools at the normal grade level for their age, so strong was their motivation for educational achievement.

In 1943, those who wished to move out to get employment in the East were allowed to. But in Toronto and elsewhere they still met with a good deal of hostility, and few jobs (except domestic service) were open to them. Nevertheless, many Nisei settled there quietly, hoping to prove to their detractors that they were good Canadians.

With the defeat of Japan in 1945, plans for repatriation were put into effect. Unless they uprooted themselves again and settled east of the Rockies they were threatened with deportation. There were violent protests by Japanese and civil rights organizations and by many white politicians. The order was at last rescinded in 1947, and the camps were wound up in the same year. But by this time some 4000 had already left for Japan, where they soon found that they were far from welcome, though some of them were useful as interpreters to the American occupation forces. British Columbia fought vigorously against any return to the West Coast, and terrorized those who tried to do so. However, by 1948 the climate of opinion had changed. More than half the total population had settled outside British Columbia and Alberta, and even those in British Columbia mostly stayed inland. In fact greater numbers were living in Ontario than in British Columbia by 1951. Compensation was supposedly paid for their losses of property, boats, etc., but actually the average settlement amounted only to 23% of what the Japanese claimed.[2] With remarkably little opposition, the right to vote in federal elections was granted in 1948, and in 1949 even British Columbia followed suit, with general approval from the press. Renewed immigration was allowed, but the numbers were very small—about 100 a year between 1949 and 1965. At last in 1967 entry was accorded on the basis of sponsorship, education, and training, and the numbers of arrivals rose slowly to about one thousand a year by 1974. Much of the rise in total numbers was due, of course, to the natural birthrate; in addition, numerous students arrived with the expansion of Canadian

[2]Sunahara (1977) gives more details of compensation, and concludes that 56% of the 1941 value of goods and property was repaid by 1950, presumably in devalued dollars.

universities.[3] Table 8.1 shows that there had been considerable dispersal of the Japanese around the country, though hardly the even distribution that Mackenzie King had envisaged. Approximately one-third of all the Orientals in Canada were living in Ontario in 1971.

Many Japanese nowadays admit that, in the long run their hardships helped to improve their status in Canada. Evacuation enabled most of the Nisei to escape from the domination of the Issei, and to follow their own desires to become fully acculturated. But their spectacular rise since the war into largely middle-class status doubtless owed a great deal to the qualities that their parents had instilled into them—educational motivation, ambition, patience, self-restraint, and willingness to comply with the white majority norms. Their own children, the Sansei, went still further in Canadianization, but sometimes lacked these qualities essential to success. Actually some of them reverted to a stronger belief in the value of their Japanese culture. However, assimilation has proceeded apace, and in recent years over half of Japanese marriages have been with non-Japanese (as against barely 1% in 1941). Both Chinese and Japanese (apart from recent immigrants) are accepted as Canadians rather than foreign Orientals. Naturally they are still regarded by Caucasians as "different" in some respects, cultural as well as physical, but there is practically no racist ill-feeling.

ABILITIES AND ACHIEVEMENTS

What was probably the first cross-cultural study of Canadian Orientals was carried out by Sandiford and Kerr (1926) in Vancouver. Five hundred Chinese and Japanese children in Grades 1 to 6 were given the Pintner–Paterson performance test scale. The median IQs for both sexes and ethnic groups appear in Table 8.2. The instructions were in English, but the tests themselves involve no language. The method of arriving at IQs for this battery have always been somewhat dubious, and when recalculated by an alternative method, these figures were considerably reduced. But the authors conclude that Chinese were already as able as whites in nonverbal intelligence, and that Japanese were superior to both—in fact, the most intelligent group in British Columbia. They suggest that the original immigrants from China and Japan were more resourceful and able than the general population. This could hardly be true of the Chinese, since their ancestors were originally of poor peasant stock. However, the Japanese Issei, though mainly farmers in Japan, were better educated and able to take up skilled or commercial jobs soon after arrival. Adachi (1976) states that

[3]For a further analysis of Asian and other immigration into Canada after the war, see Richmond (1967).

TABLE 8.2
Median IQs of Chinese and Japanese School Children (Sandiford & Kerr, 1926)

	Chinese		Japanese	
	N	Median IQ	N	Median IQ
Males	131	107.7	144	115.4
Females	93	107.0	132	112.8
Combined	224	107.4	276	114.2

they represented the upper layer of the working class, including some from middle class. Another possibility, not mentioned by Sandiford and Kerr, is that many Oriental children at that time did not attend school at all, hence those that did so would tend to be above average, and to come from families with better knowledge of English.

The work of Kline and Lee (1972) and Peters and Ellis (1970) in Vancouver with Grades 1–3 Chinese children is described more fully in Chapter 11. Their main finding (at this much later date) was that there was very little retardation in English reading achievement beyond Grade 3, although a large proportion of the sample were being taught Chinese reading at the same time. Also they were mostly children of quite recent immigrants, generally in low SES jobs, and Chinese was spoken almost exclusively at home. The WISC test was given to all the children and the mean IQs were Verbal 99, Performance 112—a very remarkable result.

STUDY OF CHINESE CHILDREN IN CALGARY

Since I could find no further published research in Canada, I sought and obtained access to the school printouts covering all Calgary public schools. Various standardized tests had been given in different grades, and I extracted the scores of all children with Chinese names in Grades 3, 4, 7, and 9—539 in all, together with a white control group. Classification by name is somewhat unreliable, since some names that appear to be Chinese may be Korean or Indochinese. Also, some Chinese may be missed; for example, Young and Lee are common in Chinese and Caucasians, but they had to be classed as Caucasian since they are the majority. However, two Chinese colleagues assisted me in deciding on doubtful cases.

There has been a large influx of immigrants to Calgary in the past 10 years, partly from other provinces or the United States, and attracted by the economic prosperity of Alberta. Those from abroad came mostly from Hong Kong, where English is quite widely spoken and is taught in all schools. It has been claimed

TABLE 8.3
Significance of Differences between Chinese and White Children on Achievement and Ability Tests

Grade	Median age	Nos. of Chinese	Tests		*t* values	
					Boys	Girls
3	8:8	148	Stanford Reading Comprehension		+1.039	+1.328
			Arithmetic Problems		+0.702	+0.950
4	9:8	137	Canadian Tests of Cognitive			
			Abilities:	Verbal	−0.169	+0.044
				Nonverbal	+1.460	+2.546
7	12:10	132	CCAT:	Verbal	−0.300	−2.295
				Quantitative	+3.127	+1.745
				Nonverbal	+4.444	−0.770

that in 1979 there were 19,000 Chinese in a population of some 500,000, that is, about 3.8% (Warden, 1979); but as I found only 139 in the average grade, it seems likely that the figure is nearer 2%, or a total of 12,000.[4] There is still a Chinatown in Calgary, but it is mainly occupied by the elderly, and the majority are dispersed widely over the city area. Many adults speak Chinese among themselves, though few children do so. There are two language schools operating out of ordinary school hours to train children in speaking and reading Mandarin or Cantonese, but these reach scarcely more than 10% of young children.

Table 8.3 gives the *t* values for the differences between Chinese and Caucasian controls: + signifies that Chinese were superior. It may be seen that there were no more than chance differences in Verbal abilities among boys. But the girls (and combined sexes) are higher on Grade 4 Nonverbal at the .01 level of probability.

In grade 7, girls are a little lower on Verbal ability ($< .05$ probability). But boys and sexes combined are significantly superior in Quantitative and Nonverbal.

The most extensive data were obtained in Grade 9, where Bennett's Differential Aptitude Tests yielded scores on seven types of ability (unfortunately, the Clerical aptitude test was not given). Table 8.4 shows the mean raw score differences between Chinese and Caucasians. All asterisked means are significant at the 0.1 level. Also, the Chinese means have been converted to an IQ scale with standard deviation 15. It can be seen that there are no differences among

---

[4]Approximately 23% of the Calgary school population are Catholics who attend separate instead of public schools. But as there is no reason to expect a larger or smaller proportion of Orientals in the separate schools, their omission in my investigation does not affect the percentage or total figures given here.

TABLE 8.4
Differences between Chinese Students[a] in Grade 9 and White Controls on D.A.T. Battery

	Mean differences			Chinese quotients	
Test	Boys	Girls	Combined	Boys	Girls
Verbal Analogies	−0.26	−2.50	−0.88	99	94
Number Computation	+4.26[b]	+4.66[b]	+4.55[b]	110	111
Nonverbal Reasoning	+5.40	−0.77	+2.80	109	98
Mechanical Comprehension	+1.47	−2.47	+1.23	103	94
Spatial Ability	+8.13[b]	+2.81	+6.05[b]	110	103
Spelling	+7.93 [b]	+5.88	+6.06[b]	107	105
English Usage	+0.56	−1.60	−0.93	101	97
			All tests	105	100

[a] Numbers of Chinese: 80 boys and 42 girls.
[b] Significant at .01.

boys on the Verbal, Mechanical, and English Usage tests, and girls are somewhat lower than whites on these. The Mechanical Comprehension test is based on verbal statements about pictures of mechanical objects. But on all the other tests the boys are very significantly superior, at a level corresponding to an IQ of about 110. Girls are above average on Number and Spelling, that is, subjects that involve a good deal of rote learning, and less verbal reasoning.

It should be noted that these results reflect superiority to Calgary whites. But the average SES and education of white families in Calgary is distinctly higher than the Canadian average; their mean IQ on standardized tests is probably at least 105. This means then, then the Chinese average even on verbal tests is above 100 relative to Canadian norms. On nonverbal, number, spatial, and spelling tests, the boys' mean would be approximately 114, the girls' 109. Incidentally, the proportion of girls in Grade 9 has dropped from 50% to 34%. This suggests—though there is no direct evidence—that Calgary Chinese parents still see less need for girls to obtain advanced secondary education, and even tend to remove some of the brightest ones, perhaps to help in their stores or businesses, or else to get secretarial or hairdressing training at other institutions.[5]

Only 67 Japanese names were discovered in the four grades (i.e., one-ninth as many as Chinese); hence, no attempt was made to analyze them. However, much

[5]A Chinese commentator suggested to me that Hong Kong parents would be more likely to bring their sons than their daughters with them. But I would expect this to affect elementary school numbers also.

Another complication is that quite large numbers of students from Hong Kong come to Canada for schooling in Grades 11 or 12, or for college education, and then return home. Probably these would be mainly male. Ashworth (1975) reports on 2763 such students entering in 1973. They did not get as good grades as others who had passed the Hong Kong matriculation examinations (cf. p. 125).

the same pattern of scores, relative to those of whites, was obtained as with the Chinese, except that Japanese girls more often scored higher than boys. There are small Japanese schools in Calgary: one for teaching English to recent immigrants and preserving Japanese culture, and another for coaching short-term visiting children up to the same level as in Japan.

I had hoped to be able to find out the background and language usage of these Chinese students by means of a simple questionnaire, but they were spread throughout so many schools that it was not possible to contact more than about 200, and disappointingly few of those contacted returned the questionnaire. It is commonly noted that Chinese parents tend to be reticent in such matters, but the instructions were given in Chinese as well as English, asking them to cooperate in getting their children to respond. Eventually 112 completed copies were returned, but they did provide approximately equal numbers of boys and girls and of elementary and secondary school students.

Fifty-six percent of all children had been born in Canada (usually, though not necessarily, Alberta), thus confirming the arrival of a great many immigrants since the last census. Almost all the 44% foreign-born came from Hong Kong. Close to one-half of them had lived in Canada 5 years or more, the others being more recent. Either the earlier test results or teachers' ratings were used to grade the current achievement of the students. The Canadian-born secondary students were superior in ability to the foreign-born at the .01 level, but curiously this did not hold in the elementary grades. Possibly this is because the language gap between foreign- and native-born secondary school students is greater than at elementary level.

The following table shows the percentages who said that they spoke Chinese or English at home or with friends. It may be seen that a majority of homes use Chinese mostly or all the time, but three-quarters of students speak only English with their friends.

	Spoken at home	Spoken with friends
Chinese all the time	13%	0%
Chinese mostly	48	3
English mostly	32	23
English all the time	7	74

However, no relation was found between use of English or Chinese outside school and achievement in school. Thus, although Chinese children continue to score less well on verbal intelligence tests or English achievement tests than on nonverbal tests, their bilingualism does not affect their educational progress in any consistent fashion. Finally, there were also no significant differences in achievement between those who did attend or had attended Chinese language schools and those who had not. The absence of clearcut results may be due partly to the small size of the sample, which may not have been sufficiently representative of the whole range of achievement, language usage, or birthplace.

No studies could be found dealing with Chinese or Japanese Canadian personality characteristics. However, it appears in Chapter 13 that the choice of college subjects and vocations is similar among Chinese Canadians and Americans; hence, there is no reason to think that temperamental factors, personality traits, or attitudes of Chinese will differ much between Canada and the United States.

SUMMARY

The history of Chinese and Japanese immigration to British Columbia, and later to the rest of Canada, is quite similar to that in California and the United States. The white population was extremely hostile over many years, especially when the numbers in British Columbia rose to some 10% of the population, and when they moved away from menial laboring jobs into skilled trades and commerce, where they were in competition with white immigrants. The rise and eventual decline of racial discrimination is outlined, including the disgraceful mass evacuation of Japanese from the West Coast during World War II. Although numbers of both groups have risen greatly since the war, and are still expanding, they are now accepted with very little opposition or ill-feeling. There are sizable populations of them in all provinces from Ontario to British Columbia. Their educational and vocational achievements are remarkable, and they have become very largely acculturated.

In the very early days of mental testing (1926), Chinese and Japanese elementary school children in Vancouver scored at or above white levels on nonverbal performance tests, despite their descent from mainly peasant stock and the unfavorable conditions in which they were living. More recent studies—some of them carried out by the present writer—show that they are still slightly below white average on verbal intelligence and achievement tests, but the boys at least are much superior on nonverbal reasoning and spatial abilities. Both sexes are also much above average in number work and spelling. Those born in Canada achieve somewhat better than recent immigrants, yet there seems to be remarkably little adverse effect of the still widespread usage of Chinese in the homes. A substantial number of Grade 1 and 2 Chinese have difficulties with learning to read English, especially if attending Chinese language schools in spare time. But by the end of Grade 3, the number of retardates is very small, and there seem to be virtually no cases of dyslexia (see Chapter 11).

Though there are valuable historical and sociological studies of Orientals in Canada, there has been a remarkable lack of interest among psychologists, in contrast to that shown in the United States.

9

The Abilities of Chinese Children
in Hong Kong, Singapore,
and Taiwan

INTRODUCTION

Hong Kong is obviously not part of North America. But it does provide a large sample of Chinese, who are partly westernized and partly English-speaking. A large proportion of present-day immigrants to North America come from Hong Kong. In addition, quite a lot of research has been carried out there, which is well worth our attention.

Hong Kong is a British crown colony seized as a treaty port in 1841. Although over 98% of the population are Chinese (mostly from the Canton region, though some Hakkas, some from Shanghai, etc.), it was administered entirely by the British Civil Service until the Japanese occupation of 1941–45. After the war, considerable efforts were made to democratize the government, bringing in Chinese businessmen as advisers, and a great many Chinese employees (Lethbridge, 1969).

The total area of the colony is 400 square miles, made up of Hong Kong Island, Kowloon on the mainland, and the much larger (but more mountainous) New Territories. By 1960, 80% of the population lived on 12 square miles of land, the rest being less suitable for building or agriculture. This produced one of the highest population densities in the world, up to 200,000 per square mile, though doubtless many Chinese cities are equally or more crowded (Goodstat, 1969). Hong Kong has no natural resources, but it developed a prosperous economy through export and commerce. Now there is a thriving industry, especially in manufactured clothing, and the unemployment rate is very low (Jarvie, 1969). Naturally China could take over the colony with the greatest of ease, but it suits her to use the port as a trade outlet and a source of foreign currency.

The population totaled close to one million in 1940, dropping to half a million

TABLE 9.1
1976 Hong Kong Census, Occupational Distribution of 1,209,590 Men and 657,890 Women

Occupations	Percentage	
	Men	Women
Professional (Doctors, architects, writers, etc.)	3.7	1.7
Teachers	1.2	1.7
Administrators and managers (Government and production)	3.0	0.3
Clerical workers	8.6	6.3
Sales, managers (Commercial, etc.)	13.5	4.2
Service workers (Catering, laundry, hairdressing, etc.)	15.0	7.8
Agricultural workers	1.6	0.7
Fishing	1.2	0.6
Production workers (Artisans, operatives, builders, etc.)	48.6	29.4
Laborers	2.0	0.9
Armed forces and unclassified	1.5	0.6

Note: The women's totals are also divided by 1,209,590 in order to make their percentages comparable to those of men. Presumably the remaining 46% of women were housewives, who were not classified by the census.

by 1945, but with the victory of the Communist regime over Chiang Kai-shek in 1949, there came floods of immigrants, raising the population to some three million in 1961, and about five million in 1980. In addition the birthrate is high, and the population is growing with such rapidity that there are great difficulties in supplying sufficient housing, social services, and education.[1] The New Territories are becoming more widely settled, and many small townships have been established there, but the drift from the rural areas into the city cannot be controlled.

In 1969, J. Agassi listed the occupational distribution of the population, pointing out the widely diversified nature of the economy. Later census figures (1976) give the following classification of the main types of employment.

The social class distribution in the colony, together with the educational standards, remain fairly stable despite the continuous influx of additional immigrants. The probable reason for this is that, although the majority of immigrants are unskilled workers, they range all the way up to businessmen and professionals.

[1]In 1980 a fence was erected between the Hong Kong and Chinese frontiers, and the regulation that illegal immigrants should be deported back to China was more strictly enforced. But there are still intolerable numbers arriving in the colony.

While there is a good deal of poverty in Hong Kong, due to the low wages and large families, it is much less noticeable than, say, in India. There is no widespread malnutrition; the infant mortality rate has dropped to 12 in 1000. However, tuberculosis is still a serious threat; some 2% of all adults require treatment. And the appalling overcrowding, together with the intractability of providing an adequate sewage system, certainly constitute a danger to health. The crime rate is quite low compared with, say, the United States. In 1978 the total rate of violent crimes against persons and property was 3.7 per thousand population.[2] Admittedly smuggling, gambling, drugs, and prostitution are still rife.

There have been tremendous efforts to catch up with housing needs. The government has built numerous low-rent six-story blocks of flats, holding up to 3000 persons each. Many of them, though, could well be called slums, since they provide only 24 square feet of space per person, and sanitation is quite inadequate. In some tenements, as many as 60-70 persons live in a three-room flat, taking turns at sleeping. Housing associations supply somewhat better quality accommodation, with 35 square feet per person. But in addition, an estimated one million of the population are squatters who build shacks on any vacant land or live on the streets or on boats. The Chinese appear much less sensitive to such crowding than Caucasians would be, but the health hazards have already been mentioned. It is astonishing how clean and neat are the great majority of the school population, despite such conditions.

Anderson (1972) has discussed overcrowding in Hong Kong, trying to explain why it does not lead to undue social conflict or crime (see also Baldassare and Feller, 1975). From interviews with 4000 parents and some of their children, Mitchell (1971) concludes that the lack of space as such does not increase tensions or hostility within families or between families in the same unit. However, when two or more families share a unit that is on the sixth floor or higher, there is noticeable strain, since those who are high up cannot readily get away from the unit.

EDUCATION

Schooling has improved greatly since the 1940s. According to government statistics, 100% of children attend primary schools (6-11 years), 89% junior secondary (12-14), and 64% senior (15-16). Roughly 10% or more are getting higher education in universities, colleges of education, polytechnics, etc. I myself feel doubtful as to the possibility of making a complete enumeration of school attenders under the above-mentioned conditions. There may actually be quite a lot of children (e.g., those of illegal immigrants) who do not go to school.

[2]The figures for 1978 are quoted from a government pamphlet: *Hong Kong in Figures,* 1979.

Certainly there are a lot of drop outs by the age of 14 and, though illegal, many do leave and go to work before they reach 15. At the time when Godman and Rowe's research were carried out (see page 119), government schools were mostly bisessional, that is, half the children attended from 8 A.M. to 1 P.M., the other half from 1:30 P.M. to 6:30 P.M. Many of the classes numbered 45 children, and no special programs were available for the treatment of seriously retarded or maladjusted children. However, such special programs are now being developed.

In the 1960s, all schools charged fees, though those in government schools were quite low. But such schools were quite insufficient to provide for all children, and many were sent to government-aided (subsidized) or private schools. By the late 1970s, compulsory and free education up to the age of 14 was provided in all three types of schools.

The Cantonese dialect of Chinese is the medium of instruction throughout government elementary schools, though some English is taught from Grade 3 on. But several private and aided elementary schools use English. Anglo–Chinese secondary schools use English throughout, and these are extremely popular since knowledge of English is generally recognized as the key to the best jobs in business, commerce, professions, public service, etc. But the switch in languages at about 12 years is unfortunate, since the children are just reaching the stage at which they could read Chinese for pleasure or curiosity. Instead, the difficulty of the English medium leads to some stagnation in education, and reinforces the tendency to learn purely by rote. Students read word by word instead of going straight to the meaning. Learning becomes the acquisition and regurgitation of facts. Even at the university, students cling to the authority of the printed word or the professor, and are unwilling to discuss or show any initiative in class (Cansdale, 1969). Questioning the teacher would mean that he might "lose face," and the questioner would lose face if his questions were stupid. Students accept British or American ideas, but often do not understand and do not evaluate them. Also, they seem to get no pleasure or satisfaction out of their studies. Nevertheless it is obvious that a great many able Chinese, who are also fluent in English, survive the system.

Kvan (1969) tested University of Hong Kong students and found that 50% of them were reading at a speed of less than 150 words/minute. On Schonell's Reading Comprehension Test B, they scored at the 12- to 13-year level for British children. Kvan compared their reading skills to those of American college students reading French. In the early 1960s, 90% of the population spoke only Chinese, and much smaller numbers could read or write it; only some 9% were fluent in both English and Chinese. But the literacy rate has been rising rapidly. When J. Chan (unpublished observations, p. 122) devised a group intelligence test in the English medium for University of Hong Kong matriculation students, I was astonished at the capacity of these students to comprehend and think in a foreign language, apparently at much the same level as many higher education students in England. But of course they were a very highly selected group, and they had undergone tremendous pressure from home and school to achieve university places.

A large proportion of children in Hong Kong are sent to kindergarten, even as early as 3 years, and they are given an examination for entry to primary school, which requires knowledge of, say, 100 to 160 Chinese characters, together with some English vocabulary. After school hours children are not usually encouraged to go out and play; parents regard this as a waste of time, and they may arrange for additional coaching, as well as seeing that some 2 hours of homework are done every night.[3]

The Hong Kong Chinese are obviously very similar to Chinese elsewhere, and yet there is the interesting difference that they are becoming acculturated, or westernized, although they are not, as in Hawaii or the United States, a minority culture. There tends to be a large generation gap. The parents, especially those in the rural areas, cling to Chinese traditions, but the younger generation, who go to school or get jobs in the cities, are deserting them. Family life is becoming more nuclear, less extended; the father's unquestioned authority and the arrangement of marriages by the parents are breaking down. The young accept American films, music, tastes in dress, etc. Yet, it is still necessary to remember that the Chinese think of themselves as solidly Chinese, not as British subjects. Despite intergenerational conflicts, there has been far less student violence in Hong Kong than in Japan. There have been occasional riots (in 1956, 1966, and 1967), not led, but participated in, by students. But considering the conservatism and rigidity of the elders, the strains of schooling, and the pull of the West, one might well have expected a good deal more activism (Jarvie, 1969).

RESEARCH ON THE ABILITIES OF HONG KONG CHILDREN

In the early 1960s, N. K. Henderson, professor of education at the University of Hong Kong, set up the Hong Kong Council for Educational Research. This body produced two rather comprehensive investigations by Godman (1964) and by Rowe (1966) and some subsequent publications. Rowe's study will be described in Chapter 11.

Godman surveyed the Primary 4 children (mostly aged 9–11 years) in five representative government schools. Four objective tests were prepared in English, Chinese, Mechanical and Problem Arithmetic, and these were given to 1007 children along with the Raven Matrices, Cattell's Culture-Fair tests, Forms

---

[3]Goodnow, Young, and Kvan (1976) quote the following advertisement from a Hong Kong newspaper: "English-speaking lady wanted to tutor 4-year-old for 2 hours each evening for primary entrance examination."

A and B, and a locally produced nonverbal test by K. A. Spelling. The instructions were given in Cantonese. The intercorrelations between achievement and nonverbal tests were in the range .30 to .47 (except the two Arithmetic tests correlating .64). These figures seem rather low, suggesting that Hong Kong children were quite unsophisticated with written group tests, especially as their answers had to be entered on IBM sheets. Moreover, the correlation between the two forms of the Cattell Test, 1 month apart, was only .65.

The median score for the total group on the Raven Matrices was 30, which is close to the published British norm for age 10:0 years. However, these norms have become too lenient over time, and a restandardization by Kyle (1977) indicates that the current median at 10 years is 36.[4] The Cattell Scale B mean score of 28 is somewhat superior to the American norm for 10-year-olds, indicating a mean nonverbal IQ of about 105.

The main finding, which is very difficult to explain, was that, when the sample was divided up by chronological age, there was remarkably little difference between the means and standard deviations among 8½-, 9½-, 10½-, and 11½-year-old children. The correlation of total attainment scores with age was only .14. In an ordinary American or British school one would naturally think that the younger children were brighter ones who had been accelerated, and the older were duller ones who had been kept back a year or two. Godman specifically denies this, saying that, although children enter at various ages from 6 on, they are automatically promoted one grade each year. And in only one school was there some partial streaming by ability. He hypothesizes a tendency for all pupils, regardless of age, to regress to the mean level of ability and attainment of the grade they are in. This sounds improbable, and Rowe suggests that some children are ''over-promoted''; also, that it is fairly common for children to fail a grade, and therefore have to repeat. Another possible factor is that parents who realize that their children are rather dull may enter them at more advanced ages, and vice versa if they are particularly bright.

Additional work on the Raven Matrices was reported by Li (1964). She found the median score at 12½ years to be 41, which is the same as Raven's norm. Kyle (1977) quotes 44 as the British norm for this age. But in any case the Hong Kong mean is probably boosted because the 1197 children in Li's sample were applying for entry to secondary schools, and therefore were, to some extent, self-selected.

Three studies have been published using Piaget tasks of mental development. Goodnow and Bethon (1966; also Goodnow, 1962) gave several tests of conservation and combinatorial reasoning to Chinese children in Hong Kong who had

---

[4]Probably it is unfair to expect this standard from test-unsophisticated children in 1963. Also, a time limit of 20 minutes was imposed by Godman, which is not the practice in England. This does tend to reduce the mean score, though by only quite a small amount.

not received any schooling, and also to a control group of American children of the same chronological age. There was virtually no difference on the conservation tests, but the unschooled children were significantly poorer on the reasoning test, which presumably requires complex mental processing that is assisted by schooling. The unschooled children were also below average on the Raven Matrices test.

Douglas and Wong (1977) investigated Piaget's formal operations in matched groups of Chinese and American children, aged 13 and 15 years. There were 120 in each sex, ethnic, and age group. The tasks were color combinations, invisible magnet, and projection of shadows. The mean total scores were

	Male		Female	
	13 yr.	15 yr.	13 yr.	15 yr.
Chinese	7.60	8.60	6.80	7.06
American	7.93	9.99	8.07	9.34

All the American means are higher, though not by a great amount. Chinese boys score better than girls, and in both ethnic groups scores increase with age. Analysis of variance showed all these differences to be statistically significant at the .01 level.

Jahoda, Deregowski, and Sinha (1974) studied the transition from topological to Euclidean space perception in Hong Kong, Scotland, India, and Zambia. Following Piaget, they hypothesized that children in industrially developed countries would show more Euclidean perception than those in less developed. Sets of three nonrepresentational shapes were shown, the subject being told to pick out the one that is different from the other two. The answers could be classified as topologically or Euclidean-based. Over the age range of 4 to 12 years, there was no clear trend in scores, as would be expected from Piagetian theory, and about half the children were too inconsistent in their choices to be classified under either heading. The results shown in Table 9.2 represent the mean Euclidean ($+$) scores or topological ($-$) scores.

There is no known difference between the Chinese-medium and English-medium pupils to account for the higher score of the former. But the combined group show more Euclidean perception than the Scottish, and very much more than the unschooled boat children, Indians, and Zambians.

Some work on aesthetic sensitivity was summarized in Chapter 5. Chan, Eysenck, and Götz (1980) found Hong Kong children scoring lower on Götz's test than English children, and much lower than Japanese.

Dawson, Young, and Choi (1973, 1974) have worked extensively on cross-cultural differences in visuospatial abilities, including tests that measure Witkin's concept of field dependent and independent cognitive styles. In Hong Kong, Dawson found that the Chinese children, over the 3- to 17-year-old range, were

TABLE 9.2
Differences between Euclidean and Topological Perception Scores in Different Ethnic Groups
(Jahoda *et al.*, 1974)

Group	N	Mean
Hong Kong children in Chinese-medium school	30	+6.00
Hong Kong children in English-medium school	30	+3.11
Hong Kong children living in boats	48	+0.15
Glasgow schoolchildren	120	+3.02
Indian children, nonscheduled castes	62	+1.29
Indian children, scheduled castes	53	−0.05
Zambian schoolchildren	72	−1.12

less susceptible than whites to geometrical illusions, which would be expected of field independent persons. A test of Traditional versus Modern attitudes showed the traditional to be more susceptible to illusions.

Dawson also gave tests of three-dimensional perception to Eskimos, Chinese, and African natives, and found the Chinese to perform better than Africans, though not as highly as Eskimos. These results confirm the superiority of Chinese boys in spatial ability, as noted in Chapter 2.

Recent Investigations of Abilities and Achievements

Dr. J. Chan of the Educational Research Establishment has carried out a wide range of research studies on the abilities and achievements of children in Hong Kong. His first article (1974) describes previous work by the Hong Kong Council for Educational Research, in which the Raven Matrices,[5] Cattell Culture-Fair, and WISC were adapted for application in Chinese. Heim's AH4 test (translated) has also been used, and Chan has constructed a group intelligence test, given in English to students entering the English-medium University of Hong Kong, including verbal, numerical, and nonverbal subtests. But the third section of this test gave little or no correlation with achievement, indicating that it may be unwise to rely on nonverbal tests as educational predictors in a bilingual community.

Chan (1976a) studied the effects of testing Primary 6 children (aged 9:11–14:6) in a foreign language. Cantonese (or occasionally other dialects) would almost always be used at home, but all the children would have studied English at school for several years. Two forms of a verbal and a numerical reasoning test were constructed, one in English and one with closely equivalent items in Chinese. Half of the group of 141 pupils took the Chinese first and then the English, half the reverse. The overall mean scores were

[5]See also Li (1964), who published a Chinese version of the WISC in 1962.

Verbal in English	68.67	Verbal first	78.27
Verbal in Chinese	85.85	Verbal second	76.27
Number in English	87.48	Number first	85.45
Number in Chinese	89.46	Number second	91.44

Clearly there is a large (and significant) disadvantage when taking the verbal test in English, but only a small (nonsignificant) difference in the number test. Some of the arithmetic items that involved a lot of reading did show differences. The last column shows the order effect. Taking number first in either language yields a lower mean than taking it second: that is, there is a substantial practice effect. But there is no such effect with the verbal test. At this age, then, it is preferential to test in Chinese, though later on, all the well-educated students become more or less bilingual.

Chan (1976b) also gave the Raven Matrices to 213 English students (aged about 15) in one government and one subsidized school, and to 209 Chinese in an Anglo–Chinese school. The schools were close to average level in their examination performances. But the English were children of expatriates in government or business employment, that is, higher income families, whereas the Chinese parents were mostly middle income. The mean scores were

	Boys	Girls	Total
English	50.86	49.34	50.21
Chinese	53.28	53.29	53.29

Both sexes of Chinese scored significantly higher than the English. Kyle's (1977) norm for British 15-year-olds is 49, and a score of 53 represents the 75th percentile. Chan suggests that the eye movements involved in reading Chinese may transfer to the Matrices problems, and thus give some advantage. However, I would suspect that Chinese who gain entrance to Anglo–Chinese schools are rather highly selected, because these schools have greater attraction to aspiring parents. Nevertheless the relatively poor performance of the English students is surprising considering their SES level, though perhaps understandable in terms of weaker motivation.

In a further investigation of 4500 junior high school students (median age 13:3), the median Matrices score was 51, and the percentiles are shown here:

Percentile	Chinese Score	Kyle's Norms
95	57	53
90	56	52
75	53	49
50	51	46
25	48	42
10	45	36
5	42	28

Kyle's British norms are added. Here, the Chinese performance is certainly superior, but note that the differences are greatest among the bottom 25% or so. About 84% of Hong Kong students aged 12–14 were in full-time education, so there was a certain degree of selection. Thus, the bottom tail of the high age group was not representative.

Other unpublished studies have used the AH4 test, which has Verbal (including some numerical), and Nonverbal sections. Over 3000 secondary students aged around 16 years were tested. There were variations between different sub-groups, but the overall medians are shown in Table 9.3. Heim does not provide age norms, but her large group of naval recruits would be nearest to a representative sample of young British adults. The grammar school students listed here would be much more highly selected than the secondary modern school. It would appear that the Hong Kong students are distinctly lower on the verbal part, and higher on the nonverbal than comparable English students and another group of Canadians (MacLean and McGhie, 1980). The verbal part was taken in English, though with Cantonese instructions, which would naturally reduce their scores. Taking the Nonverbal Part 2 alone, the Chinese are much the highest; though, as before, one should realize that they would be selected to some extent.

TABLE 9.3
Median Scores on AH4 Intelligence Test

Group	N	Part 1	Part 2	Total
Hong Kong high school students	5209	29	50	79
Heim's figures for English groups:				
Naval ratings	1183	34	41	75
Secondary modern school, 14-year-old	565	26	34	60
Grammar school, 14-year-old	533	39	46	85
Canadian Grade 11, 16-year-old students	296	38	45	83

These findings of the equality, or even superiority, of Hong Kong students on nonverbal intelligence tests are all the more striking when it is considered that the per capital income (in U.S. dollars) was about $487 in Hong Kong, $1298 in United Kingdom, and $2562 in the United States at that time.[6]

Achievement Tests

Two series of achievement tests in Chinese, English, and Mathematics were constructed by Chan (1976c, 1978). These are used by primary school teachers

[6]In more recent years the income figures have risen considerably. In 1978 the Hong Kong per capita income was equivalent to US $2904. But as the American and British figures approximated $10,000, Hong Kong is still far lower.

of Grades 4, 5, and 6 to help in guidance and promotion of pupils. Each test is normalized to a mean of 100 and a standard deviation of 15. Samples of 10 to 18 thousand have been drawn to establish regional and sex differences, and differences between three different types of school. The mean scores in Hong Kong Island, Kowloon, and New Territories for combined tests were 102.0, 101.2, and 95.2, respectively. The New Territories schools are less advanced, partly because a large proportion of the population are recent immigrants, and partly because the more prestigious schools are on Hong Kong Island and, to a lesser extent, in Kowloon. The three types of schools described above are the government, the subsidized, and the private; their median quotients in 1978 were 94.9, 99.5, and 106.2. These figures probably reflect the aspirations of more ambitious, able, educated, and usually wealthy parents who believe that they can get the best education for their children in the private schools. In each comparison the differences were greatest on the English test, and relatively small on Chinese and mathematics. Consistent sex differences were found: the girls being 3.63 points above boys in English, 1.14 in Chinese; and boys better in mathematics by 2.08 points. In single-sexed schools the means for girls were higher than those for boys on all tests, including mathematics. Boys' and girls' single-sexed schools surpassed the coeducational, probably because they are private schools, and therefore are more selective.

At the high school level, Chan (1981) compared students attending Anglo–Chinese and middle schools (i.e., Chinese-medium). No objective achievement tests were available, but both types of school had taken the territory-wide departmental examinations. The middle school students obtained higher average marks in Chinese and mathematics, both of which tend to be taught by rote and to require little or no English. But the Anglo–Chinese students do better in biology, chemistry, physics, geography, and history, which are taught in a more free style, and probably use more English materials and books. Again, it is the parental aspirations rather than the quality of schooling as such that probably account for the superior results of Anglo–Chinese schools.

A general inference from the above reports is that Chinese students from Hong Kong, especially those from Anglo–Chinese schools and universities, are better prepared for graduate work in the United States, Canada, or United Kingdom, than those from other schools, or from Taiwan or mainland China. Dawson (1970) points out that secondary schooling in Hong Kong derives from the English Sixth Form, which produces high school graduates whose standards of achievement are comparable to those of first-year university students in many countries. The Chinese are clearly at least as able as whites on noverbal ability, and their education does give them considerable knowledge of English. At the same time one should remember Cansdale's (see p. 118, this volume) warning about the inadequate English reading skills of University of Hong Kong students. It is probable that those who do get visas to study abroad at graduate level in North America or Britain would generally be above average level in English. But a lot of Hong Kong undergraduates in overseas universities are those who have failed to gain entry to the University of Hong Kong.

SINGAPORE

Singapore is another ex-British colony, now self-governing and independent of the Malay States. In 1970 the population of two million lived on the 225-square-mile island. Since it is not closely adjacent to China, the population is more mixed—about three-quarters Chinese, but with large minorities of Malaysians, Indians, and others. Like Hong Kong it is predominantly a trading center, and it has as high a literacy rate and living standards as any Asian country (except Japan). The dictatorial powers of the government have controlled population growth more successfully than in other southeast Asian countries.

Phua (1976) investigated the two main ethnic groups, Chinese and Malays. Taking 337 boys aged 13 years in representative Singapore schools, she obtained the following means on the Raven Matrices test:

	Chinese	Malaysian
N	147	190
Means	47.9	41.9

Kyle's median for this age is 47, so the Chinese are closely the same (unless a selective factor was operating). The Malaysian mean corresponds to an IQ difference of some 10 points—a figure comparable to that which separates blacks and whites in the United States (Lynn, 1977a).

As in Hong Kong, the delinquency rate of Chinese is low. Murphy (1963) recorded the numbers of court referrals of 10- to 15-year-old boys as follows:

White and Eurasian	4.4 per thousand
Chinese	12.3
Malaysian	12.8
Indian	44.6

Another investigation in Singapore by Torrance, Wu, Gowan, and Aliohi (1970) has come to notice. The Torrance Tests of Creative Thinking are well known, and three of these are based on inventiveness in drawings; that is, they are nonverbal. Torrance hypothesized that children who were brought up as bilinguals would experience some conflict between their two languages, and this might reduce the Fluency and Flexibility scores on his test battery. On the other hand, Originality and Elaboration scores might be raised by acquaintance with two languages and two sets of concepts.

Over one thousand third to fifth grade children in Singapore were given the nonverbal tests with Chinese or Malaysian instructions. Approximately one-half were bilingual, that is, Chinese or Malays attending English-medium schools, and the other half unilingual, attending schools in their own mother tongues. The mean scores over all grades were as follows:

	Monolingual	Bilingual
Figural Fluency	46.22	41.80
Flexibility	46.56	42.82
Originality	37.57	37.10
Elaboration	36.07	36.74

As predicted, the monolinguals are significantly superior on Fluency and Flexibility. There are no significant differences in Originality or Elaboration. However, relative to their own Fluency level, the bilinguals are superior to the monolinguals on these variables.

CHINESE IN TAIWAN

Taiwan (or Formosa) is a large island, 100 miles off the coast of mainland China. It was seized by Japan after the first Sino–Japanese war in 1946, but was returned to China in 1946. In 1949 after his defeat, Chiang Kai-shek, his army, and many refugees settled there, and called it the Republic of China. Almost the entire population is Chinese, but Taiwanese and Nationalist Chinese cultures do differ to some extent.

Rodd (1959a) gave an extensive battery of tests to 765 eleventh grade students of Taiwanese descent and 525 of mainland descent. The battery included Cattell's Culture-Fair tests Scale 3, Forms A and B, the Harry–Durost Achievement tests in Mathematics and Science, the Watson–Glaser Critical Thinking test, and the Allport–Vernon–Lindzey Study of Values (all appropriately translated).

The 16-year-old students obtained mean IQs of 104 (Taiwanese) and 106 (Chinese) on American norms, and small groups of 15-year-olds in the same grade averaged 114 and 117, respectively. Both Rodd and Cattell (1959) cite these results as evidence that the C–F tests are not culturally biased. And Cattell considers his test series as superior to the Raven Matrices in containing four varied subtests, instead of the single type of item used in the Matrices. The total working time of 12½ minutes is shorter, but this may be a disadvantage in terms of reliability. Thus, the correlation between Forms A and B given a few weeks apart was only .57. However, there was a rise with practice from 24 points on Form A to 28 points on Form B, indicating that the students were quite unfamiliar with such tests at first administration, and therefore likely to perform better at the second test.

Cattell admits that children in developing countries do sometimes score lower on his C–F tests than American whites. But he suggests that such factors as poor motivation, lack of experience in working at speed, unfamiliarity of tests, and imperfect three-dimensional visual perception may adversely affect their performance. But it would be premature to claim that Taiwanese students are as high as, or higher than, whites in nonverbal intelligence, since no indication of the degree of selectivity of the students is provided (except that the sample was drawn from five urban secondary schools). Probably, as in almost all countries outside the United States, there is a large drop-out of the duller students before Grade 11 is reached. And the 15-year-olds with even higher IQs were presumably the brighter ones who had been further selected and accelerated. This criticism might be countered by Godman's (see p. 120, this volume) finding of much the same degree of superiority to white norms on Cattell Form B in his fourth and fifth grade Hong Kong students, who would not have been highly selected. We cannot decide the interpretation of these results without more information on the nature of the samples.

On the Mathematics Achievement test, both Chinese groups were superior to American norms by the same amount. Rodd suggests that they were helped by good teaching in the Taiwan schools. They were about equal in the Science test, although this test tries to avoid rote-learned factual information. The Chinese group scored higher than the Taiwanese here, as they did on the Cattell test. On both tests the males obtained much higher marks than the females, and this is generally found in the United States also. Performance on the Watson–Glaser test was also quite similar to that of American students. Again, though, we cannot interpret the high achievement test scores without knowing whether the students were a highly selected or more representative group.

A very different approach—namely a study of cognitive "styles"—was used by Chiu (1972), who worked with 221 Grade 4–5 children in Taiwan. Their performance was compared with that of 316 American children of the same age and comparable SES; that is, they consisted mainly of middle and working class children in rural communities. Chiu argues that several factors in Chinese upbringing might be expected to stimulate a reflective rather than impulsive type of thought, as described by Kagan, Moss, and Sigel (1963). However he did not use Kagan's well-known test of impulsivity—Matching Familiar Figures, but applied Sigel and Kagan's categorizing test. This consists of 28 items, each showing three pictures. The children are told to pick out two pictures that are alike, and one unlike in each item, and to state why the two are similar. This test was group-administered, and children wrote their own answers. Four main types of categorization were scored:

1. Descriptive–analytic. For example, classifying two human figures together because "they are both holding guns."
2. Descriptive–holistic. Two humans together because "they are both small."

3. Relational–contextual. For example, classifying a mother and a baby together because "the mother takes care of the baby."
4. Inferential–categorical. Classifying on the basis of inferred similarities. For example, a saw and an axe "are to cut with," or "both are tools"; or a horse and a cow "both live on a farm"; and so on.

The results were generally similar in the two grades, also in both sexes. The dominant style of categorization among the Chinese was relational–contextual, and the least popular the descriptive–analytic. The white children's dominant style was inferential–categorical, and they were high in descriptive–analytic, but low in relational–contextual. Or, more generally, the Chinese prefer to categorize stimuli on the basis of interdependence and relationship, whereas Americans prefer to analyze the components of stimuli and to infer common features. These differences were statistically significant.

As with most cognitive style tests, it is difficult to say how generalizable are the results. That is, we do not know the sorts of situations (outside the actual test) in which children use relational or inferential thought. There is much evidence that Chinese are particularly able in physical science and technology, less inclined to abstract or theoretical fields. Surely then, one might expect them to favor analytic and inferential categorization. (For a further experiment on reflective–impulsive style in Hawaii, see Ayabe and Santo, 1972.)

SUMMARY

A brief history is given of Hong Kong, which, although a British colony, is inhabited almost entirely by Cantonese-speaking Chinese. All schools teach English, and some secondary and higher-level schools use the English medium of instruction, since most commerce, government, and professional work are conducted in this language. Thus, there is considerable acculturation to Western habits, attitudes, etc., and very strong motivation and parental pressure for students to do well in school, including English. In spite of serious over-crowding, health hazards, and poverty, family incomes and education are superior to anywhere else in Asia, except for Japan.

Research between 1964 and 1976 covering large numbers in elementary and secondary schools showed little difference between Chinese performance and the British norms on nonverbal intelligence tests like the Raven Matrices. Indeed, in one study of 15-year-olds, Chinese students, mainly from middle-income families, scored more highly on this test than white students from high-income expatriate families. However, the Matrices norms have become too lenient, and need to be revised upwards. Also, at secondary levels, a good deal of selection occurs for entry to the most prestigious Hong Kong schools, so that the samples tested may not have been fully representative. The AH4 test has also been used, and on the verbal section Hong Kong students were below the probable English norm, but above it on the nonverbal section. Cattell's nonverbal Culture-Fair tests were applied to large numbers of eleventh grade students in Taiwan (both Taiwanese natives and Chinese émigrés). Their mean IQ on American norms was 105, but here also it is highly probable that high school students would be a selected group. Another comparison was made on the Raven Matrices between Singapore Chinese and Malaysian students aged 13. The Chinese mean was close to the British norm, and the Malaysian considerably below, by an amount equivalent to some 10 IQ points.

There is evidence that nonverbal group tests are of little use in predicting school or college grades in the Asian setting. If verbal tests are used, Hong Kong elementary school children are considerably handicapped when these are given in English, but quite able to cope with number or mathematical tests (unless the items require a lot of reading). Even at the English-medium University of Hong Kong, a considerable proportion of the Chinese students are slow readers whose comprehension of English textbooks and teachers may be inadequate. The better students tend to come from Anglo-Chinese or other secondary schools where English is the medium of instruction throughout. In national examinations they are superior to government or Chinese-medium school students in Natural and Social Science subjects, though inferior in mathematics and Chinese, which tend to be taught by rote.

In a test devised to measure Piaget's formal operations, given in English to 13- and 15-year-olds, Chinese did score somewhat below white American standards. On the other hand, with tests of visuospatial abilities and with Witkin's concept of field-independence versus dependence, such as susceptibility to geometrical illusions, and three-dimensional depth perception, Chinese children and adolescents were equal or superior to whites.

10

Oriental Languages

CHINESE

The differences between oriental and European languages are very much greater than those between, say, English and French. European languages are phonetic, in the sense that certain combinations of the 26 letters usually correspond to the same sound in different words or parts of words, though admittedly there is much irregularity of grapheme–phoneme correspondence in English. Chinese, however, represents every different word by an ideograph, or pictorial character, and there are some 3500 of these characters to be learned in order to read an ordinary book or newspaper, and far more for uncommon words. Each character contains two parts: one is the stem, which gives the phonetic element, or sound; the other is the radical, which gives the semantic element, or meaning. Though there are many thousands of phonetics, a much smaller number is required for most reading and writing. A knowledge of these, therefore, makes it possible to pronounce a great many new words. Likewise, some 80% of characters contain one of 214 radicals. Words that are related in meaning usually contain the same radical. Thus, there are many regularities or general rules that help in reading Chinese. Moreover, the basic sentence structure of subject–verb–object is followed in Chinese sentences, so that there is a certain isomorphy between Chinese and western languages (Kvan, 1969; Leong, 1973).

One might well ask why an alphabetic version of Chinese has not been invented. It is difficult to devise a satisfactory system since there are such subtle variations in vowel and consonantal sounds, inflections, and pitch, which cannot readily be expressed in an alphabetic transliteration. Nevertheless, there is now an official system called *Pin Yin* that is used, for example, in street names, railway stations, etc. Some simplification of Chinese characters has also been tried, but this is a dubious advantage, since it necessarily reduces the amount of information provided by the complex ideographs. More progress has been made in transliteration of Japanese, as it is partly phonic.

For the most part, each character has to be learned as a whole by rote, though in view of the phonetic components and the regularities noted above, reading is quite largely a rational process. Children may learn a few characters at home from around 3 years, or begin some elementary instruction at kindergarten at 4 or 5 years, if one is available. In Hong Kong the children are supposed to know about 100 characters before they gain entry to primary school. But in most of the People's Republic they start reading at first grade, and they are expected to learn some 500–600 characters in each year at school, thus reaching about 3500 characters by the end of elementary schooling.

It is generally known that Chinese characters are written or printed from top to bottom of a column, starting with the right-hand column on the page. It might seem that the eye movements required are totally different from those involved in reading European languages. However, in the 1950s Chinese books began to be printed with horizontal lines, read from left to right; apparently there is no difficulty in making the transition from one pattern to the other. Taiwan and Hong Kong have retained the traditional columns much longer than the People's Republic.

Writing Chinese is even more complicated since the characters are made up of a lot of brush strokes, possibly 30 or more in a single character, though the average number is about 11. I have not come across any references describing the motor difficulties of performing these brush strokes. Obviously the task is much more complex than that of the copying items in the Binet scales. Yet apparently the necessary skills are taught from age 6 onwards. Indeed, Chinese children show remarkably little difficulty in learning to read and write. According to Kline and Lee (1972), Chinese Canadian children who continue to study Chinese as well as English, are well motivated, docile, happy, and interested, not restless nor fatigued by this repetitive task. There may be some backward readers in Grades 1 and 2, but scarcely any beyond Grade 3. Kline and Lee state that there are no "hard-core" dyslexics among Chinese children.

Another complication is that there are several Chinese dialects that differ considerably in pronunciation, inflections, etc., and vocabulary. However, the greater part of the northern provinces (together with Taiwan) use a dialect derived from traditional Mandarin. But the great majority of Chinese people in America or Canada come from the southern provinces or from Hong Kong, where the Cantonese dialect is spoken. However, there is only one written or printed form, which is more closely allied to Mandarin than to Cantonese. After 1911, the Nationalist government introduced a common national language called *Guo-Yu,* now termed *Pu Tong Hua* (generally understood speech), which is used in all schools of the People's Republic.

JAPANESE

Though the Japanese language has borrowed many characters from Chinese, it is very different in many respects (Sakamoto & Makita, 1973). Indeed it differs from all other languages except Korean. There are four systems of writing Japanese: *Kana,* which uses two alternatives—*Hiragana* and *Katakana; Kanji,* which is derived, with some modifications from Chinese ideographs, or characters; and *Romaji,* which uses the Latin alphabet.

Hiragana is based on 46 symbols, that is, phonetic signs. These cover all the vowel and consonantal sounds and—unlike English—they are invariant, having the same sounds wherever they appear. Thus they are easily learned and easily written since they embody only a few pen or brush strokes. All Japanese words can be written in Hiragana. It is usually learned in Grade 1, though sometimes it is taught at home or in kindergarten. Katakana has the same symbols, but written in more cursive form. This is chiefly used for foreign words and names, and it is taught in Grade 2.

Kanji is ideographic and, like Chinese, has to be learned chiefly by rote. But it gradually replaces Kana as children grow older, since each Kanji character (or small group of characters) covers a word or a concept that would require a lot of Kana symbols, and these would have to be integrated by the reader. Thus, it is more economical, and the characters are readily recognized since they usually occupy a square shape. In a typical sentence, some 30% of the characters would be Kanji. Children are expected to learn about 100 Kanji characters by second grade, and nearly a thousand by sixth grade. In everyday Japanese, some 2400 characters are generally used. Any modern book, magazine, or newspaper will be found to contain Kanji, Hiragana, and Katakana, mixed together and often in the same sentence. Though usually printed or written vertically like Chinese, some modern books employ horizontal lines from left to right, like English. School textbooks, technical or scientific journals, and book titles are often printed horizontally.

The teaching of Japanese is similar to the whole-word method used in Western countries. As in Chinese, analysis and synthesis may be required, since two or more words related in meaning may be differentiated only by a few detailed strokes. It is often accompanied with tracing, and then writing, the characters. Saito, Inoue, and Nomura (1979) describe the complex nature of information processing that applies to the graphemic, phonemic, and the semantic components. Their experiments show that these three aspects are closely intertwined in Kanji, whereas in Kana (or indeed any phonetic language) the processing is much more straightforward. By presenting Hiragana or Kanji symbols tachistoscopically to the right or left visual field, Hatta (1978) has shown that Hiragana is mainly processed in the left hemisphere, like most language functions. Kanji, which is more complex and involves more recognition of shapes, is mainly processed in the right hemisphere.

The Japanese language contains only five vowels and 16 consonantal sounds—hence, the difficulty Japanese have in distinguishing *l* from *r,* and their confusion by some other English consonants.

Romaji is an attempt to represent Japanese words by an alphabetic system, which is printed from left to right. The American mission in Japan after World War II recommended the development and use of Romaji. But it has not proved a satisfactory substitute for the traditional systems. The same Kana symbols can have many different meanings, which are distinguished by the accompanying Kanji. Thus it is very difficult to translate Kana plus Kanji into Romaji. Where it is used is in guidebooks, notices, etc., for Western visitors, and particularly for English–Japanese or other dictionaries.

DIFFERENCES BETWEEN ORIENTALS AND CAUCASIANS IN READING ABILITIES

Makita (1968) describes the reading task expected of Japanese children and states that, despite its difficulties, the numbers of backward readers are lower in Japan than in the West, and similar to those in China. He admits that a few pathological cases of dyslexia can be found. But when he asked 247 teachers of 9195 children (first to fourth grades) to note those who showed specific difficulties in learning to read, only 1.2, 1.1, 0.8, and 0.4% were so nominated in successive grades. Kanji did cause more trouble than Kana. As no exact criterion of the amount of retardation was specified, the figures should be treated with caution. Even Japanese child guidance clinics mentioned very few cases, whereas estimates of serious reading problems in European and American schools generally range around 10%. Sakamoto and Makita (1973) claim that 99% of the Japanese population are literate, and that no specialist teachers or reading clinics are needed, since ordinary teachers can handle any difficulties. However, they do add that there are some problem cases, and that the numbers of nonreaders have risen seriously in recent years, especially in secondary schools. More boys than girls fall into this category. The authors attribute this mainly to lack of motivation rather than cognitive difficulties or to insufficient support at home (e.g., too much television or going out to play, instead of reading).

It is difficult to account for the apparently superior ability of oriental children to learn to read what, to us, are much more complicated scripts than English. Sakamoto and Makita reject any kind of genetic racial differences in aptitude for the reading task. But Makita (1968) has also pointed out that there is unlikely to be much difference between Japanese and American children in the numbers with brain damage or in the amount of emotional maladjustment. In Western countries these two conditions are usually regarded as major sources of backwardness. But if they do not so operate in Japan, it suggests that they are not particularly important.

Another interesting point in regard to writing oriental languages is that very few Chinese appear to be lefthanded, either in writing, eating, or other activities. This might suggest that there are neurological differences between oriental and white races. However, the incidence of lefthandedness in Japan is more nearly similar to that of whites. Hatta and Nakatsuka (1976) gave a questionnaire to 1200 Japanese college students, and found 4.3% of males and 2.25% of females to be lefthanded. Whereas Clark (1957), who studied some 6000 Scottish children, concluded that 8% of boys and 6% of girls write with the left hand. However, self-descriptions, as used in the Japanese research, do not necessarily coincide with actual motor behavior. And I am told that the pressures by oriental parents and teachers to use the right hand are much stronger than in the West.

Sakamoto and Makita conclude, then, that the main reasons for superior reading achievement in Japan (or China) are, first, that the apparently monumental task of learning characters is not as great as that of the western alphabetic system. To a large extent the pupil goes straight from the Chinese or Kanji character to the meaning, without requiring much internal processing. Indeed, Chinese has less redundancy than any other language, according to Kvan (1969). This is not true of Kana, since several symbols usually have to be synthesized to make a word, but they are simple enough to be learned quite thoroughly in first grade.

Second, the early introduction of children in oriental countries to formal education by their parents, the strong motivation to learn in almost all families, and the compliance to teachers' demands induced by oriental childrearing, are also involved.

The Work of T. Tsunoda

Mention should be made of an alternative neurological theory put forward by Tsunoda, whose work is little known in the West, although he has published several articles in American journals (1969, 1971, 1975). His book *The Japanese Brain* (1978) is being translated, but the most accessible source is two reviews of the book by Sibatani (1980a, b). He has developed certain techniques for determining whether various kinds of sounds are processed mainly in the left or right cerebral hemisphere. Magoroh (1980) summarizes seven of these, but the most widely used is based on delayed auditory feedback.

The subject is first instructed to carry out a simple, repetitive tapping task. Brief sound stimuli, such as a 1000-cycle tone or the vowel *a* (as in *Ah*), are transmitted directly to one ear, and with 0.2-second delay to the other ear. The amplitude of the sound is increased until the tapping performance is interfered with. If, say, the left ear is more sensitive to such interference, this means that that sound is processed in the right hemisphere, and vice versa. The beauty of the technique is that it does not involve introspective reports by the subject; the aural effect is shown objectively by breaks in the tapping rhythm.

In his 1975 article, Tsunoda determined the lateralization of these two sounds in 92 Japanese adults. Seventy-two percent showed the consistent pattern of left dominance for vowels, right dominance for tones. Eight percent reversed the pattern, and the other 20% either showed no consistent differences or used the same hemisphere for both sounds.

From such experiments he concludes that the lateralization of auditory functions in Japanese is different from that in Westerners. It is generally accepted that, in the majority of Caucasians, verbal functions are located in the left, or dominant, hemisphere, but spatial, musical, and creative functions are mainly located in the right hemisphere. According to Tsunoda it is chiefly consonantal sounds that are processed in the Caucasian left brain, but vowels, musical, and mechanical sounds are processed in the right. Among Japanese, however, both consonants, vowels, and natural human or animal sounds are processed in the left brain; mechanical sounds including Western music in the right. A fairly complete list of the functions of the two hemispheres in the two ethnic groups (based on Sibatani, 1980b) is as follows:

Western Subjects

Left hemisphere	*Right hemisphere*
Consonants	Isolated vowel sounds
Words	Nonverbal human and animal sounds
Language	Mechanical sounds (e.g., pure tone)
Calculations	Emotional stimuli
Analytical functions	Music
	Spatial and holistic functions

Japanese Subjects

Left hemisphere	*Right hemisphere*
Vowels	Mechanical sounds
Consonants	Pure tones
Language	Western music
Calculations	
Human and animal sounds	
Emotional stimuli	
Japanese music	

Not all Japanese or Westeners show these differences, but a large proportion are claimed to do so. Tsunoda does not regard the phenomena as genetically determined, but as resulting from the nature of the Japanese language. Its peculiarities are said to determine the neurological pathways of auditory processing. Thus, Japanese Americans of second or later generations, who are brought up to speak English, follow the Western model. Vowel sounds play a very large part in

Japanese; indeed some words consist wholly of vowels. The same tendency is found in some Polynesian languages; hence, the abundance of vowel sounds in Hawaiian. Chinese is listed as a non-Japanese language like English, though this seems curious since vowel sounds tend to dominate in Chinese also (Leong, 1973), whereas in European languages, consonants play a larger part in word recognition. Also one might ask how did the Japanese language develop so differently from European unless there was, and still is, some underlying biological difference?

Tsunoda's book has achieved remarkable popularity in Japan, possibly because it seems to support the notion that Japanese are, in this respect, unique and unlike any other nation. However, his work has not been adequately replicated by other Japanese or by Western psychologists. So it should be regarded as an interesting theory rather than fact. But it may help to explain why the Japanese, after early childhood, have great difficulties in learning Western languages and pronouncing them correctly. Sibatani suggests that the Japanese left brain may be overtaxed by its responsibility for so many functions, especially if an additional language is being learned.

A little relevant evidence is available regarding Caucasians. Gordon (1975) summarized work on the lateralization of musical perception, and concluded that melodic stimuli are processed in the left hemisphere of trained musicians, but are more likely to involve the right hemisphere in the musically naive. In other words, melodies can be recognized either analytically or holistically. Besides a melodic recognition test, he gave a test of musical chords to adult subjects, and found that these were chiefly processed in the right hemisphere; but a few subjects used the left hemisphere, and they were not more trained or better scorers than the rest.

Johnson, Cole, Bowers *et al.* (1979) gave a test of recall of digits to 73 Caucasian adults, aged 50 and over. Two different sets of three digits were sounded in the two ears. It was found that these sounds were more effectively processed in the left hemisphere (like verbal stimuli). Left-ear stimuli could be processed in the right hemisphere, but this capacity declined rapidly with age, in the same manner as spatial abilities.

Also of some relevance are studies of sex differences among Caucasians, which often show superiority of females in many verbal skills, including language learning. These have recently been reviewed by Ekstrand (1980), and he points out the inconsistency of the results of many investigators, partly because they use very diverse measures of language skills. Nevertheless, the weight of the evidence does indicate female superiority in some elements of language, which might be largely accounted for by differences in cultural expectations of the two sexes. But Ekstrand favors a theory of genetic differences interacting with cultural and environmental differences. He also accepts the view that there are biological differences in lateralization, females showing less pronounced asymmetry. This would imply greater representation of some of their speech functions in the right brain. This too is controversial; but if it is confirmed, it might link up with Tsunoda's work and suggest (contrary to his own view) that genetic neurological differences are involved in racial differences in word processing.

While this discussion is quite inconclusive, it is clear that there are very fundamental differences between oriental and Western languages. Thus, we might expect that oriental children trained to read their own language should have greater difficulties with printed or written English, and verbal tests, than do English monoglots. For example, they might show more reversals of letters or words, which commonly occur among younger or duller white children. One experimental investigation of this problem is worth summarizing here. Other surveys or investigations of reading in Japanese children, carried out by Japanese psychologists, are described in Sakamoto and Makita's article (1973).

Smith's Study of Directionality of Eye Movements

Smith's first publication in 1932 dealt with the directionality or orientation of eye movements among adults and children who had some experience of both Chinese and English. She prepared a card consisting of 25 pictures of familiar objects, arranged in five rows and five columns. These were shown to each subject, with instructions to name all the objects, but without telling them where to begin or what order to use. Quite a number of eye movement patterns were found:

A. English, that is, left to right
B. Right to left, as in reading Hebrew
C. Reversed directions in alternate lines, that is, LR, RL. This occurs in some Roman inscriptions, hence she called it Old Latin
D. Vertical, as in Chinese, top to bottom, starting on the right
E. Vertical reversed, from bottom to top
F. Other variants of vertical patterns, for example, starting with the left-hand column
G. Mixed, or no clear pattern at all. The subjects might start anywhere, and jump around haphazardly.

Her subjects included 50 adults who read English only, and 50 who could read either language, together with large groups of children from kindergarten to Grade 2 (aged 2 to 7).

The numbers of adults using different patterns were

English readers: A, 41, that is, 82%; B and C, 14%; E, 4%.
Chinese readers: A, 19, that is, 38%; B and C, 20%; D, 16%; E, 22%; F, 4%.

Clearly, familiarity with reading and writing Chinese has produced many more unusual patterns in the second group.

Among the children, none of the 2-year-olds used any systematic pattern; they tended to pick out any picture that appealed to them. However by 7 years, the great majority were using a regular pattern, provided that they were not attending a Chinese language school, as well as an English-medium school. One hundred such attenders and a control group of similar nonverbal intelligence were compared, and 28% of attenders versus 48% of controls followed the A pattern, whereas 25% of attenders and 10% of controls used vertical patterns. The results are not classified under the types listed above and are difficult to follow. But Smith seems to have been chiefly concerned with regular or systematic versus more random or inconsistent patterns. One hundred and sixty-eight regulars obtained a mean score of 8.7 on the Gates Reading Test, whereas 44 irregulars averaged 3.5—a highly significant difference. The research indicates that the establishment of regular directionality is essential to progress in reading English among oriental children. The degree of consistency also correlated positively with age and intelligence (as measured by the Pintner–Cunningham Nonverbal and Draw-a-Man tests). Other differences between attenders at Chinese schools and nonattenders were that the former made more reversal errors and were more confused between letters in reading English. It is not suggested that Orientals should receive special training in directionality, but it does seem that new immigrant children in English-medium schools, who continue to study Chinese reading and writing, are going to have greater difficulties in English.

11

Problems of Bilingualism

INTRODUCTION

The nature and the effects of bilingualism have proved far more complex than might be expected; though a great deal of research on the topic has been published, many of the results have been quite contradictory. Before we discuss the acquisition of English by Chinese and Japanese, it is important to try to define bilingualism and its variations and to summarize the present state of our knowledge.

In the strictest sense bilingualism signifies equal fluency in two languages. But the term is generally extended to people who have been brought up in their mother tongue (which we will refer to throughout as Language 1, or L1), but have also acquired a working competence in a second language (to be referred to as L2). Most second and later generations of Orientals in North America should, therefore, be described as bilinguals, though there are wide variations in their understanding and use of English. But eventually they become English monoglots.

Dornic (1980) and other writers refer to equal fluency in L1 and L2 as "balanced bilingualism," whereas most immigrant or minority ethnic groups are decidedly "unbalanced." A variety of tests, questionnaires, etc., have been employed to assess degrees of bilingualism, and naturally the results of such measures often differ quite widely, thus accounting for part of the confusion in the literature. Lambert (1975) distinguishes two main types that he labels:

1. Additive. The newly acquired L2 and culture are added on to the original cultural background and L1.
2. Subtractive. The individual's progress in L2 results in the decay of L1 and the original culture.

3. A third type is Retractive bilingualism. The individual reacts against L2. He is forced to learn it in order to adjust to the majority culture, but reverts to L1 whenever possible. Dornic has shown that partial bilinguals, when faced with a difficult task in L2, tend to translate the problem into L1 and, after solving it, retranslate the answer into L2. Naturally there is some waste of time in this roundabout information processing.

Cummins (1979) likewise distinguishes two constrasting situations. In the first of these the children's L1 is a minority language, and they have to acquire L2 (English) in order to become assimilated into the majority culture. L1 is regarded by the school as a weakness, which accounts for slow progress in L2, and the pupils are liable to be reprimanded either for failure in L2 or for reversion to L1. The second situation occurs when L1 is English, and the pupils are trying to gain some fluency in a foreign language (e.g., French). Here the L2 is additive since it constitutes an addition to the children's linguistic skills, and they are likely to be commended for any progress they make. But it by no means follows that the second situation is more effective than the first; though it might be expected that English students learning French (a language with very similar structure and many words in common) should have much less difficulty than Chinese or Japanese students learning the totally different English language.

EARLY FINDINGS OF ADVERSE EFFECTS OF BILINGUALISM

When children are acquiring two languages simultaneously, the question naturally arises—Do they not interfere with one another, and thus retard development in one or both? Early investigations were summarized by Arsenian (1937), Darcy (1953), and Peal and Lambert (1962). Many different studies including Italians, Spanish, American Indians, Orientals, and Welsh (Jones, 1959) showed that the partially bilingual children scored lower than monoglots on intelligence and achievement tests. In some studies they even scored below monoglots on relatively culture-free nonverbal intelligence tests; in others, the children were equal or superior to monoglots on nonverbal, but markedly lower on verbal intelligence and English achievement tests. This occurred with Orientals (Chapters 2 and 5), also with American Indians in studies by Havighurst and Hilkavitch (1944), MacGregor (1946), and Havighurst, Gunther, and Pratt (1946). These used the Arthur Scale of Performance Tests or the Goodenough Draw-a-Man. Teachers' reports likewise showed immigrant and minority children to be backward at school, often having behavior problems and dropping out early. In some studies of minority group children, even their proficiency in the mother tongue fell below that reached by monoglots who were not trying to learn any L2.

In all these studies, however, the non-English speaking children came from families of low SES. The parents of Italian, Spanish, and Welsh-speaking children were largely peasants or semiskilled laborers. Some attempts have been made to correct the children's test scores for SES. But this begs the question— Are the parents in lower-grade jobs partly because they are below average in intelligence? I have discussed this tricky issue elsewhere (Vernon, 1979). Also, such children frequently hear and use nothing but their L1 mother tongue at home. In other respects also the bilinguals and monoglots were not adequately matched.

Two fairly recent studies confirmed the adverse effects of bilingualism on educational progress. Macnamara (1966) investigated 11-year-olds in the Irish Republic. Those who attended predominantly Irish-speaking schools scored lower than children in English-speaking schools, not only on English and problem arithmetic tests, but even on nonverbal intelligence tests. His explanation was that the more time given to L1, the less there was to stimulate progress in L2 or other skills. Again, Torrance et al. (1970) studied bilingualism in Singapore (see p. 142, this volume), and concluded that negative transfer occurred between L1 (Chinese or Malaysian) and L2 (English), which affected their fluency and flexibility scores on divergent thinking tests, though not their originality and elaboration scores. Torrance suggests that the formation of new associations between words and meanings in L2 competes with the familiar associations required in L1.

LATER FINDINGS OF POSITIVE EFFECTS

Though scarcely any reports of positive effects of bilingualism were published until the 1960s, it has long been known that young children who hear two (even three) languages in infancy seem to have no difficulty in acquiring both, and in switching from one to the other, according to the language used by their interlocutor. More recently, it has been found that an almost complete or balanced bilingualism is possible if two languages are used in the school they first attend, say, from the age of 4 or 5, provided they are actually taught various subjects in the second language, and use it in play activities at least 50% of the time. Thus, Canadian English-speaking children in "immersion programs," where half the teaching is in French, maintain the same standards in English as children in English-speaking schools, or even surpass them, and at the same time develop remarkable competence in French. But if they do not start until 7 years or later, they tend to lose this flexibility. Their mother tongue has become so engrained that they can learn the second language only as a school subject, and few of them progress to reasonable fluency unless, perhaps, they spend a year or two in a foreign language environment, where they have to use it in order to make their needs known.

Positive evidence of the advantages of bilingualism has been obtained in several countries, but some of the most convincing studies have been done in Quebec (where French is the L1 of the majority of the population), and Ontario (where so many immigrants settle that, in 1971, 31% of the Toronto school population did not have either English or French as their native language). Peal and Lambert (1962) compared 10-year-old French-speaking children who were nearly balanced in their knowledge of English and French, with others who were learning English in the same schools, but were virtually monoglots in French. The bilinguals scored higher on verbal and nonverbal intelligence tests and achieved better at school. In particular they were superior on tests involving flexibility in manipulating ideas and tests of concept development. The authors believe that these qualities are promoted by having two labels for every concept, by their exposure to a wider range of experiences, and by switching easily from one language to the other.[1] They are more aware of the existence of alternative languages, and more tolerant to other ethnic groups. Peal and Lambert also studied the homes and found that parents of bilinguals tended to have higher education and SES and to encourage their children to learn English, than the parents of monoglots. When samples of bi- and unilingual children were matched for SES, the differences in their achievements were reduced, but were still in the same direction.

Bhatnagar (1980) compared Italian immigrant children attending either English or French Schools in Montreal with children speaking only English or only French.

Those using mixed Italian *and* French or English at home with siblings or with friends were superior in academic achievement in English or French, in fluency and classroom participation, to those who chiefly used either Italian, English, or French outside school. Lambert (1975) quotes a study by Scott (1973) of English-speaking Canadians who attended French-immersion schools, or were monoglots. In Grade 1, they were matched for intelligence, SES, and parental attitudes toward French. When given Torrance-type divergent thinking tests over the following 7 years, the bilinguals obtained substantially higher flexibility scores.

Summarizing, we can say that with suitable school programs and suitable motivation to learn, children can achieve well in a second language without detriment to their original language; continued use of L1 need not affect progress in L2, and may even help intellectual development generally.

---

[1]Peal and Lambert factor-analyzed 31 tests of abilities and attitudes in both groups and found considerable differences in mental organization or structure. In particular, the bilinguals displayed more independent ability factors, that is, their intellectual capacities were more diversified.

How far does this depend on the children's intelligence and home background? James (1960), in a useful discussion of bilingualism in Wales, found that Welsh-speaking children of high intelligence benefited from a bilingual program in Welsh and English; but those of low intelligence had very great difficulties in coping with two languages. Children of average intelligence were generally neither helped nor hindered. Certainly, middle-class children from cultured and educated families, where the parents are favorable to bilingualism, are more likely to succeed than lower-class children. Yet we have seen that such programs can work even when SES effects are held constant. In any case, intelligence should not be regarded as the main cause of bilingual achievement. It is usually associated with good background, and it may even be stimulated further by bilingual schooling. Cummins (1979) considers it necessary for children to have reached a fairly advanced stage in their L1, including some analytic understanding of words and their meanings, which they can transfer to the acquisition of L2. Thus, children of below-average ability who have not progressed far in their L1 and who are faced with learning a second language, may end up semiliterate, with little competence in either L1 or L2. Cummins's view may be true for children of, say, 7 years upwards, but it clearly does not apply to preschoolers, who make better progress in two languages the younger they are. Lambert particularly stresses introducing the L2 early, not waiting until first grade. He adds that parents and teachers should avoid pressuring children to use one language or the other. Preferably, they should use their L1 with adults or other children of the same ethnicity, but use L2 when the people around them are speaking L2. Also, children should be discouraged from using sloppy mixtures of both languages in the same sentence.

Current opinion does not regard bilingualism as a purely cognitive problem. It is one aspect of cultural adjustment. A minority or immigrant group naturally holds on to its own language and culture and regards the acquisition of the majority language as a threat to its existence. Yet the families of immigrants certainly want to adjust to and achieve well in their new cultural environment; clearly they cannot communicate other than by learning the second language. But at the same time, the introduction of the second language, especially to younger kindergarten or elementary pupils, should be gradual. If they are at first taught in their mother tongue, this helps to maintain security, avoid maladjustment, and instill confidence to work with the new language. At least this is the policy of the Toronto schools, where so many children enter with no knowledge of English nor experience of a modern urban environment (Lambert, 1975). This approach also engenders favorable attitudes to both languages; both are seen to be of social value in their own right. There must, however, be some identification of the immigrant family with the new culture if the children are to learn. At the same time it should not be assumed that all new immigrants should become acculturated forthwith, and give up their native culture and language completely. Beck (1975) discusses these issues and points out that a certain amount of diversity is valuable in any society. In much the same way as subgroups within our own society (artists, for example) are allowed to deviate to some extent from the general norm, there should be the same kind of tolerance and respect for the values and norms of the new immigrants. Multiculturalism and multilingualism are more appropriate for contemporary Canadian society than the American policy of complete assimilation. This policy has been notably successful in the United States, though it does not seem to have worked with Spanish Americans or American Indians. When, however, the minority group opposes the majority culture (as with many blacks who continue to speak Negro dialect) or when the new language is seen as an unpleasant chore (as in French courses at most English-medium secondary schools), it is improbable that there will be any useful learning.

Cummins (1980) has surveyed over 200 foreign-born ''New Canadian'' children in the Toronto area who had been referred to educational psychologists on account of learning problems. He brings out the difficulties of using psychological tests such as WISC-R for predicting their likely progress, and for suggesting the best means of helping them other than by putting them into special classes or schools for the educationally retarded. Cummins argues that continued use of their L1 at home does not hinder but helps the children because, by using this medium, the parents can develop their understanding of concepts, and this will transfer to their acquisition of L2. I would hesitate to accept this view without further direct evidence, for continued use of L1 by parents and children seems to indicate a lack of identification of the family with the new culture and L2. Also, in the case of the Chinese, the correlations of English achievement with amount of use of Chinese at home, though small, are negative.

W. C. Lambert, R. C. Gardner, and their colleagues have carried out numerous investigations of high school or college Anglophones (i.e., English speakers) and Francophones, who were learning the other language (Clement, Gardner, & Smythe, 1980). Some of these studies used factor analyses of batteries of achievement, aptitude, and attitude tests. An important factor or dimension, which they named the ''integrative motive,'' was generally found. This included favorableness to the second language and to the culture of its speakers, persistence in learning it, and seeking contacts and using the second language with others who speak it. In a recent study by Clement, Gardner, and Smythe, it appeared that the achievement of Francophones in learning English depended on a second factor called ''self-confidence with English.'' This included low anxiety about speaking English, and high self-ratings of proficiency. The authors point out that Francophones are likely to have more problems with English than Anglophones have with French, since the former are much more aware that they constitute a minority in Canada and therefore feel threatened if they put much effort into learning English, whereas the latter, even if living in the province of Quebec, feel no such danger of losing their ethnic identity and language.

LEARNING OF ENGLISH BY ORIENTAL CHILDREN

Immigrant oriental children are observed to learn and speak English surprisingly quickly, though they still tend to score lower on verbal intelligence and English achievement tests than on nonverbal and mathematical tests. They fulfill the condition of being highly motivated; even if no special introductory classes are arranged for new immigrants, they are effectively in immersion programs at English-medium schools, since their teachers and peers speak nothing but English. Thus although the Japanese Issei clung to their culture and language longer than many batches of immigrants (especially in Hawaii), the third generation Sansei were almost wholly English-speaking, except insofar as their parents or grandparents spoke Japanese at home and tried to teach the children, or sent some of them to private schools whose aim was to preserve the culture and language of their forebears.

The Chinese showed a less regular pattern of progress, because the earlier immigrants were seldom able to bring wives or have families. Many of them returned home to China eventually, but even more fresh immigrants arrived. Hence, it is unlikely that the level of English in the total Chinese American population improved much until after 1924, when almost all further immigration was prohibited. From then until 1954 there probably was a continuous rise; but with the abolition of anti-Oriental immigration, much larger numbers were admitted on a basis of vocational skills and/or relationship to Chinese already living in the United States or Canada. Again, therefore, the English competency of the total oriental populations became diluted with the addition of non-English speaking immigrants. But by now a considerable proportion of immigrants had learned some English in their countries of birth or—in the case of Chinese—in Taiwan or Hong Kong. Also many Orientals on the United States mainland came from Hawaii, where the use of English is much more widespread. As a result of these variations in language background, samples of Chinese who have been tested in the past or recently may include individuals ranging all the way from those with little or no experience of English, to those whose families have been predominantly English-speaking for several generations. With rare exceptions, the authors of studies of oriental abilities give little or no information on the language background of their subjects, their homes, and neighborhoods, and this obviously vitiates any comparison of one oriental sample with another or with white control groups or American test norms. However, some tests are always less dependent on knowledge of English than others, even though none can be accepted as wholly culture-fair (Vernon, 1969). And despite the influx of large numbers of immigrants over the past 15 years, the standards of scholastic and occupational achievement do seem to have remained steady or to have improved gradually.

RELEVANT RESEARCH

We turn now to studies that have been concerned directly with learning by oriental children, or with the effects of living in a mainly oriental environment at home.

One of the earliest studies of language conflict was carried out with Japanese American children by Yoshioka in 1929. The National Intelligence Test (a group verbal test) was translated as accurately as possible into Japanese and restandardized on over 8000 children in Tokyo. (Incidentally, the Japanese norms at about 10 to 11 years were somewhat higher than the American; that is, the Japanese means were greater.) In Yoshioka's American experiment, 17 Japanese American children, aged 9–11, attending a Japanese language school took the Japanese version first, and the English version next day. Then 21, aged 12–15, took them in the reverse order. According to the author the combined group means averaged some 30 points below the American norms, and 40 points below the Japanese. The second group scored more highly than the first, but presumably because it was older. No indication is given regarding the background or SES of the children, not even whether they were American-born; thus these low scores are difficult to interpret. Probably the children were Nisei who might have acquired a fair competence in English by the ages of 10–15, but their parents would use Japanese at home almost exclusively. The younger group was more retarded than the older, presumably having even less experience of English. Yoshioka admits also that some test items may not have been quite equivalent in Japanese and English. Thus, the correlation of .75 between the two versions is lower than one might expect for tests given only one day apart.

M. E. Smith (1932, 1939, 1949, 1957) carried out a series of studies between 1932 and 1957 on language development in Hawaii. In 1939 she compared the use of English and proportions of errors in the speech of seven main ethnic groups. Twenty-five children from each group, aged 2–6 years, were observed at home and with other children, and 50 remarks by each child were recorded. The Chinese and Japanese groups were the highest in SES (indeed both were above the American white mean); Korean and Portuguese came next; and Hawaiian and Filipino last. The percentages of English words in the conversations, together with the mean total speech errors, are shown in Table 11.1. The third column, taken from the 1930 census, shows the percentages of children above 10 years who could speak English in the island population.

TABLE 11.1
Use of English by Hawaiian Ethnic Groups
    (Smith, 1939)

Ethnic group	Percent English words	Errors	Percent English-speaking
Japanese urban	52.4% ⎞		
	⎟	540	70.1
Japanese rural	33.1 ⎠		
Chinese	82.2	407	77.5
Korean	96.9	453	70.4
Portuguese	98.6	379	94.8
Hawaiian urban	96.7 ⎞		
	⎟	425	96.7
Hawaiian rural	90.0 ⎠		
Filipino urban	93.0	478 ⎞	
		⎟	46.0
Filipino rural	80.7	587 ⎠	

It seems surprising that Korean, Portuguese, Hawaiian, and even urban Filipino children were using more English than the Chinese, and that Japanese (especially rural dwellers) were lowest of all. However, the Chinese are second best in having few errors, and Filipinos are definitely the lowest. Presumably the figures mainly reflect the rapidity of acculturation. Many of the Japanese parents would be Issei, some Nisei, and they may have resisted more strongly the intrusion of English into their homes until the 1940s. It was observed that the numbers of children with Anglicized given names ranged from 94% for Hawaiians to 30% for Japanese. The length of sentences spoken by the children was also recorded, and here the Japanese had the highest mean of 5.0 words; Hawaiian, 4.2; both Chinese and Portuguese, 3.6; Filipino and Korean, 3.1 and 2.5, respectively. The inconsistency between these various measures brings out the difficulties of arriving at any simple statement regarding the effects of bilingualism.

Other tables in Smith's monograph list sentence types and functions, parts of speech, typical errors, etc., together with breakdowns by age, sex, and parental SES. Ratings were made of several home variables, and these were correlated with amount of English speech. Negative factors included the use of pidgin, living in an area of concentration where all one's neighbors use the same language, and the extent of use of the native language at home. Positive factors were use of English at home, sending children to kindergarten instead of teaching them at home, parents born in Hawaii or mainland United States, and parental education.

In a later study (1949) Smith developed a picture vocabulary test for young

TABLE 11.2
Percentages of Vocabulary Words Known by Chinese children in Hawaii (Smith, 1949)

Age	N	Known in English	Known in Chinese
3:5+	6	55	37
4:6+	12	53	31
5:6+	6	66	50
6:0+	6	58	43

children, and standardized it for Americans. This could also be given in Chinese. Thirty Chinese children in Hawaii, aged 3-6 years, were tested first in English and the next day in Chinese. The percentages of vocabulary words known in English were much below American norms for unilinguals; the percentages known in Chinese were lower still. The scores for different age groups are given in Table 11.2. It will be seen that there is little improvement with age in either language, but the numbers are too small to be reliable. Smith admits that it is useful to the children to be able to converse in both languages. But she believes that on entry to Grade 1 at age 6, their command of English is insufficient for them to understand the teacher, and it might be better to start them off in the Chinese language, which they chiefly hear out of school. She cites an additional study where the English vocabulary of Chinese entering kindergarten at 5½ was barely 40% of that of whites. But within 1 year the figure rose to 62%.

However, a repetition of these studies in 1957 showed remarkable progress. Fifty Chinese American children, aged 3-5, were tested. Their use of English in the playground had risen from 82 to 98.7%; the numbers of sentences using mixed languages dropped from 17 to 2.4%; and pidgin was rarely used and then only by small numbers of children. The use of Chinese in the homes had almost died out, except in homes where there were grandparents. All the parents had been born in Hawaii or on the mainland, and all their children had Anglo given names. Nevertheless, on several indices of English achievement the children were at or below the norms for 3-year-old white unilinguals. Thus, Smith expected them still to be handicapped to some extent on entering elementary school.

According to Ciborowsky and Choy (1974), almost all Honolulu children in 1974 still knew and used a certain amount of pidgin, which they picked up from their friends. This did not much affect their ability to cope with tasks in English. The authors selected 12 Grade 5 children who were more fluent in English than pidgin, and 12 of those more fluent in pidgin than English. Two stories were read to them (one in English, one in pidgin), and they were tested for recall in the appropriate language. The mean points recalled were

	English stories	Pidgin stories
Children fluent in English	7.3	5.5
Children fluent in pidgin	6.3	7.2

The mainly English-speaking children did badly with pidgin stories, but the pidgin-fluent ones scored not much below the others on English stories.

Another important study of scholastic retardation was carried out in Hong Kong elementary schools by Rowe (1966). As shown in Chapter 9, over 90% of the parents are Chinese-speaking, and elementary schooling uses the Chinese medium. But a lot of time is given to teaching English. All the Grade 3 children in five such schools were given tests in English, Chinese, Mechanical and Problem Arithmetic. The 20 lowest scoring students in each school were compared on numerous environmental and other factors with the 10 highest scorers. The major differences between the groups were on the English test. This procedure yielded 38 very backward boys and 62 girls, also 28 successful boys and 22 girls. This sex difference is surprising since, in British and American schools, boys usually make up most of the seriously retarded. Probably it results from the greater pressures put on Chinese boys by their parents for educational achievement.

The ''bottoms'' differed greatly from the ''tops'' in having parents of poor cultural background and education, who were more traditional, for example, in keeping up ancestor worship. The ''bottoms'' also did less reading at home, more television watching, and their parents were more easygoing, imposing less strict discipline. In addition, the children were less often engaged in jobs outside school hours. To a lesser extent the bottoms came from homes that were more neglectful, where parental income was lower, and there were more broken families. The top group did more studying outside school, and had attended school for more years. However, their parents were found less likely to overpressure than average. The amount of English spoken at home was the same in the two groups, as also were the type of housing, family size, age, and years of residence in Hong Kong. There were also marked personality differences, according to teacher and parent ratings. The ''tops'' were more confident, persistent, and sociable; the ''bottoms'' more lethargic, shy, poor in concentrating, and showing behavior problems.

Kline and Lee's Research in Canada

Peters and Ellis (1970) reported on the WISC profiles of Chinese Canadians who had reading problems. Those with reading difficulties in Chinese did not differ from normal readers in English. But those with reading problems in English were below average on Vocabulary, Similarities, and Picture Assembly. A more complete study of 277 Grades 1–3 Chinese children was published by Kline and Lee (1972).

TABLE 11.3
IQs and Test Results of Successful and Backward Readers among Chinese Children
(Kline and Lee, 1972)

Percentages	72 Controls; no problems	13 problems with Chinese	9 problems in English	6 problems in both	Total group
Mean WISC Verbal IQ	101	100	92	86	99
Performance IQ	113	113	110	105	112
Full Scale IQ	107	107	101	95	105
Bender–Gestalt, low scores	21%	33	55	83	29
Draw-a-Man, abnormalities	24%	38	50	77	31
Monroe Auditory Discrimination, errors	23%	16	15	39	22

About half of these attended Chinese full-time private schools where both English and Chinese were studied. The remainder attended a public elementary school where 81% of all children were Chinese. Of these, 43% attended a Chinese language school for 2 hours a day, out of school hours. Almost all the families were recent immigrants from Hong Kong or China, and Chinese was used almost exclusively in the homes. The fathers were mostly in low-SES jobs, but are described as responsible and thrifty. Though not authoritarian, they did expect their children to show traditional Chinese respect for their elders.

Monroe's Oral Reading Test was given, and a similar test constructed in Chinese. Taking account also of school grades and parental reports of reading problems, 13% were found to be backward in Chinese only, 9% in English only, and 6% in both, making a total of 28%. Notice that there is not much tendency for backwardness in one language to be associated with backwardness in the other.[2] As in Makita's study of Japanese, the numbers with problems declined with age. By the end of Grade 3 there were only 5%, 3%, and 2%, respectively, in the three groups: 10% in all. It was also observed that boys with problems exceeded girls by 4 to 1. The main results appear in Table 11.3.

Those with problems in both languages are clearly lower in general, and especially verbal ability. The Problems-with-English group are poor on Verbal WISC, but those with problems in Chinese differ little from the control group. The WISC subtests most affected among poor readers were Vocabulary, Information, and Digit Span (*not* Coding). All problem groups are noticeably poorer in visuospatial, drawing, and auditory discrimination tests, especially those backward in both languages. Though no differences were found in handedness or eyedness, certain personality differences were observed. The parents of retarded

[2]Tetrachoric $r = .40$.

children reported them as being restless, bashful, lazy, watches too much television though at the same time hardworking, interested in school, and liked by peers.

Kline and Lee conclude that their results do not show an adverse effect of studying two languages simultaneously, since the numbers of backward are small, and they tend to disappear by third grade. The overall standard of achievement in the public school attended by 136 of their cases is one of the highest in the city of Vancouver. This must mean that even children from quite a poor Chinese background overcome initial difficulties quickly, when they are, in effect, taking an immersion program in English. They achieve at least as well as unilingual whites. There was no indication, as in Smith's study 40 years previously, of difficulties attributable to having learned Chinese.

Other Recent Investigations

In view of the often inconsistent results of different studies of bilingualism, Yee and LaForge (1974) set out their own hypotheses regarding the background influences that affect Chinese children's educational and intellectual development in English-medium schools. Their subjects were 53 American-born Chinese with a mean age of 9½ years in fourth grade of a private school in San Francisco. Most of the fathers were skilled workers. By interviewing the parents, 30 environmental variables were assessed, and these were correlated with WISC Verbal and Performance IQs. The mean IQs were 98.6 and 110.7, and 104.8 for Full-Scale; thus the children were of at least average ability. The amount of English used in the homes was estimated at 28.3% by the fathers, 16.8% by the mothers, and 75.6% by the children. Some of the more interesting correlations are shown in Table 11.4.

The percentage of English used at home does not correlate appreciably with child IQ, though it does correlate .44 with educational and occupational level of the parents, and .43 with distance of home from Chinatown. Again, SES as such is not associated with child intelligence. It is curious that the largest coefficients

TABLE 11.4
Correlations of Environmental Conditions with WISC IQs (Yee and LaForge, 1974)

Environmental Conditions	Verbal	Performance	Full Scale
Overall amount of English used at home	.05	−.16	−.10
Child's free time, including television	.26	.14	.22
Distance of home from Chinatown	−.35	−.35	−.42
Amount of studying at home	.15	.33	.32
Social class (Occupation and residence)	(All close to zero)		

in this table are negative ones between IQ and Distance of Home from Chinatown. Surely the families that have moved away from Chinatown would be higher in SES, and speak more English. Their children would be expected to be more, not less intelligent. However, the amount of studying at home does correlate positively (to a small extent), suggesting that the more formal and traditional type of childrearing does assist intellectual development. But it seems contradictory that children who get more free time are also a little above average. The authors' initial hypotheses were not confirmed, and the overall results are contradictory. But they suggest that the sample may have been unduly homogeneous in intelligence, although the standard deviations of IQs were 17 and 18.

Two studies of Chinese children were described in Chapter 2. Jensen's research in Chinatown schools showed virtually no relation of father's occupational level to children's achievement, and only small negative correlations between use of Chinese at home and scores on tests of English. In my own investigation of Chinese in Canada, there was some tendency for Canadian-born to achieve better than recent immigrants, but no consistent effect of language used outside school.

Kuo (1974) reports on a study of 47 Chinese preschool children in Minnesota. Their ages ranged from 2½ to 6 years. Most of the parents were American-born, though five had come from Taiwan. All had been residents in the United States for at least 1 year. Nevertheless, the Chinese language was still chiefly used in the home. The Peabody Picture Vocabulary Test (PPVT) was administered both in English and in Chinese at a session when the parents were interviewed. As an index of English versus Chinese skills, the formula

$$\frac{\text{English score } - \text{ Chinese score}}{\text{English } + \text{ Chinese}}$$

was used. This could range from $+1$ to -1.

The use of Chinese by the parents was assessed by the Hoffman Bilingual Schedule, and this correlated $-.645$ with the Child Index. It correlated .573 with Chinese PPVT score, but only .159 with English score. Other indexes of acculturation that were significantly associated with Child Index included parental naturalization as Americans, time in the country, and habitual use of Chinese between mother and father or mother and child. The children's ages gave a low correlation with the Index, but a high .71 with English scores. This suggests that the children were rapidly improving in oral English with age, probably as a result of experiences outside the home.

Tsushima and Hogan (1975) studied American children at an American school in Japan, rather than Japanese in America. Most of them were unilingual, both parents being white. But some had a Japanese mother, and these were effectively bilingual. The Lorge–Thorndike intelligence test and certain achievement tests were given to the Grade 3–5 children. The mean scores of uni- and bilinguals are shown in Table 11.5. The authors point out that there were no differences at

TABLE 11.5
Test Score Means of Unilingual and Bilingual Children, Grades 3–5
(Tsushima and Hogan, 1975)

	Grade 3		Grade 4		Grade 5	
	Unilingual	Bilingual	Unilingual	Bilingual	Unilingual	Bilingual
Numbers of children	92	50	88	49	85	43
Lorge–Thorndike Nonverbal	40.2	41.5	47.0	47.4	44.3	44.7
Lorge–Thorndike Verbal	39	40	50	47	54	49
Reading English	33	32	44	42	58	54
Total Language score	33	34	46	45	60	58
Total Arithmetic	32	33	41	42	51	50

third grade, but that by fifth grade the bilinguals had noticeably dropped behind on verbal tests, not on nonverbal or Arithmetic. Apparently the use of Japanese at home with the mother at around 9 years (perhaps also with Japanese neighbors' children) does interfere with progress in English. However, the differences are not large, and only those for Lorge–Thorndike Verbal and Reading are significant. These findings of adverse effects of bilingualism are unusually positive, but the circumstances of American children receiving an English education in a Japanese environment may well be atypical.

IMPLICATIONS FOR TEACHING ENGLISH
TO NON-ENGLISH-SPEAKING ORIENTAL IMMIGRANT
CHILDREN, INCLUDING INDOCHINESE

Ashworth (1975) has surveyed the policies and practices in most of the major Canadian cities in teaching new immigrant children with little or no English. She considers the difficulties of the Chinese as being more serious than those of, say, Italians, Greeks, or West Indians, because of the extreme dissimilarity of their languages and English. I would suggest that the situation of Chinese and Japanese is improving, partly because so many parents and children nowadays have acquired some English in their native lands, and partly because they can mingle with families of the same ethnic origin who have been residents long enough in Canada to have become acculturated to Canadian living and speech. The difficulties facing the Vietnamese and other Indochinese refugees are likely to be greater because the children and most of their parents will seldom know any English, and the culture from which they come differs even more from the Canadian than do the cultures of Hong Kong or Taiwan. However, in most cities where these immigrants arrive concerted efforts are being made to help them over the initial cultural hurdles, and to make special provision for coaching both adults and children in English.

Ashworth's main conclusion is that the education of new immigrants throughout Canada is very haphazard, varying greatly from one school board to another. (The same is probably true of the United States.) Financial funding is patchy and usually inadequate, and there is a serious shortage of teachers trained in handling such pupils, and teaching English as a second language. The numbers able to speak the language of the newcomers are even fewer, though this can to some extent be made up by employing parent aides who are bilingual. A further adverse factor is the widespread ignorance among Canadian teachers of the cultures from which immigrant children come. They can hardly be expected to understand the children's difficulties if they know nothing about their background, values, and language (Ramcharan, 1975).

Many districts do have reception classes in which pupils with the same mother tongue can use their own language initially; they are sent on to regular classes as soon as they have acquired a minimum of English. There may or may not be schemes for following them up and continuing to provide part-time remedial English instruction. But the issue of segregation in native-language groups versus immediate placement in wholly English-medium classes is controversial. Despite the arguments cited earlier that favor study of both languages, it is claimed that such oriental (or other) groups will continue to speak their own language among themselves and will be less motivated to acquire English. They should, of course, be encouraged to mix with English-speaking Orientals or Caucasians in the playground and other school activities.

If they are immediately sent to regular classes, few teachers will have the time or indeed the skills to give them extra coaching. They are more likely to dub them "slow learners," place them in classes 2 years or more below their age-grade level, or try to shunt them off into special education classes.[3] It has been found useful to appoint volunteer English-speaking children as buddies to each oriental child, despite the initial difficulties of communication. While most Canadian children are willing to be helpful, there are unfortunately many incidents of Orientals being ridiculed, teased, or attacked. I would have thought that much more use should be made of older immigrant children who arrived a few years earlier and who have become good English speakers. Knowing the difficulties that they themselves experienced should help them to advise and teach newcomers.

While it is still true that the majority of immigrants pick up English more

---

[3]Some academic secondary schools refuse to accept any immigrant children who have shown difficulties in learning to read English in primary school. Hence, they are sent to vocational schools, and they are denied any opportunity to acquire an advanced secondary education.

rapidly than one might expect, it will usually take them at least 2 years to catch up with English-speaking children.[4] They may become fairly fluent in everyday communication with peers in a shorter time, but be unable to use the language for understanding the teachers' instruction or the books they have to read. Pupils of secondary school age are much more seriously handicapped than younger ones, since the language used in school is more advanced, the timetable more complex, and they are taught by many different teachers. Provision for preschool education is almost nonexistent, but it has been found that just dumping oriental children in a nursery school or kindergarten does nothing to develop their usage of English. A major difficulty for all age groups is that the children arrive at any time in the school year; they cannot just join Canadian classes in September.

It is natural that the parents of oriental immigrants are often disappointed at their slow scholastic progress. Being downgraded means that many of them fail to get the advanced academic education that the parents had hoped would be superior to that available in their home country. But to some extent the parents themselves must take the blame, since mothers particularly are reluctant to take classes in English, hence the children hear only the native language at home. They also tend to prevent their children from joining in extracurricular activities, especially those of a coeducational nature, and this cuts them off from making friends with Canadian peers.

Li (1976) has described her work in Calgary with new Chinese immigrants. In 1974 alone, 176 children, aged 6–13 years, entered Calgary elementary and junior high schools. Some of them, chiefly those with well-educated parents, had learned some English before arrival. When the parents had had 8 years or less schooling, only one out of three children had a good knowledge of English; but for those with more than 8 years, four out of five were competent. The immigrants from mainland China showed greater difficulties of adjustment and language learning than those from Hong Kong. This problem is likely to be exacerbated with the Indochinese.

Li comments on the importance for both parents and children of favorable attitudes toward the Canadian culture and toward learning English. On the basis of her clinical experience with Chinese problem children, she concludes that what are required are individual diagnosis and treatment, which take account of previous background and present proficiency. Thus, some children react better to immersion programs, while others react favorably to native-language classes in which English is taught by the ordinary translation approach. Among younger children, play methods and role-playing are often appropriate. In Calgary the teaching of English as a second language is decentralized; that is, a body of trained teachers take small groups of oriental children in many of the city's elementary and secondary schools.

---

[4]Cummins (1980) concludes that English-medium tests like Binet or WISC do not give reliable results until the immigrants have lived for 5 years or more in Canada.

In addition to the Chinese, Calgary has received about 5000 Indochinese (boat people) in 1980 and 1981, scarcely 10% of whom spoke any English.[5] The majority are Vietnamese, some of whom are Chinese-speaking, and others are from Cambodia or Laos. It is too early to judge their progress, but it is clear that those sponsored by community groups and given continuous help are adjusting better than those allocated by the government. The children have settled down well and seem extraordinarily resilient, despite the traumatic circumstances that many have experienced. But they are more handicapped than the Chinese because their previous education has been much interrupted or even nonexistent; this especially affects students of high school age. On the other hand, the written or printed Vietnamese language is alphabetical, not ideographic. It uses Roman letters, supplemented by a number of accents to indicate phonetic variations. Thus, the transition to reading and writing English is easier. It may be that most of those who escaped from Indochina were above average in wealth and education, but the children appear to show much the same distribution of abilities as Hong Kong immigrants, and they are, if anything, more strongly motivated to learn English. Thus, there are as good prospects of their becoming acculturated and accepted in Canadian society as the present-day Chinese immigrants.

SUMMARY OF CHAPTERS 10 AND 11

A description of the oral and written (or printed) Chinese and Japanese languages indicates very great differences from European languages, though there are some structural similarities. Hence, it is surprising that oriental children learn to read and write their own languages more easily than Euro–American children. Anything corresponding to dyslexia is almost nonexistent (except in cases of brain pathology). Genetic racial differences seem unlikely as an explanation, though there is some evidence suggesting that lateralization of language functions in the left and right cortexes may be involved. Neither emotional maladjustment nor minimal brain damage, which often underlie reading difficulties among Western children, are likely to occur less frequently in Orientals. Probably therefore, the reading of Chinese ideographs and Japanese Kanji, which looks so difficult to us and has to be learned largely by rote, is actually more straightforward than that of alphabetic languages. Japanese may also be easier because many of the symbols used (Kana) are phonetic, and are more invariant than English spellings.

When the children of oriental immigrants transfer to speaking and reading English, there is again less difficulty than might be expected from having to acquire a totally different pattern of eye movements, as well as new phonemes

---

[5] A considerable proportion of them come from other Canadian provinces where, presumably, they have begun to acquire some English.

and syntactical structures. The findings of studies of oriental achievements in English and verbal intelligence are often inconsistent, partly because the composition of the tested samples may differ in such respects as length of time in North America and in English-medium schools, amount of English spoken at home or with peers, etc. Thus, most generalizations about oriental second-language learning are dubious. A review of theories and research on bilingualism shows that early conclusions as to the adverse effects of bilingualism on achievement were unjustified. Poorer achievement was found largely because the children whose mother tongue was non-English came chiefly from low SES and poorly educated families. The remarkable ease with which very young children acquire two languages in bilingual households, and the success of ''immersion programs'' in which the children receive half their education in the mother tongue, half in a second language, demonstrate that there is no necessary interference or confusion attributable to bilingualism. Indeed, recent investigations have shown positive gains among bilinguals, especially when the children are of good intelligence, are well motivated, and are favorably disposed toward the second language and culture.

In some studies of oriental achievements—mainly those in the 1920s to 1950s—the children were much behind monoglot whites in their use and understanding of English, and always scored lower on verbal than nonverbal intelligence tests. In more recent studies, including those of Jensen and Vernon (Chapters 2 and 8), achievements were better, though the verbal versus nonverbal pattern persisted, and there was very little effect of parental language or SES on child achievement. The parents' own education, their length of residence in English-speaking countries, and their identification with the second culture seemed to have more influence. It is possible that exposure to English either at home or at school is less important than the free mixing of oriental children with whites and other English-speaking Orientals. Smith's (1939) and Rowe's (1966) studies provided useful information on the environmental factors that do tend to differentiate between high and low oriental school achievers. Positive factors included use of some English at home, encouragement of English reading (and less television), early introduction by parents to verbal skills, and sending preschoolers to nursery schools and kindergarten. Adverse factors included persistence of traditionalism among the parents, use of pidgin English with other children (in Hawaii), and neglectful (rather than strict) home upbringing.

Some suggestions are made as to the education of newly arrived immigrants with very little English, such as the Indochinese.

12

Oriental University Students
and Adults

INTRODUCTION

Investigations of college students naturally do not give us much information about Chinese and Japanese achievements in North America generally, since they are mostly based on highly selected groups. Nevertheless, the numbers who go to college and get degrees can be compared between Orientals, whites, or other groups. It also is of interest to observe whether the patterning of abilities found among children still persists at selected adult levels. Another topic that has received considerable attention is whether the structure or organization of abilities using factor analysis give similar results for Orientals as for whites.

The first study noted was that by Walcott (1920). This was carried out at a university in China, where the students had learned English as well as Chinese subjects. Sixty-three of them were tested with the Stanford–Binet 14-year and adult items. The range of IQs was 81–122. The mean is not given, but 44 of the 63 reached 100 IQ or over.[1] Comparable white American students would certainly show a much higher proportion. The Chinese were superior to Americans on some items such as arithmetical, ingenuity, etc., but they were lower on others, especially those that presented language or cultural difficulties. A group verbal test by Walter D. Scott was also given, and comparisons made with 190 United States students. There were nine subtests, and the Chinese were superior on Arithmetic Problems, Opposites, and Complex Completion, whereas the Americans excelled on Predicate Completion, Genus–Species, and especially Directions. Overall, the Americans scored 81% correct, the Chinese 70.5%. However, the Chinese had a smaller number of incorrect items. It was their speed of work that mainly pulled down their scores. Walcott points out that over and

---

[1] The 16-year divisor of Mental Ages was used. Had the commonly adopted 14-year divisor been substituted, the mean would have been about 15 points higher.

TABLE 12.1

Comparison of Chinese and Caucasian Students on the Ohio State
University Intelligence Test (Wang, 1926)

1. Arithmetic Problems	Chinese equal to Caucasians
2. Proverbs	Chinese a little higher
3. Same–Opposite	Chinese a little below
4. Mixed Sentences	Chinese below
5. Number Series	Chinese much higher
6. Analogies	Chinese higher
7. General Information	Chinese much lower

above the obvious difficulties of handling items in English, the Chinese would
certainly be less test-sophisticated than the American students.

Porteus and Babcock (1926) gave the Thorndike Intelligence Test in 1922 to
groups of Hawaiian university students: 63 whites, 60 Japanese, and 43 Chinese.
The respective average scores were 70.2, 61.6, and 59.7. The authors remark,
however, that Japanese students had higher academic grades than the whites.
Presumably these test scores were adversely affected by language difficulties and
lack of familiarity with objective tests.

In another early study at Ohio State University, Wang (1926) compared students of three minority groups with Caucasians on the university's group test of
intelligence. There were 34 Chinese, 158 blacks, 45 students born in Russia, and
paired white students. Actual scores are not listed, but the main results on the
seven subtests are shown in Table 12.1. Again, we find the Chinese obtaining
low scores on the most verbally loaded tests (though not invariably, since Prov-
erbs and Analogies show somewhat higher Chinese means). They are most
successful on the Number test, and are equal to whites in Arithmetic. There were
no outstanding differences between the blacks and Russians and the Caucasians.
Wang admits that all the groups were highly selected, so that their results should
not be taken as representative of minorities in the total population.

MORE RECENT INVESTIGATIONS OF COLLEGE STUDENTS

Backman (1972) studied 2925 twelfth grade high school students who had
been included in the PROJECT TALENT research, and had also completed a
follow-up questionnaire 5 years after graduation. All of these fell in the middle
range of SES. Project Talent analyses had yielded 11 orthogonal factors, and
scores on the six major factors were compared between four ethnic groups:
Jewish, non-Jewish whites, Negroes, and Orientals. These scores are shown in
Table 12.2, the highest mean on each factor being italicized.

TABLE 12.2
Mean Factor Scores of Four Ethnic Groups (Backman, 1972) [a]

	Jewish	Non-Jewish	Negro	Oriental	Males	Females
Numbers of students	1236	1051	488	150		
Factors						
Verbal Knowledge	*57.1*	51.9	46.0	49.0	*53.7*	48.3
English Language	50.8	51.1	47.5	*52.5*	40.9	*60.0*
Mathematics	58.6	52.1	47.3	*59.1*	*63.9*	44.6
Visual Reasoning	46.0	*51.8*	45.1	49.4	*54.5*	41.7
Perceptual Speed						
and Accuracy	*51.0*	49.5	50.9	50.3	49.1	*51.7*
Short-term Memory	47.8	50.9	50.4	*51.6*	44.3	*56.0*
Averages	51.9	51.4	47.9	52.0	51.1	50.4

[a] The italicized figures represent the highest mean factor scores.

It may be seen that the Orientals are highest in Mathematics, English Language, and Short-Term Memory, and close to average or slightly below on other factors. The Jews are much the highest in Verbal Knowledge, and almost as high as Orientals in Mathematics, but low on Visual Reasoning and Short-Term Memory. On all factors combined the Orientals obtain the same average score as Jews. Backman also lists sex differences, and these show wider variations than do the ethnic figures. In fact, analysis of variance found sex differences to account for 69% of variance, ethnicity and SES only for 13 and 2%, respectively. However, these figures are much distorted by the restriction in range of SES, and but for this there is no doubt that ethnicity and SES would have been much more influential, sex less so. It is unfortunate that the numbers of Orientals were too small to list Chinese and Japanese separately. But this research provides very strong evidence that Oriental American abilities and achievements are, on the average, somewhat superior to those of Caucasians.

Hsia (1980) has reported on several tests used for undergraduate or graduate selection, such as the Scholastic Aptitude Test (SAT), the Graduate Record Examination (GRE), and the Medical College and Law School Admissions tests (MCAT and LSAT, respectively). In every instance the oriental applicants were superior to general American norms in mathematics or quantitative subtests, but were below average on verbal ability subtests. The following means were obtained on the 1971–72 SAT for 503,323 high school whites and 10,098 Orientals.

	Verbal	Quantitative
Whites	474	505
Orientals	442	517

The Verbal deficiency of 32 points would correspond to some five IQ points. But it should be pointed out that the number of oriental applicants, relative to their total population figures, is more than three times that of white applicants. Had the same proportion of both ethnic populations applied, the oriental verbal mean would certainly be higher than the white.

Other studies (e.g., Goldman & Hewitt, 1976) have shown that the SAT is at least as reliable and valid a predictor of college grades for Orientals as for whites.

Sue and Kirk (1972, 1973) discuss the abilities of oriental students at the University of California, Berkeley. Of the student body, the Chinese constitute some 10% and Japanese 5%, compared with only 2% of the California population (Table 1.2). In 1966, over 3000 freshmen, including 236 Chinese and 106 Japanese of both sexes, were given the School and College Ability Test (SCAT). The results confirmed that relative to whites both oriental groups were lower on verbal than quantitative abilities, and the two groups did differ significantly. Other useful data were obtained on the Strong Vocational Interest Blank and on a personality inventory, but these are considered in Chapters 14–16.

Connor (1974b, 1975) studied the achievements of Sansei Japanese in college. He interviewed 130 males and females at the California State University, Sacramento. Some 84% of these had participated in extracurricular activities in high school; the males mostly in athletics, the females in clubs. It is also interesting that 69% of males and 79% of females claimed that more than half of their friends were Caucasians.

The males concentrated mainly in business (37%) and sciences (26%). Their mean GPAs are shown below, and these were closely similar to those of whites.

	Japanese	Caucasian
Business	2.63	2.70
Sciences	2.78	2.80
Others	2.60	2.79

Females in both ethnic groups obtained similar grades, though both were a little superior to males. Connor concludes therefore that the college achievements of Orientals in the 1970s were not greater than those of whites, thus confirming Kitano's (1962) view that the Sansei had fallen below the standards of the Nisei. But this is partly explained by the larger proportion of Japanese than of whites entering college. Some 30% of all California whites entered college at that time, whereas 74% of Sansei males and 58% of females did so. This would certainly lower their mean GPA. Likewise the Nisei may have been outstanding academically partly because they were a more highly selected group than the Sansei, and partly because of their extremely high motivation.

Meredith (1965) notes that the University of Hawaii considers it necessary to arrange remedial English courses for many of its students, mainly Oriental. About 21% of entrants are regarded as below standard, despite the almost complete disappearance of Chinese and Japanese usage in daily life. But he adds that Hawaiian Oriental students may be handicapped because a good deal of pidgin English is still commonly used outside school. Similarly Watanabe (1973) found that oriental students at the University of California fail the English proficiency test twice as often as whites (50% versus 25%).

They have considerable difficulties in reading and comprehension; hence their tendency to prefer scientific or technical courses to those involving more language. He suggests that this handicap does not arise mainly from parental use of the traditional language, but rather from restrictions on talking in oriental homes, where the father always lays down the law and permits no argumentation. Even during infancy, Japanese mothers talk less to their babies than do white mothers. Verbal reticence may also have been encouraged by racial discrimination in the past, which isolated Orientals from American society and led to fatalism and resignation, especially among Chinese. Similarly Sue and Frank (1973) mention that Orientals are brought up not to express strong feelings in public.

Klein, Miller, and Alexander (1974) have described the difficulties of adjustment among Chinese students from Taiwan, Hong Kong, or mainland China, who come to work at American universities. They mix very little with white students and make no real friends. Often they lack confidence in their English skills and are afraid of being misunderstood. They seldom join in class discussions because of their traditional reverence for the teacher.

Hutchinson, Arkoff, and Weaver (1966) recorded the numbers of contributions to class discussions at the University of Hawaii, where JA are the largest ethnic group. Forty-six Caucasian and 73 JA students were observed in three psychology courses. The mean numbers of classroom responses were

	Caucasians	Japanese
Male	26.35	1.71
Female	11.04	1.00

Klein *et al.* add that Chinese, especially those from abroad, do not share the white students' view of university education as contributing to self-realization, for working out one's philosophy with new friends, and for breaking loose from one's family. Oriental students are working in the United States to honor their parents' wishes, not to enjoy life. They look on the university as a place to learn, work, and sleep. They live in solitude and constant anxiety in dormitories or else in rooming houses with their own kind. They are strongly motivated also, because their families have often deprived themselves and saved so as to send them to college. Hence, it is unthinkable that they should not do well in all their courses. Those who do adjust to some extent to American norms may become ostracized by other oriental students. And when they return home, they are likely to have serious conflicts over parental control and traditional values.

Bochner, Lin, and McLeod (1980) gave a questionnaire to 15 students from several Asian countries who were studying in America and had just completed their M.A. or Ph.D. (see Bennett, Passin, and McKnight, 1958; p. 46, this volume). They were asked what happy and unhappy incidents they anticipated when they got home. Eighty percent of the incidents were concerned with family relations, job prospects, and peer group relations. Much smaller numbers mentioned concerns about the lower standards of living or about political difficulties. Some typical responses indicating their worries were:

"Convincing my parents that study is not just to get more money."

"Can't apply knowledge gained." "Have to start all over again."

"Friends may view me differently." "Few I can talk to."

Even American-born Chinese, though much more acculturated, tend to keep to themselves and take little part in extracurricular activities. CA students have few contacts with CC from abroad. Commonly they are working their way through college and therefore have little time for social, athletic, or political activities. All these factors may be involved in their relatively poor verbal competence.

A footnote is provided by Hwang and Dizney (1970). Sixty-three Chinese students who had come to do graduate work in America had all had from 7 to 13 years of instruction in English in their home country. They were given the ETS test of English as a Foreign Language. Twenty of them took a course in English, and the ETS test scores correlated .66 with first-term English grades. But for the whole group there was no significant correlation with GPA. This suggests that once some minimal level is reached, initial fluency in English does not greatly affect advanced work in the English medium. Presumably the cultural and attitudinal variables referred to in the preceding paragraphs are more important for academic achievement.

Despite these many problems, there is no doubt as to the high degree of success attained by Orientals, whether American- or foreign-born, in English-speaking universities. Yee (1976) states that by 1974, 25% of all Chinese completed college degrees versus 13% for the United States as a whole. The figure for Chinese women was lower, namely 17%, but this too is double that for American females. One-third of all employed Japanese and 40% of Chinese were in professional occupations, though there was still much underusage of their qualifications and some persisting racial discrimination. More data on college enrollments and choice of subjects, and on professional employment, are given in the next chapter.

COMPARISONS OF ADULT SAMPLES

Bloom and Goldman (1962) reported on the Wechsler Adult IQs (WAIS) of two samples of 63 male hospital patients. One hospital was in Connecticut, the other Hawaii, but no indication is given of the racial makeup of the patients.

Probably the Hawaiian group was about one-half Oriental. The samples were matched for age (range 17 to 53 years), and education, though apparently not for nosology. The mean IQs were

	Connecticut	Hawaii
Verbal	96.78	90.77
Performance	89.81	93.53

The Hawaiian group show the familiar pattern of rather low verbal ability, but higher than Caucasians on performance tests. The Hawaiians were superior on Kohs Blocks and Object Assembly, while the Caucasians excelled chiefly on Information, Similarities, and Vocabulary.

The comparison by Lynn (1977b) of Japanese and American norms on some of the WAIS subtests was described in Chapter 5.

FACTORIAL STUDIES OF STUDENT AND ADULT ABILITIES

In cross-cultural studies there is always the problem that test items or questions about attitudes, etc., may not convey the same meaning to members of Culture B as they do to Culture A for whom the tests or questionnaires were made up. Several precautions can be taken to improve accuracy when translating into a foreign language (see Brislin, Lonner, & Thorndike, 1973), but these do not guarantee that the scores arrived at measure the same psychological variables in both groups. One of the most fruitful ways of studying this is to apply factor analysis to a considerable number of tests given to representative samples of As and Bs. Statistical analysis enables one to discover the underlying dimensions of the variables in each group or, to put it more simply, to find whether the variables cluster together in the same manner.[2] For example, verbal intelligence and visuo-spatial tests always yield moderate positive intercorrelations among whites, showing that they measure a general factor or component of intelligence. But the verbal tests usually intercorrelate more highly among themselves than they do with the spatial, which suggests the presence of a separate verbal cluster or group factor. Similarly, those that depend on spatial manipulation (perceiving how the visual shapes would look if turned around, etc.) involve another more specialized type of spatial or visualization ability. Now if the tests cluster in the same way in Culture B as in Culture A, this provides useful evidence that the organization or underlying structure of abilities is essentially the same in both cultures. Also, one can examine whether the same tests, which are the best

---

[2]The methods of factor analysis and its results are explained in many standard texts such as Cronbach (1970), Anastasi (1958), Tyler (1965), and Vernon (1960, 1961). Several applications have been referred to in earlier chapters; see pp. 21 and 60, also the Glossary.

measures of verbal intelligence or of the spatial component, in one group are at the top of the list in the other group. One can intercorrelate the sets of factor loadings for the A and the B samples, and one would generally expect to find high "congruence coefficients" of .90 and over if the factors in each group are essentially the same.

I will point out some weaknesses of factor comparison below; but I will first summarize a number of applications to Orientals and whites. Vandenberg (1959) gave 20 of Thurstone's original Primary Mental Abilities tests, along with four English language tests and some Chinese tests (35 tests in all) to students from China (presumably mainly from Taiwan) working at several American universities. There were 56 males and 36 females. They scored somewhat lower than white students on certain tests, for example, English Vocabulary, but were higher on others. Thirteen factors were extracted, and these were rotated to maximum congruence with the original American factor loadings of the 20 tests among American students. Strong evidence was obtained of close identity in the case of Spatial, Verbal, Number, Rote Memory, and Perceptual Speed factors. However, there were seven additional smaller factors, especially in the Chinese tests, which were less clearly defined. Vandenberg points out that there may be enough similarity between educational and cultural influences in America and China to bring about this common structure, but adds that "It seems more plausible to assume that, at least for factors S, N, V, P, and M, there exists potentialities in the human neuropsychological organization that are independent of one another, that limit the performance on certain types of task, regardless of the kind of educational experiences undergone, and provided there have been enough such experiences to develop their potentialities" [p. 301].

In a further similar study (Vandenberg, 1967), much the same test battery was given to 92 South American students attending a summer school program in English at the University of Michigan. Instead of Chinese tests, 11 tests in Spanish were included, some identical in content with the Chinese ones. Again 13 factors were extracted and rotated, and some of the same Thurstone factors reappeared: Verbal, Perceptual Speed, and Rote Memory. Spatial and Reasoning factors showed only moderate resemblance to Thurstone's primaries, and number ability split up into two independent factors. Additional native language factors appeared, as they had with the Chinese. Ahmavaara's technique for rotating factor matrices to maximal congruence was applied to the seven main factors in the Chinese and South American samples, and this yielded high congruence on Native language, V, M, S, and P, and lower on N and R.

It is difficult to know how to interpret such findings. How high must the congruence be if one is to accept that virtually the same major dimensions of ability or personality operate in two or more cultures? When such agreement is lacking, what does it tell us about the cultures? The fact that a particular set of tests tends to cluster in Culture B, but not in Culture A, might be interpreted in terms of the cultural influences that gave rise to it; but this would be little more than subjective speculation. Probably one should refrain from making comparisons between the abilities of two or more racial–ethnic groups unless high congruence has been demonstrated. Fortunately this condition is usually met when the same tests are analyzed among American whites and the main minority groups.

In Flaugher and Rock's study (1972) of 18,000 high school juniors in Los Angeles (p. 20) the intercorrelations of nine ability tests were factor analyzed separately among whites, blacks, Mexicans, and Orientals. When rotated by Varimax, essentially the same factors were found in all four groups.

Marsella and Golden (1980) gave the Educational Testing Service Kit of 20 Cognitive Factor tests to 118 JA students and 101 whites at the University of Hawaii. These were of pure Japanese and Northern European descent, respectively. Eight factors were extracted in each group, and half of these were quite similar. They were labeled as: (1) Symbolic Fluency, (2) Creativity–Originality, (3) Verbal Fluency, and (4) Visual Spatial Organization. However, in several instances the highly loaded component tests differed between the groups, and the other four factors were largely dissimilar. The authors did not compute congruence coefficients, but they believe that when essentially the same dimensions are recognizable, they probably derive from genetic sources that are common to both cultures. On the other hand, when the specific components of these factors differ, this is due to different cultural influences. I would suggest that the contradiction between the considerable consistency in Flaugher and Rock's study, and the greater divergence in Marsella's, may have arisen because the former's population covered a wide range of ability and were mostly below average, whereas the latter's population was highly selected and therefore more homogeneous; thus their high-level abilities would be more differentiated.

In Marsella and Golden's study, most of the mean scores showed only small differences between Caucasians and Japanese. But the Japanese were significantly higher on Perceptual Speed and Number Facility tests, and also on Spatial Orientation (nonsignificant). The Caucasians were higher on Verbal Comprehension, Ideational and Expressional Fluency, and Syllogistic Reasoning. Generalizing, the Japanese excel in rapid learning of repetitive tasks, Caucasians in tasks involving verbal facility.

An earlier study by Marsella and Higginbotham (1976) investigated cognitive differences between Japanese and Caucasians by means of nine tests of visual, auditory, and tactile-kinesthetic sensitivity (see also Shizuru and Marsella, 1980). These were given individually to 114 Japanese American and 57 Caucasian students at the University of Hawaii. Most of the tests yielded several scores, and these were combined to give 16 variables, which were factor-analyzed in each group. Seven main factors were extracted and rotated, and these showed considerable differences in organization or structuring of cognitive processes. Four of them gave only moderate congruence coefficients of .42 to .76. The overall sensitivity scores in the two groups were quite similar, but ethnic differences were chiefly shown by the greater purity of the Japanese factors. That is, most of these factors were confined to a single sensory modality, whereas the Caucasian factors were much more mixed, indicating that the various modalities were more integrated. The Japanese relied most heavily on spatial–kinesthetic processes, while the Caucasians were more visually oriented (in combination with other modalities).

A long series of studies was carried out during the 1970s by J. C. DeFries, S. G. Vandenberg, and J. R. Wilson of the University of Colorado, and R. C. Johnson, K. W. Wilson, M. P. Mi, and others at the University of Hawaii. These were based mainly on Caucasian and Oriental Hawaiians. Thirty-four tests were chosen as good measures of cognitive factors. These were given to a mixed group of 172 whites, Japanese, and Chinese. Factor analysis indicated that the clearest ability dimensions were Verbal Ability, Spatial Visualization, Perceptual Speed and Accuracy, and Visual Memory; 15 tests were chosen that were most highly loaded on these. This shorter battery was given to 5077 members of 1490 families, aged between 14 and 60 years. These were mainly whites and Japanese Americans, though with some Chinese and part-Hawaiians.

DeFries *et al.* (1974) and DeFries *et al.* (1976) showed that the four factors were nearly identical in whites and Japanese. (Note that, as in Flaugher and Rock's study, the subjects were quite heterogeneous in range of ability.) Wilson *et al.* (1975) extended this to show that the factor structure was the same for three different age groups. However, when the 14- to 20-year olds and the 36- to 60-year olds were compared, the Japanese Verbal and Perceptual scores increased more slowly with age than did those of the whites, and on the other two factors the Japanese declined more rapidly. No explanation of these findings is offered.

DeFries *et al.* (1976) studied the heritabilities of the 15 tests from the parent–offspring correlations found in 739 Caucasian and 244 Japanese families. The Japanese heritability coefficients tended to be distinctly lower than the Caucasian ones (for no obvious reason). But the rank order correlation between the two sets of 15 coefficients was .77, indicating that there was considerable congruence in heritability in the two groups.

Wilson (1977) collected assessments or indexes of some 44 environmental and attitudinal variables by means of questionnaires to fathers, mothers, and offspring. The analysis was based on 1120 Caucasian and 379 Japanese offspring who had also taken the 15-test battery measuring the four ability factors. Many of the environmental variables gave substantial correlations with factor scores in both ethnic groups. The correlations for each factor were rank-ordered, and the congruence coefficients between Caucasian and Japanese were as follows:

Verbal ability	.74
Spatial ability	.64
Perceptual Speed	.47
Visual Memory	.01
All tests combined	.69

Thus, there was fair similarity between the two groups regarding the pattern of environmental variables related to Verbal, Spatial, and combined tests. But the similarity was low for Perceptual, and near zero for Memory. None of the figures is as high as those obtained for ability factor comparisons, but they do indicate that to some extent the environments of Caucasian and Japanese students in Hawaii act in much the same way to affect certain major abilities.

Obtained in the 1970s, these results obviously would be influenced by the considerable homogeneity of environments and cultures in the two largest Hawaiian groups. They should not be taken to mean that primary mental abilities are biologically the same in two races, as suggested by Vandenberg in 1959, and Marsella and Golden in 1980. Also, we do not know how great the similarity would have been between whites and Chinese, Hawaiians, Filipinos, and other minorities.

Several other studies by these authors, not based on factor analysis, gave useful results. The mean ability scores of spouses, parents, and offspring, and even uncles and aunts, could be intercorrelated on large samples. This provided data on genetic influences in the four ability factors. Two major findings were, first, that heritability coefficients are higher, not only in Caucasians versus Japanese, but also in children versus adults. And second, that the theory of spatial ability as dependent on a sex-linked gene was not confirmed (see DeFries *et al.*, 1978).

13

Academic Preferences
and Professional Employment
of Orientals

INTRODUCTION

Several articles mentioned in previous chapters have pointed out the tendency of Chinese and Japanese college students to select particular kinds of course work and university degrees (Sue and Kirk, 1972, 1973; Watanabe, 1973; Connor, 1975; Yee, 1976). Perhaps the most extensive survey is that published by McCarthy and Wolfle (1975). This dealt with doctoral degrees received by minority group students, the award of which probably constitutes the most reliable indication of outstanding scholastic talent in the United States. In my view, intelligence and other objective tests are much less accurate measures of ability among young adults than success in higher degree work.

McCarthy and Wolfle collected lists of all doctoral students in 1969–1972 from almost all the major American universities. Table 13.1 shows the percentages of doctoral degrees obtained by four minority group students.

Apart from whites, blacks produce the greatest total of Ph.D. students. But they are, of course, drawn from a much larger number in the American population than the other minorities. The percentages in the total population, taken from the 1970 census, are listed in the middle column. The last column shows the productivity of Ph.D. students in each group. The Orientals produce 10 times as many per head of population as blacks, and even 3 times as many as whites. Unfortunately, Japanese and Chinese are not distinguished. Possibly the oriental figures are exaggerated insofar as many of the students came from abroad on immigrant or student visas. However, the authors state that such foreign students are "generally not included" in the university reports.

Other Ph.D. statistics were collected from 650 institutions of higher education

TABLE 13.1
Percentages of Doctoral Degrees in 1969–72 Obtained by Minority Group Students

Group	Percentage of Ph.D. Students	Percentage in 1970 Population	Ratio of Ph.D. Students to Population
Blacks	3.9	11.11	0.35
Asians	1.7	0.50	3.40
Spanish	1.1	0.52	1.92
Indians	0.2	0.39	0.51
Minority totals	6.9	12.52	0.55
Whites	93.1	87.47	1.06

by the National Research Council and DHEW. In 1973, it was found that only 37% of minority group members were American citizens; 29% came with immigrant visas, and 34% with other types of visa. Table 13.2 shows, for citizens and immigrant visa holders, the percentages of doctoral degrees obtained by each minority group. Corresponding figures for whites were not available.

The table shows, for example, that 11% of doctorates in engineering and physical sciences were obtained by Asians. These figures are *not* corrected for numbers in the total American population. Clearly, the Asians obtained far more doctorates, both absolutely and relatively, than the other three groups. They are high, also, in life sciences, but tend to avoid psychology, education, and arts and humanities. According to Yee (1976) they contribute fewer in education because they think of schoolteaching as a feminine job. They prefer "tangible" occupations in which they can succeed despite some weaknesses in verbal skills. The

TABLE 13.2
Percentages of Minority Group Students in Different Courses of Study

Course of Study	Black	Indian	Asian	Spanish	Total
Engineering, math, and physical science	1.0	0.3	11.0	0.6	12.8
Life sciences	1.9	0.5	7.0	0.9	10.3
Psychology	1.3	0.6	1.3	0.9	4.1
Social sciences	1.9	0.5	3.8	0.6	6.9
Arts and humanities	1.7	0.5	1.2	1.4	4.8
Education	6.9	0.7	0.8	0.9	9.3
Other programs	2.2	0.1	2.6	0.2	5.1
All fields combined	2.7	0.5	4.6	0.8	8.7
All students	16.9	3.2	27.7	5.0	53.3

only field in which blacks play a major role is that of education. The other black, Indian, and Spanish figures are too small for any reliable inferences to be drawn.

At a still higher level, ten times as many Orientals have been elected to the National Academy of Sciences as would be expected from their numbers in the population (Havender, 1980). At the undergraduate level, Walsh (1980) reports the following figures for the percentages of different ethnic groups admitted to the University of California:

Caucasian	16.5
Oriental	39.0
Black	5.0
Spanish	4.7

This university only takes the top 12½% of the United States population. But more than 2½ times as many Orientals gain entry to this highly select group as do other groups combined, relative to population figures.

FURTHER ANALYSES OF UNIVERSITY DEGREES

University of Hawaii

I carried out similar analyses for all degrees (not only higher) at the Universities of Hawaii, Calgary (Alberta), and British Columbia. At the University of Hawaii, the convocation lists for 1978–1979 totaled 4920 students. For each degree their names were classified into Caucasian, Chinese, Japanese, and "Other." Since the classification was inevitably somewhat subjective, a considerable proportion of doubtfuls were called "Other," along with miscellaneous small groups such as Hawaiians, East Indians, etc. They amounted to about one-quarter of the total. The lists included the place of residence of each student, and this helped in classification. It was also possible to distinguish students who came from other American states or foreign countries, and they amounted to nearly one-quarter of the total (11% of bachelors, 38% of masters, and 40% of doctors). But as it was not possible to tell how many Hawaiian students were working at mainland or foreign universities, it was decided to include the non-Hawaiians with the residents.[1] The sexes were combined throughout.

Table 13.3 lists the results. A few smaller categories of degrees were grouped together, for example, fine arts, music, and architecture.

The percentage figures in the last three columns represent the percentage of the total numbers in each row. Thus, 302 out of 1067 B.A. students, or 28%, were

---

[1]Numbers and percentages for Hawaiian residents only were also calculated, but they yielded essentially the same pattern of choices.

TABLE 13.3
Numbers and Percentages of Oriental and Other Students Taking Degrees at the University of Hawaii, 1978–79

Degree	Numbers					Percentages[a]		
	Caucasian	Chinese	Japanese	Other	Total	Cauc.	Chin.	Jap.
All bachelors	656	442	1193	691	2982	22%	15%	40%
B.A.	302	129	390	246	1067	28	12	37
B.Arch., Fine arts, Music	41	17	68	36	162	25	10	42
Education	54	24	115	71	264	20	9	44
Business admin.	69	146	265	141	621	11	24	43
B.Sc.	48	29	79	41	197	24	15	40
Engineering	19	41	80	43	183	10	22	44
Agriculture	36	9	42	23	110	33	8	38
Social work, Nursing	36	7	31	22	96	38	7	32
Human resources	51	40	123	68	282	18	14	44
All masters	706	149	346	428	1629	43	9	21
M.A.	190	28	67	108	393	48	7	17
M.Arch., Fine arts	24	3	8	19	54	44	6	15
Education	144	36	117	87	384	38	9	30
Library studies	37	2	8	17	64	58	3	12
Business admin.	44	14	21	18	97	45	14	22
Public health	83	13	21	51	168	49	8	13
M.Sc.	117	38	65	83	303	39	13	21
Social work	48	14	33	25	120	40	12	27
Urban and regional planning	19	1	6	20	46	41	2	13
All doctors	135	38	48	88	309	44	12	16
Ph.D. Science	35	12	3	20	70	50	17	4
Social science, Economics, Psychology, Arts	74	5	7	34	120	62	4	6
Medicine	12	15	22	16	65	18	23	34
Law	14	6	16	18	54	26	11	30
Total for all degrees	1497	629	1587	1207	4920	30	13	32

[a] Italicized figures represent percentages above or below the ethnic averages.

Caucasian. The significance of differences in percentages were not calculated, but the italicized figures, showing percentages much above or below the ethnic averages, are mostly significant.[2] These columns therefore indicate the degree subjects in which Caucasians, Chinese, and Japanese are most or least numerous. No account was taken of the population figures for these groups, but the 1970 census figures for Hawaii yielded 38.8% of Caucasians, 6.77% of Chinese, and 28.27% Japanese. Thus, the 13% of Chinese obtaining all degrees combined is nearly twice what would be expected from their population figure (i.e., 13/6.77). Caucasians obtained only 77% of expectation, but it is probable that many of the apparently missing white students were at mainland universities. Japanese were only a little more numerous than expected.

Note first that Orientals constitute a much larger percentage of bachelors degrees (55%) than of masters (30%) or doctors (28%), despite the influx of many students from overseas at the higher degree levels. In other words, more Caucasian bachelors go on to higher degrees than do Orientals. However, one cannot precisely specify without information about Hawaiians attending other universities. At the bachelor level, Chinese are most strongly represented in business administration and engineering, and least interested in education, agriculture, social work, nursing; they are also low in the arts. Japanese, however, are outstanding in education, as well as in engineering and human resources. They too are low in social work and nursing. Naturally, the Caucasians tend to be highest in areas that the Orientals avoid; thus, Caucasians are lowest in business administration and engineering.

At the masters level there is much the same pattern—Chinese are high in M.Sc. and business administration, low in arts, library studies, and urban and regional planning. The Japanese are again high in education and in social work, low in much the same subjects as the Chinese. Caucasians make up most of the M.A.s in library studies and public health, and are low in education.

At the doctoral level, Chinese are especially strong in science and medicine, and are very low in social studies. Japanese are rare in science and social studies, but especially high in medicine and law. These results very generally confirm those of earlier commentators, such as McCarthy and Wolfle. One would naturally expect some substantial differences between Japanese in Hawaii and on the mainland, since the former, with their very large numbers, play a much more prominent role in the community.

---

[2]The level of significance naturally depends on the total number of cases, hence the Chinese differences are the least reliable. With small degree groups, such as 70 students taking Ph.D. in Science, the 17% of Chinese in this group is *not* significantly higher than the 13% for all degrees. Also, the 23% of Chinese with M.D., out of a total of 65, only just reaches .05 significance. But when the degree attracts large numbers, such as 4% of Chinese out of 120 doing nonscience Ph.D., this figure *is* significantly lower than 13%, at <.001 level.

University of Calgary

My first study of Chinese students in Canada was based on convocation lists of 4677 students who graduated at the University of Calgary in 1977 and 1978. The surnames were classified as follows:

Chinese of Canadian origin	4.04%
Chinese from abroad (mostly Hong Kong)	1.88
Japanese	0.60
West Indians, Africans, Asians, or Middle Easterners	2.40
Non-Anglo names (Ukraine, French, German, etc.)	25.60
Anglo and Scottish names	65.48

It may be seen that 4% of the total group were Chinese with Canadian addresses, and 1.9% more came from abroad. Only 0.6% (28 in all) were Japanese. Sex could not be guessed from Chinese given names, but three-quarters had an English given name, and the sex ratio for these was two males to one female. We can deduce then that approximately 5.0% of all male graduates are Chinese and 2.5% of females, as compared with the (approximately) 4% of Chinese in the population of Calgary and environs. In other words, the numbers of male Chinese students does not greatly exceed the population figure, and the proportion of females is below expectation.

In Table 13.4 the actual numbers of each oriental group in each degree category are listed, but all the non-Orientals are combined. The last column gives the percentage of Orientals in each row. The results are quite clearcut. As in Hawaii, the proportion of Orientals taking higher degrees is much smaller than that of bachelors, despite the inclusion of Chinese from abroad. However at masters level, Orientals opt for science and engineering more frequently than for arts or education.

At the bachelor level they avoid arts, education, and social welfare, but a fair number do take social science, and very large numbers take science, commerce, business, and most of all, engineering. In fact, in the last three faculties Orientals constitute 17% of all undergraduates versus 2.2% in all other faculties.

There are too few Japanese to yield any reliable conclusion. But, like the Chinese, they seem to prefer social science and science degrees, and avoid the arts—with the exception that they may be more ready to become teachers, as occurred also in Hawaii.

The concentration of Chinese Calgarians in business and engineering may arise partly because so many of their parents are engaged in business and mer-

TABLE 13.4
Numbers and Percentages of Oriental Graduates at the University of Calgary

Degree	Calgary Chinese	Other Chinese	Japanese	Others	Percentage of Orientals
B.A. Humanities and Fine arts	9	2	2	341	3.7
B.A. Nursing, Physical education	3	0	0	225	1.5
B. Social welfare	3	1	0	238	1.7
B. Education, Educational diploma	8	3	6	1293	1.3
B.A., B.Sc. Social science	22	8	6	552	6.1
B.Sc. Physics, Biology	50	16	6	455	13.7
B. Commerce, Business	35	30	2	360	15.7
B.Sc. Engineering	44	22	2	187	26.7
M.A. Education, Arts, and Social work	2	2	2	298	2.0
M.Sc. Science, Engineering	6	4	1	219	4.8
Ph.D., all subjects	3	0	1	77	4.9
M.D.	4	0	0	127	3.1
All degrees	189	88	28	4372	6.5

chandising. In addition, Calgary is known as an oil center, hence many Chinese residents and foreign students are attracted to science and engineering courses. But the total number of local Oriental students is lower than is usually found in the United States, suggesting that Calgary parents do not aspire so strongly to higher educational and professional qualifications as do Chinese Americans, and they persist in the traditional belief that daughters need much less education than sons.

University of British Columbia

One further analysis was made of graduates at the University of British Columbia in 1980. Though they represented only 1 year's output, they provided larger numbers of higher degree students than at Calgary (913 versus 746), and especially of Japanese (69 versus 28). There were also greater variations in the type of degree (e.g., only 21.2% took education versus 33.3% at Calgary), and more detailed breakdowns were possible. Out of 4647 names in the convocation lists, 7.5% were Chinese with Canadian residence, only 0.4% foreign, and 1.5% Japanese In the 1971 census, the proportions of Chinese and Japanese in Vancouver and Burnaby were 5.9 and 1.0 (see Table 8.1), that is, quite close to the proportions among university graduates.

The sex ratio also differed greatly from Calgary—52% male versus 48%

TABLE 13.5
Numbers and Percentages of Oriental Graduates at the University of British Columbia

Degree	Chinese	Japanese	Other	Percentage of Orientals
B.A. Fine arts, Music, Architecture	12	3	185	7.5
Languages and Literature	13	2	212	6.6
Social sciences, Anthropology, Psychology, Asian studies	20	7	168	13.8
Miscellaneous: Geography, History, Philosophy	6	3	181	4.7
Economics, Political science	10	1	93	10.6
Education, Physical education	24	18	796	5.0
Home economics, Social work	9	0	139	6.1
Law	2	1	223	1.3
Business, Commerce, Accounting	64	7	348	17.0
Total B.A.	160	42	2345	7.9
B.Sc. Physical sciences	24	4	87	24.4
Botany, Zoology	6	2	106	7.0
Other biological sciences	70	7	221	26.4
Agriculture, Geography, Forestry	6	3	194	4.4
Nursing, Dental hygiene	8	1	187	4.6
Applied science, Engineering	38	3	220	15.7
Total B.Sc.	152	20	1015	14.6
M.A. Art, Music	0	0	25	0.0
Languages, Literature, Library	1	1	100	2.0
Law	0	0	6	0.0
Social work, Social sciences	1	1	86	2.3
Education	2	2	146	2.7
Business administration	13	0	78	14.3
Total M.A.	17	4	441	4.5
M.Sc. Physical sciences	5	0	39	11.4
Biology	3	1	52	7.1
Agriculture	2	0	34	5.6
Applied science, Engineering	5	0	51	8.9
Total M.Sc.	15	1	176	7.8
Ph.D., all subjects	8	1	135	6.2
M.D.	7	1	71	10.1
Medicine, Dentistry	9	0	27	25.0
Total doctors	24	2	233	10.0
All degrees	368	69	4210	9.4

female, indicating that Orientals in British Columbia are decidedly less traditional, or more Canadianized, in their attitudes than at Calgary. However, there are far more males in doctoral and masters programs (both M.A. and M.Sc.), 80%; and the bachelors level in biological, agricultural, and applied and engineering science, 70%; and Bachelor of Commerce, 64%. But many more females are found in nursing, fine arts, languages, social studies, education, and home economics—78% versus 22% males.

Table 13.5 gives the raw numbers for Chinese (including foreign), Japanese, and all others combined, and the percentages of all Orientals. Though the Orientals obtain large proportions of doctor and dentist degrees, B.Sc.s in Physical and Biological Sciences, and engineering, and business degrees, they also produce more than 10% in a wide range of subjects: M.Sc. in Physical Science, M.A. in Business Administration, B.A. in Social Sciences, Economics, and Political Science. This suggests that they are more acculturated and ready to study a greater variety of topics than the Calgarian Orientals. A curious exception is that some biological subjects at the B.Sc. level, namely botany and zoology, are far less popular than biology, biochemistry, physiology, and pharmacy (7% versus 26%). Possibly these are regarded as less useful for vocational purposes. Note that law and fine arts are right at the bottom in popularity, followed by all other M.A. subjects (except business).

There are still too few Japanese to allow much distinction from Chinese. But there are some pointers. Relative to Chinese, they are very low in doctorates and M.Sc. and, at the bachelor level, in nursing, economics, home economics, and social work. They seem to be more interested in botany, zoology, agriculture, and the social sciences, and especially in education. Indeed, they are more similar in their likes and dislikes to Canadian and American students in general than are the Chinese. This was tested by ranking the 28 types of degree in order of popularity in Table 13.5. For example, among Chinese, B.Sc. in Biology is highest; M.A. in Arts and in Law, the lowest. The correlations between the rank orders were Chinese–Japanese, .57; Chinese–Others, .61; and Japanese–Others, .78. Clearly, despite the unreliability of the Japanese choices, they resemble those of whites more than they do those of Chinese.

PROFESSIONAL OCCUPATIONS

The most interesting data on the professional occupational achievement of different ethnic groups in the United States are those published by Weyl (1969); they are based on the 1960 census. Weyl calculated the proportional representation of four groups in each of 12 major professions. These were converted to an index that averages 100 if a certain ethnic group is represented in a profession in accordance with its numbers in the total population. But when the number

TABLE 13.6
Proportional Contributions of Five Ethnic Groups to American Professions in 1960 (Weyl, 1969)

Professions	Whites	Negroes	Indians	Japanese	Chinese
Accountants	112	7	38	166	174
Architects	110	5	0	232	506
Artists and writers	110	16	133	209	136
College professors	107	32	0	143	537
Schoolteachers	103	76	86	120	318
Engineers	111	5	57	124	303
Natural scientists	109	20	0	205	438
Lawyers and judges	111	11	19	54	53
Clergymen	104	66	124	89	23
Physicians	108	21	10	182	302
Nurses	106	54	124	116	76
Technicians	107	36	86	201	197
Averages	108	29	56	155	256

reaches, say 200, that group provides twice as many as would be expected from its population size; at 50 that group provides only half as many as expected. The results are shown in Table 13.6.

It will be seen that Chinese provide, on average, 2½ times as many professionals as would be expected from their population numbers. The Japanese are next highest with 1½ times expectation. Chinese produce 5 times as many architects and college professors, and are greatly overrepresented as school teachers, engineers, natural scientists, and physicians. But they are below average as lawyers and clergymen (both highly verbal occupations), and nurses. The Japanese produce twice the expected figure as architects, artists and writers, natural scientists, and technicians, and are again low as clergymen and lawyers.[3]

In a supplementary study, Weyl included Jews as one of his ethnic groups. Their overall index in 11 major professions was 282. Since Jews are generally regarded as the most intellectual of all white groups, it is interesting to find that the Chinese are very little below them at 262. Weyl suggests that Chinese, like Jews, have been bred selectively for intelligence over generations; thus they have become outstanding in jobs requiring the most advanced training and abstract reasoning. But an explanation in terms of parental aspirations and valuation of

[3]There is a curious contradiction between Weyl's finding that Chinese produce far more schoolteachers than Japanese, and my own finding in three universities that Japanese are more attracted to education than Chinese. Possibly this represents a change in attitudes over the past 18 to 20 years since Weyl's census data were published. Alternatively, the universities that I covered were not representative of American universities in general.

education seems equally possible, except that it could not easily explain the higher proportions of Chinese in nonverbal than verbal abilities.

Lind (1967) published some figures on proportions of professionals in the population of Hawaii in the 1960 census, according to racial–ethnic grouping:

Caucasian	17.9%
Chinese	16.6
Japanese	10.1
Filipino	1.8

Koreans and part-Hawaiians also produced substantial numbers. Here again, the Chinese contribute more than twice as many as expected from their 7% in the Hawaiian population.

I collected some similar, though much less extensive, data by analyzing the names given in the Yellow Pages of the telephone directories for Oahu and Calgary. Only four specimen professions were chosen: architects, attorneys or lawyers, dentists, and physicians and surgeons. The telephone book is a somewhat unreliable source since many persons in the four professions have double or triple listings, for example, they may work for a firm or partnership, as well as individually. As far as possible, these extra listings were omitted. Thus, all specialist medical categories, for example, gynecologist, heart, etc., were omitted since almost all these doctors appeared already under physicians and surgeons. As in the University of Hawaii analysis, the names were classified as Caucasian, Chinese, Japanese, and Others (doubtful or miscellaneous).

Table 13.7 gives the percentages of each group in each profession. The 1970 census figures for the Hawaiian population are listed at the bottom. Once again, note that the Chinese appear some 2½ times as frequently in these professions as in the total population. Their outstanding performance is as physicians. But even more striking is the fact that over half of all dentists are Japanese, while the

TABLE 13.7
Percentages of Different Racial Groups in Selected Professions in Hawaii

Profession	N	Caucasians	Chinese	Japanese	Other
Architects	266	44	14	26	16
Attorneys and lawyers	973	48	15	21	16
Dentists	376	14	18	53	16
Physicians and surgeons	901	41	20	18	21
Total, and Averages	2516	37	17	29	12
Hawaiian population percentage		39	7	28	26

proportion of Caucasian dentists is very small. But Caucasians exceed Chinese and Japanese combined as architects, attorneys, and physicians.

The population of Calgary is roughly comparable to that of Honolulu, and the Yellow Pages provided 1717 professionals in these four areas, compared with 2516 in Oahu. However, the numbers of oriental professionals are much smaller, largely, of course, because Chinese and Japanese constitute only some 4% of the population, versus 35% in Hawaii. There were 21 Chinese and 13 Japanese names in all, one-half of them physicians and surgeons, and very few architects or lawyers. This total of 34 constitutes 2% of the 1717 names, which is somewhat lower than their proportion in the city population. Thus, there is no tendency as yet for Chinese or Japanese to become especially prominent in the professions. They might, of course, be more frequent as technologists. Probably, also, these findings in one large Western city do not apply to cities such as Toronto and Montreal, where the oriental populations are much larger.

SUMMARY OF CHAPTERS 12 AND 13

Almost all of the studies on Chinese and Japanese adults have been conducted with college students or with people in professional employment. Both of these groups are, of course, highly selected, and therefore give us little reliable information on the abilities or other qualities of representative adult populations. However, some studies of oriental student performance on group intelligence tests in the 1920s revealed the same pattern as with children, namely below-average verbal but above-average quantitative and nonverbal scores. Probably the oriental groups were handicapped by unfamiliarity with the English language and by the emphasis of objective tests on speed of response.

Studies in the 1970s, when all oriental college students (except those from abroad) were entirely fluent in English, tend to show either very little difference from whites or superiority on some tests, especially quantitative. But in all these comparisons, the proportion of oriental students at college has been much greater than that of whites, relative to their numbers in the general population. This leads to a reduction in mean scores; if the same proportions of Caucasian and oriental students had been tested, the superiority of the latter would be obvious.

Several writers have drawn attention to the difficulties of oriental students (especially those from abroad) in adjusting to university life. Despite their superior ability, a great many are anxious about achieving well, and show no enjoyment of social activities. Even in the 1970s, about twice as many oriental students as whites were poor readers, and had to be sent to remedial classes in English. Hence, they tend to choose science or mathematical or engineering programs, which make less demands on verbal abilities than arts courses.

Much use has been made of factor analysis for bringing out similarities and differences in the organization or structure of mental abilities between whites and Chinese or Japanese. With fairly heterogeneous populations (i.e., a wide range of ability), the factors turn out to be very similar. But among more homogeneous groups, such as college students, there are much greater divergences, which are difficult to interpret.

Objective tests of intelligence and other abilities at college level are rather poor predictors of academic achievement and professional competence. Hence, actual examination results, the award of bachelors' and higher degrees, and entry into professional careers give a better indication. Several studies have shown that when allowance is made for the numbers of Orientals in the total population, they are 2 to 3 times more likely than whites to achieve professional employment. Particularly striking was the work of Weyl on the representation of four United States minority groups in a dozen professions. Here, the Chinese were outstanding, since they produced 2½ times as many professionals as would be expected from their population numbers; indeed, there were even 5 times as many in certain professions. Japanese were also above average, though they produced only 1½ times as many overall. I made a similar analysis of selected professions in Oahu and in Calgary, on the basis of names listed in the Yellow Pages of the telephone directory. In Oahu the Chinese were greatly overrepresented. The Japanese were found to be just about as numerous as whites, but they provided over one-half of all the dentists on the island. In Calgary, however, there was no tendency for Orientals to be overrepresented in these professions.

I also analyzed the numbers and types of degrees awarded to Chinese, Japanese, and whites (or others) in the convocation lists of three universities— Hawaii, Calgary, and British Columbia. Over four thousand graduates were tabulated in each university. In all of them the proportion of bachelor degrees was higher among Orientals than whites, but relatively fewer graduated with masters or doctoral degrees. The main finding was that the Chinese were very largely concentrated in business administration, engineering, and natural science degrees, and very few took education, social welfare, or arts degrees. The numbers of Japanese in the two Canadian universities were too small to yield reliable differences, but in Hawaii they were strongly represented in education and medicine, as well as in engineering and business. In British Columbia the pattern of courses chosen or avoided by the Japanese resembled that of whites more than it did Chinese. In the same university there was much greater diversity of Chinese choices than in Calgary. Women students were about as numerous as males, whereas in Calgary only one-third were women, suggesting that the Chinese were more traditional in their attitudes to education than in Vancouver or Honolulu.

14

Personality Studies of Japanese

INTRODUCTION

In the 1960s and 1970s, much more work was published on the personality traits, attitudes, interests, and values of Japanese (and less frequently, of Chinese), both residing in the mainland United States or Hawaii or in their own countries, than on abilities and achievements. Most of it has been carried out with self-report questionnaires or inventories, though in some instances observations of behavior, projective techniques, or ratings by others were employed. Such self-report tests are open to many weaknesses such as social desirability, or "faking good" (i.e., choosing the socially respectable answers), and other distortions (see Vernon, 1964), even when given to Orientals who are fully conversant with English, and still more so if translated and given in Japan or Taiwan.

Ho (1972) cogently criticizes the application of American-constructed personality tests in other cultures, especially among Chinese and Japanese, who are typically more concerned with "saving face" than with giving information. Researchers also often fail to recognize that Orientals who live in different regions or countries are not necessarily the same everywhere. Questions concerning personal values, social and emotional problems, etc., are quite likely to mean something different to persons reared in different cultures. However, several investigators have applied "back translation" (Brislin *et al.*, 1973) in an attempt to minimize this difficulty. This means that one person fluent in English and Chinese translates the English items; a second equally bilingual person translates this Chinese version back into English, and this is checked with the original English. When there are discrepancies, the difficulties are discussed by the author and the translators.

Others have carried out factor analyses of questionnaire items or intercorrelated and analyzed a battery of tests including the questionnaire in both English-speaking and oriental groups. And when substantially the same factors turn up in the two cultures, this provides some evidence that the questionnaire is measuring much the same variables in both cultures (Gordon and Kikuchi, 1966).

Another weakness is that over three-quarters of all research cited in the following pages were based on college students as subjects or—still more restricted— on students taking psychology courses. Obviously, we should not regard the results of these as applicable to all Japanese, Chinese, or Americans.

Because of the large number of publications, I will not attempt to outline each one in as much detail as the investigations of abilities and achievements. Where convenient, the more detailed technical information on numbers and types of subjects, scores, or correlations, etc., are tabulated in Appendixes B and C. When the author's name or date is followed by ($p.$ *000*), this means that the appendix should be consulted. Thus, Chapters 14–16 contain a more general account of the objects and results, together with a few of the more interesting tables. We start with the Japanese instead of the Chinese because far more research has been done with the former. Many studies of Japanese were carried out in Japan, whereas those of Chinese in Taiwan or elsewhere are relatively few.

STUDIES OF NEUROTICISM, ANXIETY, AND OTHER PERSONALITY TRAITS IN JAPAN

There are many personality questionnaires or self-report tests that purport to measure emotional stability–instability, or psychoneurotic tendency, or—what comes to much the same thing—general anxiety. For example:

Thurstone's Psychoneurotic Inventory (college level)
Children's Manifest Anxiety Scale (CMAS), by Castaneda
Frost's Self-Description Questionnaire (FSDQ)

Other tests refer to extraversion–introversion or aim to cover several different traits with the same instrument. For example:

Bernreuter's Personality Inventory measures Neuroticism, Introversion, Dominance, and Self-sufficiency (college level).
Eysenck's Personality Inventory measures Neuroticism and Introversion and Lie Scale (EPI). Adult and children's forms. Eysenck Personality Questionnaire (PEN test) also measures Psychoticism.
Cattell's 16 PF test, measuring 16 personality factors. Adult form and other versions for children.
California Personality Inventory (CPI), measures numerous traits (college level).
Omnibus Personality Inventory measures numerous traits (college level).
Minnesota Multiphasic Personality Inventory (MMPI); adult level scored for various psychopathological tendencies, for example, Depression.

Ohmura and Sawa (1957) summarized several studies in Japan that used translations of the Children's Manifest Anxiety scales. These generally showed Japanese students to express more anxiety than Western ones, but the authors do not cite actual figures. An investigation by Iwawaki *et al.* (1967, p. 231) contradicted this by finding lower CMAS scores in Japan than among United States or French children. It might be thought that the children would be influenced by the social desirability tendency, but they also had lower than average Lie Scale scores, which are supposed to show such distortion. The authors suggest that the children were all born more than 10 years after World War II, when Japanese parents were beginning to treat their offspring more permissively. Moreover, the students would not have reached the age at which severe pressures for achievement are customary.

Gotts (1968) likewise argues that young Japanese children have greater freedom to express aggression and sexuality than do the Americans or French, but he presents no evidence. Caudill and Frost (1974) stress the security engendered by the strength of mother–child bonds in Japanese families. Ruth Benedict (1946) also noted considerable permissiveness with regard to aggression up to age 9, though thereafter it is strongly suppressed.

Kaneda (1971, p. 231) gave the CMAS by Sarason to Japanese boys, and found no overall difference from American norms. More specifically, they were less anxious about school, but rather more so about taking tests, and they showed poor self-evaluation.

The Frost Self-Description Questionnaire (FSDQ) consists of 14 short personality scales, derived from factorization of responses among English 11-year-olds. These provide scores for eight types of Anxiety, three types of Aggression, Denial of Anxiety, Affiliation, and Submissiveness (Frost, Iwawaki, and Fogliatto, 1972). The questionnaire was given to 610 Canadian, 1027 Japanese, and 332 Latin American 11-year-old children. In both sexes combined, the Japanese scored lower than the other two groups on Test Anxiety, Social Anxiety, and to a lesser extent on four other Anxiety scales. But they were higher in Concentration Anxiety and Spatial Separation Anxiety, both of which differences seem plausible. They were also lowest on all types of Aggression, but higher than Canadians (and lower than Latin Americans) on Denial and Affiliation. The results for Anxiety tend to confirm other studies such as Iwawaki *et al.* (1967). The very low aggressive tendency may be due to the thorough suppression by the parents of any overt expression of aggression in their children.

Two studies have used the Cattell 16 PF test with Japanese college students and other ethnic groups (Cattell and Scheier, 1961, p. 231; Tsujioka and Cattell, 1965, p. 231). In addition to the separate factor scores, Cattell provides for scoring more general, or "second order," factors, chief of which are identified as Anxiety and Exvia–Invia (similar to Extraversion). The following are the mean scores on Anxiety of seven national groups.

	N	Mean		N	Mean
United States	108	7.1	France	422	14.1
United Kingdom	91	9.8	India	350	15.1
Japan	321	12.5	Poland	113	16.1
Italy	308	13.5			

Clearly, the Japanese appear more anxious than the Americans or British, but less so than students in India and some other European countries.

From the Cattell 16 PF, Tsujioka and Cattell extracted four second-order factors which showed a very similar structure in Japanese and American subjects. On the first two factors, Japanese were significantly higher in Anxiety and Invia (Introversion). The third and fourth factors are less reliable.

The most extensive surveys, covering Japanese and English college students, children, and adult psychiatric cases, were those of Iwawaki, Oyama *et al.* (1970, p. 232), using the Maudsley Personality Inventory (MPI); and Iwawaki, Eysenck, and Eysenck (1977, 1980, p. 232), using the Eysenck Personality Questionnaire (EPQ or PEN test). In the first of these, Japanese college students were a little more extraverted and much more neurotic than English students. Results are given also for high school students, mature adults, patients, and criminals. Psychoneurotics and psychosomatics averaged 31 points on the Neurotic scale versus 24 points among students, which suggests that this scale at least is as valid a discriminator in Japan as in England.

In the 1977 investigation with the EPQ, Iwawaki and Eysenck found that Japanese students had higher scores on all three scales: Neuroticism (N), Introversion (I), and Psychoticism (P). Among Japanese children, N and P scores were higher at most ages, but elementary school children tended to be more extraverted, and secondary students more introverted. In both countries, the psychotics, especially the Japanese, were high on the P scale.

Iwawaki and Eysenck (Iwawaki *et al.*, 1980) gave the Junior EPI to large groups of Japanese and English children, respectively. All items were factor-analyzed within each group and within sexes and rotated by Varimax to yield the four factors covered by the test—N, E (extraversion), P, and Lie (L) Scale. Comparisons of the factor loadings in the different groups yielded congruence coefficients of .945 to .999, with three minor exceptions: namely, .86 to .89 for the L and P scales, which are known to be less reliable than N and E. Thus, it can be claimed that virtually the same factors appear in both sexes and both ethnic groups. This contrasts with wider-ranging tests like the Cattell 16 PF, where the primary factor structure sometimes differs considerably in different countries. However, several Eysenck items showed some variations in factor loadings, and a new, abbreviated version of the test was drawn up, consisting only of items that had been shown to have high and consistent loadings in all groups. Rescoring these items yielded means for the ethnic and sex groups that are directly comparable. The main result was that the Japanese scored much the same as English in neuroticism, though there were some differences on the other three scales.

Two other studies by Nishiyama (1973, p. 232) and Mahler (1976, p. 232) used the California Personality Inventory and Tennessee Self-Concept scale, respectively. Japanese college students were found to be less socially adjusted and poorer in Self-Esteem than Americans.

Finally, Hama (1966) reported on the Minnesota Multiphasic Personality Inventory in Japan. He gave it to 80 college students and 30 depressive patients. The latter group showed the same score pattern as is commonly found in the United States, namely high Depression, Psychasthenia, and Schizophrenia. The normal controls scored in the normal range on all scales apart from a slight tendency for the men to show abnormal Depression.

Thus, there is considerable consistency between different investigations in this area. All of them tend to show Japanese as more neurotic (or anxious) and introverted, except those that involve children of 8 to 15 years. Moreover, several different tests were used. Almost all the studies were conducted between 1961 and 1977, so the findings are, presumably, still valid. At the same time, one still has doubts as to whether Japanese subjects react in the same way to personal questions as whites, and whether the tests are measuring the same qualities. Iwawaki *et al.* (1980) claim that this is true of the EPQ. Fortunately, some more objective indicators of anxiety and introversion have been used in two studies of national differences by Lynn (1971) and Lynn and Hampson (1975).

STUDIES OF NATIONAL DIFFERENCES IN PERSONALITY

Lynn collected a number of medical, social, and other statistics from 18 Western-type countries (including Japan, but not China). The various indexes showed substantial intercorrelations that, when factor analyzed, yielded a bipolar factor with Suicide rate, Alcoholism, and Vehicle Accident rate at one pole, and low Mental Illness (Psychoses), Coronary Death rate, and Calorie Consumption at the opposite pole. From other sources, Lynn provides considerable evidence that this factor corresponds to a personality factor of anxiety (or neuroticism) versus stability. The highest anxiety scores were found in Japan, Germany, Austria, and France, and the lowest in Canada, United States, New Zealand, United Kingdom, and Ireland (bottom). He also found a high correlation between Anxiety and Rate of Economic Growth, though not with an index of Need for Achievement. In 8 of the 18 countries, samples of college students had taken Cattell's 16 PF test or his Anxiety questionnaire, and here too, France, Japan, and Germany obtained the highest means; Canada, United States, and United Kingdom were the lowest. Lynn believes that his data support the view that there are underlying genetic temperamental (as well as cultural) differences between nations, though he admits that there is some possibility that climatic differences in different parts of the world might be partly involved.

In a further study, Lynn and Hampson (1977) added a number of demographic variables which were available for the 18 countries and which were believed to be associated with extraversion–introversion and bear little relation to neuroticism or anxiety. Factor analysis of all these variables did indeed show two orthogonal factors, the first being anxiety, while the second loaded most highly on cigarette consumption (already known to be related to extraversion), crime, murder and divorce rates, and illegitimacy. When the 18 nations were scored on both, those highest in neuroticism were Austria, Japan, and France (as before); the lowest New Zealand, United Kingdom, and Ireland. On the new factor the United States was much the most extraverted, whereas Japan was lowest, that is, most introverted, accompanied by Holland and Norway.

It would be difficult to define precisely what is meant by the neuroticism or introversion of the Japanese nation. But Lynn's variables were chosen for probable relation to these personality traits, and they did fall into the hypothesized clusters and yielded national differences that agree closely with those suggested by the more subjective and questionable self-report techniques. Another striking point is that the two factors covered 50% of the total variance between national means, which is a high figure for personality research.

Some further studies of national groups, using different tests, are described later (e.g., McClelland, 1961; Morris and Jones, 1955).

Another relevant investigation by Eysenck (1977) was based on blood groups. Apparently three times as many Japanese as English belong to the *AB* group. Also, the Japanese *B/A* ratio is much higher. These physiological differences are certainly genetic, and Eysenck claims that *AB* individuals tend to be introverted, andf *B > A* to be highly emotional. This would fit in with Lynn's findings. But even if confirmed it would not, of course, mean that cultural factors are not also involved in group personality differences.

ALCOHOLISM

Many surveys have found much less drunkenness and alcoholism among Chinese and Japanese than whites in America (Wolff, 1972; Ewing, Rouse, & Pellizzari, 1974; Sue, Zane, & Ito, 1979). This is generally attributed entirely to differences in cultural norms. Many Orientals do drink alcohol, but only in moderation, and they strongly disapprove of drunkenness. But the previously mentioned authors state that there are good grounds for believing that Orientals differ biologically in autonomic reactivity. As with Eskimos and native Indians, fairly small amounts of alcohol have adverse effects—flushing, dizziness, and muscular incoordination. Even young babies flush more than white babies when administered small doses of alcohol. It may be then that the cultural norms have developed in order to control this weakness.

Ewing *et al.* compared 24 Caucasians and 24 Asians (including 11 Chinese and 5 Japanese), working at an American university. They were given controlled amounts of alcohol, proportional to their body weights, and were tested with a breathalyzer and observed before and up to 2 hours after. Seventeen Asians, but no Caucasians, showed flushing and increased heart rate up to 1 hour after. They reported dizziness, weakness, etc., whereas the Caucasians reported feeling happy and relaxed. Similarly, Wolff found flushing among 76% of 117 Chinese, Japanese, and Korean adults and infants, whereas this occurred in only two cases out of 54 Caucasians. A questionnaire that dealt with personal and parental drinking habits and attitudes given to 24 JA, 23 CA, and 77 whites indicated 43% of Orientals and 14% of whites to be abstainers or light drinkers; 34 and 66% respectively, were heavy or very heavy drinkers (Sue *et al.*, 1979). The length of time since their ancestors immigrated, and the inability to speak an oriental language, correlated positively with drinking, presumably because the more frequent drinkers were more acculturated to American habits. Finally, Sue reports a marked increase in drunkenness in present-day Japan.

JAPANESE AMERICANS AND HAWAIIANS

Studies of the emotional stability or anxiety, and extraversion of Japanese Americans in Hawaii or mainland United States have yielded quite similar results to those of JJ. Strong (1934) cited results obtained by University of Hawaii students on the Bernreuter Personality Inventory in the early 1930s, finding them to be less self-sufficient and dominant than whites, and more introverted. Smith (1938) verified this by giving the Thurstone Inventory to 675 students who were of mixed race at the same university. The mean scores are of interest; high scores represent more neurotic.

	N	Mean
Part-Hawaiian	121	61.4
Portuguese	77	57.1
Chinese	125	56.2
Japanese	208	54.4
Caucasian	114	51.6
Other groups	30	—

Both Japanese and Chinese were more neurotic than whites, but less so than Hawaiians or Portuguese. However, the differences are fairly small (mostly not significant), indicating much overlapping. Smith also describes differences on different types, or clusters, of items. The Japanese were subject to many specific fears, somatic complaints, and difficulties in family relations. But they were close to whites in self-confidence and social adjustment. The Chinese were similar, but oversubmissive and fearful.

In 1943 she gave an abbreviated form of the inventory to 285 students, mostly female (Smith, 1945). Increases were expected in neurotic scores because of wartime anxieties. But actually almost all ethnic groups scored lower. However, Japanese women showed no change, and Japanese men did increase from the 1938 mean, suggesting that they were more affected than other groups. But we should recognize that the samples attending college in 1943 were unlikely to be representative ones.

In 1945 (p. 232), Kuhlen used a different instrument that has now gone out of fashion—the Pressey Cross-Out Test. The subjects cross out from long lists of words things that they disapprove of, worry about, or are interested in, etc. By contrasting the responses of different age groups, a score for Emotional Immaturity can be obtained. Much greater immaturity was found among Japanese and Chinese high school students in Hawaii than among whites. Their maturity level at Grade 12 was equivalent to that of Caucasians at Grades 7–8. They also crossed out many more worries. Kuhlen noted that Japanese were more concerned with concrete specific items (e.g., Crime), whereas whites of the same age were more concerned with abstract, general concepts (e.g., Immodesty). However, the differences are so big that one wonders whether the Orientals understood the instructions to cross out items in the same way as whites.

Meredith (1966) discusses the Japanese concept of *amǎe*—the basic need for dependency, love, and emotional bonds with people—as the cause of adjustment difficulties among Japanese students, and their apparent lack of leadership potential (see also Meredith & Meredith, 1966; Takahashi, 1974). He gave the Cattell 16 PF test to 154 JA and 140 whites, including both sexes, and found significant differences on the following traits or factors. Japanese males, as contrasted with white males, were more:

submissive (E−)	tense (Q4+)
diffident (H−)	affected by feelings (C−)
reserved (A−)	conscientious (G+)
serious (F−)	socially precise (Q3+)
regulated (M−)	unpretentious (N−)
apprehensive (O+)	

Females were also high in E−, H−, A−, O+, Q4+, and in L+ (suspicious) and Q2− (group dependent). He argues that these findings confirm the theory of *amae*. But it would have been more convincing had he been able to hypothesize beforehand just which traits or factors would be stronger or weaker in Japanese than whites, and then see if these were confirmed. The same criticism applies to several other studies involving tests of multiple traits. It is far too easy to read into a pattern or profile of scores what one believes about the oriental personality.

Earlier (1964, p. 233), Meredith had given the 16 PF test to college students in Hawaii, and found the JA to get higher Anxiety and Invia (Introversion) scores than the Americans. He also tested Japanese students who were taking a remedial speech course to reduce their usage of pidgin English. These obtained even higher scores on the two factors than the normal Sansei. Meredith interprets this as a reaction against the majority culture and its speech.

Sue and Kirk (1972, 1973, p. 233) and Sue and Sue (1974, p. 233) studied oriental personality characteristics at the University of California, Berkeley, where all incoming students took a battery of ability and personality tests. According to the Omnibus Personality Inventory, Japanese preferred structured situations, and disliked unconventionality or novelty; they avoided social contacts. The Chinese were similar, and both groups were predominantly introverted. On the MMPI orientals tended to obtain higher psychotic scores, showing many somatic complaints, family problems, and social introversion. Sue suggests that oriental college students show more pathology than whites because they are under abnormal pressures to get good degrees, knowing that they will need higher qualifications than whites to obtain comparable jobs. Sue and Sue (1971) point out, though, that they seldom make use of facilities for psychological counseling or therapy, since they and their families try to conceal such weaknesses, which nevertheless find expression in the answers to personality questionnaires.

The only relevant study of children seems to be that of Werner et al. (1968), described in Chapter 7. No personality tests were given, but on the basis of clinical interviews of 10-year-old children in Kauai, she found that the proportion of Japanese with emotional and behavior problems was 18.6%, compared with 27.8 to 34.8% of Hawaiians, Caucasians, Filipinos, and Portuguese. However by that date (late 1960s) the Japanese in Hawaii had become highly acculturated. In the 1930s and 40s there might well have been more strain, and conflicts within Japanese families, as well as with other ethnic groups (see also Tuddenham, 1970, p. 203).

In Chapter 7, I mentioned the early work of Porteus and Babcock in Hawaii in the 1920s, showing Japanese to be the best socially adjusted group in Hawaii (followed by the Chinese). This finding was based on ratings given by experienced educators and others, and it referred to ethnic groups as a whole rather than to the actual test scores of children or adults. However, in another much later study of personality ratings by teachers (Dixon, Fukuda, & Berens, 1968) Japanese high school students did not differ significantly from other ethnicities in such traits as initiative, leadership, and self-confidence. It is difficult to reconcile these findings with the emotional instability claimed by Smith, Kuhlen, Meredith, Sue, and others. The differences do not seem to be associated with the date of testing, nor the degree of acculturation of successive generations. However, as with Japanese subjects in Japan, investigations based on unselected groups of children are more favorable to Japanese mental health than those derived from oriental college and high school students, who are likely to be highly selected, and to be working under great strain.

EDWARDS PERSONAL PREFERENCE SCHEDULE

Because of the susceptibility of most personality questionnaires to faking, or giving socially desirable responses, a great deal of research has been done with the Edwards Personal Preference Schedule (EPPS). This yields scores for 15 of Murray's needs. Each item involves a choice between two statements, which express different needs. But the statements in each pair were chosen to be of approximately equal social desirability, so that it was hoped that subjects would be forced to choose on a basis of need, not of acceptability.

The earliest comparison of needs between Japanese and white Americans by Fujita (1957, p. 233) failed to reveal any significant differences. But subsequent studies by Arkoff, Meredith, Berrien (pp. 233–234) and collaborators between 1959 and 1967 have yielded a fairly consistent pattern. Most of them were conducted at the University of Hawaii. It would be far too voluminous to reproduce the results for both sexes in all these studies. But in Table 14.1, I have extracted the mean scores for three groups of Japanese males, two white groups, and one Chinese group. These were rank-ordered (i.e., highest to lowest need scores in each group), and intercorrelations are given in Table B.1 (p. 233).

The first two groups of Japanese Hawaiians are closely similar ($\rho = .85$), as are the two sets of Caucasian figures ($\rho = .82$); the Chinese show quite a similar pattern to the Japanese (mean $\rho = .81$). But the third Japanese group, tested in Japan, differs considerably from Hawaiian Japanese and Chinese (mean $\rho = .52$), and still more so from whites (.27). Let us pick out the needs showing greatest differences. Japanese Hawaiians, compared with whites, are higher in Abasement, Deference, Nurturance, Endurance, and Order. But they are lower in Dominance, Achievement, Exhibition, and Heterosexuality.

This fits in quite well with the common stereotype of Japanese as being overpolite and submissive, but high in persistence and carefulness. The high Nurturance score confirms Meredith's views on the importance of *amae*, or dependence. They also do not want to show off or display sexual feelings, as westerners do. Their low Achievement score will be commented on later.

The Japanese in Japan differ from those in Hawaii in being high in Succorance, Heterosexuality, Autonomy, and Endurance, and lower in Nurturance, Deference, and Exhibition.

This does not sound so plausible but—as pointed out by Merdith (1965)—cultural norms in Japan have changed since 1946 in the direction of more independence and less submissiveness.

TABLE 14.1
Scores of Japanese and Other Student Groups on the Edwards Personal Preference Schedule

Needs	Samples					
	137 JA[a]	560 JA[b]	458 JJ[c]	155 CA[b]	US Norms[a]	146 Whites[b]
Deference	13.28	12.24	10.08	12.70	11.21	10.63
Dominance	13.28	13.17	12.49	13.22	17.44	14.92
Abasement	15.75	15.91	16.31	15.02	12.24	13.73
Aggression	12.38	12.27	13.05	11.88	12.79	14.49
Nurturance	17.31	16.39	13.04	15.20	14.04	13.24
Succorance	11.28	11.61	15.09	11.47	10.74	10.81
Affiliation	15.46	15.68	15.04	14.92	15.00	13.69
Autonomy	13.35	12.35	15.23	11.78	14.34	14.73
Achievement	13.17	14.15	12.65	13.70	15.66	14.93
Exhibition	11.55	12.93	10.17	13.80	14.40	16.17
Order	11.60	12.09	10.73	13.47	10.23	9.89
Change	15.92	16.78	16.19	17.18	15.51	17.32
Endurance	13.91	15.58	16.49	15.88	12.66	13.92
Intraception	16.83	14.22	16.05	14.22	16.12	14.61
Heterosexuality	14.83	14.14	17.35	14.63	17.65	17.74

[a] Arkoff (1959)
[b] Fenz & Arkoff (1962)
[c] Berrien (1966)

Compared with whites, JJ are strong in Abasement, Succorance, and Endurance; low in Dominance, Achievement, and Exhibition. These are quite similar to the differences mentioned between Hawaiian Japanese and whites. But Berrien (1966, p. 234) believes that the high Abasement score in all Japanese groups indicates a continuing reluctance to take leadership and responsibility. He quotes a study of local volunteer firefighters in the United States and Japan. In the former, local initiative and leadership are encouraged, whereas in Japan the units are bureaucratically organized from above.

Other points of interest from investigations with the EPPS include Arkoff's (1959, p. 233) comparison of Nisei and Sansei students in Hawaii. In many respects the Sansei were moving closer to the American pattern. Another generational study by Berrien, Arkoff, and Iwihara (1967, p. 234) compared sons and daughters at college (both JA and JJ) with their fathers and mothers. Again, the trend was for the younger generation to approximate more closely to whites. Arkoff, Meredith, and Jones (1961, p. 234) found few if any significant differences in EPPS scores between Sansei students from rural and from urban families.

Dixon, Fukuda, and Berens (1970, p. 234) factor analyzed EPPS and ability scores, and teachers' ratings among JA high school boys and girls. Though no sex differences in means are reported, there were certain differences in the underlying factor structures.

Arkoff, Meredith, and Iwihara (1962, p. 234) constructed a short scale of 20 items that contrasted Dominance with Deference only. As would be expected, the whites were highest in Dominance, while JJ came next and Hawaiian JA last. Differences among females were in the same direction, but smaller.

A recent study by Connor (1974a,b, 1976, p. 234) included several hundred Caucasians and JA. The Japanese represented three generations—Issei, Nisei, and Sansei—whose mean ages were 72, 49, and 24 years. Caucasians were chosen to match the Japanese age distributions. This was the first EPPS study to be based on mature adults as well as college students, and it showed very large age changes in JA and Caucasians. The younger the generation, the greater the decline (among males) in Deference, Order, Abasement, and Endurance, and the higher the scores in Exhibition, Intraception, Change, Heterosexuality, and Aggression. All these differences apply to females also, except for Aggression.

The Sansei scores approximate fairly closely to the figures for JA, given in Table 14.1. Though there has clearly been some acculturation, this resemblance is partly due to the groups being of the same age.

Connor (1974b) claims that the major needs of Japanese in Japan are collectivity, duty, obligation, hierarchy, deference, and dependence. Whereas the major needs of Americans are individualism, rights and privileges, equality, self-reliance, and self-assertion (see Chapter 4). These, he considers, overlap quite closely with Edwards' 15 needs, and the scores obtained by JJ generally bear out his expectations, with a few exceptions.

An investigation of Japanese values by Scanlon, Dixon et al. (1980, p. 235) gave the EPPS scores of 132 JJ secondary school students. These closely resembled the figures reported by Berrien in 1966, with the exception that Heterosexuality had dropped from top of the list to ninth place. The only explanation that comes to mind is that 15- to 17-year-old students may be more apt to conceal sexual need than Berrien's college students.

We may conclude that the various studies of JA students show considerable stability in EPPS scores, though there are marked differences between JA and JJ, and also between generation and age groups.

After Berrien completed his extensive survey in Japan (1966), he turned to criticizing cross-cultural applications of tests like EPPS or Gordon's Personal Values test (Berrien, 1968). He found that items that had been paired for social desirability in the American standardization often obtained very different desirability values in Japan. He suggests overcoming this by rearranging the items in a Japanese version to yield more closely matched pairs. This seems a wise precaution, though it would imply that comparisons between JJ and whites would be based on nonidentical tests.

In two other studies by Fujita (1957), and Klett and Yaukey (1959) the social desirability of individual items was rated by various groups of students. Fujita found JA and United States ratings to be quite similar. Klett and Yaukey compared JA, American, and Norwegian students, and Arabs at the American University of Beirut, and obtained correlations ranging from .74 to .96 between the item ratings of different groups. This substantial agreement between different cultures indicates that the test can be used cross-culturally.

NEED FOR ACHIEVEMENT

In view of the high educational and occupational motivation of Japanese in Japan or in the United States, it seems curious that their Need for Achievement scores are consistently lower than those of whites. However, this is confirmed by McClelland's (1961) well-known study of achievement motivation in 30 different countries, based on content analysis of children's stories. In 1950, the mean scores of American and Japanese students were 2.24 and 1.29 (in standard deviation units).[1] Hayashi and Habo (1962) applied McClelland's method of testing to Japanese students in an achievement-oriented situation, and they claim similar results.[2]

However, Maloney (1968) points out that both McClelland's concept and the EPPS items involve social recognition of high achievement. This egocentric motivation is quite foreign to Japanese values, which stress collective obligations to the family or firm (see also Berrien, 1965). Connor (1976) adds that Japanese strive to achieve goals laid down for them by others, rather than by self-choice.

Sloggett, Gallimore, and Kubany (1970, p. 235) gave a TAT-like test of 12 pictures to small groups of Hawaiians, Japanese, and Filipinos, and scored them for Need for Achievement by McClelland's method. Here the Japanese did obtain the highest mean, and the Hawaiians the lowest. But the Hawaiians were collected from two schools, one with a very high reputation for achievement, the other very low. Yet there was no significant difference between them on the TAT test, suggesting that the test does not measure the same need in different cultures. Subsequently, Gallimore (1974) scored for Need for Affiliation, and found that this correlated better with achievement among Hawaiians than did the Achievement score.

An attempt was made by Hayashi, Rim, and Lynn (1970, p. 235) to explore some aspects of McClelland's theories by obtaining occupational preferences of

---

[1]Berrien (1965) quotes the means as +0.32 and −0.95, respectively. I could not find these in McClelland's book, but they also show that Japanese are lower than whites on this measure of Need for Achievement.

[2]Seen in abstract only.

students in two high-economic growth countries—Japan and Israel, and in two low-growth countries—the United Kingdom and Ireland. It was predicted that young adults in the former countries would prefer business to professional occupations. However, the Japanese rated Teacher, Professor, and Artist as highly as they did Independent Businessman. It was also predicted that students in high-growth countries would give higher ratings to their most preferred occupation. Actually, the Japanese figure was insignificantly higher than the British or Irish. The Israeli students did confirm this prediction because, working at a technological university, they gave very high ratings to the occupation Engineer. Here too, then, the Japanese failed to show Need for Achievement in a situation designed for Occidentals.

One further study of achievement motivation by Ōnoda (1976, p. 235) required 144 JA high school students to pick out adjectives that fitted them from Gough's Adjective Checklist. By comparing their school grades with their intelligence test scores, they were classified into High or Low Achievers. It was found that the Highs claimed significantly more positive traits than the Lows. For example, the former stressed self-controlled, serious, sober, responsible, intelligent, confident, strong-willed, forceful, and dominant, whereas the Lows were more often rebellious, arrogant, careless, conceited, cynical, headstrong, irresponsible, complaining, disorderly, impulsive, etc. The research was not intended to provide any comparisons between Japanese and other cultures, but the results do suggest that present-day Japanese High Achievers have retained much of the traditional Nisei values, though at the same time they are no longer typically quiet or meek.

RESPONSE SETS

It has been shown by Cronbach (1970) and others, that people who take self-report tests, which offer a range of possible responses (e.g., Strongly Agree, Agree, Doubtful, Disagree, Strongly Disagree) may differ consistently in their usage of the scale. For example, some may accept many items, while others disagree with more. This is referred to as the *acquiescence response set*. Again, some may use the Strongly answers more frequently, and others the Doubtful or Undecided responses. This is referred to as the *extremeness, or Impulsive versus Cautious, response set*. Note that these sets are quite independent of the content of the items or the object of the test.

Iwawaki and Cowen (1964) obtained ratings (on a 7-point scale) of the social desirability or undesirability of 148 adjectives referring to personality characteristics. Sixty-five JJ college students and 39 whites were compared. The Japanese gave more cautious or middling ratings, whereas the Americans gave more Highly Desirable or Highly Undesirable ratings. Though there was very close agreement between the mean ratings of the adjectives in the two groups (r = .895), it was noticeable that the Japanese tended to give high ratings to adjectives suggesting cautious, meticulous, suppressive traits, whereas the Americans favored traits implying frankness and impulsiveness.

In a similar study by Zax and Takahashi (1967, p. 235), JJ and American students rated Rorschach inkblots on Semantic Differential scales. They showed that Americans of both sexes gave more extreme responses than Japanese, and fewer neutral or cautious responses. Iwawaki, Zax, and Mitsuoka (1969) found increasing cautiousness from Grade 4 to Grade 12 children (see also Stricker, Takahashi, & Zax, 1967).

In all of these studies the raters were not rating themselves or other people, only items or pictures. But Gordon and Kikuchi (1970, p. 235) obtained similar results with a self-report test. The numbers of extreme responses did not differ significantly between ethnic groups, but the percentage of undecided responses was much higher among Japanese. The authors suggest that this "cautiousness" might be due partly to Japanese politeness; that is, they respond with "Undecided" when they really mean "Disagree," but do not want to criticize the test or the tester.

Similarly Chun, Campbell, and Yoo (1974, p. 235) gave a 133-item attitude scale to Korean and American college students. Each item was answered on a 5-point scale. Thus, the standard deviation (S.D.) of responses to any item would give a measure of extremeness, or middlingness. The mean S.D.s were higher among Americans than Koreans.

Ayabe and Santo (1972) hypothesized that Japanese and Chinese children would be more cautious than whites in responding to Kagan's Matching Familiar Figures test. Groups of 30 Japanese, Chinese, Filipino, Hawaiian, Portuguese, and Samoan children in Grade 2 were given the test with one of three sets of instructions:

1. Work as fast as possible.
2. No mention of speed.
3. Work slowly and think about your answers.

No reliable ethnic differences were found under instructions 2 and 3, but under instruction 1 (fast conditions) the oriental groups gave significantly fewer wrong answers.

Hatano and Imagaki (1976) gave the Matching Familiar Figures and another perceptual choice test, along with two conceptual choice tests to 51 JJ children aged 5-6 years. They were mainly concerned to establish that there was some generality or consistency among different tests of impulsiveness–reflectiveness, and this was confirmed. The reflective child is one who spends some time searching for fuller information before he commits himself to a decision. The authors also state that, in an earlier experiment, Japanese children were found to be much more reflective and cautious than American white children.

OBJECTIVE TESTS

Some studies have been based on more objective measures of behavior than self-report tests, ratings, or interviews. McMichael and Grinder (1964) compared resistance to temptation and guilt feelings among 15 JA and 8 white students in Hawaii, aged 12–13 years. The first test involved aiming a gun at a rotating target. This was done unsupervised, so that it was easy to fake good scores. The second test consisted of stories about transgressions, and the children's reactions to these were scored for guilt feelings. The Japanese obtained slightly higher scores on the guilt test, but showed less cheating in the aiming test. However, neither difference was statistically significant, which is only to be expected with such small numbers.

Cattell, Schmidt, and Pawlik (1973, p. 236) applied some of Cattell's 440 objective or behavioral tests of personality factors. Seventy-one of these, together with the CPQ or HSPQ (personality quizzes) were given to JA, white American, and Austrian boys, aged 12–14. Twelve personality factors were found to match one another in the three groups and to agree with previous studies. However, some of the congruence coefficients, showing agreement between factors in different groups, dropped to quite low values; the median figure was only .36. No comparisons were made between group scores, since Cattell's aim was only to demonstrate similar personality structures across cultures.

In order to explore the general belief that Japanese tend to hide their feelings, Lazarus, Opton, Tomita, and Kodama (1966) studied the psychogalvanic reactions (GSR) of 80 JJ students and 48 adults to emotionally stressful stimuli. First, an innocuous 10-minute film of rural life was shown, and the subjects rated on a 7-point scale their "degree of distress" at several time intervals. This was followed by a very stressful film of mutilation of adolescent genitals, and the ratings were repeated. In addition, some MMPI scales, including Denial of Symptoms, were given. In an earlier study in the United States, Americans showed enormous rises in distress ratings and GSR inductance at the second film. But only a small proportion of the Japanese reacted so strongly, and the relation of their responses to film content was less marked than in the whites. Indeed, they actually showed a larger initial rise in GSR during the benign film. Yet at the same time, the distress ratings did closely resemble those of whites. No interaction was found with MMPI scores. The authors believe that the anomalous Japanese reaction occurred because they always tend to feel threatened and anxious in situations where they are observed and evaluated by others, and this outweighed any variations attributable to the film content.

EXPRESSION OF EMOTIONS

It is generally believed that Orientals express (or conceal) emotions very differently from Caucasians. But several studies appear to show considerable consistency of emotional expressions across cultures, thus confirming Darwin's theory. Vinacke (1949b) and Vinacke and Fong (1955) collected from periodicals pictures of 20 Caucasian and 28 oriental persons in emotional situations. These were shown to Japanese, Chinese, and white students at the University of Hawaii. A list of 30 names of emotions was provided, and the subjects chose the name they regarded as most appropriate to each picture. The faces alone were shown first, and then the whole person and situation. The most common response for each photograph was determined, and the percentage of judges who gave these responses were as follows. With Caucasian faces, 25% of subjects (judges) agreed, and with the situations, 34% did so. The corresponding frequencies for oriental faces were 29 and 46%. The three ethnic groups were quite similar in their overall agreement, though the degree of consensus for particular pictures often varied. Each group included males and females, and the two sexes gave more consistent responses than did the three ethnic groups. Also, Japanese and Chinese agreed more closely than did either with whites.

Boucher and Carlson (1980) used similar materials—namely, photographs of six emotional expressions portrayed by both Americans and Malaysians. These were judged by 53 American and 30 Malaysian students, who tried to identify the correct names for 67 photos in all. Correct labeling was as follows:

	American judges	Malaysian judges
American faces	84.8%	68.8
Malaysian faces	68.9	60.0

Although the Malaysian students were less accurate, the majority of both groups correctly identified all emotions but Fear. Thirty-one Temuan aboriginals judged the American faces by a simpler method, and they obtained 79.5% correct, though they had had scarcely any experience with Caucasians. This close similarity in judging facial expressions of emotions by three very different ethnic groups could hardly be explained by any kind of social learning theory of emotional recognition.

Iwawaki and Lerner (1976) measured the agreement between Japanese and Americans and between the sexes in attributing personality traits to particular kinds of body physique. A set of side views (without heads) of a mesomorph male, an ectomorph, and an endomorph was prepared, together with a list of 56 trait-names. The subjects—180 JJ college students—were asked to assign each trait to one or another of the pictures. The percentages of agreement on different traits were converted to correlations and factor analyzed to yield three principal components. After rotation these components corresponded closely to the traits normally attributed by Caucasians to persons of mesomorphic, ectomorphic, and endomorphic physique. As in earlier studies (Lerner & Korn, 1972), mesomorphic received the most positive qualities, endomorphic the least. The congruence coefficients between the factor loadings in the different sex, age, and ethnic groups mostly exceeded .90. Indeed the median correlation was .93 between Japanese and American factors. This again shows an unexpected degree of cross-cultural consistency.

Engebretson and Fullmer (1970) studied the "territoriality" of JJ, JA, and American students, that is, the distance that two persons who are intercommunicating prefer to keep from one another (see also Engebretson, 1972). Both Japanese and Americans are rather "low-contact" people, but probably Japanese keep their distance more than Americans. Fifty-six JJ studying in Hawaii, 50 JA, and 44 American students placed six pairs of silhouette figures on felt pads, according to the distance that they preferred. The persons included two students, two friends, student with father, and student with professor (usually the most distant). The actual mean differences in twelfths of an inch were 29.3, JJ; 23.3, JA; 24.1, United States. There is a significant difference between JJ and JA or Americans, but not between JA and the United States. The JA students were Sansei, who still think of themselves as culturally different from Caucasians, and yet they do not differ in this aspect of social behavior.

OBSERVATIONAL AND INTERVIEW STUDIES

The development of young children and their behavior at play are best studied by direct observation, preferably in the home. Or, the mothers' accounts of behavior can be gathered by interview, though we should be prepared for these to be considerably distorted. In the elementary school years, children can answer oral questions about their preferences, etc., but written questionnaires are inappropriate until later, when their reading and writing are adequate.

Caudill and Winstein (1969) and Caudill and Schooler (1973) observed 30 JJ babies, and 30 middle-class white babies, all aged 3–4 months. Each child was watched for 4 hours on 2 days, and time sampling was used; that is, their behavior was recorded under 12 headings at regular intervals, and the behavior of the mother or caretaker under 15 headings.

Presumably the biological needs of the two groups of infants are the same,

TABLE 14.2
Percentages of Preferences for Different Types of Play among Japanese and American Children (Seagoe and Murakami, 1961)

	JJ		US		JA	
Type of Play	Grade 1	Grade 6	Grade 1	Grade 6	Grade 1	Grade 6
Dramatic	22	11	17	2	28	0
Group activities	50	36	18	17	27	9
Individual activities	13	4	27	11	22	19
Team competitions	5	29	17	40	35	42
Individual competition	3	11	4	5	3	5
Passive participation	7	9	5	1	7	5

actual IQs at 6 years correlated with mother expectations. Thus, this investigation of differences between Japanese and Western young children accords well with the previous ones using more direct observation.

Tuddenham, Brooks, and Milkovich (1974) carried out an extensive study of mothers' ratings of their 9- to 11-year-old children by administering questionnaires when the mothers attended the Kaiser Foundation Health Clinic. (All children had been born at Kaiser Plan hospitals.) There were 2212 whites, 641 blacks, 117 Orientals, and 79 Chicanos (total, 3049). Obviously, such a sample would tend to be better able to take a relatively objective view of their offspring, and about one-third did in fact report unfavorable aspects of behavior. Printed on cards, one hundred questions could be answered "True," "Not True," or "Uncertain." The whole procedure took only about 15 minutes per parent. A few of the main demographic statistics appear in Table 14.3. Clearly, the oriental parents have somewhat superior SES and education to the whites.

TABLE 14.3
Characteristics of Kaiser Plan Parents of Different Ethnicity (Tuddenham *et al.*, 1974)

Characteristics	Whites	Oriental	Black	Chicano
Father's occupation				
Professional or semiprofessional	42.8%	52.2%	16.3%	13.9%
Unskilled, manual, or unemployed	38.8	27.3	66.6	73.4
Graduate education or some college				
Father	58.3	71.9	33.0	19.0
Mother	52.5	65.8	43.6	15.2
Less than eighth grade education				
Father	1.2	0.0	8.2	16.5
Mother	0.6	0.0	4.1	13.9
Mean income	$15,349	$16,005	$11,613	$10,911

TABLE 14.4

Problem Behaviors of Children in Four Ethnic Groups as Assessed by Mothers (Tuddenham et al., 1974)

Behavior	White		Oriental		Black		Chicano	
	Boys	Girls	Boys	Girls	Boys	Girls	Boys	Girls
Wets bed occasionally	14.6%	5.6%	8.8%	0.0%	18.0%	9.9%	19.6%	0.0%
Bites nails	16.9	19.6	8.8	6.1	16.3	25.8	19.6	27.3
Hates to sit still, restless	38.9	26.5	35.3	30.6	52.5	43.6	47.8	36.4
Often seems tired	8.6	9.8	2.9	14.3	14.1	12.1	17.4	15.2
Not truthful, tells lies	10.8	8.2	8.8	8.2	30.7	23.6	23.9	18.2
Stays away from home without permission	6.9	4.1	0.0	0.0	15.6	8.3	15.2	9.1
Lot of fears and worries	11.7	11.3	17.6	6.1	9.2	8.6	15.2	15.2
Shy, bashful	18.9	23.1	35.3	42.9	30.4	33.4	28.3	42.4
Flares up, gets mad easily	25.6	16.2	13.2	10.2	28.7	23.6	41.3	18.2
Likes to tease others	34.2	18.2	20.6	12.2	37.0	32.5	41.3	30.3

A few of the questionnaire items, dealing with maladjustment and troublesome behavior, are shown in Table 14.4. These also differed considerably between ethnic groups. Sex differences also are indicated.

On most items the oriental children show less maladjustment and better behavior. But Shy, Bashful did occur more frequently than among the whites, blacks, and Chicanos.

A similar study was carried out by Kurokawa (1969) on the basis of interviews of 130 Kaiser Plan oriental mothers of boys or girls, aged 10–15 years. There were 151 such children. From the mothers' reports the liability of their children to any kind of accident was assessed, and this was related to various background factors. Generally, the oriental children had lower accident-susceptibility than whites of the same age group. This the authors attribute to the greater restrictiveness of childrearing, and the lack of encouragement for independence, venturesomeness, or aggressive behavior. In those families that were most acculturated, these American-type qualities were more evident, and they were associated with greater exposure of the children to dangerous situations and more accidents. If the parents were judged to be cold or detached, their children showed greater proneness, and the same occurred with tense or anxious children. It should be remembered that all these findings were derived from mothers' verbal reports, but, as in Tuddenham's study, the mothers were mostly middle- or upper-class and well educated, so their reports should be reasonably objective.

15

Japanese Attitudes, Values, and Interests

INTRODUCTION

It is impossible to distinguish precisely between personality traits, attitudes, values, and interests. Many personal characteristics may belong under more than one of these headings. For example, the "needs" that were discussed in the preceding chapter seem to partake both of traits and attitudes. But I will try to indicate the sense in which I intend to use the terms.

A trait usually describes a certain kind of behavior that is prominent in some persons or lacking in others, for example, irritability or leadership. An attitude more commonly means an emotional reaction (either positive or negative) to certain objects, people, etc., for example, antisemitism. Values are even more equivocal, though they chiefly refer to the more generalized attitudes underlying people's beliefs, or—colloquially—their philosophies of life. Like attitudes, interests are expressive of values; for example, an individual may strongly value aesthetic experience, and this finds expression in his interest in drawing and painting. But an interest differs in having more cognitive content; the individual has a body of knowledge about art and technical skills as well as an emotional reaction to it.

In eliciting and trying to measure these characteristics, psychologists rely very largely on the same methods as are used in studying personality traits, that is, self-report tests and questionnaires, whose weaknesses—especially in cross-cultural research—have already been described. However, quite a wide range of techniques may be employed, some relatively objective, and others that are highly subjective, such as projective techniques.

ATTITUDES

Masculinity–Femininity

Several standard tests such as Strong's Vocational Interest Blank, the MMPI, and the California Personality Inventory yield masculinity versus femininity scores, based on differences in attitudes, feelings, and behavior between the sexes. But the Terman–Miles Attitude-Interest Analysis Test, containing seven varied subtests, gives the greatest coverage. Another approach uses projective devices, such as Franck and Rosen's test based on drawings. It should be noted, however, that the correlations between different instruments are often moderate or even low; hence, it is dubious to interpret scores on any one of them as measuring masculinity–femininity in general.

All of these tests are strongly culture-bound; that is, they mostly reflect the tastes, etc., of Americans. Thus we cannot accept at its face value a score that shows Japanese males to be more effeminate than westerners, since the Japanese do not happen to value many masculine qualities that are conventional in the West.

Meredith (1969, p. 236) compared Japanese and Chinese American and white students on the Terman–Miles test. The American males scored most highly in masculinity, and the females were less feminine than the other groups. Japanese students were the reverse, the males being least masculine, females most feminine. Chinese of both sexes were intermediate between JA and whites.

Using the California Personality Inventory, Gough, Chun, and Chung (1968, p. 236) likewise showed Korean men to be more feminine than Americans, but the women were less feminine. The authors suggest that Korean women are more emancipated and outspoken than elsewhere in Asia. Nishiyama (1975, p. 236) compared the masculinity scores of large groups of students in eight countries. The same difference was found between JJ and American males. The JJ women were more feminine, but American women were quite close to them.

Blane and Yamamoto (1970, p. 237) used Gough's test (abbreviated) with JJ, JA, and whites, together with Franck and Rosen's Drawing Test. The JA male students were closer to whites in masculinity on both tests than the JJ. The authors suggest that males in Japan are recognized as such without having to prove their manliness. Hence, they accept several items that, among whites, go with femininity. But JA females were more feminine than JJ, since the former have retained more of the Meiji tradition, whereas JJ women have become more emancipated since 1946.

Other Marital and Sex Attitudes

Three studies of females emancipation versus male dominance have given quite similar results, with the Japanese males (JJ and JA) being less favorable to emancipation than white males or Japanese females (Arkoff, Meredith, & Dong, 1963, p. 237). But JJ males were more progressive than JA (Arkoff, Meredith, & Iwihara, 1964, p. 237). The difference between JA males and females is probably involved in the much higher marriage rate of JA women to non-Japanese than that of JA males. In a more recent study of JA and white students by Meredith and Ching (1977, p. 237), all groups showed greater acceptance of female emancipation, and there were no significant differences between ethnic groups. But men were still less egalitarian than women.

In a further investigation by Inagaki (1967, p. 237), JJ female students were asked to rate a set of personality items three times: first, for how true of their own self-concept; second, their ideal self; and third, for men's concept of the ideal woman. The items were intended to measure self-oriented versus other-oriented. The results and their interpretation are difficult to follow, but the author claims that they show persistence of the traditional submissive role in present-day Japan. Yet at the same time, many Japanese women wish to copy the more modern American-type role.

Two studies of attitudes to premarital sex or other unconventional sexual activities (Church & Insko, 1965, p. 237; Maykovich, 1976, p. 237) indicated that JA men and women are still more traditional than whites, though they are breaking away from this. Maykovich interviewed 100 JJ and 100 white females, finding that approval or disapproval does not necessarily coincide with actual extramarital activities. Twenty-seven percent of the Japanese women had experienced such sex, very little less than the 32% of American women.

Asayama (1975) studied large groups of JJ adolescents and adults with a questionnaire on sexual behavior. Puberty changes had accelerated between 1950 and 1960, though still lagging 1 or 2 years behind Kinsey's findings for whites. Many activities, such as petting and kissing, and early intercourse, seem to have been taken over from American culture. Premarital sex, birth control, and abortion were more widely accepted, but extramarital sex occurred among 75% of males, and only about 5% of women. Love marriages, rather than arranged marriages, occurred among some 14% of couples in prewar days, but in 31% of couples nowadays.

Inomata and McGinnies (1970, 1971) carried out an even more wide-ranging study of adolescent JJ attitudes, ideals, and values. Over 1500 boys and 2000 girls, aged 11–18, were compared with large American groups. Very detailed tables, which are hard to summarize, are given. Japanese boys had achieved less autonomy or self-determination than American boys; they had fewer responsibilities in the home, and were behindhand in planning a vocation and in dating behavior. Methods of control in the home showed differences, Japanese parents making more use of psychological methods, Americans more use of withdrawal of privileges and, occasionally, physical methods.

Childrearing

Three investigations by Kitano (1961, 1964, p. 238) and Higa (1974, p. 290) used the Parental Attitude Research Instrument (PARI) to assess traditionalist and restrictive versus progressive beliefs about childrearing among Japanese mothers, both JJ and JA. Kitano showed that JA Issei were highly traditional and the Nisei more similar to whites, and that this disagreement led to considerable intergenerational conflicts about child upbringing within the families (see also De Vos, 1955). The younger women were more progressive than the older ones in both countries. Higa tested "war brides," that is, women born in Japan but now living in Hawaii, and found them more progressive than either JJ or JA. Again, the JJ were somewhat more progressive than the JA.

Conroy, et al. (1980) interviewed 58 JA and 67 white mothers of young children, who were matched for SES. The median age of the children was 3:8 years. Six incidents involving conflict between child and parent were presented, and the mothers asked how they would control the child in each situation. Japanese were found to use persuasion and reasoning more frequently than Americans, while the latter resorted more to imperative or moderate demands, sometimes accompanied by external rewards or punishments.[1] The responses were classified as follows:

	JA	Caucasians
Imperative demands	58%	68%
Moderated demands	11	13
Discussion	25	2
Yielding to child	6	7

Matsumoto and Smith (1961) gave a questionnaire to 50 JJ and 18 American elementary school children (Grades 5 and 6). The questionnaire asked about their parents' roles in upbringing, for example, in caretaking, disciplining, playing, and educating. The Japanese perceived the mother's and father's roles as more differentiated, whereas the Americans reported more equality between the parents.

Takahashi (1974) studied the dependency of Japanese girls and women upon their parents and other persons. The author regards this trait as basic in Japanese of all ages (see Meredith's discussion of *Amae*, 1966, p. 190). After analyzing the components of dependency, Takahashi devised a 24-item questionnaire asking whether, in each situation, the person would depend chiefly on Mother, Father, Sibling, Friend, and Lover or Friend of the Opposite Sex. This was given to 168 JJ female college students, 349 high school girls, and 249 junior high school girls. The Mother was rated as high at all ages, though exceeded by a Close Friend in high school, and by Lover in college. Father or Sibling received very few votes. These results are taken from students who nominated the same person for all items; naturally many of the subjects referred to different persons in different situations.

Johnson (1977) studied the family attitudes of 61 Nisei and 43 Sansei by lengthy interviews. In Hawaii, even as late as 1977, there is a great deal of family solidarity and mutual support. The families are nuclear, but numerous kin tend to

---

[1]Note that the classification of Conroy et al. (1980) omits shaming or ridicule as a means of control, which other writers have stressed (see p. 53).

live close together. The Japanese males are still continuously concerned with the favors they receive from others, and how to repay them. Such obligations were stressed by 75% of Nisei and 58% of Sansei. The younger generation even yet do not regard independence as an important goal. They feel less bound by duty towards their parents than in earlier days, but nevertheless do care for them.

Identification with Japan

Meredith constructed an attitude scale for JA on their feelings of identity with Japan. This was given by Masuda, Matsumoto, and Meredith (1970, p. 236) to over 300 Issei, Nisei, and Sansei in Seattle. The expected decline in scores with age was obtained in successive generations. There were no significant sex differences. But when Matsumoto, Meredith, and Masuda (1970) gave the same instrument to 260 JA in Honolulu, they found the Nisei scoring considerably lower than those in Seattle. Indeed, their identification with Japan was little greater than that of Sansei. The authors point out some differences between the two JA samples. In Seattle they constitute a much smaller proportion of the population, and they have not increased much in numbers through further immigration. Probably then the Nisei in Hawaii have become acculturated more rapidly.

Masuda, Hasegawa, and Matsumoto (1973) translated and slightly modified the scale for application in Japan. Three age groups of subjects were chosen to match the Issei, Nisei, and Sansei in the United States. These groups obtained mean scores almost identical with the JA in Seattle. It would seem that JJ have changed in their attitudes over the past 50 years as much as, and in the same direction as have the JA. But it should be pointed out that both the Seattle and Honolulu JA Sansei still retained their pride in many aspects of their traditional culture, and answered several items of the 50-item test in the pro-Japanese direction. JJ youth showed less acceptance of family ties and obligations, and were more individualistic and rebellious than the JA.

Okana and Spilka (1971, p. 236) compared the strength of identification with Japan of JA adolescents, whose mothers adhered to Buddhism, with others whose mothers were Methodists (i.e., likely to be more acculturated). While the Buddhist mothers themselves scored more highly, the difference between the two groups of offspring was not significant. However, the Buddhist children had somewhat higher achievement motivation, and also showed more symptoms of alienation, presumably because there was greater value-conflict between adolescents and parents in the more traditional homes.

Delinquency

Two studies of juvenile delinquents in Japan (Mizushima and De Vos, 1967, p. 238; Gough, DeVos, and Mizushima, 1968, p. 238) used the Socialization and other scales from the California Inventory. In the first of these, the delinquent youth obtained lower scores than normal high school and young adult groups. In the second, delinquents were lower on several scales indicative of Social Maturity, especially Socialization, Responsibility, Self-Control, Tolerance, and Intellectual Efficiency. By combining these scales, 88% of normals and delinquents could be correctly diagnosed. Thus, the California scales developed in the United States were found to be equally valid in Japan.

Conformity

Studies of traditional childrearing in Japan suggest that adults would be highly conformist to authority and to group pressures; though with the greater radicalism of postwar students, this might be reversed. Frager (1970, p. 239) applied Asch's well-known conformity test of judging the lengths of lines along with three stooges, who sometimes give intentionally wrong answers. This was taken by 128 JJ students, who also took a test of traditional authoritarian versus alienated attitudes, and another intended to measure need for social approval. The Japanese males were somewhat less conformist than American students, but many did yield to group pressure, whereas others did not yield or even counter-reacted by disagreeing wrongly with the stooges. Females were similar. There was no correlation between conformity and need for approval, but students with traditional attitudes were more conformist than the others, and the anticonformists were more likely to be alienated.

A different approach was used by Klauss and Bass (1974, p. 239) in a study of managerial trainees in several countries. At the end of the course the students rated its value three times: first, individually, second, after group discussion, and finally, individually again. Comparing the first with the third rating, 49% of all subjects showed a tendency to conform, 38% retained their individual views, and 13% reacted against group pressure. West Germans and Swiss were the most conformist, and British and Australians the least (the United States was not included). Japanese were close to average in conformity, but also produced the greatest proportion of anticonformists as in Frager's investigation.

Maykovich (1973) did not apply any conformity tests, but was interested in the heterogeneity of attitudes among Sansei, as contrasted with the more conformist Nisei parents. He interviewed 508 JA college students in California, and classified them on two dimensions: (1) Traditionalist versus Modern or Rebellious, and (2) Involved in social issues or activies versus Noninvolved. This gave four types designated as Liberated (Traditional–Involved), Conformist (Traditional–Not Involved), Militant (Rebellious–Involved), and Alienated (Rebellious–Not Involved). There were roughly equal numbers of each type. In general, the Sansei saw their fathers as holding similar views to their own, but the Militants sometimes reacted against parental pressure. The Liberal and Militant were highest in self-esteem and leadership, whereas the Alienated had low self-esteem. The Conformists tended to come from upper-SES homes.

Radicalism–Conservatism

Larsen, Arosala, Lineback, and Ommundsen (1973) report on a test of radical attitudes given to students in the United States, Japan, Norway, and Finland. There were considerable ethnic differences in the factor structures underlying the 78 test items. But generally the Japanese and Norwegians were more left-wing than the Finnish or Americans.

Wilson and Iwawaki (1980) gave the Wilson–Patterson Attitude Inventory to 219 Japanese college students and 112 school students. It had already been used in England, United States, Germany, South Africa, and Korea. The inventory covers approval–disapproval of various social issues, including, for example, Coeducation, Pornography, Working Mothers, Modern Art, Birth Control, Socialism, Death Penalty, and Race Discrimination. When the responses of western students were factor analyzed, four main clusters of items were identified: (1) Puritanism; (2) Antihedonism; (3) Ethnocentricity; and (4) Religiosity.

But among the Japanese there was much more specificity of attitudes to particular issues. Only some rather small factors (covering 19% of variance in males, 16% in females) could be labeled as General Conservatism versus Radicalism, and Idealism versus Realism.

The items in which males chiefly differed from females were quite similar in Japan and the United Kingdom, males being more sexually permissive and more tough, females more religious and traditionalist. The authors suggest that besides similarity in the sex role norms of the two ethnic groups, there might be some underlying constitutional differences in male and female hormones.

Locus of Control

Caudill and De Vos (1956) described the Japanese as more strongly regulated by external sanctions than by internal controls, and this is backed up by the high EPPS scores for Deference and Abasement. They do not, like Americans, stress the value of self-reliance, individualism, and independence. Likewise, Hsu (1971) and Potter (1969) indicate that the Chinese tend to believe in luck or fate rather than self-determination. These conceptions closely resemble Rotter's (1966) notion of external versus internal control (his 29-item questionnaire has been quite widely applied in the 1970s). However, some studies have indicated that there are three kinds of attitude rather than a single dichotomy; namely, belief in luck or fate; belief that one is controlled by other powerful people or spirits; and belief in one's own decisions and responsibility.

Six studies are outlined in Appendix B (pp. 239–240): Bond and Tornatsky

(1973); McGinnies, Nordholm, Ward, and Bhanthumnavin (1974); Mahler (1974); Reitz and Groff (1974); Hopkins, Lo, Petersen, and Seo (1977); and Boor (1976). There is remarkable unanimity among them. JJ subjects, mostly college students, accept more external beliefs than whites, whether of the Powerful Other or Chance type, and Japanese females usually show more Externality than males. JJ industrial workers are more External than American counterparts, and students in relatively underdeveloped countries (Thailand and Mexico) also get high External scores. The research of Hopkins *et al.* (1977), using a different instrument, indicated that JA follow the United States' pattern of being low in "fatalism." JJ adults were higher than whites in authoritarianism as well as fatalism. Boor (1976) hypothesized that countries with high Externality would have higher suicide rates, and this was confirmed by tests in 10 countries, where Japan and Sweden were in the top three on both variables.

A related attitude might be termed sense of responsibility. Shaw and Iwawaki (1972) constructed a test based on Heider's notion of primitive versus mature levels of attributing responsibility. This consisted of 40 short stories of incidents happening to a boy, each ending with the question: Was the boy responsible or not? This was given to 20 children in Japan, aged 9–10; to 20 children aged 11–13; and to equal numbers of Americans. The design was too elaborate to be described here, but there was no overall superiority or inferiority in maturity of responsibility between the ethnic groups. The most significant difference was that Americans attributed a high level of responsibility in negative incidents involving wrongdoing, and less high in positive incidents involving achievement, whereas the Japanese showed no such discrimination. The interpretation of these results in terms of ethnic differences in childrearing does not seem very convincing.

Machiavellianism

A rather different, yet overlapping, attitude has been described by Christie and Geis (1970) as *Machiavellianism* (or *Mach* for short), that is, the view that other people can be manipulated for one's personal gain. They have developed a 20-item attitude scale. Dien (1974) hypothesized that high-Mach parents would exert more control over their children, and not let them get away with transgressions. Thus, their children would be lower-Mach than others who had been indulged by low-Mach mothers. She devised a ball game in which children could cheat (without being caught) in order to raise their scores. Forty-eight Japanese kindergarten children, aged around 5.0 years, all being firstborns or only children, played this game and were observed through a one-way screen for any cheating. The hypothesis was confirmed, though only at the .05 level; when later-born children and their parents were tested, and association of high-Mach mothers with low-Mach children broke down. In 27 families where the father also answered the scale, high-father–low-mother children cheated most whereas high-father-and-mother children cheated least (p = <.02).

Six years later (Dien and Fujisawa, 1979), 76 parents and children took the same scale. This time the hypothesis was that girls develop their own techniques of gaining their ends. This was borne out by correlations of .35 and .56 between girls and their fathers and mothers, but there were no significant correlations for boys. However, boys obtained higher Mach scores than girls, namely 94.03 versus 88.90 (as found also with Chinese by Oksenberg, 1970). No correlation was found with the 5-year scores for cheating.

VALUES

There are two instruments most frequently used for assessing values. First is Allport, Vernon, and Lindzey's Study of Values, which is based on E. Spranger's *Types of Men*. This measures relative preference for Theoretical (Scientific), Aesthetic (Artistic), Economic (Utilitarian), Religious (Spiritual), Social (Humanitarian), and Political (Power-seeking) attitudes. Second, there is C. Morris's Ways to Live, in which subjects react to 13 short paragraphs describing different views of life.

Nobechi and Kimura (1957, p. 241) list the mean value scores for male and female JJ college students. Americans score close to 40 on each value. The table in Appendix B shows that Japanese of both sexes are much more aesthetically inclined and less religious. But the latter result might be better interpreted as showing that the Japanese are not much concerned with Western notions of what is spiritually valuable. Sex differences between the six scores are quite similar to those consistently obtained in the United States.

In Morris and Jones's work with Ways to Live (Morris and Jones, 1955; Morris, 1956) over four thousand students from five countries, including Japan and China, rated each value on a 6- or 7-point scale for acceptance–rejection. Marked differences in profiles of responses were found between the different ethnic groups. For example, number 13, advocating ''Submissiveness to Cosmic Purpose,'' was most strongly accepted by Chinese, but most strongly rejected by Americans and Japanese.

Next, using factor analysis, the authors tried to reduce the ways to a few more general dimensions. The five factors extracted were named as follows:

A. Social restraint and self-control
B. Enjoyment and progress by action
C. Withdrawal and self-sufficiency
D. Receptivity and sympathetic concern for others
E. Self-indulgence and sensuous enjoyment

The students were scored for these factors, and the main features of the profiles for different nations were

United States: B and A, high; E, moderate; D, low; C, very low
China: B and A, high; D, moderate; E, low; C, very low
Japan: A, high; B, D, and E, low; C, very low

Results are also given by Ando (1965) for India, Norway, and the Philippines. It will be seen that the profiles for Americans and Orientals are fairly similar, though both Chinese and Japanese put D higher and E lower than Americans do. Perhaps these factor dimensions have become too generalized, and Morris's original 13 Ways might have been more discriminative.

Kilby (1971) broke down Morris's Ways to Live into 32 more specific values. These were rated on Semantic Differential evaluative scales by JJ, Indian, and American students (both males and females). The main values rated highly by Americans and Japanese were

Americans only	Japanese only	Both
Highs		
Openness to change	Achievement	Helpfulness to others
Self-develop-ment	Vigorous action	Individuality
Friendship and affection		Equality and tolerance
		Solving the nation's problems
Lows		
Let oneself be used	Enjoyment	Averageness
Community living	Acceptance of things	Solitariness
Avoiding problems	High esteem	Adapting to nature
Preserve tradi-tional values		
Possessiveness		

These brief names are inadequate to convey the essence of such values. But even if one quoted the full descriptions, it is still probable that Japanese and Americans might interpret them differently.

Another Survey of Personal Values was constructed by Gordon (1967) to cover the following variables: (1) Support from others, (2) Conformity, (3) Recognition from others, (4) Independence, (5) Benevolence to others, and (6)

Leadership. Preferences for these were collected in a number of ethnic samples, and several distinctive groups of Americans, such as nurses, managers, prisoners, Army officers, and Peace Corps volunteers were tested, giving 35 groups in all. By intercorrelating and carrying out a Q-type factor analysis,[2] the following main types were obtained:

1. Self-determination and independence. High in American students and gifted individuals. Low in Indians and Samoans.
2. Conformity to institutional restraints. High in Chinese, Japanese. Low in prisoners and delinquents
3. Control and leadership of others versus reciprocal support. High in American army, managers, etc. Low in white female students.
4. Service to others. High in Chinese, Indians, medical students, teachers, and Peace Corps volunteers.

This method seems to be a promising one for differentiating ethnic, occupational, and other groups, though not, as yet, suitable for mapping individual differences.

Later, Kikuchi and Gordon (1970) devised a test of 30 four-choice items to measure a different list of values: P (Practical-minded, materialistic), A (Achievement need), V (Variety, change, and discovery), D (Decisiveness), O (Orderliness), and G (Goal orientation or persistence). These six variables had been identified by factor analysis, and the same patterning was confirmed among Japanese students. Large groups of male and female students in Japanese high schools and universities were compared with similar American subjects. In both sexes and both age groups, Japanese were higher than whites on O & G, and lower on A, V, and P. However, Berrien (1968) criticizes Gordon's studies and the identification of his six value types with EPPS needs, because of the difficulties of ensuring that self-report items measure the same thing in English and Japanese.

Meredith (1976) used the FIRO-B—Fundamental Interpersonal Orientation Behavior Scale (Schutz, 1961). This is claimed to measure six types of relations to others, namely: Expressed Control, Inclusion, and Affective relations; and Wanted Control, Inclusion, and Affection. When given to 154 JA Sansei and 84 white students at the University of Hawaii, both sexes of Japanese were higher than whites on Wanted Control (e.g., accepting such statements as: "I want people to control me"). Females only were high on Expressed Inclusion (e.g., "I initiate interactions with people"). The variables seem too peculiar to throw any light on ethnic differences.

Two additional surveys of goals and values were carried out with school

---

[2]Q-type factorization analyzes the correlations between several peoples' or groups' ratings of, for example, values, instead of the correlations between several tests given to one group of persons. This technique yields types of people instead of types of abilities or attitudes, etc.

students (i.e., mostly younger than college level). Schwartz's (1971, p. 241) questionnaire, given to JA students in Los Angeles and to other groups, showed the former to be the most highly motivated toward educational and occupational goals. They are still more imbued with traditional Japanese values than with Caucasian American ones, that is, they are not so acculturated to Western middle-class norms as is usually believed.

Gallimore, Weiss, and Finney (1974, p. 241) asked Japanese and part-Hawaiian high school students to write what they would do if given $1500. The Japanese much more frequently wished to use the money for some significant, long-term purpose, whereas the Hawaiians more often mentioned some immediate use. Some 40% of both groups mentioned personal uses, but 41% of JA and 26% of Hawaiians opted for educational or personal advancement. And 53% of Hawaiians versus 35% of JA listed family, friends, or charity. Obviously the subjects' responses were hypothetical, not actual behavior, but they fit in with the accepted cultural differences, that is, the value that Japanese place on education and the Hawaiians on family and social cooperation.

The Semantic Differential Technique

The Semantic Differential is not any kind of personality test. It is a technique developed by Osgood, Suci, and Tannenbaum (1956) for exploring the connotative (i.e., the affective) meanings of concepts in one or more groups of people. One example was cited in Chapter 4, where Marsella *et al.* used the technique for bringing out differences in the meanings attached to the word *shame* by Japanese, Chinese, and Caucasians. It has been much used in cross-cultural research, since it can throw light on differences in attitudes and values of contrasted groups.

Usually it consists of a series of concepts, for example, Mother, Self, Teacher, The Future (or any other area of interest), and a number of adjectival scales, usually about 20: for example, Good–Bad, Beautiful–Ugly, Strong–Weak, Active–Passive. Each concept is rated from 1 to 7 on each scale by a group of subjects. The mean ratings for all concepts are intercorrelated, and Osgood generally finds that there are three main factors running through such scales: (1) Evaluation (like–dislike), (2) Potency, and (3) Activity. The scores of each concept on these dimensions can be calculated, and much can be learned about the structure of people's attitudes by measuring how the concepts resemble or differ from one another. Osgood and his collaborators have applied this technique in many different countries, usually to groups of college students (Osgood, May, & Miron, 1975). A considerable degree of consistency is found, that is, the same factors tend to arise, though there are some variations, for example, the appearance of other dimensions, such as Intelligence, or Rationality (Clever–Stupid), or Familiarity–Unfamiliarity.

Sagara, Yamamoto, Nishimura, and Akoto (1961) queried the suitability of

American concepts and scales among Japanese subjects, and chose 120 and 50, respectively, which had high frequency of usage in Japan. When these were rated by groups of students (48 men and 48 women in all), and the scale factors analyzed, four factors were found that did differ from Osgood's: (1) Evaluation, but this mainly referred to accuracy and moral correctness, rather than to liking-disliking. (2) Magnitude, for example, long–short, deep–shallow, large–small. (3) Sensory pleasure—another type of evaluation—happy–sorry, soft–hard, hot–cold. The Good–Bad scale had a high loading on this factor as well as on number (1). (4) Dynamism, a combination of Potency and Activity.

In 1965 Takahashi had the 10 Rorschach inkblots, rather than verbal concepts, rated on 21 scales. Seventy-nine college students, and 79 delinquents from a reformatory, all of similar age, were compared. Here, the students' factors closely resembled Osgood's, except that there was a fourth minor factor combining elements of Potency and Activity in a Dynamism dimension. The delinquents showed the same Evaluation and Dynamism factors, but their second and third factors were closer to Sagara's Magnitude and Sensory Pleasure. The author suggests that delinquents rely more on sensory perception and less on evaluation than the students. Several differences were found in the loadings of certain traits. For example, Tense versus Relaxed is positively evaluated by the delinquents and negatively evaluated by the students (i.e., the latter favor Relaxed).

Kumata and Schramm (1956) compared 25 Japanese, 22 Korean, and 24 American students, all working at an American university. The concepts presented were largely political or social (e.g., United States, Soviet Union, Police, Father). The foreign students rated 30 of these on 20 of the standard Osgood scales both in English and in their own languages. In all sets of ratings the same two factors were dominant: Evaluation and Dynamism. Factor loadings in the three ethnic groups were intercorrelated, and all congruence coefficients were high, from .87 to .95 (average .92), which is about as large as the coefficients between two sets of ratings provided by each group. Thus, in this study the dimensions of attitudes or opinions are virtually the same across three cultures, though the factor scores of particular concepts sometimes varied.

Another study by Tanaka (1972) explored the affective meanings of a large number of social, political, and other concepts among samples of about 40 high school seniors in 15 ethnic groups, including Hong Kong Chinese, Japanese, Americans, English, and Germans. The semantic factors differed a good deal in content in different groups, but the following four factors were fairly consistent among Japanese and German students: (1) Pleasantness (happy, sociable, etc.); (2) Development (sophisticated, quick, active); (3) Stability (calm, quiet, moral); and (4) Strength (big, strong, heavy).

General evaluative scores for the concepts were calculated in all groups, and some of the more interesting ones are listed in Appendix B-2, for US + UK, Hong Kong Chinese, and JJ groups. For example, the Japanese are very much antigovernment, Labor unions, and Atom bomb. Chinese give the highest evaluation of Yellow races, as opposed to Whites and Blacks, and they are strongly in favor of Democracy and Work. In a further investigation in 1973, Tanaka obtained Semantic Differential ratings on several concepts connected with nuclear development. Ninety American and 169 Japanese students took part. The main factors appeared to be (1) Favorable-unfavorable to nuclear development; (2) Feasibility of banning development; and (3) Dynamism (e.g., fast, strong, sturdy). While the Japanese subjects were mainly unfavorable to military and civilian uses, only about one in three strongly rejected any uses of nuclear power. Also some 30 to 40% believed that Japan would "go nuclear" within about 10 years. American students were more discriminating between military and civilian uses, but as many as 79% believed that Japan would soon "go nuclear." (In fact, within 8 years there were 21 nuclear power plants in Japan.)

An elaborate investigation was reported by Triandis, Tanaka, and Shanmugam (1966). This dealt with the interpersonal attitudes of white, Japanese, and Indian students (100 in each group). A number of types of persons were rated on Semantic Differential scales, and on what Triandis calls Behavior Differential scales. These were factor analyzed in each ethnic and sex group. The major factor structure was quite similar in all groups, though there were some quite marked inter-ethnic differences on minor factors. Thus, all groups displayed the general Evaluation dimension, but the Potency and Activity factors once again condensed to a Dynamism factor in the Japanese, who also stressed the importance of age in evaluating others. The main Behavioral factor among whites was termed "Respect," but among the Japanese this carried a strong flavor of subordination toward people whom they respected. Another "Marital Acceptance" factor indicated that Japanese women expected to be obedient to their husbands, though desiring more equality.

Clearly the technique has many other potentialities in cross-cultural research yet to be explored. But it is necessary to bear in mind that we are dealing with a limited range of affective responses to certain concepts or issues and, as with all attitude scales, they do not necessarily accord with how people actually behave when confronted with these issues.

INTERESTS

In earlier chapters, mention was made of the preference of Oriental Americans for scientific, mathematical, and business jobs, and their avoidance of literary or social occupations. This has been confirmed by studies using formal tests of interests such as the Strong Vocational Interest Blank. Two of these studies, by Sue and Kirk (1972, 1973, p. 242) and Sue and Frank (1973, p. 242) dealing with Japanese and Chinese students at the University of California, are outlined in Appendix B.

A pictorial test of 11 types of vocational interests was devised by Geist (1969,

p. 242). The results for large groups of JA and white secondary and college students are shown in Table 15.1. The three most-liked and the three least-liked occupations are listed, and those that are common to both ethnic groups are italicized. There is more overlapping between the groups than expected, 7 out of 12 choices being identically placed, whereas there is no overlapping between the sexes in Japanese, and only 2 out of 6 are the same in white students. Some of the results seem to contradict expectation, for example, Japanese males putting Literary high and Musical low. Geist also found that age differences were small, apart from the tendency among college women to choose professional interests more than did high school girls.

Stereotypes and Ratings

Stereotypes refer to widely held generalizations about the psychological characteristics of particular groups (e.g., Japanese), or types of people (e.g., artists, hippies). Often these contain a modicum of truth, and they are undoubtedly useful in our everyday social contacts—for example, we react differently to old adults and to young adults. But frequently the stereotypes are derogatory and are indicative of discrimination or prejudice against the group. Characteristically the stereotype is believed to apply to all members of the disliked group, for example, "All Japs or all Chinks are. . . ." Yet, any rational person would admit that there are wide individual differences, and that some personal acquaintances do not show these qualities. Clearly, we should not regard them as valid assessments of the personalities of other ethnic groups or only with the greatest caution. But they are of interest in bringing out those qualities in which an ethnic minority is seen as acculturated or not acculturated to the majority norms.

The study of stereotypes was set off by Katz and Braly (1933), and several other investigations have followed their method. They provided a list of 84 traits,

TABLE 15.1
Liked and Disliked Occupations among Japanese and White Students (Geist, 1969)[a]

	Japanese		Whites	
	Most liked	Least liked	Most liked	Least liked
Males	*Computational*	*Musical*	*Computational*	Dramatic
	Literary	Mechanical	*Scientific*	*Social service*
	Scientific	*Social service*	Personal service	*Musical*
Females	*Persuasive*	Personal service	*Persuasive*	*Dramatic*
	Clerical	*Dramatic*	*Clerical*	Literary
	Literary	Outdoor	Social service	Musical

[a] Occupations italicized represent those common to both ethnic groups.

or adjectives, and got 100 Princeton University students to pick out those that they thought most appropriate for 10 nationalities or ethnic groups. The authors list the 12 adjectives most frequently attributed to each group. The top six are given here for four groups:

Americans: industrious, intelligent, materialistic, ambitious, progressive, pleasure-loving

English: sportsman-like, intelligent, conventional, tradition-loving, conservative, reserved

Chinese: superstitious, sly, conservative, tradition-loving, loyal to family, industrious

Japanese: intelligent, industrious, progressive, shrewd, sly, quiet.

Other psychologists have reported similar findings, but as might be expected, they change markedly when there is some notable social change. Thus, Meenes (1943, p. 242) reported the stereotypes of Orientals held by Negro students in 1935, and again in 1942. In 1935 the Japanese were intelligent, industrious, tradition-loving, nationalistic, ambitious, alert, artistic, progressive. But in 1942 they had become sly, treacherous, nationalistic, intelligent, deceitful, shrewd, tradition-loving, industrious. By contrast, the Chinese showed little change, or even improved by 1942.

1935: tradition-loving, superstitious, loyal to family, quiet, shy, physically dirty, conventional, treacherous, industrious, conservative.

1942: tradition-loving, loyal to family, quiet, religious, reserved, courteous, conservative, faithful, superstitious.

Smith's study (1943) was similar. Forty-four University of Hawaii students in 1938, and 51 in 1942, were asked to rank 20 nations or cultures according to the degree of prejudice felt by average whites (that is, they were not asked for their own opinions. Many of the students were Chinese or Japanese, but this had little effect on their judgments.)

In 1938, the bottom six were Chinese, Jewish, Turkish, Hindu, Japanese, Negro. In 1942, Chinese had risen to eighth, and the bottom six were Jewish, Hindu, Negro, Italian, German, Japanese. Note that there is rather little difference in the placement of Japanese, but this is because they were already so low in 1938, even at the University of Hawaii.

In contrast, Kashiwa and Smith (1943, p. 242) showed that Japanese students rated their own group very highly, and Chinese quite low.

Morgan (1945) gave a 50-item questionnaire to 170 midwestern psychology students, asking for opinions about Japanese. Thirty-four percent agreed that the Japanese are not assimilable in the United States; 19% said they were inferior; 24% untrustworthy; and 15% inherently more cruel than whites. Since this was carried out during the war in 1943, and the proportions of unfavorable responses are generally below 50, it does not seem to demonstrate strong racial prejudice. However, Morgan went on to show that there was a great deal of confusion and loose thinking in the students' opinions.

Probably the most extensive research in this area was that of Vinacke (1949a). The study elicited stereotypes for the eight major ethnic groups in Hawaii. One hundred and seventeen descriptive traits were selected, and 375 mixed students were asked to pick out those most characteristic of each group. The main results that concern us are the traits most frequently applied to:

Whites—luxury-loving, sociable, expressive, confident, outspoken, progressive
Japanese—polite, close-knit family, industrious, clean, traditional, quiet, clannish
Chinese—good businessmen, traditional, industrious, thrifty, shrewd, money-conscious, intelligent, scholarly, close-knit family, clannish.

By contrast, Hawaiians were musical, easygoing, happy-go-lucky, friendly, generous, lazy, superstitious. Vinacke noted that ratings of one's own group were generally very similar to ratings by others, though the more unfavorable traits tend to be omitted.

In another study at the University of Hawaii (Harrigan et al. 1961, p. 242), oriental female students tended to show greater tolerance to other ethnic groups than whites did, though the numbers were too small to be of much significance. Abate and Berrien (1967) gave the EPPS to large groups of JJ and American white college students. They were then provided with descriptions of the 15 needs, and asked to rate Americans and Japanese in general on each of these. The ratings of Americans by Americans and by Japanese correlated quite highly, as did the ratings of Japanese by Japanese and Americans (.56 to .89). But when comparisons were made with the actual EPPS scores of each group, American ratings of their own and of Japanese needs agreed moderately well ($r = .40$ to .64), whereas the Japanese ratings, both of themselves and Americans, showed virtually zero correlations with the test scores. The data are difficult to follow and interpret, but the authors suggest that the lack of validity in Japanese ratings may arise because of current changes in Japanese values, and uncertainty over their identity in the postwar world. I would be inclined to add that the various needs probably do not mean the same to Orientals as to whites (see also Berrien, 1969, p. 243).

Maykovich (1971, p. 243) used Katz and Braly's list of 84 traits. One hundred each of white, black, and Japanese students were asked to pick out the traits that they thought appropriate to each group. As described above, Meenes (1943) found that Negroes held very unfavorable stereotypes of Japanese. But by 1970 the most frequently listed were ambitious, industrious, loyal to family, courteous, reserved, and quiet. The Japanese themselves listed almost the same traits, but put Tradition-loving at the top of the list. Whites were seen by Japanese as materialistic, pleasure-loving, ambitious, aggressive, impulsive, talkative. The white students chose almost the same list of traits for themselves. There seems, then, to be quite close agreement between stereotypes of a nation as seen by nationals and by members of other nations, except when there are strong prejudices, as against Japanese in the 1940s. But the rationality of college students' views is presumably somewhat higher than that of the general population.

Kumagai (1977) studied 104 JJ males who had worked for 2 to 3 years at American universities. They were given attitude scales for measuring favorableness to America and to Japan. Each scale was taken four times: first, just before going to America, next shortly after arrival, then after 1 year, and finally upon return. Their favorability to America rose slightly on each occasion, from a score of 3.5 to 4.2 (on a 6-point scale). The attitude to Japan remained stable around 3.8, which implies that on return, they were more favorable to America than to their home country. Incidentally, they also took the Japanese version of the California Personality Inventory on the first and last occasions, and this showed very little personality change; but Sense of Well-being, Achievement via Conformance, and Femininity rose significantly.

Despite the surface harmony between Hawaiian ethnic groups, there are still considerable preferences for or against certain groups, and persistent stereotypes about them. In the most recent study to be cited, Wong (1979) got 45 university students—18 Japanese (JA), 16 Caucasian, and 11 CA—to make paired comparisons between eight groups and to rate them on a Semantic Differential scale. The overall rank order of preference or popularity was Japanese, Chinese, Hawaiian, Caucasian, Filipino, Korean, Black, Samoan. However, the application of multidimensional scaling indicated that the groups differed along two main dimensions:

1. SES; Caucasian students being highest, Koreans lowest.
2. Oriental versus Black; Japanese and Chinese being contrasted with blacks and Samoans. Obviously, the preferences would vary in different ethnic groups, and no mention is made of whom, say, the blacks and Samoans would have liked best.

Iwawaki, Sonoo et al. (1978, p. 243) used a very different approach to assessing racial bias in Japanese kindergarten children. It is well known that children from an early age choose pictures of whites in preference to black persons. Two color-bias tests were constructed, each consisting of 24 pictures that provided choices between black and white. For example, one picture showed a black and a white cat, and the children were asked: Which is the bad cat? The other test showed human figures. Even black children made more white than black choices, though their scores were much nearer to the neutral point of 12 than those of American and British whites. The younger Japanese showed less antiblack bias than all other ethnic groups. But it was found that scores rise with age, from 11.43 at 3½ years to 19.0 at 6 years. In other words, they do learn to follow white prejudices. It would have been interesting to use colored pictures, including yellow as well as black and white figures. Iwawaki *et al.* account for the widespread dislike of black partly in terms of fear of the dark. Japanese children might be expected to be less fearful since the rooms they sleep in are not darkened, and they are in close proximity to adults.

Two cross-cultural studies have made use of ratings of personality by acquaintances, rather than stereotype judgments. Bond, Nakazato, and Shiraishi (1975) used a rating scale developed by Norman (1963) for assessing five personality factors or general traits, namely: (1) Extraversion; (2) Agreeableness; (3) Conscientiousness; (4) Emotional Stability; and (5) Culture. Each factor score was based on ratings for four more specific traits, for example, Sociable versus Reclusive, as part of Extraversion. Groups of students who knew one another (e.g., in a college dormitory) rated their peers on these 20 traits. The groups included 91 Japanese (JJ), 100 Filipino, and some 600 American students. Factor analyses within the three groups showed much the same dimensions numbers 1–4, with good congruence coefficients ranging from .79 to .97. But the fifth factor, Culture, showed more discrepancies with congruence coefficients of .41 to .72. There were some substantial differences in factor loadings for particular traits, and the strength of the factors varied in the three groups. Thus, among Filipinos, the Agreeableness factor was the dominant one. However, I would suggest that the consistency of factors across cultures may be exaggerated in this study by the authors' choice of the specific traits to be rated. Had a more representative sample of traits been provided, it is quite likely that there would be greater factor differences between cultures.

In a similar investigation, Hama and Plutchik (1975) chose four main bipolar dimensions: (1) Trustful–Distrustful; (2) Timid–Aggressive; (3) Depressed–Gregarious; and (4) Controlled–Impulsive. About 100 pairs of specific traits were grouped under these headings, and subjects chose which member of each pair more closely applied to themselves. Five hundred JJ males and 500 females carried out these self-ratings, and data were available from American students. The main ethnic difference among males was that Japanese were more Timid and Depressed, and less Impulsive than Americans. Japanese females were more Depressed, less Gregarious, and less Impulsive. The methodology of this study seems somewhat crude. No attempt was made to show that the trait-pairs did measure the four factors, nor that the factors were congruent in the two groups. However, the results do accord with those obtained on standard personality questionnaires in the previous chapter.

Projective Techniques

Advocates of the Rorschach Inkblot and Thematic Apperception Test (TAT) would claim that these instruments are particularly appropriate for cross-cultural comparisons, since the subjects give their own fantasy responses, instead of reacting to a Western-type questionnaire that limits them to responses that may seem to them unrealistic. Lindzey (1961) advocates the use of projective techniques, but points out many difficulties. For example, the actual test materials are not culture-free, and the interpretation of responses by a Western psychiatrist or psychologist may introduce ethnocentric bias.

A number of studies have been published, notably by Caudill and De Vos, who clearly have a deep acquaintance with Japanese culture (see also Kodamo, 1957). Caudill (1952), and Caudill and De Vos (1956) report on 70 JA (30 Issei, 40 Nisei) and 60 whites who were given the Rorschach and TAT. No quantitative results are provided, but the Japanese tended to give more W (whole) responses than whites. Illustrative protocols are given for some of the TAT pictures, which were analyzed for "press" (environmental pressures) and defense mechanisms. The Nisei showed powerful superego and guilt responses, and also need for achievement. Indeed they surpassed the Issei in achievement-related responses, which appeared in 83% of Nisei, 55% of Issei, 48% of white middle class, and 30% of lower class. (Note the difference from the findings of verbal need for achievement tests, described above.) Both the Japanese generations showed high persistence in the face of obstacles.

Norbeck and De Vos (1961) summarized various Rorschach and TAT studies, stating that Japanese subjects generally give below average numbers of Rorschach responses, with several rejections. Low Color score total was held to indicate difficulties in the expression of affect. However, high percentages of good Form responses and complex, integrated Whole responses, suggest a strong drive for organization. Connor (1976) gave 12 TAT pictures to 31 JA Sansei and 21 whites. He refers to the well-known picture of "Boy with Violin." Japanese tend to interpret this in terms of parental expectations, whereas more whites mention revolt against parental wishes.

Connor tested another group of 95 JA (Issei, Nisei, and Sansei) with an Incomplete Sentences test. Older Japanese expressed far more emotion in responding to: "When he thinks of his mother. . . ." Sansei and whites treated it more objectively. In relation to the father, Nisei more often mentioned respect and discipline, while Sansei and whites were more neutral. Finally, in responding to: "If a person finds himself in difficulties, he . . . ," 40% of Issei and Nisei expected help from family and friends, but Sansei, like whites, more often said that they would work it out for themselves.

Incomplete Sentences were also used by Takahashi (1974, cf. p. 209) to supplement his questionnaire on Dependency. This consisted of such items as: "For me, father is . . . ."

De Vos (1955) gave the Rorschach inkblots to Issei, Nisei, and Kibei in Hawaii, and to normal whites, neurotics, and schizophrenic patients. The responses were scored for maladjustment on the basis of associative blocking, Whole-detail imbalance, Color responses, few Movement responses, poor Form,

Confabulation, Sex, and Anatomical content. Another rigidity score was derived from slow reaction time, few total responses, high Animal percent, W, Dd, F+, and Shading responses. Table 15.2 shows that the Issei were more stereotyped and rigid even than the pathological groups, and are the most highly maladjusted after the schizophrenics. The Nisei are much closer to whites, though still rather high in maladjustment; they showed some signs of breakdown of ego functions. The Kibei (who had been educated in Japan for at least 5 years) are close to midway between Nisei and Issei (see also De Vos, 1956).

Bennett, Passim, and McKnight (1958) used a shortened TAT and Incomplete Sentences in studying young JJ adults who had studied abroad, mainly in the United States. No quantitative results are quoted, but the authors believe that these tests provide a lot of information about conflicts, emotionality, dependency, and authoritarianism in their subjects' personalities.

De Vos and Murikami (1974, p. 243) compared the TAT responses of Japanese and American youths, both normal and delinquent. The stories were scored for (1) Violent and Aggressive content, and (2) Unusual physical states, for example, Dead. The differences between ethnic groups were greater than those between delinquents and nondelinquents. The American boys produced more violent themes, though fewer unusual states. But the Japanese made more references to underlying motives, and consequences, such as guilt or reconciliation.

Finally Gardiner (1969, p. 243) scored children's drawings of a man for weapons, wrestling, boxing, kicking, and cowboy or military emblems, as signs of hostility. Samples of 11- to 13-year-old boys were obtained in several countries. Hostility themes were most frequent in Thai children (35%), and Gardiner ascribes this to their being brought up to repress any aggression. Taiwan Chinese and Germans were also high. But it seems surprising that both Japanese and Americans had very few, since repression of aggression is as characteristic of Japanese culture as of Chinese.

TABLE 15.2
Rorschach Syndromes in Groups of Japanese and Whites (De Vos, 1955)

	N	Maladjustment	Rigidity
Issei	50	66.5	45.2
Nisei	60	45.7	28.0
Kibei	30	56.2	37.4
White normal	60	32.1	27.3
Neurotic	30	59.4	33.4
Schizophrenic	30	86.7	35.0

SUMMARY OF CHAPTERS 14 AND 15

Any reader who has struggled through these two chapters (with their nearly 200 bibliographical references) is likely to be surprised at the amount of work done in personality testing of Japanese, and/or is likely to be disappointed that such work seems to give us so little fresh or psychologically valuable information. Some of it is quite plausible, that is, it just confirms what general observation had already indicated. Often it is not plausible, in which case we tend to search for an explanation in terms of the unrepresentativeness of the samples or the differences in meanings that the Japanese read into the test questions from those intended by the test author. Both of these are subjective and speculative. Also, the great bulk of studies are based on college students, and therefore cannot be applied to the population in general, though a few have sampled more representative groups of adults or school and preschool populations. Nevertheless, some of the conclusions from some of the investigations are of positive value. In many instances the availability of test results from Japanese in Japan, as well as Japanese Americans of several generations, is quite helpful in interpretation. The differences between JJ and JA groups can be seen to be due to the increasing Americanization of the JA; yet sometimes it is found that contemporary JJ have become more westernized than the JA (especially those resident in Hawaii) who have retained many of the traditional Japanese Meiji values and beliefs. This was confirmed by C. L. Johnson in 1977.

Out of 19 published investigations of college students and adults, all but two showed JJ and JA to be more anxious, or neurotic, and/or introverted than Caucasians. It has been suggested that Japanese methods of childrearing engender greater dependency than do Western methods. But an additional reason may be that so many studies have been based on college students, either in Japan or the United States, who are living under great strain and anxiety to succeed in their courses. Investigations of children often show no Japanese–Caucasian difference; indeed sometimes JJ and JA children are found to be less anxious than American children. The large-scale enquiry into mothers' ratings of their own children by Tuddenham et al. (1974) generally showed JA to have fewer emotional problems than those of whites, blacks, and Mexicans, except that they tended to be unduly shy and bashful. And Werner, Bierman, and French's (1971) assessments of maladjustment by clinical interview in the late 1960s found 10-year-old Japanese children in Kauai to have fewer such problems than any other ethnic group in Hawaii. This fits in with Porteus and Babcock's early conclusions (1926) that the Japanese in Hawaii were the best socially adjusted, and potentially—along with Caucasians—the leaders in the community. On the other hand there is very strong evidence from Lynn's demographic studies (1971; Lynn & Hampson, 1975) that the Japanese nation is one of the most anxious (and the most introverted) of 18 techologically developed countries. This was not based on questionnaires or other subjective techniques, but on statistics available for crime rates, nutrition, disease, death, and economic growth, etc., which were already known to be indicative of neuroticism or extraversion–introversion. No satisfactory resolution of these contradictory findings has been put forward.

A great deal of use has been made of Edwards's Personal Preference Schedule, which claims to measure 15 basic human needs. This shows JJ and JA males to score high in needs for Abasement, Endurance, Affiliation, and Change, and low in Dominance and Aggression. Further, the JA profile is quite similar to the CA (Chinese), though less so with JJ and with whites. The Japanese do not score high on Need for Achievement, as might have been expected, but this can be attributed to the differing interpretations of "achievement" in the two cultures. On other tests of masculinity–femininity, Japanese males consistently come out with low masculine scores, but again this probably represents cultural differences in sex roles. The greatest degree of unanimity between different studies occurs in the tendency of Japanese (and Chinese) to attribute successes and failures to Fate or Luck (i.e., external causes), rather than to their own efforts (internal).

JJ males still tend to be more authoritarian and opposed to female emancipation than Americans, and they are more conservative about unusual sexual activities. But these characteristics are breaking down, indeed even more so among JJ than JA. The latter are now showing a very high rate of cross-ethnic, or mixed, marriages. Many differences have been found between the more rigid and maladapted Issei generation of JA, the more dynamic and adaptive Nisei, and the largely acculturated Sansei and later generations. The upbringing of children is still rather restrictive in Japan, but JA mothers tend to combine some traditional features with modern American practices. It is reasonable to regard the Japanese emphasis on deference to authority, social obligations, and motivation to succeed educationally and vocationally as a major causal factor in the continuing advancement of Japanese nationals and Japanese Americans. Direct observational studies of Japanese babies and young children are much more illuminating than most research studies based on formal personality tests. They indicate that Japanese infants are temperamentally more placid, less excitable, than whites; the mothers give them more soothing and affection than stimulation to become independent. Hence, they tend to be slower in motor and linguistic development, though they catch up later. In their play Japanese children are not lacking in spontaneity and boisterousness, but they are more group-oriented and compliant, less competitive and aggressive than whites. Adults do not turn out to be more conformist to social pressures than Americans, though the available tests are somewhat artificial. However, tests of "response sets" uniformly show Japanese to be more cautious, and less decisive or extreme in their expression of opinions or judgments. And the children tend to be more reflective, less impulsive in making decisions.

The differences found between Japanese and Caucasian babies at birth suggest that there are some genetic factors in basic temperament; one could call these racial insofar as Chinese children seem to react very similarly to Japanese. Lynn's work with demographic statistics tends to confirm this, as does the greater susceptibility of Orientals to the effects of alcohol. This view does not, of course, deny that child upbringing and cultural norms play the major part in observed differences in personality, but there is probably an interaction between genetic and environmental factors. Another surprising finding is that Japanese, whites, and other cultural groups agree quite closely in their interpretations of emotions shown in pictures. This contradicts the view of most psychologists that person perception and interpretation of others is entirely based on social learning.

Other studies include the demonstration of unfavorable stereotypes about Japanese Americans in the 1930s and 1940s, and the later improvement in their public image. Tests of interests confirm the conclusions reached in Chapter 13 on educational and occupational preferences. Studies of values have shown differences from Americans, for example, the Japanese (JJ) being more Economically (Utilitarian) and Aesthetically minded, and less Socially (Humanitarian) or Religious-minded. Projective techniques have had some limited success in probing the underlying dynamics of Japanese American motivation, though drawn on by several psychologists such as Caudill and De Vos. Other workers in the field of personality have used advanced techniques such as factor analysis to show similarities and differences in personality structure among different ethnic groups, and also the Semantic Differential for exploring the meaning of concepts in such groups.

Appendix B

Personality Studies of Japanese

Abbreviations

adol.	adolescent	elem.	elementary
anx.	anxiety	Gd.	grade
assim.	assimilation	hs	high school
author.	authoritarian	Ind.	Indian
CA	Chinese American	intro.	introversion
CC	Chinese in China	JA	Japanese American
coll.	college	JJ	Japanese in Japan
del.	delinquent	N Ach.	achievement need
neur.	neurotic(ism)		
prim.	primary		
psychiat.	psychiatric		
sec.	secondary		
stud.	student(s)		
univ.	university		
UK	United Kingdom		
US	United States		
yr.	year		

Author(s) and Dates	Samples Studied	Main Tests Used	Main Results
Personality Questionnaires in Japan			
Iwawaki et al. 1967	150 Gd. 3 JJ, 169 Gd. 3 US, 132 Gd. 3 French	Children's Manifest Anxiety Scale	
			Anxiety / Lie Scale: JJ 15.88 / 3.38; US 21.85 / 4.46; French 20.49 / 5.14
Kaneda (1971)	86 JJ boys, aged 10–12 yr.	Sarason's Anxiety Test	No overall differences from US.
Cattell and Scheier (1961)	108 US; 91 UK; 321 JJ; and other nationalities	16 PF short measure of anxiety	(See text.)
Tsujioka and Cattell (1965)	300 JJ and 117 US stud.	16 PF, Forms A and B, second-order factors	Mean Factor Scores: JJ / US — Anxiety 13.49 / 10.66; Exvia–Invia 8.24 / 12.64; Cortertia 13.81 / 15.73; Inde-pendence 17.07 / 15.62

(continued)

Author(s) and Dates	Samples Studied	Main Tests Used	Main Results
Iwawaki (1970)	458 JJ stud. and other groups. UK norms.	Maudsley Personality Inventory	Means: Introvert Neurotic JJ male 25.4 23.3 JJ female 26.3 24.4 UK 24.9 19.9
Iwawaki et al. (1977)	557 JJ stud., 1400 UK; 110 JJ psychiat. cases, 310 UK; 649 Gd. 2–9 JJ children, 5467 UK	Revised Eysenck PEN, adult and children's forms	(See text.)
Iwawaki et al. (1980)	1091 JJ, 2320 UK children, aged 10–15 yr.	Junior Personality Questionnaire	JJ boys and girls higher on P; no differences on N. JJ boys higher on introversion and Lie Scale.
Nishiyama (1973)	300 male and 300 female JJ coll. students	California Personality Inventory (18 scales)	Most Japanese scores below US norms, except males higher on Femininity and Good Impression.
Mahler (1976)	345 JJ and 75 US students	Tennessee Self-Concept Scale	Japanese lower on Self-esteem; more defensive on total and several sub-test scores. Less extreme, more cautious responses.

Japanese–American Personality Tests

Author(s) and Dates	Samples Studied	Main Tests Used	Main Results		Emotional Immaturity		Worries	
					Boy	Girls	Boys	Girls
Kuhlen (1945)	1589 JA, 690 CA, 1547 US, Gd. 10–12	Pressey Interest-Attitude (XO) Test		JA	67.5	63.4	35.3	37.6
				CA	57.2	61.0	32.1	40.6
				US	28.0	15.0	17.0	17.1

		16 PF Test	ExVia		Anxiety	
			Male	Female	Male	Female
Meredith (1964)	79 JA stud. with poor speech, 72 normal, and 60 Caucasians	Poor speech	3.7	3.6	7.0	7.1
		Normal JA	4.8	5.2	6.3	6.5
		Caucasian	7.5	6.0	5.6	5.4
Sue and Kirk (1972, 1973)	106 JA, 236 CA, over 2000 Caucasians	Omnibus Personality Inventory	(See text.)			
Sue and Sue (1974)	48 Oriental stud., 120 white stud.	Minnesota Multiphasic Personality Inventory (MMPI)	(See text.)			

TABLE B.1
Rank Order Correlations between EPPS Means in 6 Groups of Male Students

Mean Correlations

Arkoff (1959), JA						
Fenz and Arkoff (1962), JA	.85					
Berrien (1966), JJ	.54	.48				
Fenz and Arkoff (1962), CA	.73	.90	.46			
Arkoff (1952), whites	.37	.42	.23	.25		
Fenz and Arkoff (1962), whites	.14	.31	.32	.22	.82	

JA with JA	.85	JJ with white	.27
JA with JJ	.51	Wh. with white	.82
JA with CA	.81	JJ with CA	.46
JA with white	.31	CA with white	.23

Edwards Personal Preference Schedule

Fujita (1957)	50 male, 50 female Nisei coll. stud.	Edwards Personal Preference Schedule (EPPS)	Social desirability of items similar in the sexes. No significant differences from American norms.
Arkoff (1959)	137 Nisei, 183 Sansei stud. at Univ. of Hawaii	EPPS	Male results in text. Sansei generally closer to US than Nisei. Female score pattern similar to male.

(continued)

233

Author(s) and Dates	Samples Studied	Main Tests Used	Main Results
Fenz and Arkoff (1962)	1015 hs seniors, 560 JA, 155 CA, 146 white	EPPS	Numerous significant differences between main ethnic groups, also between sexes.
Berrien (1966)	458 male, 504 female JJ coll. stud.	EPPS	Males higher than US on Abasement, Succorance, Endurance; low on Achievement, Dominance, Deference. Females similar.
Berrien et al. (1967)	100 each JA and JJ sons, daughters, and parents. 150 whites	EPPS	Sons less Deference, Order, Endurance, more Heterosexual than fathers. Daughters and mothers similar. Small differences from whites.
Arkoff et al. (1961)	32 JA rural stud., 54 urban stud.	EPPS	No significant differences, except rural females higher on Abasement than urban.
Dixon et al. (1970)	48 JA males, 54 females, 59 mixed-race hs stud.	EPPS, SCAT, and teachers' ratings	All variables factorized. Different factor patterns between sexes. No ethnic differences reported.
Arkoff et al. (1962)	76 Sansei, 113 JJ, and 63 US stud.	Dominance versus Deference scale only	Mean Dominance Scores Male Female JA 3.6 3.4 JJ 4.5 3.7 US 5.2 4.0
Connor (1974a b, 1976)	483 JA (Issei, Nisei, and Sansei) coll. stud.; 670 Caucasians, similar ages	EPPS	JA males high in Affiliation, Order, Abasement, Succorance, Endurance, Low Exhibition, Autonomy, Change, Dominance, Heterosexuality. Similar for females. Large generational differences in both races.

Scanlon et al. (1980)	182 JJ boys and girls, and 15–17 yr.	EPPS	Similar profile to Berrien (1966), except lower Heterosexuality. Omitting this, rho = .74.

Need for Achievement

Sloggett et al. (1970)	13 JA, 15 Filipino, 48 high-achieving and 31 low-achieving Hawaiian boys	TAT scored for N Ach.	Means: JA 4.77; Filipino 4.13; High-ach. Hawaiian 2.27; Low-ach. Hawaiian 1.79
Hayashi et al. (1970)	110 JJ, 50 Israel, 154 UK, 140 Irish coll. stud.	Preference ratings for 23 occupations	High and low economic growth countries compared. Predicted differences not confirmed.
Onoda (1976)	75 JA boys, 69 JA girls, Gd. 10	Gough Adjective Check List; Lorge–Thorndike and Grades	Students classified as High Achievers claim more positive traits than Low Achievers.

Response Sets

Zax and Takahashi (1967)	40 each JJ male and female stud., 40 each white male and female stud.	Ratings of Rorschach Inkblots	Responses: Neutral Extreme; JJ males 46.55 26.73; JJ females 50.83 30.35; US males 36.43 33.15; US females 36.48 47.45
Gordon and Kikuchi (1970)	189 JJ, 172 white Gd. 12 stud.	Agreement with 24 statements on traditional versus modern beliefs	% of middling (undecided) responses: Male Female; JJ 26.7 29.1; US 15.4 14.4
Chun and Campbell (1974)	204 So. Korean, 187 US stud.	130-item attitude questionnaire with 5-choice responses	Mean standard deviation of item responses: 1.12 US and 0.86 Korean (the latter more cautious).

(continued)

Author(s) and Dates	Samples Studied	Main Tests Used	Main Results
Objective Tests			
Cattell *et al.* (1973)	175 JA boys, 275 white and 218 Austrian, aged 12 yr.	71 objective tests and personality factor quizzes	23 factors found in each group, the first 12 being fairly congruent.
Observational Studies			
Arai *et al.* (1958)	776 JJ babies	Gesell Schedules, 1–36 months	Motor, social, and language development close to US norms up to 16 weeks, then fall markedly behind.
Seagoe and Murakami (1961)	300 JJ, Gd. 1 and 6; samples of whites in Japan and US	Interviews regarding types of play preferred	(See text.)
Masculinity–Femininity			
Meredith (1969)	98 JA, 40 CA, 60 US coll. stud.	Terman–Miles MF test	Mean Masculinity Scores Male Female JA 34.66 −53.62 CA 42.80 −50.65 US 49.19 −26.15
Gough *et al.* (1968)	311 Koreans, Gd. 8 and 9	California Personality Inventory Femininity Scale	Mean Femininity Scores Male Female Korean 18.05 21.18 US norms 16.26 23.36
Nishiyama (1975)	600 JJ stud., and large groups in 8 other countries	California Personality Inventory Femininity Scale	Mean Femininity Scores Male Female JJ 18.88 22.16 US 16.26 23.36

			Femininity Means			
			Gough		Franck and Rosen	
			Male	Female	Male	Female
Blane and Yamamoto (1970)	289 JA, 93 JJ, 80 US hs stud.	Gough's M-F and Franck and Rosen's Drawing Test				
		JA	10.29	15.87	4.79	6.88
		JJ	13.08	14.78	6.09	7.56
		US	8.91	14.88	4.38	6.75

Marital Attitudes

Arkoff et al. (1963)	75 JA and 60 whites in Hawaii	Jacobson's Scale for Female Emancipation	White males and both groups of females support emancipation. Japanese males significantly less favorable.
Arkoff et al. (1964)	145 JJ, 75 JA, 60 white stud.	Female equality versus Male Dominance Scale	Equality Means Male JJ 81.5 JA 77.6 US 84.4
Meredith and Ching (1977)	41 JA, 31 white stud.	Jacobson's Scale for Female Emancipation	Similar results to Arkoff et al. (1964), but all scores for female equality have risen.
Inagaki (1967)	289 JJ female stud., 75 US	Steinmann's Scale for Self-oriented versus Other-oriented	(See text.)
Church and Insko (1965)	96 Hawaiian stud., including male and female JA and whites	Ratings of desirability of 99 sex activities	Little ethnic difference, but JA women most conservative.
Maykovich (1976)	100 JJ and 100 US females, aged 35–40	Questionnaire on Premarital Sex	JJ women more traditional, though many alienated.

(continued)

Author(s) and Dates	Samples Studied	Main Tests Used	Main Results
Childrearing			
Kitano (1961)	26 JA Issei, 43 Nisei mothers	PARI test of pro-gressive attitudes	Issei highly traditional; Nisei similar to whites.
Kitano (1964)	JA and JJ mothers, aged 30–40 or 50–80	PARI test of progressive attitudes	Mean Restrictiveness Scores Older Younger JJ 16.0 14.1 JA 16.9 12.9
Higa (1974)	44 JJ, 45 JA mothers, and 40 war brides	PARI test of progressive attitudes	Item means: 2.17, 2.59, and 1.99, re-spectively. War brides are the most liberal.
Identification with Japan			
Masuda et al. 1970)	125 JA Issei, 114 Nisei, 94 Sansei in Seattle	Meredith Ethnic Identi-ty Questionnaire	Mean Age Score Issei 69.3 162.34 Nisei 41.6 153.46 Sansei 23.1 143.76
Okana and Spil-ka (1971)	38 JA adol. and mo-thers (Buddhists), 25 JA adol. and mothers (Methodists)	Ethnic Identity Scale; Alienation and N Ach. Scale for children	Stronger identification in Buddhist mothers, not in children. Their children more alienated, but have higher motivation.
Delinquency			
Mizushima and De Vos (1967)	64 nondel. JJ males, 36 del. hs stud. and adults	CPI Socialization Scale	Means Nondelinquent 35.7 Delinquent 24.3

Study	Sample	Measure	Results
Gough *et al.* (1968)	113 JJ hs, and 36 del. boys	CPI Social Maturity Index	Means Nondelinquent 47.39 Delinquent 40.08
Conformity			
Frager (1970)	128 JJ coll. stud.	Asch's conformity test; Authoritarian and Need for Approval Scales	27% did not yield at all; 16% conformed once, 16% twice, 42% three or more times. Anticonformists significantly more alienated.
Klauss and Bass (1974)	Managerial trainees in 13 countries	Ratings on value of course, freely and under group pressure	JJ men about average in conformity, but also produce most anticonformists.
Locus of Control			
Bond and Tornatsky (1973)	117 JJ male and 58 JJ female; 59 and 60 whites	Internal versus External Control	Means for Externality 　　Male　Female JJ　13.42　12.67 US　11.31　11.88
McGinnies *et al.* (1974)	719 males, 819 female stud. in US, Japan, etc.	Internal versus External Control	Females more External than males. Japanese mean, 11.72; higher than US, 10.31, but lower than Swedish, 14.59.
Mahler (1974)	194 JJ and 120 US coll. stud.	3 sets of 8 items	Means for Japanese 　　Male　Female Internal　26.96　26.41 Powerful Others　17.18　19.01 Chance, or Luck　22.94　25.16

(continued)

239

Author(s) and Dates	Samples Studied	Main Tests Used	Main Results	
				Means for US
			Internal	33.42	32.98
			Powerful Others	16.47	16.72
			Chance, or Luck	18.58	17.51
Reitz and Groff (1974)	503 US industrial workers, 716 Japanese, 469 Mexican, 258 Thai	Rotter Scale; items divided by content	Asian countries higher on Fate or Luck; Japanese most External, US most Internal.	
Hopkins et al. (1977)	10 JA, 32 JJ, 24 white managerial trainees	Questionnaires for Fatalism and Authoritarianism	Fatalism Mean	Authoritarian
			JA −1.30	Not stated
			JJ +1.00	29.34
			White −1.35	25.75
Boor (1976)	Coll. stud. in 10 countries	Internal versus External; and Suicide Rate	Correlation of .68 between External Means and Suicide	

Values

Author(s) and Dates	Samples Studied	Main Tests Used	Main Results	
				Means
Nobechi and Kimura (1957)	131 male, 390 female JJ stud.	Allport-Vernon-Lindzey Study of Values	Male	Female
			Theoretical 41.09	39.42
			Aesthetic 42.17	39.87
			Economic 45.80	46.67
			Social 38.30	37.64
			Political 40.11	39.87
			Religious 32.53	36.52

| Schwartz (1971) | 254 JA Gd. 6, 9, and 12. Some 2000 whites. | Questionnaire on goals, aspirations, values | JA more motivated by traditional Meiji values. |
| Gallimore *et al.* (1974) | 49 JA and 202 part-Hawaiian hs stud. | Written responses to "What would you do if given $1500?" | Japanese superior on delayed gratification; also personal rather than social uses. |

TABLE B.2
Semantic Differential Evaluation Scores for Selected Concepts in 3 out of 15 Ethnic Groups (Tanaka, 1972)

	US + UK	H.K. Chinese	JJ
Regions and Races			
Asia	-0.2	1.3	0.3
North America	2.1	0.8	0.5
Blacks	-0.1	0.3	-0.2
Whites	1.4	-0.1	0.2
Yellows	0.1	2.3	0.5
Political–Economic			
Democracy	1.6	2.4	1.2
Power	1.6	0.7	-0.4
Competition	1.0	1.0	0.3
Labor unions	1.2	0.5	0.0
Salary	2.2	1.4	1.3
Work	0.8	2.1	1.0
War and Peace			
Atom bomb	-1.3	-1.5	-2.4
Army	1.4	0.9	0.0

(*continued*)

Author(s) and Dates	Samples Studied	Main Tests Used	Main Results
Interests			
Sue and Kirk (1972, 1973). Also, Sue and Frank (1973)	216 CA, 106 JA coll. stud., both sexes; 104 CA, 50 JA, coll. males	Strong Vocational Interest Blank	Combined Orientals prefer business, applied science, and biology to jobs requiring linguistic skills. A few differences between JA and CA: JA less favorable to Physical, more to Social sciences. Females similar.
Geist (1969)	Some 400 JJ hs and coll. Some 400 US white hs and coll.	Geist's Picture Inventory, covering 11 types of job	(See text.)
Stereotypes			
Meenes (1943)	160 black Harvard stud. in 1935, and 137 in 1942	Pick out characteristics of 10 ethnic groups	Chinese viewed mainly positively on both occasions. Japanese more unfavorably in 1942.
Kashiwa and Smith (1943)	100 JA, aged 9–13 yr.	Thurstone-type attitude scale	Mean favorable scores: Japanese 9.3, Chinese 3.6.
Harrigan et al. (1961)	19 JA females, 9 CA, 19 white coll. stud.	Adorno Ethnocentric Scale. Picture Frustration, and Bogardus Social Distance Scale	Less bigotism and ethnocentricity among oriental students than white.

242

Study	Sample	Method	Results
Berrien (1969)	480 JJ stud., 343 US whites	15 EPPS items rated for 16 national groups	Whites ascribe traits to disliked groups unlike their own group; Japanese do not. Also, knowledge about a group has different effects.
Maykovich (1971)	100 each white, black, and JA stud.	Katz & Braly's 84 traits	Considerable similarity between stereotypes of own ethnic group and those held by other groups.
Iwawaki et al. (1978)	143 JJ children, aged 3½–6 yr., and other ethnic groups	24 pictures showing white versus black bias	Means (out of 24) — see table below

Iwawaki et al. (1978):

	Animals	Humans
US white	17.34	18.66
US black	14.90	14.18
Japanese	15.29	15.52

Projective Techniques

Study	Sample	Method	Results
De Vos and Mu- rikami (1974)	30 each JA and white del. and nondel., aged 17–23 yr.	9 TAT cards scored for violent responses, and unusual physical states	See table below
Gardiner (1969)	2382 boys, aged 11–13 yr., in several countries	Hostility symptoms in drawing a man	Hostility found in 35% Thai, 26% German, 22–25% Taiwan CC, 1% JJ, and 0.6% US.

De Vos and Murikami (1974):

	Means for Violence		Physical States	
	JA	US	JA	US
Del.	32.2	40.7	22.6	16.9
Nondel.	34.8	40.2	21.8	11.6

16

Personality Studies of Chinese

INTRODUCTION

The earliest study of Chinese, involving personality questionnaires was (to my knowledge) that of Shen in 1936 (see Appendix C, p. 263). He gave the Bernreuter Inventory to 400 CC school students in Hangchow. The same pattern of high neuroticism and introversion was found as with Japanese. The author's summary of his results states that Chinese showed greater "modesty" than Americans.

Both Chou and Mi (1937, p. 263) and Hsu (1951, p. 263), using the Thurstone Inventory in Chinese, obtained neuroticism scores of about 80, which are higher than those of American students, and even those of mental hospital patients. However, this is not unusual, since white college students tend to be more morbidly introspective than less-educated persons. Chou and Mi, however, suggest that there was a great deal of social unrest in China at that time, and a lack of psychiatric or mental hygiene treatment for neurotics. However, Hsu emphasized the Chinese tendency to self-depreciation and humility, the small amount of social mixing, especially with the opposite sex, and the conflicts produced by family obligations. Pai, Sung, and Hsu's (1937, p. 263) study yielded a much lower score of 53 for CC students, though it is still close to the figures found for pathological mental cases in China. Smith's (1938, p. 263) results on the Thurstone Inventory for University of Hawaii students have been quoted in Chapter 14. Differences between Chinese, Japanese, and whites were quite small.

The Children's Manifest Anxiety Scale was used by Chiu (1971, p. 263) with Taiwan Chinese. These subjects showed a small but significantly greater degree of anxiety than Americans. However, they also scored above average on the Lie Scale, which indicates the tendency to give socially desirable responses. But for this, the anxiety scores might have been even higher (see also Paschal and Kuo, 1973, p. 263). Chiu attributes this anxiety to restrictive home upbringing in Taiwan. On the other hand, Li (1974, p. 264) gave Sarason's Text Anxiety Scale for Children (TASC) to fifth and sixth grade Chinese children in Hong Kong.

This scale was designed to measure anxiety about being tested at school, but it correlates very highly with Sarason's General Anxiety Scale. The overall scores for both grades and sexes are much the same in Hong Kong children as in Americans tested by Sarason, and in both groups girls were more anxious than boys. However, there was a tendency for Hong Kong Grade 5 to show less anxiety, and Grade 6 to show more anxiety than whites, quite possibly because of the stress of approaching examinations for entry to secondary school.

Kuhlen's (1945) work with the Pressey Cross-Out Test was summarized in Chapter 14. He found above average immaturity and worries among CA (Hawaiian) secondary school students, though they were a little less deviant than the Japanese. Fong and Peskin (1969, p. 264) used the California Personality Inventory to compare Chinese (CC) students working at an American university with naturalized Chinese Americans. The CC males were significantly less adjusted on several scales: Social Presence, Responsibility, Tolerance, Well-being, Communality, Achievement via Conformance and via Independence, Intellectual Efficiency, and Flexibility. The female students showed fewer differences, the CC group being lower in Responsibility and Femininity. Abbott (1974, p. 264) gave the same test to CA in California, and CC in Taiwan, including fathers, mothers, and sons, some of the latter known to be delinquents. The CC sons were higher in Self-control, Good Impression, and Femininity than the CA and American norms, but lower in Social Presence, Self-acceptance, Well-Being, Communality, Intellectual Efficiency, and Flexibility. Much the same traits differentiated between CC and CA fathers. In general, the CA scored between the Taiwan group and American norms, that is, they were more acculturated. Nondelinquent sons were much like their fathers, but greater differences were found between delinquents and nondelinquents, the former being lower on Socialization, Self-control, Responsibility, and Well-being, and more deviant from their parents.

Kadri (1971, p. 264) gave the Minnesota Personality Inventory to Chinese students in Singapore, who were attending the University Health Clinic. He claims that the mean scores are similar to those of California college students, and it is true that the means for the nine main scales combined are quite close. But when the scale means are rank-ordered, the correlations between Chinese and California orders were only .57 (males) and .20 (females). In other words, the profiles were decidedly different. Sue and Sue (1974) also used this test with oriental students (see Chapter 14). Sue and Kirk's (1972, 1973, p. 264) application of the Omnibus Personality Inventory at the University of California (Berkeley) showed the Chinese to be high on Conformity, Inhibition, Introversion, and Anxiety.

Liu and Meredith (1966, p. 264) contrasted Chinese students in Taiwan and Hong Kong on the Cattell 16 PF test. There seems to be no reason to expect any differences, but the Taiwan males were more Trusting (L−), Self-Sufficient

(Q2+), Assertive (E+), and Restrained (H−) than the Hong Kong students. No interpretation of these findings is suggested. Scofield and Sun (1960, p. 264) report numerous differences between CC students from abroad and whites on the same test. The former were lower in Intelligence (B), Maturity (C), and Adventurous (H); but higher in Dominance (E), Cheerfulness (F), Sensitivity (I), Paranoia (L), Introversion (M), Shrewd (N), and Self-Sufficient (Q2).

There seems, then, to be a fair degree of unanimity that Chinese, either in China or those not fully acculturated to life in America, tend to show somewhat above average neuroticism, anxiety, and introversion in their test responses. However the more recent studies, either in the United States, Taiwan, or Hong Kong indicate very little difference from whites. There are insufficient data to indicate whether Chinese children, like the Japanese, are less affected than college students. But it should be borne in mind that Chinese may well react differently to the kinds of questions in these tests, and we do not know how far this is due to modesty, reticence, suspicion, etc., or to misunderstanding of items.

EDWARDS PERSONAL PREFERENCE SCHEDULE AND NEED FOR ACHIEVEMENT

This test has seldom been used with Chinese, except by Fenz and Arkoff (1962), who found CA high school students very similar to Japanese, but different from whites (Chapter 14). The males were especially high in Deference, Nurturance, Order, and Endurance, and low in Aggression, Autonomy, Exhibition, and Heterosexuality. Another study by Singh, Huang, and Thompson (1962, p. 265) compared students from China and (East) India with whites at a midwest university, but dealt with three needs only. Whites were highest in Autonomy, Chinese and Indians on Nurturance, and Chinese on Succorance.

Lindgren (1976, p. 265) gave a test composed of 30 pairs of adjectives contrasting Need for Achievement with Need for Affiliation. This was given to CA adults in San Francisco. The younger males obtained the highest Achievement scores, exceeding both American college students and Chinese females.

Adkins, Payne, and Ballif (1972) developed a pictorial test of 75 pairs of drawings, designed to elicit achievement motivation in children aged 3–6 years. A total of 1588 were tested individually in many parts of the United States, mostly in Head Start classes. Though there were some changes with age, and a slight influence of response sets, 16% of the score variance was attributable to ethnic differences. Mormon and Jewish children obtained the highest mean scores, whereas 39 oriental children were in the lowest scoring groups along with American Indians, Hawaiians, and Mexicans. However, all of these were drawn from lower-class families, and the difference may be more socioeconomic than ethnic.

OBSERVATIONAL STUDIES AND INTERVIEWS

There do not seem to have been any studies of response sets nor studies based on objective experimental data. But there have been some good publications comparing the development of Chinese infants and young children with that of Caucasians. One of the main aims of such work is to throw light on possible genetic differences, or to show whether all racial–ethnic differences can be attributed to different childrearing practices between Chinese and whites.

Freedman and Freedman (1969) reported on 24 newborn infants, both CA and white, to whom they applied neurological, sensory, and motor tests at a mean age of 33 hours, that is, an age where any differences in maternal handling could not have had any appreciable effect. The main ethnic differences were found in the excitability of white babies, and the imperturbability of Chinese. The latter were more calm and impassive, even when a cloth was placed over the face. The Caucasians were better at turning the head when lying face down, though there was no difference in holding the head upright. The Chinese also habituated more readily to a blinking-light stimulus. There was no difference in amount of crying, but the Chinese stopped more quickly and were more easily consoled.

In 1974, Freedman expanded this research to include the 24 CA and 41 JA, 65 whites, 36 Navajo Indians, and 123 others (blacks, Africans and aboriginal Australians). He used the Brazelton–Freedman Neonatal Scale, which covers 28 general behavioral items (rated 1 to 9) and 17 neurological signs. The Chinese and whites were very similar in CNS maturity and sensory and motor development. But besides the excitability difference, the whites showed more rapid changes of mood from contentment to upset.

Freedman quotes other work on older children, for example, that of N. Green in 1969 with 3- to 4-year olds. Chinese children in a nursery school showed as much activity, but less intense emotional behavior, no fighting, and less noise; they were more calm and self-possessed. Reports from elementary schools in San Francisco, Hong Kong, and Shanghai have commented similarly on the more restrained behavior of Chinese. This is interesting because CA mothers are so largely acculturated to American norms, and yet their children behave in much the same manner as children reared in China. There are close similarities also to the reported behavior of Japanese children (see Chapter 14). Freedman argues that a divergence between East and West gene pools has been going on for some 300,000 years (while admitting that anthropologists' views vary). Thus, he is inclined to trace the obvious polarity between oriental and occidental art and religions to basic temperamental differences. It is also interesting that Navajo infants, whose tribe probably branched off from the Mongolians some 12,000 years ago, show much the same profile on Freedman's test as Chinese and Japanese, despite the fact that the parents are of much lower SES, and the children less well-nourished.

Freedman realizes the importance of parental expectations in the rearing of infants. For example, American mothers certainly stimulate and interact with their infants and older children more than oriental mothers do. Yet it is also the case that American infants are more "evocative" of mother intervention. His findings with children barely 1½ days old demonstrate the presence of innate differences. These differences are reinforced by the different cultural conventions of childrearing to produce the observed behavioral differences between older white and oriental children. Freedman also mentions the wide range of differences in personality within any ethnic group, and the large amount of overlapping between different groups. In other words, different groups of mankind are very much more alike than they are different. These facts that he has recorded could not possibly be dubbed "racist."

Another very extensive investigation of Chinese and Caucasian children was carried out by Kagan, Kearsley, and Zelazo (1978). The authors' main concern was whether daycare outside the home, from the age of 3½ to 29 months, had any different effects from normal care by the mothers at home. Thirty-two white infants and 32 CA were matched for age, sex, and SES; and half of each sample received the contrasted types of care. (Additional cases, making a total of 116, were involved in some of the comparisons.) The Chinese daycare sample were looked after by bilingual Chinese nurses at a center. This center was well equipped and well staffed, and the infants were brought there each weekday from about 8:00 A.M. to 5:00 P.M. Every infant was looked after for about 14 months by a single caretaker, and then—as toddlers—by another for the remaining period. The teacher–child ratio was 1:3 for babies, and 1:5 for toddlers. On eight different occasions tests and observations were carried out with the children at the center and with the controls in their own homes.

Standard situations were arranged to elicit Attentiveness to new Stimuli, Affective Excitability, Vocalization, Smiling, Fretting or Crying, Reacting to Strange Adults or Children, Mother Separation, and Cognitive Functioning. More than 200 comparisons between Chinese and whites are listed, many of them statistically significant. The white children were more vocal and smiled more. But the stability of the characteristics from one age level to another was quite low, though becoming more consistent from 9 months on. Variability in heart rate was also measured, and the difference between whites (large variation) and Chinese (small) was one of the major ethnic attributes.

Memory for Hidden Objects, Embedded Figures, Recognition Vocabulary, and Growth of Concepts showed no marked ethnic differences. Scores on the Bayley Nonlanguage Scale were lowest in the Chinese children reared at home.

Playing close to mother (when present) versus play near other adults was much more common among Chinese. Also the latter were more inhibited, apprehensive, and wary in playing or talking with a strange peer child. The Chinese from 7 months on were more apt to fret and cry when their mothers departed.

Mothers reported on the characteristics of their own children at home. The white mothers most often stressed talkativeness, laughing easily, activity, and fighting with peers, whereas the Chinese more often stressed staying close to mother. Overall there were larger interethnic differences than differences attributable to type of care or parental SES. The authors conclude that some of the wide individual and group differences have a genetic and temperamental basis. But the influence of cultural norms and parental childrearing pressures must also have been considerable, partly because many of the major differences were not noticeable until the second half of the first year, and because any differences were generally more marked among middle-class children in both groups, and less so among working class.

Masculinity versus Femininity

This topic has been explored only in Meredith's study (1969, Appendix B, p. 236), in which the CA college students were intermediate between JA and whites in feminine tendencies. However, Sexual Permissiveness was measured by Rashke (1976, p. 265), using a 7-item attitude scale. He found that Hong Kong Chinese of both sexes were much less permissive than whites or Chinese studying in America. Also, the Americans had had much more experience of premarital sex than had the Chinese.

Childrearing Attitudes

Childrearing has been studied with the PARI test of parental attitudes in research by Kriger and Kroes (1972, p. 265) and Li (1974, p. 265). The former found CA mothers much more restrictive in their treatment of children than either Jewish or Protestant white mothers. By means of an Anxiety scale and a TAT-type projective test of Achievement Motivation, Li classified 40 Hong Kong Chinese children into those who were high or low in Anxiety, and high or low in Motivation (there being 10 in each subgroup). There were interesting differences between the attitudes of the mothers of these groups. Dominant mothers tended to have low-need achievement sons; and mothers who fostered obedience and dependance had more high-anxious boys. Those who stressed comradeship had low-anxious boys. There were quite different relationships between maternal attitudes and the personalities of daughters, probably because of the low pressure put on girls in Hong Kong for high achievement, and the less strict discipline.

An extensive research by Chan (1976d, 1977) was carried out with 160 Hong Kong Chinese students in Form 4 (i.e., Grade 10). This explored the effects of parental attitudes, as seen by the children. Ginsburg's Parent Image Differential (PID) asks how the child's father and mother treated him or her, taught him, and disciplined him, as a child. Each question is accompanied by a Semantic Differential of 14 or 15 adjectives, which yield measures of Concerned–Warm versus Restrictive–Stern treatment; Democratic versus Demanding teaching; and Autocratic versus Rational discipline.

It was found that these qualities of upbringing were significantly associated with child IQ, achievement in different school subjects, and the adolescents' own attitudes to home and school. Factor analysis of each set of adjectives yielded similar results in Hong Kong and Singapore, but different structures in American and Mexican adolescents. The Father and Mother Concerned and Democratic and Rational factors covered much more variance among Chinese than whites or Mexicans. It is difficult to interpret such variances, for they do not represent the extent to which the parents in different countries applied Concerned or Restricted Treatment, etc.; the mean scores for these variables are not reported.

The effects of family structure on the personalities of Chinese children, together with the persistence of traditional attitudes among immigrants and their descendants (CA), have been discussed in Chapter 1. In addition to the references cited there, the following are helpful: Wright (1964); Sue and Sue (1971, 1973); and Fong (1973). Sollenberger (1968) interviewed 69 parents in New York's Chinatown and describes the upbringing and socialization of their young children. Scofield and Sun (1960) gave a questionnaire on rearing practices to 40 CC students in the United States, and found that they were more severe than American parents in weaning, toilet training, and control of aggression and sex. Most of the above writers draw attention to the increasing problems of delinquency among lower-class CA children living in overcrowded slums.

A similar study of 1187 students in six different countries, including Taiwan, was reported by Ryback, Sanders, Lorentz, and Koestenblatt (1980). A questionnaire was given regarding childrearing practices in their own countries. A few of the items that were rated as very frequent or very infrequent by the Chinese were as follows:

	Chinese %	United States %
Is the mother near to the young child most of the time?	92%	83%
Is the child made to feel loved?	75	93
Is toilet training a gradual process?	75	93
Is weaning by sudden withdrawal rather than by gradual steps?	19	34
Is aggressive behavior encouraged in fighting with other children?	16	23

There seems to be fair similarity between Chinese and Americans, but some of the other countries—India or Israel—often gave very different responses. The results fail to yield a clear picture of how Chinese parents differ from other groups. But it may be that the groups of students understood the questions differently, or their responses may be distorted because they were allowed to answer only "Yes," "No," or "Doubtful."

School Children's Attitudes

Jensen (1973) (see Chapter 2) gave the questionnaire on student attitudes used in the Coleman *et al.* (1966) survey to his Berkeley sample of oriental children. In Grades 4–6 there were 1526 whites, 1181 blacks, and 252 Orientals, the majority of whom were probably Chinese rather than Japanese. The percentages endorsing six items (out of 21) are listed below:

	White	Black	Oriental
1. I like school.	66.1%	68.1%	73.7%
2. I would go to another school rather than this one if I could.	13.9	31.0	7.6
7. People like me do not have much of a chance to be successful in life.	5.7	19.6	9.9
11. Few or none of my close friends are whites.	13.8	67.2	35.2
16. Good luck is more important than work for success.	6.0	24.8	8.4
20. The tougher the job, the harder I work.	65.6	65.7	70.1

All students give more than 60% of *Yes*'s to Numbers 1 and 20, but the Orientals are the highest on both. In Number 2, the Orientals show least dislike of their present school; blacks, the most. Numbers 7 and 16 bear on locus of control; the Chinese show very little more tendency than whites to ascribe success to luck. Finally, in Number 11, two-thirds of the blacks versus about one-third of the Orientals admit that they have few white friends. In other words, the Orientals are generally well adjusted and strongly motivated academically.

CHINESE IDENTITY AND ACCULTURATION

Kang (1972, p. 266) compared CA college students who had Anglo given names with those who had Chinese names only. The former were found to associate more with white Americans, the latter more with Chinese. Those with Anglo names read fewer Chinese publications, had higher occupational aspirations, and participated more in non-Chinese campus activities. Thus, their names gave quite a good indication of degree of acculturation. Working in Hong Kong, Podmore and Chaney (1974, p. 266) found that Chinese adolescents and adults who had had secondary education held fewer traditional opinions and more modern ones than the less educated. This especially was true of those who had attended Anglo–Chinese schools.

Three studies of Hong Kong Chinese students have shown links between modernistic versus traditional attitudes, and their usage of Chinese or English language. Earle (1969, p. 266) gave Rokeach's Dogmatism Scale both in English and Chinese to 101 students at the University of Hong Kong, where English is the medium of instruction. Scores for dogmatism were especially high on the Chinese version, suggesting that the students accepted dogmatic beliefs more strongly when using their mother tongue.

Yang and Bond (1980) tested 121 students of both sexes at the Chinese University of Hong Kong. Though Chinese is the medium of instruction, they had studied English since elementary school, and many had attended Anglo–Chinese secondary schools. The test was a 20-item scale of modernity versus traditionalism, and it was presented either in Chinese or English language by either Chinese or English experimenters. Neither the sex of the students nor the ethnicity of the testers had any consistent effect. But this time the scores for Traditionalism were significantly higher among Chinese taking the English version. The authors suggest that these students would be more closely identified with Chinese culture than those at the English-speaking university, and therefore when faced with a task in English, they would tend to reaffirm their traditional Chinese beliefs.

Earle (1967) wished to show that Chinese students who are attracted to modern English beliefs will also give similar connotative meanings to common concepts. The methodology was elaborate, and somewhat similar to that adopted by Triandis *et al.* (1966, cf. p. 219). Having rated their own acceptance of traditional beliefs, they also rated the probable acceptance of 20 attitude statements by typical Chinese and typical English people. They were then classified as Chinese-Affiliated, English-Affiliated, or no difference, and their self-ratings were found to accord with those of typical Chinese or English, respectively. In addition, the subjects had rated 12 common concepts (e.g., Work, Food, Mother, Success), given both in English and Chinese on 12 semantic differential scales. The D scores, representing the overall differences in connotative meaning were larger in the English-affiliated than the Chinese-affiliated, as hypothesized. This indicated a greater gap between English and Chinese concepts among those who were more strongly identified with English culture. The same or even greater differences were found among secondary school students as with college students.

Conformity

Meade and Barnard (1973, 1975, p. 266) gave a modified version of the Asch conformity test to male and female Chinese and white students in Hong Kong. The students stated their own opinions on six controversial attitude statements, and were then pressured to change by the opinions voiced by stooges. Though the Chinese did not show larger attitude changes than whites, they gave fewer anticonformity responses than whites did, that is, responses that moved further away from the stooge judgments. The authors conclude that the Chinese are more sensitive to group pressures than whites, and this accords with their well-known unwillingness to speak out, or contradict, in university seminars. The Chinese women shifted their opinions more than twice as frequently when the stooges were male than they did with females. It was also observed that 22 Chinese women (and only 8 American women) gave up the task, since they could not cope with standing up to group pressure.

Earlier, Meade (1970) had studied attitude change among Hong Kong and American university students. He found that the Chinese were most influenced by a discussion group under an authoritarian leader, whereas the whites were equally open to a democratic leader.

Dawson, Whitney, and Lau (1972) studied the reactions of 44 Hong Kong students to items in a Traditional versus Modern attitude scale. Considerable emotion was aroused, as shown by the GSR (psychogalvanic reflex), when their answers to the more important items were contradicted by answers purporting to be the group opinions.

Several different groups in Hong Kong, including psychiatric patients and school and university students, were tested with the same instrument by Dawson, Law, Leung, and Whitney (1971). Four possible responses to each item were classified as Traditional, Semitraditional, Semimodern, and Modern. The total Modern responses minus the Traditional provided a range of variation (RV) score. This showed modernism to correlate positively with educational achievement and SES, and negatively with neurotic disturbance and with the GSR test of anxiety when contradicted by peers. Younger students tended to give many traditional responses, but attitude reorganization (i.e., adoption of more modern views) occurred in secondary school, while at university there was a regression on certain issues to younger attitudes. Dawson and Wing-Cheung (1972, p. 266) applied the same T–M scale to sons in primary or secondary schools, and their parents. The strongest Traditional scores were found in Grade 4 students, and there was a trend toward Modernism in Grade 6. Much higher Modern scores were obtained by Chinese students in Form 4 attending either Chinese middle schools or Anglo-Chinese schools, and by their parents. Exposure to mass media, measured by time per week spent on television, radio, or newspapers, correlated significantly with Modernism scores (.69), but only among the Anglo-Chinese youth.

Chu (1960, p. 267) applied Janis's methods of studying persuasibility (developed at Yale University) to Chinese high school students and American controls. The subjects answered questions on certain controversial issues, and then repeated this after reading persuasive arguments for or against. The Chinese changed their opinions more frequently than whites, but the girls did not show greater persuasibility than boys, as in the United States. Chu admits that the results should not be taken to represent persuasibility or conformity in general, since there was considerable variation in reactions to particular items.

Huang and Harris (1973, p. 267) criticized the artificiality of the Asch procedure. They contrived a situation where Chinese or American adults waiting at bus stops were asked to choose among pictures of plants or flowers that would be suitable for a beautification project. The interviewers identified themselves as college professors or as garbage collectors, and as knowledgeable about plants, or not knowledgeable. They gave their own opinions about the pictures first. In all instances, Chinese imitated the interviewer more than Americans did. The apparent SES and competence of the interviewers also affected their judgments.

Sensitivity to Others

Several studies have been carried out in this rather unusual area. They were based on the assumption that members of one culture have difficulty in interpreting expressions, gestures, and behavior of members of another culture, though the longer they interact, the greater should be their accuracy. Adams (1937) observed changes in facial expressions and mannerisms among Orientals in Hawaii with progressive adaptation to other cultures. However, it has been pointed out that Chinese students working at American universities mix very little with other ethnic groups on campus, hence adaptation and mutual understanding are slow to emerge.

Fong (1965a,b, p. 267) constructed an inventory for measuring degree of assimilation, and gave this along with Sarbin's Stick Figures test to several generations of CA students and to some quite recent immigrants from Hong Kong. The Stick Figures consists of outline drawings of people expressing various emotions, which have to be identified. On both tests there was a continuous rise in scores from first to fifth generation Chinese. The Hong Kong immigrants were the lowest on the assimilation scale, but scored highly on the Stick Figures. Fong suggests that this is because Hong Kong inhabitants have internalized Western norms of behavior to a large extent. The Stick Figures scores also rose with living in white rather than Chinese areas, having Caucasian versus Chinese friends, and with inability to speak Chinese. Similarly Lindgren and Yu (1975, p. 267) devised an Intercultural Insight Questionnaire for Chinese, based on identifying traits that were most characteristic of Americans. This was given to 91 adults born abroad, who had been living in America for various lengths of time. Those with longer residence scored higher than those with 3 years or less; those with secondary education were better than those with elementary only. Finally, Barney and Chu (1976, p. 267) tested 30 Mormon missionaries to China with a test containing 70 items of knowledge about Chinese traditions, clothing, language, manners, etc., and found that they scored lower than Chinese (CC) adults on 29 of the items. Despite their long experience they misunderstood many aspects of Chinese values and customs.

One investigation of recognition of emotional expressions by children compared 87 Taiwan Chinese and 96 Americans in Grade 2. Borke and Sue (1972) presented stylized pictures of Happy, Afraid, Sad, and Angry faces, together with 38 short stories of situations in each of which one of the emotions would be displayed. Approximately 98% of both groups recognized Happy and Afraid, but Sad and Angry were less consistent, with approximately 70% agreement. The American children gave Sad responses more frequently, and the Chinese gave more Angry ones. Overall, the Americans obtained higher scores than the Chinese. This is attributed by the authors to the Americans being exposed to a wider range of emotions in daily life and being less sheltered. Also, they have been taught earlier to feel sad rather than angry about frustrating situations.

Locus of Control

One would expect Chinese, like Japanese, to score high on External Locus, since Chinese upbringing emphasizes kinship dependence rather than independent initiative. This was confirmed by Hsieh, Shybut, and Lotsof (1969, p. 268), using the Rotter scale with Hong Kong Chinese high school students, a group of half-Chinese, and American whites. Tseng (1972, p. 268) likewise found Asian students at an American university (presumably including some Japanese) more externally oriented than whites, especially those with less than 1 year's residence. But he was also concerned with attitude towards disabled persons, and found that unfavorable attitudes were more prevalent among short-stay Asians, and among those who scored high on Taylor's Manifest Anxiety Scale.

Lao, Chuang, and Yang (1977, p. 268; see also Lao, 1978) gave the 3-part Levenson–Rotter IPC scale, covering Internal Control, Powerful Others, and Chance. The subjects were 517 Taiwan CC students. Unlike the Japanese students tested by Mahler (1974), there was no substantial difference between the Chinese and a group of American college students. They scored higher than Japanese both on I and P, but not on Chance. Chinese males were somewhat higher in Internality and lower in Chance than females. Certain relations were obtained with background variables, Internal scores being associated with high SES, and with the students' confidence in their own ability to succeed.

Machiavellianism

Christie's Machiavellianism scale was used in Hong Kong by Oksenberg (1970, p. 268), where it was taken by 67 17-year-old students in a highly traditional Chinese secondary school, and by 146 in a more Western-type school. The latter group obtained higher Mach scores than the former, and in both groups boys scored higher than girls.

Nachamie (1970) prepared a simplified version suitable for sixth grade Chinese and other ethnic children in a poor neighborhood of New York. She also devised a disc-throwing test that could be scored for bluffing. High-Mach children were found to bluff much more often. No comparison was made with white children, and there were no significant sex differences. But the children's Mach scores were lower than those of adults, suggesting that they do not develop into competent manipulators until adolescence. Kuo and Marsella (1977, p. 268) gave the Mach scale to 64 Taiwan Chinese studying in Hawaii and to 62 Caucasians. There was no significant difference in scores. But when the items were factorized, it appeared that the scale was measuring rather different variables in the two groups. With the Americans it mainly covered deceit of versus openness to others, whereas with Chinese it implied caution and restraint in interacting with strangers.

VALUES

Rodd (1959b, p. 269) carried out a large-scale study in Taiwan with the Allport–Vernon–Lindzey Study of Values. Native and emigré Taiwanese scored much the same, but there were considerable differences from whites, as also from the Japanese tested by Nobechi and Kimura (1957). The three highest and lowest values in each group were

	High	Low
Chinese	Theor., Polit., Relig.	Aesth., Econ., Social
Japanese	Econ., Aesth., Polit.	Theor., Social, Relig.
Whites	Econ., Polit., Relig.	Aesth., Social, Theor.

In addition there were sex differences in value profiles, but these were similar to those found in the United States (see also Nobechi, Chapter 15).

Singh *et al.* (1962, p. 269) quote considerably different results on the same test, but their groups, consisting of CA, Indian, and white students, were small.

Morris's "Ways to Live" was also given, with the following values chiefly favored:

Chinese: Sympathetic, Group participation, Cosmic purpose
Indian: Sympathetic, Cosmic purpose
Whites: Integrative action, Carefree enjoyment, Adventurousness

On Sanford's Authoritarianism Scale, both Asian groups scored significantly more authoritarian than whites. On the Edwards Personal Preference Scale, Chinese and Indians scored especially high on Nurturance (i.e., sympathy and mutual help); Americans scored high on Autonomy.

Two other studies confirm high authoritarianism scores on the F scale among Chinese (CC) teachers. Ho and Yu (1974, p. 269) gave in addition a scale of Attitudes towards Filial Piety, and found that this correlated +0.50 with authoritarianism. Presumably both tests involve traditionalism. Meade and Whittaker (1967, p. 269) gave the F scale to college students in six countries, and found Chinese a little lower than Indians or Africans, but higher than Arabs, Brazilians, and especially American whites.

Quite a different form of test was devised by Lo (1942, p. 269) for studying Chinese versus white values. A list of 16 common vices and another list of desirable personality traits were ranked in order of importance by high school and college students in China, and comparisons made between the sex and age groups. The Chinese put the following vices highest: Snobbishness, Cheating, Sex irregularities, Stealing, and Selfishness. And the least serious were Vulgar talk, Swearing, Smoking, Drinking, and Dancing. The highest in the list of admired qualities were Honesty, Courage, Initiative, Cooperation, and Open-mindedness, and the least important were Thrift, Cheerfulness, Reverence, Cleanliness, and Obedience.

The same lists had been used in American studies some thirty years ago, and the correlations between Chinese and Americans were quite substantial, namely .50 to .58. The only marked difference in evaluation of traits was that the Americans put Cleanliness ahead of Courtesy; the Chinese did the opposite.

Vocational Interests

The studies by Sue and Frank (1973) and Sue and Kirk (1972, 1973), which included CA and JA, have been outlined in Chapter 12. The Chinese were generally similar to Japanese in their score profiles on Strong's Vocational Interest Blank (VIB). But Chinese were even more favorable to physical science and skilled technical jobs. Chu (1975, p. 270) obtained considerable differences on the VIB between Taiwan Chinese and American college students, but no details are available.[1]

[1]Seen in abstract only.

Bennett and Tiy (1976, p. 270) gave the Pacific Vocational Interest Analysis (similar to the Kuder Preference Record) to miscellaneous groups in Hong Kong, Fiji, etc. Chinese in Hong Kong and Fiji showed very similar interest profiles. But Fijian Chinese and Indians differed considerably, the Chinese being higher in Practical–Technical, Outdoor, and Artistic interests, while Indians were higher in Clerical, Number, and Scientific. It seems unusual for Chinese to favor Outdoor, but no interpretation is offered of these or other significant differences.

Stereotypes

In the 1870s, the conventional stereotype of the Chinese included Yellow, Slant-eyed, Pigtailed, Filthy habits, Morally evil, Shrewd and Treacherous, Low Intelligence, Cowardly, Taking White Jobs, and Unassimilable (see Chapter 1). However by the time of Katz and Braly's (1933, p. 270) study, the adjectives most frequently applied by college students were Superstitious, Shy, Conservative, Tradition-loving, Loyal to Family, and Industrious (Sue and Kitano, 1973). Other studies, already cited in Chapter 15, showed that, from the 1930s on, their reputation had become quite favorable (Smith, 1943; Vinacke, 1949a; Harrigan et al., 1961).

Three additional studies were based on Chinese (CC) self-ratings rather than judgments by non-Chinese. Since Chinese have been generally regarded as showing humility and underestimating their worth, Trow and Pu (1927, p. 270) hypothesized that their ratings of self would be less favorable than the ratings by other Chinese. This was tried out among Chinese studying in America, who rated themselves and their acquaintances on several traits. The mean self-ratings (on a scale of 1 to 5) for these traits were Trustworthy, 3.7; Intelligence, 3.6; Sociable, 3.4; Industrious, 3.3; Personal Appearance, 3.0; and Leadership, 2.9. Thus Trustworthiness and Intelligence seem to be most valued by Chinese, and the students regard themselves as relatively lacking in Leadership. The overall self-rating was 3.32, whereas the mean for ratings by others was 3.69. Thus there is only a rather slight tendency for them to understate their good qualities. However, a repetition by Luh and Sailer (1933, p. 270), using the same trait ratings, found that among 20 CC, 13 overestimated and 7 underestimated themselves as compared with the ratings by others. The authors suggest that Trow and Pu's results occurred either because the students were not fully confident of anonymity, or because those studying in a foreign country were likely to be unusually modest. In another study of self-ratings for 10 traits on a scale of 1 to 9, the majority of all ratings were above the midpoint of 5, particularly such important characteristics as Honesty and Loyalty. Thus the same trend towards self-overestimation occurs among Chinese as with whites.

Later, Yeh and Chu (1974, p. 270) compared self-ratings and the ratings of CC peers and American students by three groups of Taiwan Chinese. The first group, preparing to study in the United States, was more positive toward self and peers than a second group doing graduate work in Taiwan. They claimed to be high in Forceful, Aggressive, Spontaneous, Active, and Optimistic; they also had more favorable images of Americans. A third group, who had been studying at least a year at the University of Hawaii, gave the most negative judgments of Americans, finding them unfriendly, rebellious, and demanding.

Li and Liu (1975) found that present-day American sociology students are more self-critical and tolerant towards Chinese (in Taiwan) than are Chinese psychology students; the latter are strongly ethnocentric. Groups of 296 and 265 were given a list of 33 of Katz and Braly's traits, and they rated their own and other nationalities on each of these. The traits were classified as positive–favorable or negative–unfavorable. It was found that the Chinese gave themselves predominantly positive traits, and the Americans negative traits; Americans however gave themselves many negative traits, and the Chinese positive traits.

Very little use seems to have been made of projective techniques with Chinese, apart from Gardiner's (1969) work with children's drawings, in which the Taiwan Chinese showed high levels of hostility (see p. 226). Yeh (1972) gave the Thematic Apperception Test to Chinese American students in Hawaii. He claims that this indicated a high level of anxiety, and conflicts over self-identity and family values, but no details are provided.

SUMMARY

As with the Japanese there are numerous studies of Chinese—mainly college students—whose results mostly accord with common observation of their personality characteristics, but there were few which seem to add much to our knowledge. Several studies were based on Chinese in Taiwan or Hong Kong, but the majority involved testing of recent or long-term immigrants to mainland America or Hawaii, or their descendants. No outstanding differences between these populations have been reported, except insofar as the CA are more acculturated than the CC, and have taken on more of the traits and attitudes of Americans. Chinese Americans are seldom classified by generation, like the Japanese, but when they are, as in Fong's (1965b) research, they do show progressive approximation to American norms. Yet at the same time, some traditional Chinese characteristics persist, even among highly acculturated CA, for example, restrictiveness in upbringing of children (e.g., Kriger and Kroes, 1972).

One might have expected more comparisons between CA and JA, or CC and JJ. Those studies that have included both ethnic groups do not seem to show meaningful or consistent differences. On the whole, the Chinese tend to be somewhat less deviant from American norms than the Japanese.

Eleven studies using personality questionnaires suggest that CC and CA are more neurotic, anxious, and introverted, and less dominant than whites, but these were mostly published in the 1930s to 1950s. The more recent ones have usually shown smaller differences. Only two investigations (Chiu, 1971; Li, 1974) dealt with primary school children. Chiu obtained results quite similar to those of high school or college students, that is, greater anxiety among Taiwanese. But Li found no overall difference between Hong Kong and American children on Test Anxiety. In contrast, the oriental students covered by the Coleman Report were better adjusted to school than other ethnic groups, and were as realistic in their self-concepts as whites.

The Edwards Personal Preference Inventory did yield several meaningful differences between Chinese and whites: for example, the Chinese scored high on needs for Abasement, Deference, and Order, and low on Autonomy, Dominance, Aggression, and Heterosexuality (Fenz & Arkoff, 1962). Like the Japanese, they are higher in Femininity than whites, that is, less concerned with displaying masculinity. Again both groups tend to regard their lives as determined more by external forces than by internal standards, on Rotter's Locus of Control scale. It is interesting that the California Personality Inventory showed quite similar differences between delinquent and nondelinquent youths in Taiwan as are found in the United States, suggesting that the test is to some extent valid for Orientals as well as whites.

Some authors seem to ascribe high anxiety and introversion to strict upbringing at home, while others consider that Chinese college students are working under far more stress than whites. The most reliable investigations are those based on direct observations of child behavior, and excellent work has been done by Freedman and Freedman (1969), and Kagan et al. (1978). These included children ranging from day-old babies to 2½-year-olds in nursery schools. They provide strong evidence of genetic temperamental differences, the Chinese children being more calm, passive, and less excitable than American children. Their upbringing by the mother reinforces dependency and security, and it discourages overt displays of emotion or aggression. Thus at school they are less competitive and less apt to fight with other children, as well as more compliant to adult commands. To some extent this may help to explain the patience and passivity shown by the early Chinese immigrants when attacked by whites. But it does not suggest any basic or constitutional disposition for Chinese children and adults to be more anxious, emotional, or unstable than whites.

Some tendency for Chinese to conform to other peoples' expectations was found on three tests, but these were rather artificial and cannot be taken as applying to conformist or nonconformist behavior in other social situations. Also, it was found that Chinese, when assessing their own personality traits, tend to overestimate their standing on desirable traits, much in the same way as whites. That is, they did not display greater humility, as had been suggested by

Trow and Pu (1927). The stereotypes about Chinese held by whites showed interesting changes over time, being highly unfavorable in the nineteenth century, more realistic in the 1930s, and highly favorable in the 1940s when Japanese were most disliked.

Several studies of Chinese college students with the Strong Vocational Interest Blank showed similar preferences to those of Japanese, for example, for scientific occupations. However, certain differences in their choices of college courses and professional occupations were noted in Chapter 13. In their value patterns, the CC males in Taiwan most favored Theoretical, Political, and Religious values, whereas Japanese preferred Aesthetic, Economic, and Political. Chinese males tend to be considerably more authoritarian than whites, more disapproving of premarital sexual activities, and more restrictive in child upbringing.

Appendix C

Personality Studies of Chinese[1]

[1]For list of abbreviations used here, see Appendix B, p. 230.

262

Personality Questionnaires

Author(s) and Dates	Samples Studied	Main Tests Used	Main Results
Shen (1936)	400 CC hs stud.	Bernreuter Personality Inventory	Chinese score much above US norms on Neuroticism and Introversion, lower on Self-Sufficiency and Dominance.
Chou and Mi (1937)	855 CC coll. stud.	Thurstone Neurotic Inventory	Chinese mean, 78.45; US more usually 40 to 50.
Hsu (1951)	110 CC stud.; 144 CC at American colleges	Thurstone Neurotic Inventory	Mean, 80.83. Those in US, 53.49; with longer residence in US, 41.64.
Pai *et al.* (1937)	617 CC males	Thurstone Neurotic Inventory	Mental patients' means, 60–62; Drug addicts, 51; Medical patients, 43; Students, 55; Coolies, 23.
Smith (1938)	Univ. of Hawaii, mixed races	Thurstone Neurotic Inventory	See p. 189. Chinese more neurotic than Caucasians, especially in family conflicts, physical complaints, fearfulness, submissiveness.
Chiu (1971)	613 Taiwan Gd. 4–5; 381 US Gd. 4–5	Children's Manifest Anxiety Scale	Means: Anxiety Lie Scale CC Grade 4 22.63 4.42 CC Grade 5 20.70 4.53 US Combined 18.71 3.24
Paschal and Kuo (1973)	63 Taiwan CC coll. stud. 120 US	Anxiety tests and Tennessee Self-Concept test	Chinese higher on anxiety and conflict; lower on some self-esteem scores.

(*continued*)

Author(s) and Dates	Samples Studied	Main Tests Used	Main Results		
Li (1974)	61 boys, 72 girls, Gd. 5 and 6 in Hong Kong	Sarason's TASC Scale	Means:	Gd. 5	Gd. 6
			Hong Kong		
			Boys	7.1	10.3
			Girls	12.6	14.2
			US		
			Boys	9.3	9.3
			Girls	12.7	12.8
Fong and Peskin (1969)	42 CC studying in US; 42 CA	California Personality Inventory	CC students less well-adjusted for life in America. Both groups above US in Femininity.		
Abbott (1974)	82 CA sons and 52 Taiwan CC sons, and parents	California Personality Inventory	Comparisons between CA and CC, and del. and nondel. sons; see text.		
Kadri (1971)	200 male, 60 female Singapore coll. stud.	Minnesota Multiphasic Personality Inventory	Means for 9 scales: CC, 56.08; US, 53.05. Some score profile differences.		
Sue and Kirk, (1972, 1973)	236 CA, 136 JA coll. stud.	Omnibus Personality Inventory	Few differences from JA, but more deviant from whites.		
Liu and Meredith (1966)	298 Taiwan and 258 Hong Kong CC stud.	16 PF Test	Similar score profiles, though some significant differences.		
Scofield and Sun (1960)	40 CC students in US; 604 whites	16 PF and questions on childrearing	Significant differences on most personality factors; see text.		

Edwards Personal Preference Schedule

Study	Sample	Measures	Means:	Chin.	Ind.	White
Singh et al. (1962)	37 each CC coll. stud., Indians, and whites	3 EPPS scales, and Study of Values (See below)	Autonomy	12.59	10.50	14.43
			Succorance	11.19	6.24	8.46
			Nurturance	15.49	15.64	10.32

			Mean Achievement Scores		
				Under 30	Over 30
Lindgren (1976)	CA (San Francisco) adults	30 pairs of adjectives, Achievement versus Affiliation	Males	16.24	12.38
			Females	12.57	12.25
			White Stud.	13 to 14	

Sexual Permissiveness

Study	Sample	Measures	Means:	Men	Women
Rashke (1976)	153 Hong Kong stud., 26 CC in US, 264 whites	Reiss Premarital Permissiveness Scale	Hong Kong	2.90	2.53
			CC in US	4.31	4.23
			Whites	4.63	4.41

Childrearing Attitudes

Study	Sample	Measures	Mean Restrictiveness Scores	
Kriger and Kroes (1972)	35 CA mothers, Jewish and Protestant whites	PARI	CA	212
			Jewish	152
			Protestant	150
Li (1974)	40 Hong Kong mothers and Gd. 5-6 children	Mothers: PARI; Children: Anxiety Scale, and TAT N Ach. test	PARI Factors: I. Dominance; II. Obedience, Dependency; III. Communication, Comradeship. (See text.)	

(continued)

Chinese Identity and Acculturation

Author(s) and Dates	Samples Studied	Main Tests Used	Main Results
Kang (1972)	262 CA coll. stud.	Attitudes to Chinese and US cultures	36% had Anglicized names, and these showed greater identification with US culture.
Podmore and Chaney (1974)	1123 Hong Kong interviewees, aged 15–29 yr.	Traditional versus Modern attitude scale, SES, and Education	Those with secondary education who attended Anglo–Chinese schools expressed more modern attitudes.
Earle (1969)	101 Hong Kong coll. stud., 82 UK coll. stud.	Rokeach Dogmatism Scale	Mean Dogmatism Scores CC tested in English 177.9 CC tested in Chinese 191.7 British 141.7
Earle (1967)	36 Hong Kong coll. and 36 hs stud., all bilingual	Scale for accepting traditional beliefs. Semantic Differential for 12 concepts	Differences in connotative meaning between concepts rated in Chinese and English were lower in students rejecting traditional beliefs.

Conformity

Author(s) and Dates	Samples Studied	Main Tests Used	Main Results
Meade and Barnard (1973, 1975)	Hong Kong coll. stud.: 60 male, 60 female; 60 US whites	6 attitude statements rated for agreement, before and after pressure by stooges	Chinese slower to respond, especially with all-male stooges. More anticonformist responses from whites. CC females gave up more often.
Dawson and Wing Cheung (1972)	43 Hong Kong prim. children (Gd. 4 & 6); 41 Middle School, 22 Anglo–Chinese sec., and their parents	Traditional–Modern Scale, and Exposure of students to mass media	RV (Range of Variation) Scores Children Parents Pr. 4 children −8.0 +6.5 Pr. 6 children +8.6 +7.3 Middle school +34.5 +27.0 Anglo–Chinese +30.3 +23.0

Chu (1960)	182 Taiwan CC hs boys and girls; also US norms	Janis's test of persuasibility	Persuasibility Means	
			Chinese	US
			Boys 14.65	10.70
			Girls 14.85	12.20

Huang and Harris (1973)	80 Taiwan CC adults, 80 US whites	Number of imitations of interviewer's preferences (see text)	Interviewers	
			High Competence	Low Competence
			Chinese	
			High SES 3.90	4.30
			Low SES 3.50	2.90
			US	
			High SES 3.20	3.65
			Low SES 3.30	2.00

Sensitivity to Others

Fong (1965a, b)	336 CA stud., 1st to 5th generation; 24 recently from Hong Kong	Assimilation Inventory, and Stick Figures Test	Means	
			Assimilation	Stick
			CA 1st gener. 132.4	114.0
			2nd gener. 167.4	166.7
			5th gener. 233.3	192.2
			Hong Kong 89.7	186.4

Lindgren and Yu (1975)	91 CA, recent immigrants	Intercultural Insight Questionnaire	Means
			In US > 3 yr 13.76
			In US < 3 yr 12.39
			Sec. educ. in China 13.48
			Elem. educ. only 11.38

Barney and Chu (1976)	30 Mormon missionaries to China; 30 adult CC controls	70 items on Chinese traditions, culture, etc.	Each item rated for *agree* or *disagree*. 29 showed significant differences between Chinese and missionaries.

(continued)

Author(s) and Dates	Samples Studied	Main Tests Used	Main Results
Locus of Control			
Hsieh et al. (1969)	343 Hong Kong hs seniors, 80 part-Chinese, 239 US whites	Rotter Scale	Means for Externality Hong Kong students 12.07 Part-Chinese 9.79 US whites 8.58
Tseng (1972)	67 Asian stud. from abroad, 61 whites	Rotter I-E Scale, Taylor Anxiety, and Attitude to Disabled Scale	Chinese more External, especially if short residence in US. More positive attitude toward disabled with length of residence, and low anxiety.
Lao et al. (1977)	517 Taiwan CC coll. stud.	Scale for Internal, Powerful Others, and Chance	Females lower on Internal than males, higher on Chance. Internal related to confidence in one's success.
Machiavellianism			
Oksenberg (1967)	213 Hong Kong 17-yr.-old stud. in contrasted schools	Scale for Machiavellianism	Means: Traditional Schools / Westernized Schools Boys 91.88 / 101.21 Girls 88.96 / 96.47
Kuo and Marsella (1977)	64 CC studying in Hawaii; 62 whites	Scale for Machiavellianism	Chinese insignificantly higher scores than whites. Different factor patterns.

Values

Study	Subjects	Measure	Findings
Rodd (1959b)	525 Taiwan CC, 765 Taiwanese, 521 JJ	Allport–Vernon–Lindzey Study of Values	Two Chinese groups closely alike, but differences in value patterns from Japanese and US whites.
Singh *et al.* (1962)	37 CA stud., 37 Indians, 37 whites	Study of Values, Ways to Live, EPPS, and Authoritarianism Scale	Three highest values / Author. Mean Chinese — The.,Aes., Soc. — 26.2 Indian — Eco.,The., Pol. — 27.3 US — The.,Rel., Aes. — 23.0
Ho and Yu (1974)	135 CC teachers, in Taiwan	F-Authoritarian Scale, and Filial Piety Attitude	These intercorrelate +.50.
Meade and Whittaker (1967)	Coll. stud. in 6 countries, $N = 54$ to 85	F-Authoritarian Scale	Means Indian 5.06 Arab 4.45 African 4.91 Brazilian 4.02 Hong Kong 4.61 US 3.16
Lo (1942)	300 CC hs and coll. stud., also white groups	Ranking 16 vices and 16 ideals in order of importance	Some sex differences. Correlations of of ranks with Americans, .50 to .58.

(*continued*)

Author(s) and Dates	Samples Studied	Main Tests Used	Main Results
Tests of Interests			
Chu (1975)	1370 Taiwan CC, 2178 white coll. stud.	Strong–Campbell Vocational Interests Blank	Considerable cultural differences in items "Liked," and in vocational preferences. (No details available.)
Bennett and Tiy (1976)	177 Hong Kong stud., 89 Chinese in Fiji, 170 Melanesian and Indian	Pacific Vocational Interest Analysis	Chinese in Fiji much the same pattern as in Hong Kong. Males higher in Practical and Science, Women in Social and Clerical.
Stereotypes and Ratings			
Katz and Braly (1933)	100 US coll. stud.	Chose traits characteristic of 10 nations	Stereotypes of Japanese, Chinese, and other groups; see p. 220.
Trow and Pu, (1927)	18 CC students in US	Rated self and friends on 6 traits	Mean ratings of self, 3.32 (on 5-point scale); mean for others, 3.69.
Luh and Sailer (1933)	20 CC stud., and another grup of 75 CC stud.	Same traits rated as in Trow and Pu (1927)	13 students overestimated self versus others; 7 underestimated. The large group gave themselves mainly positive ratings.
Yeh and Chu (1974)	132 CC stud. going to US, 108 in Taiwan, 58 at Univ. of Hawaii	Ratings of self, peers, and Americans	Group 1 most positive in self-ratings and peers; Group 3 most negative about Americans.

17

Epilogue

In my book *Intelligence: Heredity and Environment* (1979) I endeavored to show that there is very strong evidence of genetic factors underlying the intellectual capacities or the efficiency of cognitive processing in the human species. This evidence was by no means derived merely from the rather dubious work on identical twins reared apart. At the same time there was also a great deal of research indicating the importance of environmental factors, including perinatal conditions and malnutrition, preschool upbringing in the family, and stimulation or deprivation throughout childhood and adolescence. Yet a purely cultural and environmental explanation of individual differences in intelligence was inadequate, and I concluded—in common with what is the view probably held by the majority of present-day psychologists—that a person's intelligence depends on the interaction between the genes and the amount of stimulation received during mental growth.

It was a good deal more difficult to reach a firm conclusion on the importance of genetic factors in group differences, as between racial or ethnic groups, because any genetically different groups always differ too in their cultures. Much evidence supports both the hereditary and the environmental explanations. But it is not sufficient to allow us to state, for example, that the higher average IQ of whites than of blacks is attributable to certain genes, nor that the differences are wholly explicable in terms of discrimination against blacks, deprivation, or differences in childrearing. I concluded that both kinds of influence are important and, as with individual differences, they interact.

As mentioned in the preface, I hoped to be able to throw some additional light on these problems by studying the abilities and achievements of Chinese and Japanese immigrants to North America and their descendants, since they too had been discriminated against and experienced much deprivation until the ending of World War II. Yet on the average, they appeared to have reached higher educational and occupational levels than Caucasian Americans and Canadians. The same kind of progress has occurred among the Japanese in their homeland, in spite of the technological backwardness of their culture in the nineteenth century.

The Chinese cultures in Hong Kong and Taiwan are less fully developed, yet the intellectual abilities and educational achievements of the children are quite comparable with those of Western countries. As might be expected, each ethnic subgroup evolved somewhat differently in Japan or China, and/or in Hong Kong, Hawaii, mainland United States, and Canada. All these groups started with values, social organization, and cognitive styles very different from those of the West, since the oriental cultures had been so largely isolated from Western influence until the latter half of the nineteenth century. Though these groups have all become acculturated in some degree to Western norms, they still show many differences in personality characteristics and in social and ethical behavior from one another as well as from Caucasians, and much of their original cultures have survived. Yet they have overtaken white Americans on intelligence as defined by American psychologists.

How has this come about? It would be possible, however unpopular, to argue that the oriental races inherit genes underlying intellectual ability that are superior to those of Caucasians, though this potentiality was unable to reach its full expression under the unfavorable environmental conditions in China and Japan, and the deprivation and language handicaps of the early immigrants to North America. But this is unsatisfactory because there is no means of proving or disproving it. Also it seems improbable because there is little doubt that the initial Chinese immigrants came from poor and uneducated peasant stock; and yet, as Witty and Lehman pointed out in 1930, even their first-generation children were making their way up the educational and socioeconomic ladder. There is more doubt regarding the intellectual potential of the first Japanese immigrants, and in both groups the later arrivals, particularly those currently entering Nortb America, contained a considerable proportion of Orientals who had shown above-average ability and had obtained good education at home. However, as I stated in 1979, one of the more telling points against genetic group differences in mentality is the apparent lack of intergenerational stability, that is, the tendency for the children of below-average parents to approximate the intelligence distribution of the new country to which they have come within a few generations. Also there seem to be no grounds for suggesting that the overall intelligence level of Orientals in North America or Japan has improved through the mechanisms of genetic dominance or selective breeding.

There are at least two strong arguments for admitting that some genetic factors are involved in mental differences between oriental and occidental peoples. The first is the consistent finding that Chinese and Japanese babies differ from Caucasian in some temperamental quality of passivity versus excitability. This can be observed so early in life that the mother's handling of the infants could not be held responsible, although it is very likely that her treatment and childrearing practices tend to reinforce this difference and thus result in the relative docility and dependence of oriental children, and the adventurousness, aggressiveness, and independence of Caucasians. Subsidiary evidence of innate differences in autonomic reactivity is provided by the greater susceptibility of Orientals than whites to the effects of alcohol. The work of Tsunoda and others interested in lateralization of brain functions suggests that there may also be some basic racial differences in information processing, although Tsunoda himself advocates a learning theory.

Second, there is the curious but unanimous finding that Orientals of all ages in any cultural setting score higher relative to Caucasians on spatial, numerical, or nonverbal intelligence tests, and less well on verbal abilities and achievements. In the earlier phases of immigration this could be attributed to the Orientals' difficulties with the English language. But it has persisted even when they have been living in North America for several generations and speak only English.

It is generally admitted that family pressures for educational achievement play a part in the intellectual growth of Jews, for example. But they are outstanding in verbal abilities and lower in nonverbal, while Orientals are the opposite. How and why should Japanese upbringing stimulate this inverse pattern? It would certainly be more explicable if literacy and numeracy are partly genetic, since we could hypothesize that Caucasians (including Jews) have stronger genes on the one, Orientals on the other. Another possibility might be a greater potentiality of the left hemisphere in Caucasians and the right hemisphere in Orientals. But if this were so, one would think that tests of lateralization would have demonstrated it.

There is some overlapping, too, with Witkin and Berry's (1975) concept of field independence and dependence. Both Berry (1966) and I (Vernon, 1969) have shown the higher scores of Eskimos and native Indians on visuospatial and field-independent abilities than those of Africans and Jamaicans. And it is by no means farfetched to suggest that Chinese and Japanese races are derived from the same Mongoloid stock as produced the indigenous peoples of North America. I hypothesized that Eskimos have been selectively bred for good visuo-spatial abilities, though Berry lays more stress on differences in social organization and upbringing that reinforce dependent behavior in Africans and independent behavior in Eskimos. But this line of argument runs into difficulties since Japanese and Chinese are certainly brought up to be dependent and socially cohesive (and not for independence) and yet, as Dawson *et al.* (1973, 1974) have shown in Hong Kong, Chinese do score well on some of Witkin's and Berry's tests.

Let us turn, then, to the theory most usually offered by writers on oriental achievements and personality characteristics, namely that the major factor in educational and occupational success is the family upbringing that stresses:

1. Adherence to accepted conventions of social behavior.
2. Cohesion not only within a family, but also with kin and the family ancestors.

3. Discouragement of egocentricity and recognition of obligations to others.
4. Loyalty and obedience to the authorities, employers, and the state.
5. Motivation for educational achievement from first entering school until maturity.
6. Firm control, not permissiveness, from about 3 years up.
7. The need for hard work to gain success and to honor the family.

Oriental immigrants and their descendants (also Japanese in Japan and Chinese in Taiwan or Hong Kong) overcome difficulties and achieve well because they have been brought up to be patient, persevering, modest, thrifty, and industrious. Among Japanese these values derive from the Meiji era, and have persisted even in North America to the present day, although a great many American practices have been accepted. In spite of the important differences between Japanese and Chinese cultures, Chinese child upbringing is similar to Japanese in most respects, and both differ greatly from Western models.

There is one troublesome discrepancy, namely that oriental mothers do less to stimulate their babies in the first year of life than do Caucasians. A good deal of contemporary work indicates that interactions between mother and child help the development of cognitive processing, language, and concept formation (see Vernon, 1979). Moreover, the most successful methods that have been found for increasing children's intellectual competence have always involved training mothers to be more effective teachers of their own babies. However, it is also true that such interventions have succeeded among 2- to 3-year-old children; that is, they do not have to start in the first few months of life. It may be, then, that oriental mothers who seem to avoid stimulation in the first year, may behave more like Caucasian middle-class mothers in the second and later preschool years. I also pointed out that the notion of critical periods in mental growth probably do not apply to young humans.

Jensen (1973), commenting on theories that try to account for low intelligence scores among American blacks in terms of deprived environment, points out the danger of hypothesizing poorly defined causal factors for which no scientifically sound evidence exists. He calls these "X-factors," that is, factors that can account for anything, but cannot be proved or disproved. Is oriental family upbringing such an X-factor? I would think not, since many of the characteristics of oriental childrearing are well documented in my chapters on Chinese and Japanese cultures, personalities, and attitudes. Two supporting investigations come to mind: first, Rowe (1966) working in Hong Kong found that high-achieving Grade 3 children mostly came from homes in which the parents were more cultured and exerted stricter discipline than those of low-achievers. Second, Onoda (1976) investigated high- and low-achieving JA students, and showed that the former described themselves as having more positive qualities, such as self-control, endurance, and order.

Admittedly my concept of oriental family upbringing, values, and personality is diffuse and poorly defined. But it should be possible to pick out the most crucial variables, and attempt to validate their influence. In several respects Orientals show characteristics similar to those that differentiate middle-class whites from minority groups such as blacks and Chicanos. There are also resemblances to the Puritan work ethic, as described by Max Weber. But Orientals would probably not accept the Calvinistic view that man is responsible for the effects of his own actions, or that he is fundamentally evil, but can overcome this and achieve both grace and economic success by building up strong internal moral controls, self-discipline, and hard work.

In other respects Orientals and blacks seem to have been equally deprived. For example, there was considerable malnutrition in the late nineteenth and early twentieth centuries. Loehlin, Lindzey, and Spuhler (1975) document the dietary deficiencies of black and Spanish Americans. Among both Chinese and Japanese the staple diet was rice, and there were probably insufficient proteins and vitamins for optimum physical and mental growth. (Hence, the improvement in physique and bodily size among present-day Japanese, and particularly Japanese Americans.) Yet, this adverse factor did not apparently prevent the advancement of the Orientals.

Poor living conditions, poverty, overcrowding, and discrimination and repression by the white majority are often cited as the major reason for the low intelligence scores of blacks. But oriental immigrants were subjected to at least as much deprivation and oppression. True, the worst period for the Chinese preceded the date when psychologists began to give tests to Chinese children, that is, about 1920. But by this date they were already scoring at much the same level as Caucasians on performance, nonverbal, and number tests, though substantially lower on verbal tests. Japanese also were ill-treated from about 1900 to 1924, but their early test results closely resembled those of Chinese. In addition, there was the evacuation of Japanese in World War II, and there is some evidence that lack of regular schooling during this period set back their educational achievement, but that this was soon made up. Nonverbal IQs remained high, and by the 1960s, the deficit on verbal tests had been largely wiped out, though children and adult students still do not score quite as highly as on nonverbal and quantitative tests. We must conclude that adverse environments during childhood do not have the expected effects on the growth of intelligence, provided that there is superior motivation to achieve academically, and personality characteristics such as docility and industriousness. Whatever the difficulties, oriental parents have continued to rear their children in much the same traditional manner (as also have the Jews in their own way). When the tradition has yielded to modern American fashions, it does appear that educational achievement is lowered, and that there is more delinquency, though still much below the white norm.

I discussed the topic of language learning at length in Chapters 10 and 11, but still found much doubt as to the conditions that help or hinder the acquisition of English by Orientals. The dissimilarities between Chinese and Japanese languages and English do not apparently affect the children's progress. Many writers, particularly in the 1920s and 1930s refer to the continued use of oriental languages at home and outside school as responsible for the relatively low scores on verbal intelligence and English achievement. Obviously, recent immigrants who arrive with no previous exposure to English will be severely handicapped for a year or more. Yet the amount of Chinese or Japanese spoken in the home has shown only quite low correlations with poor performance in English. I have suggested (though with insufficient evidence) that the parental and home influences are less potent than mixing with English-speaking Americans or Canadians outside the home. Certainly there was a great deal of racial segregation and interaction only with other Orientals in the early years of immigration up to the 1930s, when low verbal scores were reported. Another puzzling finding is that so many studies mention the generally low socioeconomic class level of immigrant families, whose children nevertheless score creditably on intelligence and other tests. Some investigations indicate that the correlation between SES of oriental parents and children's achievement is quite low. Probably this can be accounted for by the immigrant fathers having to take any kind of work that was open to them, and this was usually unskilled. But it did not mean that they could not have succeeded equally well, given more normal social conditions in much higher grade jobs.

Many writers on racial–ethnic differences mention that variations in intelligence or achievements within groups are much greater than those between groups. In other words, the finding of higher average scores in Group X than Group Y by no means implies that all members of Group X score above Group Y. To illustrate the overlapping, I have taken my own results with the Number Computation test in the Differential Aptitude Test battery, in which the superior performance of Chinese (both boys and girls) is consistently large (see p. 111). I divided the score distribution of the white control group of Grade 9 students into the top and bottom 15%, and the above and below average groups of 35%. Let us call these A, B, C, and D grades in Number Computation.

Grade	Whites	Chinese
A	15%	23%
B	35	47
C	35	27
D	15	3

The percentages of Chinese Grade 9 students scoring in these groups are shown in the above table. Clearly the Chinese get more A and B grades than the whites, and very much fewer D grades. Nevertheless, there are considerable numbers in the C (low average) group. The same kind of difference would be found on

Spelling and also on nonverbal intelligence and spatial tests, though the latter would be less marked.

My view of the primacy of family upbringing and personality qualities would appear to be contradicted by the great differences in achievement of China and Japan, although I stated above that the rearing of children was similar in the two countries. Clearly the factors that I have stressed must be considered in the light of the wider geographical and historical context. When the context is the same, as in Hawaii, Chinese and Japanese do score very similarly on intelligence and achievement tests, and are quite comparable in SES distribution, though of course there are some cultural differences in social organization and their choice of careers. But the countries of China and Japan differ enormously. China is approximately 26 times greater in area than Japan, and has some 8 times the size of population. China has a greater variety of natural resources; Japan, with very poor resources, had to build up an exporting economy in order to survive. The vast area of China meant that different regions were governed by warlords, and that there was little integration under a central government until the Communist regime. Japan likewise started with its warring daimyos, but the country was so small that all parts owed allegiance to the emperor, and effective power was in the hands of the single shogun from about 1600. China regarded itself as self-sufficient and able to work out its own political system regardless of the Western world. It therefore made little technological progress, and the overall standard of living is still very low. Japan was more forward-looking after the Meiji restoration, more outgoing, and more adaptable, and took over what it needed of Western technology. Thus the paths of the two countries have diverged further and further apart since 1880. If I tried to go further in suggesting temperamental, personality, or other characteristics to account for this differentiation, I would merely be indulging in unprofitable X-hypotheses. However, we are fortunate in being able to observe and study virtually the same race in many different environments: Japan, China, Taiwan, Hong Kong, Hawaii, the United States, and Canada. An expert historian–sociologist should be able to interpret likenesses and differences more acutely than has been attempted in this book.

Glossary[1]

Analysis of variance See *Variance*.

Beta weight The amount by which each variable must be weighted, or multiplied, in order to maximize the multiple correlation (*qv*) of a set of predictor variables with a criterion.

Congruence coefficients When the same battery of tests is factor analyzed (*qv*) in two or more populations, a comparison of the factor loadings will show how similar these populations are in the makeup of their factors. The correlation coefficients between such sets of loadings gives their congruence.

Correlation coefficient The degree of correspondence between two sets of measurements of the same individuals (e.g., IQ and achievement), expressed as a coefficient ranging from 0.0 (no correspondence) to +1.0 (perfect correspondence) or to −1.0 (complete inverse relationship). The symbol *r* refers to this coefficient.

Ethnic group A society or group of people who share the same customs, culture, traditions, language, religion, etc. Usually they are resident in a single nation or tribe. They tend to interbreed and thus share a common gene pool, but this is not a necessary condition as it is with race (*qv*).

Factor analysis, or factorization A technique for analyzing the correlations between a number of variables or measures, in order to bring out the main underlying dimensions or factors. When a certain cluster of variables correlate more highly with one another than with other variables, they can be regarded as measuring some common ability or trait. The factor loadings show the extent of dependence of each variable on this trait.

Mean, or *M* The average score of a group, obtained by summing the scores of all members and dividing by their number.

Median In a distribution of scores, the middle score that divides the top half from the bottom half. Usually close to the mean, unless the distribution is skewed or irregular.

Multiple correlation The correlation of a combination of several predictor variables with a criterion variable, each predictor being optimally weighted (see *Beta weight*).

N The number of cases tested or included in a table of results. Also, in discussing Eysenck's personality questionnaires, *N* is short for Neuroticism.

---

[1]Many of these definitions are reprinted from the Glossary of my book *Intelligence: Heredity and Environment* (copyright, 1979); with permission from the publisher, W. H. Freeman & Company, San Francisco.

Normalize To adjust a distribution of scores so that they yield a normal or Gaussian distribution, instead of an irregular or skewed curve.

Oblique and orthogonal factors Factors are usually assumed to be independent and orthogonal, that is, their axes are at right angles. Sometimes a more meaningful factor structure giving a better fit to the data is obtained by factors that are oblique to one another, and are therefore correlated.

P An index of the statistical significance, or probability of an obtained statistic (e.g., a mean, a difference between means, a standard deviation, or correlation). If the probability is high ($>.05$), this indicates that the statistic could have arisen from chance characteristics of the sample, that is, unreliability. When p is $<.001$, it is considered highly improbable that the statistic could have arisen by chance. A p of $<.01$ is considered improbable, and a p of $<.05$ (or 1 in 20) is considered moderately improbable.

Percentile score, or level The raw score (i.e., original score) on a test is expressed in terms of the percentage of people who score at or above this score. Thus the 98th percentile is the score that cuts off the top 2% of the population. The 50th percentile divides the top from the bottom half, that is, it is the same as the median (*qv*).

Principle axes and Principle components The most frequently used techniques for calculating the common factors in a set of variables (see Factor analysis).

Race A group of people who are of common ancestry and who share a common pool of genes that differ from those of other racial groups. The distinctive genes often produce characteristic physical attributes, such as skin color, height, or blood group frequencies. But many of the observed differences between races are not so much genetic as cultural.

Rho (ρ) A Greek letter sometimes used for the correlation between two rank orders, as distinct from two sets of scores (r).

Second-order factors When factors intercorrelate (see *Oblique factors*), these correlations can themselves be factor analyzed to give one or more second-order, or more generalized, factors.

Semantic differential Developed by C. E. Osgood (see p. 217), a technique for measuring the connotative or affective meaning of various concepts. Commonly the meanings are measured along three (sometimes two, or even up to four or five) dimensions or factors, such as Evaluative (approval of the concept), Potency (power or strength), and Activity.

Socioeconomic status (SES) The social class level of a wage earner or a family. This is generally assessed by the level of the father's occupation, or by occupation plus education.

Standard deviation (Often abbreviated as S.D., sigma, or σ.) The generally accepted measure of the range or dispersion of a distribution of test scores. It is calculated from the square root of the average squared deviations of all scores from the mean. In a normal distribution, almost all the scores fall within a range of $+3$ to -3 S.D.s from the mean.

Standard scores, or sigma scores A test score expressed in terms of number of standard deviation units above or below the mean, or some multiple or fraction of the S.D.

t A number derived from the ratio between a statistic and its standard error, for example, the difference between the means of two groups divided by the amount of variability of such a difference. It is a measure of the reliability or statistical significance of the statistic, and can be converted to the probability, or p (*qv*).

Variance A measure of the total individual differences between scores of a group of persons, calculated from the squares of deviations of each score from the mean. When divided by the number of cases (minus 1) we get the mean square variance, which is the same as the standard deviation squared. By Fisher's technique of analysis of variance, it is possible to partition the total variance into proportions attributable to differences between subgroups, different conditions of testing, sex, etc.

Varimax   A technique used for simplifying the obtained factors and rendering the factor structure more meaningful. It involves geometric rotation of the factors or axes to what Thurstone called "Simple Structure." That is, each variable loads, as far as possible, on a single factor; also each factor shows high loadings for one cluster of variables, and nonsignificant loadings on the rest of the variables.

References

Abate, M., & Berrien, F. K. Validation of stereotypes: Japanese versus American students. *Journal of Personality & Social Psychology*, 1967, **7**, 435–438.

Abbott, K. Psychosocial functioning, delinquency, and the family in San Francisco and Taipei. In W. P. Lebra (ed.), *Youth, Socialization and Mental Health*. Honolulu: University Press of Hawaii, 1974. Pp. 121–152.

Adachi, K. *The Enemy that Never Was*. Toronto: McClelland & Stewart, 1976.

Adams, F. N., & Osgood, C. E. A cross-cultural study of the affective meanings of color. *Journal of Cross-Cultural Psychology*, 1973, **4**, 135–156.

Adams, R. C. *Inter-racial Marriage in Hawaii*. Montclair, New Jersey: Patterson Smith, 1937.

Adkins, D. C., Payne, F. D., & Ballif, B. L. Motivation factor scores and response set scores for ten ethnic–cultural groups of preschool children. *American Educational Research Journal*, 1972, **9**, 557–572.

Agassi, J. Social structure and social stratification in Hong Kong. In I. C. Jarvie (ed.), *Hong Kong: A Society in Transition*. London: Routledge & Kegan Paul, 1969. Pp. 65–75.

Alsop, J. W., & Satter, D. *Chinaman's Chance*. Unpublished Report, 1976.

Anastasi, A. *Differential Psychology*. New York: Macmillan, 1958.

Anderson, E. N. Some Chinese methods of dealing with crowding. *Urban Anthropology*, 1972, **1**, 141–150.

Ando, N. A cross-cultural study on value pattern of seven cultural samples. *Psychologia*, 1965, **8**, 177–186.

Arai, S., Ishikawa, J., & Toshima, K. Developpement psychomoteur des enfants Japonais. *Revue de Neuropsychiatrie et d'Hygiéne Mentale de l'Enfance*, 1958, **6**, 262–269.

Arkoff, A. New patterns in two generations of Japanese Americans in Hawaii. *Journal of Social Psychology*, 1959, **50**, 75–79.

Arkoff, A., Meredith, G., & Dong, J. Attitudes of Japanese-American and Caucasian-American students toward marriage role. *Journal of Social Psychology*, 1963, **59**, 11–15.

Arkoff, A., Meredith, G., & Iwihara, S. Dominance–deference patterning in motherland-Japanese, Japanese-American, and Caucasian-American students. *Journal of Social Psychology*, 1962, **58**, 61–66.

Arkoff, A., Meredith, G., & Iwihara, S. Male dominant and egalitarian attitudes in Japanese, Japanese-American, and Caucasian-American students. *Journal of Social Psychology*, 1964, **64**, 225–229.

Arkoff, A., Meredith, G., & Jones, R. Urban–rural differences in need patterns of third generation Japanese-Americans in Hawaii. *Journal of Social Psychology*, 1961, **53**, 21–23.

Arsenian, S. *Bilingualism and Mental Development*. New York: Teachers College, 1937.

Asayama, S. Adolescent sex development and adult sex behavior in Japan. *Journal of Sex Research,* 1975, **11,** 91–112.

Ashworth, M. *Immigrant Children and Canadian Schools.* Toronto: McClelland & Stewart, 1975.

Ayabe, H. I. Deference and ethnic differences in voice levels. *Journal of Social Psychology,* 1971, **85,** 181–185.

Ayabe, H. I., & Santo, S. Conceptual tempo and the oriental American. *Journal of Psychology,* 1972, *81,* 121–123.

Backman, M. E. Patterns of mental abilities: Ethnic, socioeconomic, and sex differences. *American Educational Research Journal,* 1972, **9,** 1–12.

Baldassare, M., & Feller, S. Cultural variations in personal space. *Ethos,* 1975, **3,** 481–503.

Barney, R. D., & Chu, G. G. Y. Differences between Mormon missionaries' perceptions and Chinese natives' expectations in intercultural transactions. *Journal of Social Psychology,* 1976, **98,** 135–136.

Beck, C. Is immigrant education only for immigrants? In A. Wolfgang (Ed.), *Education of Immigrant Students.* Toronto: OISE, 1975. Pp. 5–18.

Bell, R. Public school education of second-generation Japanese in California. *Stanford University Press Monograph* **1,** No. 3, 1935.

Benedict, R. *The Chrysanthemum and the sword: Patterns of Japanese Culture.* Boston, Massachusetts: Houghton Mifflin, 1946.

Bennett, J. W., Passin, H., & McKnight, R. K. *In Search of Identity: The Japanese Overseas Scholar in America and Japan.* Minneapolis: Minnesota University Press, 1958.

Bennett, M., & Tiy, F. H. Psychosocial homeostasis and vocational interest. *Psychologia,* 1976, **19,** 35–39.

Berk, B. B., & Hirata, L. C. Mental illness among the Chinese: Myth or reality? *Journal of Social Issues,* 1973, **29,** 149–166.

Berrien, F. K. Japanese versus American values. *Journal of Social Psychology,* 1965, **65,** 181–191.

Berrien, F. K. Japanese values and the democratic process. *Journal of Social Psychology,* 1966, **68,** 129–138.

Berrien, F. K. Cross-cultural equivalence of personality measures. *Journal of Social Psychology,* 1968, **75,** 3–9.

Berrien, F. K. Stereotype similarities and contrasts. *Journal of Social Psychology,* 1969, *78,* 173–183.

Berrien, F. K., Arkoff, A., & Iwihara, S. Generation differences in values: Americans, Japanese-Americans, and Japanese. *Journal of Social Psychology,* 1967, **71,** 169–175.

Berry, J. W. Temne and Eskimo perceptual skills. *International Journal of Psychology,* 1966, **1,** 207–229.

Bhatnagar, J. K. Linguistic behaviour and adjustment of immigrant children in French and English schools in Montreal. *International Review of Applied Psychology,* 1980, **29,** 141–158.

Blane, H. T., & Yamamoto, K. Sexual role identity among Japanese and Japanese-American high school students. *Journal of Cross-Cultural Psychology,* 1970, **1,** 345–354.

Bloom, B. L., & Goldman, R. K. Sensitivity of the WAIS to language handicap in a psychotic population. *Journal of Clinical Psychology,* 1962, **18,** 161–163.

Bloom, B. S. *Stability and Change in Human Characteristics.* New York: Wiley, 1964.

Bochner, S., Lin, A., & McLeod, B. M. Anticipated role conflict of returning overseas students. *Journal of Social Psychology,* 1980, **110,** 265–272.

Boggs, J. W., & Gallimore, R. Value style and school achievement among Hawaiian Americans. In W. P. Lebra (ed.), *Youth, Socialization and Mental Health.* Honolulu: University Press of Hawaii, 1974. Pp. 96–118.

Bond, M. H., Nakazato, H., & Shiraishi, D. Universality and distinctiveness of Japanese person perception. *Journal of Cross-Cultural Psychology,* 1975, **6,** 346–357.

Bond, M. H., & Tornatzky, L. G. Locus of control in students from Japan and the United States: Dimensions and levels of response. *Psychologia*, 1973, **16**, 209–213.

Boor, M. Relationship of internal–external control and national suicide rates. *Journal of Social Psychology*, 1976, **100**, 143–144.

Borke, H., & Sue, S. Perception of emotional responses to social interactions by Chinese and American children. *Journal of Cross-Cultural Psychology*, 1972, **3**, 309–314.

Boucher, J. D., & Carlson, G. E. Recognition of facial expression in three cultures. *Journal of Cross-Cultural Psychology*, 1980, **11**, 263–280.

Boyd, M. The Chinese in New York, California, and Hawaii: A study of socioeconomic differentials. *Phylon*, 1971, **32**, 198–206.

Briggs, D. L. Social adaptation among Japanese American youth: A comparative study. *Sociology & Social Research*, 1954, **38**, 293–300.

Brislin, R. W., Lonner, W. J., & Thorndike, R. M. *Cross-cultural Research Methods*. New York: Wiley, 1973.

Broadfoot, B. *Years of Sorrow, Years of Shame: The Story of the Japanese Canadians in World War II*. Don Mills, Ontario: General Publishing Co., 1979.

Bronson, G. W. Infants' reactions to unfamiliar persons and novel objects. *Monographs of the Society for Research in Child Development*, 1972, **37**, No. 148.

Broom, L., & Kitsuse, J. I. The validation of acculturation: A condition to ethnic assimilation. *American Anthropologist*, 1955, **57**, 44–48.

Cansdale, J. S. Cultural problems of Chinese students in a western-type university. In I. C. Jarvie (Ed.), *Hong Kong: A Society in Transition*. London: Routledge & Kegan Paul, 1969. Pp. 345–360.

Carmichael, L. M., & Carmichael, R. S. Observations of the behavior of Japanese kindergarten children. *Psychologia*, 1972, **15**, 46–52.

Cattell, R. B. *Handbook for the Individual and Group Culture Free Intelligence Test, Scale 3*. Urbana, Illinois: IPAT, 1959.

Cattell, R. B., & Scheier, I. H. *The Meaning and Measurement of Neuroticism and Anxiety*. New York: Ronald Press, 1961.

Cattell, R. B., Schmidt, L. R., & Pawlik, K. Cross-cultural comparison (United States, Japan, Austria) of the personality factor structures of 10- to 14-year-olds in objective tests. *Social Behavior and Personality*, 1973, **1**, 182–211.

Caudill, W. Japanese-American personality and acculturation. *Genetic Psychology Monographs*, 1952, **45**, 3–102.

Caudill, W. The influence of social structures and culture on human behavior in modern Japan. *Ethos*, 1973, **1**, 343–382.

Caudill, W., & DeVos, G. Achievement, culture and personality: The case of the Japanese Americans. *American Anthropologist*, 1956, **58**, 1102–1126.

Caudill, W., & Frost, L. A comparison of maternal care and infant behavior in Japanese-American, American, and Japanese families. In W. P. Lebra (Ed.), *Youth, Socialization, and Mental Health*. Honolulu, Hawaii: University Press of Hawaii, 1974. Pp. 3–15.

Caudill, W., & Lin, T-Y. (Eds.) *Mental Health Research in Asia and the Pacific*. Honolulu, Hawaii: East-West Center Press, 1969.

Caudill, W., & Schooler, C. Symptom patterns and background characteristics of Japanese psychiatric patients. In W. Caudill & T-Y. Lin (Eds.), *Mental Health Research in Asia and the Pacific*. Honolulu, Hawaii: East-West Center Press, 1969. Pp. 114–147.

Caudill, W., & Schooler, C. Child behavior and child rearing in Japan and the United States: An interim report. *Journal of Nervous & Mental Diseases*, 1973, **157**, 323–338.

Caudill, W., & Weinstein, H. Maternal care and infant behavior in Japan and America. *Psychiatry*, 1969, **32**, 12–43.

Chan, J. Intelligence and intelligence tests in Hong Kong. *New Horizons,* 1974, **15,** 82–88.

Chan, J. Problems of psychological testing in two languages in Hong Kong. In R. Lord (Ed.), *Studies in Bilingual Education.* University of Hong Kong Language Centre, 1976. Pp. 110–113. (a)

Chan, J. Is Raven Progressive Matrices Test culture-free or culture-fair? *Proceedings of the Third IACCP Congress,* Tilburg; 1976. (b)

Chan, J. *Hong Kong Attainment Tests (Series 1): Analysis of Results.* Unpublished Report, Hong Kong Education Department, 1976 (c)

Chan, J. Parent–child interaction and education: A cross-cultural comparative study. *New Horizons,* 1976, **17,** 69–81. (d)

Chan, J. Parent–child interaction variables as predictors of academic attainment. *New Horizons,* 1977, **18,** 60–67.

Chan, J. *Hong Kong Attainment Tests (Series 2).* Unpublished Report, Hong Kong Education Department, 1978.

Chan, J. A crossroads in language of instruction. *Journal of Reading,* 1981, **1,** 411–415.

Chan, J., Eysenck, H. J., & Götz, K. O. A new visual aesthetic sensitivity test. III. Cross-cultural comparison between Hong Kong children and adults, and English and Japanese samples. *Perceptual & Motor Skills, 1980,* **50,** 1325–1326.

Chen, J., & Goon, S. W. Recognition of the gifted from among disadvantaged Asian children. *Gifted Child Quarterly,* 1976, **20,** 157–164.

Ching, C. C. Psychology in the People's Republic of China. *American Psychologist,* 1980, **35,** 1084–1089.

Chiu, L-H. Manifested anxiety in Chinese and American children. *Journal of Psychology,* 1971, **79,** 273–284.

Chiu, L-H. A cross-cultural comparison of cognitive styles in Chinese and American children. *International Journal of Psychology,* 1972, **7,** 235–242.

Chou, S. K., & Mi, C-Y. Relative neurotic tendency of Chinese and American students. *Journal of Social Psychology,* 1937, **8,** 155–184.

Christie, R., & Geis, F. L. *Studies in Machiavellianism.* New York: Academic Press, 1970.

Chu, G. C. Culture, personality and persuasibility. *Sociometry,* 1960, **29,** 169–174.

Chu, P-H. Cross-cultural study of vocational interests measured by the Strong–Campbell Inventory. *Acta Psychologica Taiwanica,* 1975, **17,** 69–84.

Chun, K. T., Campbell, J. B., & Yoo, J. H. Extreme response style in cross-cultural research: A reminder. *Journal of Cross-Cultural Psychology,* 1974, **5,** 465–480.

Church, J., & Insko, C. A. Ethnic and sex differences in sexual values. *Psychologia,* 1965, **8,** 153–157.

Chyou, N. T-I., & Collard, R. R. Parental discipline of aggressive behaviors in four-year-old Chinese and American children. *Proceedings APA Conference,* 1972, **7,** 95–96.

Ciborowski, T., & Choy, S. Nonstandard English and free recall. *Journal of Cross-Cultural Psychology,* 1974, **5,** 271–281.

Clavell, J. *Shogun.* New York: Athenaeum, 1975.

Clark, M. M. *Left-handedness.* London: University of London Press, 1957.

Clement, R., Gardner, R. C., & Smythe, P. C. Social and individual factors in second language acquisition. *Canadian Journal of Behavioural Science,* 1980, **12,** 293–302.

Coleman, J. S. *et al. Equality of Educational Opportunity.* Washington, D.C.: U.S. Office of Education, 1966.

Comber, L. C., & Keeves, J. P. *Science Education in Nineteen Countries.* Stockholm: Almquist & Wiksell, 1973.

Connor, J. W. Acculturation and changing need patterns in Japanese-American and Caucasian-American college students. *Journal of Social Psychology,* 1974, **93,** 293–294. (a)

Connor, J. W. Value continuities and change in three generations of Japanese Americans. *Ethos,* 1974, **2,** 232–264. (b)

Connor, J. W. Changing trends in Japanese American academic achievement. *Journal of Ethnic Studies,* 1975, **2,** 95–98.

Connor, J. W. Family bonds, maternal closeness, and the suppression of sexuality in three generations of Japanese Americans. *Ethos,* 1976, **4,** 189–221.

Conroy, M., Hess, R. D., Azuma, H., & Kashiwagi, K. Maternal strategies for regulating children's behavior. *Journal of Cross-Cultural Psychology,* 1980, **11,** 153–172.

Cronbach, L. J. *Essentials of Psychological Testing* (3rd ed.). New York: Harper & Row, 1970.

Cummings, W. K. The effects of Japanese schools. *Eighth International Congress of Sociology,* 1974.

Cummins, J. Linguistic interdependence and the educational development of bilingual children. *Review of Educational Research,* 1979, **49,** 222–251.

Cummins, J. *Psychological Assessment of Minority Language Students.* Unpublished Report, Toronto: OISE, 1980.

Daniels, R. *The Decision to Relocate the Japanese Americans.* New York: Lippincott, 1975.

Daniels, R. American historians and East Asian immigrants. In N. Hundley (Ed.), *The Asian American: The Historical Experience.* Santa Barbara, California: Clio Books, 1976. Pp. 1–25.

Darcy, N. T. A review of the literature on the effects of bilingualism upon the measurement of intelligence. *Journal of Genetic Psychology,* 1953, **82,** 21–57.

Darsie, M. L. The mental capacity of American-born Japanese Children. *Comparative Psychological Monographs,* 1926, **3,** 1–89.

Dawson, B. The Chinese experience in frontier Calgary. In A. W. Rasporich & H. C. Classen (Eds.), *Frontier Calgary.* Toronto: McClelland & Stewart, 1975. Pp. 124–140.

Dawson, J. L. M. Psychological research in Hong Kong. *International Journal of Psychology,* 1970, **5,** 63–70.

Dawson, J. L. M., Law, H., Leung, A., & Whitney, R. E. Scaling Chinese Traditional–Modern attitudes and the GSR measurement of ''important'' versus ''unimportant'' Chinese concepts. *Journal of Cross-Cultural Psychology,* 1971, **2,** 1–27.

Dawson, J. L. M., & Wing-Cheung, W. N. Effects of parental attitudes and modern exposure on Chinese Traditional–Modern attitude formation. *Journal of Cross-Cultural Psychology,* 1972, **3,** 201–207.

Dawson, J. L. M., Whitney, R. E., & Lau, R. T-S. Attitudinal conflict, GSR, and Traditional–Modern attitude change among Hong Kong Chinese. *Journal of Social Psychology,* 1972, **88,** 163–176.

Dawson, J. L. M., Young, B. M., & Choi, P. P. C. Developmental influences on geometric illusion susceptibility among Hong Kong Chinese children. *Journal of Cross-Cultural Psychology,* 1973, **4,** 49–74.

Dawson, J. L. M., Young, B. M., & Choi, P. P. C. Development influences in pictorial depth perception among Hong Kong Chinese children. *Journal of Cross-Cultural Psychology,* 1974, **5,** 3–22.

DeFries, J. C., Ashton, G. C. *et al.* Parent–offspring resemblance for specific cognitive abilities in two ethnic groups. *Nature (London)* 1976, **261,** 131–133.

DeFries, J. C., Johnson, R. C., Kuse, A. R. *et al.* Familial resemblance for specific cognitive abilities. *Behavioral Genetics,* 1979, **9,** 23–43.

DeFries, J. C., Vandenberg, S. G., McClearn, G. E. *et al.* Near identity of cognitive structure in two ethnic groups. *Science,* 1974, **183,** 338–339.

Dennis, W. Goodenough scores, art experience, and modernization. *Journal of Social Psychology,* 1966, **68,** 211–228.

DeVos, G. A quantitative Rorschach assessment of maladjustment and rigidity in acculturating Japanese Americans. *Genetic Psychological Monographs*, 1955, **52**, 51-87.

DeVos, G. Japanese value-attitudes assessed by application of Sargent's Insight Test method. *American Psychologist*, 1956, **11**, 410.

DeVos, G., & Murakami, E. Violence and aggression in fantasy: A comparison of American and Japanese lower-class youth. In W. P. Lebra (Ed.), *Youth, Socialization, and Mental Health*. Honolulu, Hawaii: University Press of Hawaii, 1974. Pp. 153-177.

DeVos, G., & Wagatsuma, H. Minority status and deviancy in Japan. In W. Caudill & T-Y. Lin (Eds.), *Mental Health Research in Asia and the Pacific*. Honolulu, Hawaii: East-West Center Press, 1969. Pp. 342-357.

Dien, D. S-F. Parental Machiavellianism and children's cheating in Japan. *Journal of Cross-Cultural Psychology*, 1974, **5**, 259—270.

Dien, D. S-F., & Fujisawa, H. Machiavellianism in Japan: A longitudinal study. *Journal of Cross-Cultural Psychology*, 1979, **10**, 508-516.

Dixon, P. W., Fukuda, N. K., & Berens, A. E. The influence of ethnic grouping on SCAT, teachers' ratings, and rank in high school class. *Journal of Social Psychology*, 1968, **75**, 285-286.

Dixon, P. W., Fukuda, N. K., & Berens, A. E. Cognitive and personalogical factor patterns for Japanese-American high-school students in Hawaii. *Psychologia*, 1970, **13**, 35-41.

Doi, L. T. Japanese psychology, dependency need, and mental health. In W. Caudill & T-Y. Lin (Eds.), *Mental Health Research in Asia and the Pacific*. Honolulu, Hawaii: East-West Center Press, 1969. Pp. 335-341.

Doppelt, J. E., & Kaufmann, A. S. Estimation of the differences between WISC-R and WISC IQs. *Educational & Psychological Measurement*, 1977, **37**, 417-424.

Dornic, S. Information processing and language dominance. *International Review of Applied Psychology*, 1980, **29**, 119-140.

Douglas, J. D., & Wong, A. C. Formal operations: Age and sex differences in Chinese and American children. *Child Development*, 1977, **48**, 689-692.

Draguns, J. G. Comparisons of psychopathology across cultures. *Journal of Cross-Cultural Psychology*, 1973, **4**, 9-47.

Earle, M. J. Bilingual semantic merging and an aspect of acculturation. *Journal of Personality & Social Psychology*, 1967, **6**, 304-312.

Earle, M. J. A cross-cultural and cross-language comparison of dogmatism scores. *Journal of Social Psychology*, 1969, **79**, 19-24.

Ekstrand, L. H. Sex differences in second language learning? Empirical studies and a discussion of related findings. *International Review of Applied Psychology*, 1980, **29**, 205-259.

Engebretson, D. Relationship of perceived cultural influence to informally learned cultural behaviors, interaction distances, among Sansei Japanese and Caucasians in Hawaii: A study of acculturation. *Psychologia*, 1972, **15**, 95-100.

Engebretson, D., & Fullmer, D. Cross-cultural differences in territoriality. *Journal of Cross-Cultural Psychology*, 1970, **1**, 261-269.

Ewing, J. A., Rouse, B. A., & Pellizzari, E. D. Alcohol sensitivity and ethnic background. *American Journal of Psychiatry*, 1974, **131**, 206-210.

Eysenck, H. J. Factors determining aesthetic preferences for geometric designs and devices. *British Journal of Aesthetics*, 1971, **11**, 154-166.

Eysenck, H. J. National differences in personality as related to ABO blood group polymorphism. *Psychological Reports*, 1977, **41**, 1257-1258.

Eysenck, H. J., & Iwawaki, S. Cultural relativity in aesthetic judgments: An empirical study. *Perceptual & Motor Skills*, 1971, **32**, 817-818.

Eysenck, H. J., & Iwawaki, S. The determination of aesthetic judgment by race and sex. *Journal of Social Psychology*, 1975, **96**, 11-20.

Feldman, D. H. Map understanding as a possible crystallizer of cognitive structures. *American Educational Research Journal,* 1971, **8,** 485–501.

Fenz, W. D., & Arkoff, A. Comparative need patterns of five ancestry groups in Hawaii. *Journal of Social Psychology,* 1962, **58,** 67–89.

Fersh, S. Orientals and orientation: An examination of changing attitudes toward Oriental culture in the U.S. *Phi Delta Kappan,* 1972, **53,** 315–318.

Flaugher, R. L., & Rock, D. A. *Patterns of Ability Factors among Four Ethnic Groups.* Princeton, New Jersey: Educational Testing Service Research Memorandum, No. 7, 1972.

Fong, S. L. M. Assimilation and changing social roles of Chinese Americans. *Journal of Social Issues,* 1973, **29,** 115–127.

Fong, S. L. M. Cultural influences in the perception of people: The case of Chinese in America. *British Journal of Social & Clinical Psychology,* 1965, **4,** 110–113. (a)

Fong, S. L. M. Assimilation of Chinese in America: Changes in orientation and social perception. *American Journal of Sociology,* 1965, **71,** 265–273. (b)

Fong, S. L. M., & Peskin, H. Sex-role strain and personality adjustment of China-born students in America. *Journal of Abnormal Psychology,* 1969, **74,** 563–567.

Forbis, W. H. *Japan Today.* New York: Harper & Row, 1975.

Frager, R. Conformity and anticonformity in Japan. *Journal of Personality & Social Psychology,* 1970, **15,** 203–210.

Freedman, D. G. *Human Infancy: An Evolutionary Perspective.* New York: Wiley, 1974.

Freedman, D. G., & Freedman, N. A. Differences in behavior between Chinese-American and European-American newborns. *Nature (London),* 1969, **224,** 1227.

Freeman, R. B. Discrimination in the academic marketplace. In T. Sowell (Ed.), *Essays and Data on American Ethnic Groups.* Washington, D.C.: The Urban Institute, 1978. Pp. 196.

Frost, B. P., Iwawaki, S., & Fogliatto, H. Argentinian, Canadian, Japanese, and Puerto Rican norms on the Frost Self-description Questionnaire. *Journal of Cross-Cultural Psychology,* 1972, **3,** 215–218.

Fujita, B. Applicability of the Edwards Personal Preference Schedule to Nisei. *Psychological Reports,* 1957, **3,** 518–519.

Fukada, N., Vahar, M., & Holowinsky, I. Z. Qualitative interpretation of Draw-a-Person reproductions by Japanese children. *Training School Bulletin,* 1965, **62,** 119–125.

Fukuda, T. Some data on the intelligence of Japanese children. *American Journal of Psychology,* 1923, **34,** 599–602.

Gallimore, R. Affiliation motivation and Hawaiian-American achievement. *Journal Cross-Cultural Psychology,* 1974, **5,** 481–491.

Gallimore, R., Weiss, L. B., & Finney, R. Cultural differences in delay of gratification: A problem of behavior classification. *Journal of Personality & Social Psychology,* 1974, **30,** 72–80.

Gardiner, H. W. A cross-cultural comparison of hostility in children's drawings. *Journal of Social Psychology,* 1969, **79,** 261–263.

Garth, T. A., & Foote, J. The community of ideas of Japanese. *Journal of Social Psychology,* 1939, **10,** 179–185.

Gehric, M. J. Childhood and community: On the experience of young Japanese Americans in Chicago. *Ethos,* 1976, **4,** 353–383.

Geist, H. A comparison of vocational interests at different levels in schools in Japan and a comparison with United States counterparts. *Psychologia,* 1969, **12,** 227–231.

Gensley, J. The most academically talented students in the world. *Gifted Child Quarterly,* 1975, **19,** 185–188.

Glazer, N. Ethnic groups and education: Towards the tolerance of difference. *Journal of Negro Education,* 1969, **38,** 187–195.

Godman, A. *The Attainments and Abilities of Hong Kong Primary IV Pupils. A First Study.* Hong Kong: Hong Kong University Press, Educational Research Publication No. 2, 1964.

Goldman, R. D., & Hewitt, B. N. Predicting the success of black, Chicano, oriental, and white college students. *Journal of Educational Measurement,* 1976, **13,** 107-117.

Goodenough, F. L. Racial differences in the intelligence of school children. *Journal of Experimental Psychology,* 1926, **9,** 388-397.

Goodman, M. E. Japanese and American children: A comparative study of social concepts and attitudes. *Marriage & Family Living,* 1958, **20,** 316-319.

Goodnow, J. J. A test of milieu effects with some of Piaget's tasks. *Psychological Monographs,* 1962, **76,** No. 555.

Goodnow, J. J., & Bethon, G. Piaget's tasks: The effects of schooling and intelligence. *Child Development* 1966, **37,** 573-582.

Goodnow, J., Young, B. M., & Kvan, E. Orientation errors in copying by children in Hong Kong. *Journal of Cross-Cultural Psychology,* 1976, **7,** 101-110.

Goodstat, L. F. Urban housing in Hong Kong, 1945-1963. In I. C. Jarvie (Ed.), *Hong Kong: A Society in Transition.* London: Routledge & Kegan Paul, 1969. Pp. 257-298.

Gordon, H. W. Hemisphere asymmetry and musical performance. *Science,* 1975, **189,** 68-69.

Gordon, L. V. Q-typing of oriental and American youth: Initial and clarifying studies. *Journal of Social Psychology,* 1967, **71,** 185-195.

Gordon, L. V., & Kikuchi, A. American personality tests in cross-cultural research: A caution. *Journal of Social Psychology,* 1966, **69,** 179-183.

Gordon, L. V., & Kikuchi, A. Response sets of Japanese and American students. *Journal of Social Psychology,* 1970, **82,** 143-148.

Gotts, E. E. A note on cross-cultural by age-group comparisons of anxiety scores. *Child Development,* 1968, **39,** 945-947.

Götz, K. O., Lynn, R., Borisy, A. R., & Eysenck, H. J. A new visual aesthetic sensitivity test. I. Construction and psychometric properties. *Perceptual & Motor Skills,* 1979, **49,** 795-802.

Gough, H. G., Chun, K., & Chung, Y-E. Validation of the CPI Femininity Scale in Korea. *Psychological Reports,* 1968, **22,** 155-160.

Gough, H. G., DeVos, G., & Mizushima, K. Japanese validation of the CPI Social Maturity Index. *Psychological Reports,* 1968, **22,** 143-146.

Graham, V. T. The intelligence of Chinese children in San Francisco. *Journal of Comparative Psychology,* 1926, **6,** 43-71.

Greulich, W. W. A comparison of the physical growth and development of American-born and native Japanese children. *American Journal of Physical Anthropology,* 1957, **15,** 489-515.

Grodzins, M. *Americans Betrayed.* Chicago, Illinois: University of Chicago Press, 1949.

Gulick, A. The problem of right and wrong in Japan and some of its political consequences. *Journal of Social Psychology,* 1947, **26,** 3-20.

Hama, H. Evaluation of clinical depression by means of a Japanese translation of the Minnesota Multiphasic Personality Inventory. *Psychologia,* 1966, **9,** 165-176.

Hama, H., & Plutchik, R. Personality profiles of Japanese college students: A normative study. *Japanese Psychological Research,* 1975, **17,** 141-146.

Hao, Y. T. The memory-span of six hundred Chinese school children in San Francisco. *School & Society,* 1924, **20,** 507-510.

Harrigan, J. E., Dole, A. A., & Vinacke, W. E. A study of indignation-bigotry and extrapunitiveness in Hawaii. *Journal of Social Psychology,* 1961, **55,** 105-112.

Harris, D. B., De Lissovoy, V., & Enami, J. The aesthetic sensitivity of Japanese and American children. *Journal of Aesthetics Education,* 1975, **9**(4), 81-95.

Hata, D. T., Hata, N. I. (Eds.). Articles on Asian and Pacific Americans. *Civil Rights Digest,* 1976, **9**(1), 64.

Hatano, G., & Imagaki, K. Reflection–impulsivity in perceptual and conceptual matching tasks among kindergarten children. *Japanese Psychological Research,* 1976, **18,** 196–203.

Hatta, Recognition of Japanese *Kanji* and *Hirakana* in the left and right visual fields. *Japanese Psychological Research,* 1978, **20,** 51–59.

Hatta, T., & Nakatsuka, Z. Note on hand preference of Japanese people. *Perceptual & Motor Skills,* 1976, **42,** 530.

Havender, W. R. Individual versus collective social justice. *The Behavior & Brain Sciences,* 1980, **3,** 345–346.

Havighurst, R. J., Gunther, M. K., & Pratt, I. E. Environment and the Draw-a-Man test: The performance of Indian children. *Journal of Abnormal & Social Psychology,* 1946, **41,** 50–63.

Havighurst, R. J., & Hilkevitch, R. P. The intelligence of Indian children as measured by a performance scale. *Journal of Abnormal & Social Psychology,* 1944, **39,** 419–433.

Hayashi, T., & Habu, K. A research on achievement motive: An experimental test of the "thought sampling" method by using Japanese students. *Japanese Psychological Research,* 1962, **4,** 30–42.

Hayashi, T., Rim, Y., & Lynn, R. A test of McClelland's theory of achievement motivation in Britain, Japan, Ireland, and Israel. *International Journal of Psychology,* 1970, **5,** 275–277.

Hess, R. D., Kashiwagi, K., Azuma, H. *et al.* Maternal expectations for mastery of developmental tasks in Japan and the United States. *International Journal of Psychology,* 1980, **15,** 259–271.

Higa, M. A comparative study of three groups of "Japanese" mothers in attitudes toward child rearing. In W. P. Lebra (Ed.), *Youth, Socialization and Mental Health.* Honolulu, Hawaii: University Press of Hawaii, 1974. Pp. 16–25.

Hilger, M. I., Klett, W. G., & Watson, C. G. Performance of Ainu and Japanese six-year-olds on the Goodenough–Harris Drawing test. *Perceptual & Motor Skills,* 1976, **42,** 435–438.

Ho, D. Y-F. Field studies in foreign cultures: A cautionary note on methodological difficulties. *Psychologia,* 1972, **15,** 15–21.

Ho, Y-F., & Yu, L. L. Authoritarianism and attitude toward filial piety in Chinese teachers. *Journal of Social Psycholgoy,* 1974, **92,** 305–306.

Hopkins, M. E., Lo, L., Peterson, R. E., & Seo, K. K. Japanese and American managers. *Journal of Psychology,* 1977, **96,** 71–72.

Hsia, J. Cognitive assessment of Asian Americans. *Symposium on Bilingual Research,* Los Alamitos, California, 1980.

Hsiao, H. H. The mentality of the Chinese and Japanese. *Journal of Applied Psychology,* 1929, **13,** 9–31.

Hsieh, T. T-Y., Shybut, J., & Lotsof, E. J. Internal versus external control and ethnic group membership. *Journal of Consulting & Clinical Psychology,* 1969, **33,** 122–124.

Hsu, E. H. The neurotic score as a function of culture. *Journal of Social Psychology,* 1951, **34,** 3–30.

Hsu, F. L. K. *Under the Ancestor's Shadow: Chinese Culture and Personality.* New York: Columbia University Press, 1948.

Hsu, F. L. K. *The Challenge of the American Dream: The Chinese in the United States.* Belmont, California: Wadsworth, 1971.

Huang, L. C., & Harris, M. B. Conformity in Chinese and Americans. *Journal of Cross-Cultural Psychology,* 1973, **4,** 427–434.

Hundley, N. (Ed.) *The Asian American: The Historical Experience.* Santa Barbara, California: Clio Books, 1976.

Husén, T. *International Study of Achievement in Mathematics.* Stockholm: Almquist & Wiksell, 1967.

Hutchinson, S., Arkoff, A., & Weaver, H. B. Ethnic and sex factors in classroom responsiveness. *Journal of Social Psychology,* 1966, **69,** 321–325.

Hwang, K. Y., & Dizney, H. F. Predictive validity of the test of English as a foreign language for Chinese graduate students at an American university. *Educational & Psychological Measurement*, 1970, **30**, 475–477.

Iga, M. Kyoto and university student suicide. *Psychologia*, 1971, *14*, 15–23.

Inagaki, T. A cross-cultural study of the feminine role concept between Japanese and American college women. *Psychologia*, 1967, **10**, 144–154.

Inomata, S. Review of J. Stoetzel, *Without the Chrysanthemum and the Sword*. New York: Columbia University Press, 1955; *Psychologia*, 1957, **1**, 132–135.

Inomata, S., & McGinnies, E. Social attitudes among Japanese and American teenagers. I. Girls. *Psychologia*, 1970, **13**, 88–101.

Inomata, S., & McGinnies, E. Social attitudes among Japanese and American teenagers. II. Boys. *Psychologia*, 1971, **14**, 158–169.

Ishii, K. Backgrounds and suicidal behaviors of committed suicides among Kyoto university students. I. *Psychologia*, 1972, **15**, 137–148. *Ibid*. II. *Psychologia*, 1973, **16**, 85–97. *Ibid*. III. *Psychologia*, 1977, **20**, 191–205.

Ito, P. K. Comparative biomedical study of physique of Japanese women born and reared under different environments. *Human Biology*, 1942, **14**, 279–351.

Iwao, S., & Child, I. L. Comparison of esthetic judgments by American experts and by Japanese potters. *Journal of Social Psychology*, 1966, **68**, 27–33.

Iwao, S., Child, I. L., & Garcia, M. Further evidence of agreement between Japanese and American esthetic evaluations. *Journal of Social Psychology*, 1969, **78**, 11–15.

Iwawaki, S., & Clement, D. E. Pattern perception among Japanese as a function of pattern uncertainty and age. *Psychologia*, 1972, **15**, 207–212.

Iwawaki, S., & Cowen, E. L. The social desirability of trait-descriptive terms: Application to a Japanese sample. *Journal of Social Psychology*, 1964, **63**, 199–205.

Iwawaki, S., Eysenck, H. J., & Götz, K. O. A new visual aesthetic sensitivity test (VAST). II. Cross-cultural comparison between England and Japan. *Perceptual & Motor Skills*, 1979, **49**, 859–862.

Iwawaki, S., Eysenck, S. B. G., & Eysenck, H. J. Differences in personality between Japanese and English. *Journal of Social Psychology*, 1977, **102**, 27–33.

Iwawaki, S., Eysenck, S. B. G., & Eysenck, H. J. The universality of typology: A comparison between English and Japanese schoolchildren. *Journal of Social Psychology*, 1980, **112**, 3–9.

Iwawaki, S., & Lerner, R. M. Cross-cultural analyses of body-behavior relations. III. Developmental intra- and inter-cultural factor congruence in the body build stereotypes of Japanese and American males and females. *Psychologia*, 1976, **19**, 67–76.

Iwawaki, S., Oyama, T. *et al.* Development and validation of the Japanese version of the MPI (Maudsley Personality Inventory). *Japanese Psychological Research*, 1970. **12**, 176–183.

Iwawaki, S., Sonoo, K. *et al.* Color bias among young Japanese children. *Journal of Cross-Cultural Psychology*, 1978, **9**, 61–73.

Iwawaki, S., Sumida, K. *et al.* Manifest anxiety in Japanese, French, and United States children. *Child Development*, 1967, **38**, 713–722.

Iwawaki, S., Zax, M., & Mitsuoka, S. Extremity of responses among Japanese and American children. *Journal of Social Psychology*, 1969, **79**, 257–259.

Jahoda, G., Deregowski, J. B., & Sinha, D. Topological and Euclidean spatial features noted by children. *International Journal of Psychology*, 1974, **9**, 159–172.

James, C. B. E. Bilingualism in Wales: An aspect of semantic organization. *Educational Research*, 1960, **2**, 123–136.

Jarvie, I. E. (Ed.) *Hong Kong: A Society in Transition*. London: Routledge & Kegan Paul, 1969.

Jensen, A. R. *Educability and Group Differences*. New York: Harper & Row, 1973.

Jensen, A. R., & Inouye, A. R. Level I and Level II abilities in Asian, white, and black children. *Intelligence*, 1980, **4**, 41–49.

Johnson, C. L. Interdependence, reciprocity and indebtedness: An analysis of Japanese-American kinship relations. *Journal of Marriage & the Family,* 1977, **39,** 351-363.

Johnson, F. A., & Marsella, A. J. Differential attitudes toward verbal behavior in students of Japanese and European ancestry. *Genetic Psychological Monographs,* 1978, **97,** 43-76.

Johnson, F. A., Marsella, A. J., & Johnson, C. L. Social and psychological aspects of verbal behavior in Japanese-Americans. *American Journal of Psychiatry,* 1974, **131,** 580-583.

Johnson, R. C., Cole, R. E., Bowers, J. K. *et al.* Hemispheric efficiency in middle and later adulthood. *Cortex,* 1979, **15,** 109-119.

Jones, W. R. *Bilingualism and Intelligence.* Cardiff: University of Wales Press, 1959.

Kadri, Z. N. The use of the MMPI for personality study of Singapore students. *British Journal of Social & Clinical Psychology,* 1971, **10,** 90-91.

Kagan, J., Kearsley, R. B., & Zelazo, P. R. *Infancy: Its Place in Human Development.* Cambridge, Massachusetts: Harvard University Press, 1978.

Kagan, J., Moss, H. A., & Sigel, I. E. Psychological significance of styles of conceptualization. *Monographs of the Society for Research in Child Development,* 1963, **28,** No. 86, 73-112.

Kalisch, R. A., & Moriwaki, S. The world of the elderly Asian American. *Journal of Social Issues,* 1973, **29,** 187-209.

Kaneda, T. Introduction of the test anxiety scale for children to Japanese subjects. *Japanese Psychological Research,* 1971, **13,** 97-102.

Kang, T. S. Name and group identification. *Journal of Social Psychology,* 1972, **86,** 159-160.

Kashiwa, Y. I., & Smith, M. E. A study of the attitudes of some children of Japanese descent toward the Chinese and Japanese. *Journal of Social Psychology,* 1943, **18,** 149-153.

Kato, T. Political attitudes of Japanese adolescents (in comparison with the American). *Psychologia,* 1961, **4,** 198-200.

Katz, D., & Braly, K. W. Racial stereotypes of one hundred college students. *Journal of Abnormal & Social Psychology,* 1933, **28,** 280-290.

Kikuchi, A., & Gordon, L. V. Japanese and American personal values: Some cross-cultural findings. *International Journal of Psychology,* 1970, **5,** 183-187.

Kikumura, H., & Kitano, H. H. L. Interracial marriage: A picture of the Japanese Americans. *Journal of Social Issues,* 1973, **29,** 67-81.

Kilby, R. W. Values of Indian, American, and Japanese university students. *Psychologia,* 1971, **14,** 53-66.

Kim, Y., Anderson, H. E., & Bashaw, W. L. The simple structure of social maturity at the second grade level. *Educational & Psychological Measurement,* 1968, **28,** 145-153.

Kitano, H. Differential child-rearing attitudes between first and second generation Japanese in the United States. *Journal of Social Psychology,* 1961, **53,** 13-19.

Kitano, H. H. L. Changing achievement patterns of the Japanese in the United States. *Journal of Social Psychology,* 1962, **58,** 257-264.

Kitano, H. H. L. Inter- and intragenerational differences in maternal attitudes towards child rearing. *Journal of Social Psychology,* 1964, **63,** 215-220.

Kitano, H. H. L. *Japanese Americans: The Evolution of a Subculture.* Englewood Cliffs, New Jersey: Prentice-Hall, 1969.

Kitano, H. H. L. Mental illness in four cultures. *Journal of Social Psychology,* 1970, **80,** 121-134.

Kitano, H. H. L. Japanese Americans: The development of a middleman minority. In N. Hundley (Ed.), *The Asian American: The Historical Experience.* Santa Barbara, California: Clio Books, 1976. Pp. 81-100.

Kitano, H. H. L., & Sue, S. The model minorities. *Journal of Social Issues,* 1973, **29,** 1-9.

Klauss, R., & Bass, E. M. Group influence on individual behavior across cultures. *Journal of Cross-Cultural Psychology,* 1974, **5,** 236-246.

Klein, M. H., Miller, M. H., & Alexander, A. A. When young people go out in the world. In W. P.

Lebra (Ed.), *Youth Socialization, and Mental Health.* Honolulu, Hawaii: University Press of Hawaii, 1974. Pp. 217–232.

Klett, C. J., & Yaukey, D. W. A cross-cultural comparison of judgments of social desirability. *Journal of Social Psychology,* 1959, **49,** 19–26.

Kline, C. L., & Lee, N. A transcultural study of dyslexia: Analysis of language disabilities in 277 Chinese children simultaneously learning to read and write in English and in Chinese. *Journal of Special Education,* 1972, **6,** 9–26.

Kodamo, H. Personality tests in Japan. *Psychologia,* 1957, **1,** 92–103.

Kriger, S. F., & Kroes, W. H. Child-rearing attitudes of Chinese, Jewish, and Protestant mothers. *Journal of Social Psychology,* 1972, **86,** 205–210.

Kubo, Y. The revised and expanded Binet–Simon tests, applied to the Japanese children. *Journal of Genetic Psychology,* 1922, **29,** 187–194.

Kuhlen, R. G. The interests and attitudes of Japanese, Chinese, and white adolescents: A study in culture and personality. *Journal of Social Psychology,* 1945, **21,** 121–133.

Kumagai, F. The effects of cross-cultural education on attitudes and personality of Japanese students. *Sociology of Education,* 1977, **50,** 40–47.

Kumasaka, Y., Smith, R. J., & Aiba, H. Crimes in New York and Tokyo: Sociocultural perspectives. *Community Mental Health,* 1975, **11,** 19–26.

Kumata, H., & Schramm, W. A pilot study of cross-cultural meaning. *Public Opinion Quarterly,* 1956, **20,** 229–238.

Kuo, E. C-Y. The family and bilingual socialization: A sociolinguistic study of a sample of Chinese children in the United States. *Journal of Social Psychology,* 1974, **92,** 181–191.

Kuo, H. K., & Marsella, A. J. The meaning and measurement of Machiavellianism in Chinese and American college students. *Journal of Social Psychology,* 1977, **101,** 165–173.

Kuroda, J. Application of the colored Progressive Matrices Test for the Japanese kindergarten children. *Psychologia,* 1959, **2,** 173–177.

Kurokawa, M. Acculturation and childhood accidents among Chinese and Japanese Americans. *Genetic Psychological Monographs,* 1969, **79,** 89–159.

Kvan, E. Problems of bilingual milieu in Hong Kong: Strain of the two-language system. In I. C. Jarvie (Ed.), *Hong Kong: A Society in Transition.* London: Routledge & Kegan Paul, 1969. Pp. 327–343.

Kyle, J. G. Raven's Progressive Matrices—30 years later. *Bulletin of the British Psychological Society,* 1977, **30,** 406–407.

Lambert, W. E. Culture and language as factors in learning and education. In A. Wolfgang (Ed.), *Education of Immigrant Students.* Toronto: OISE, 1975. Pp. 55–83.

Lao, R. C. Levenson's IPC (Internal–External Control) Scale: A comparative study of Chinese and American students. *Journal of Cross-Cultural Psychology,* 1978, **9,** 113–124.

Lao, R. C., Chuang, C-J., & Yang, K-S. Locus of control and Chinese college students. *Journal of Cross Cultural Psychology,* 1977, **8,** 299–313.

Larsen, K. S., Arosalo, D., Lineback, S., & Ommundsen, R. New Left ideology: A cross-national study. *Journal of Social Psychology,* 1973, **90,** 321–322.

Lazarus, R. S., Opton, E., Tomita, M., & Kodama, M. A cross-cultural study of stress-reaction patterns in Japan. *Journal of Personality & Social Psychology,* 1966, **4,** 622–633.

Lebra, T. S. Intergenerational continuity and discontinuity in moral values among Japanese: A preliminary report. In W. P. Lebra (Ed.), *Youth, Socialization, and Mental Health.* Honolulu: Hawaii: University Press of Hawaii, 1974. Pp. 247–274.

Lebra, T. S., & Lebra, W. P. (Eds.) *Japanese Culture and Behavior.* Honolulu, Hawaii: University Press of Hawaii, 1974.

Lee, R. H. *The Chinese in the United States of America.* Hong Kong: Hong Kong University Press, 1960.

Leiter, R. G. *General Instructions for the Leiter Performance Scales.* Chicago, Illinois: Stoelting, 1969.

Leong, C. K. Reading in Hong Kong. In J. A. Downing (Ed.), *Comparative Reading.* New York: Macmillan, 1973. Pp. 383-402.

Lerner, R. M., & Korn, S. J. The development of body-build stereotypes in males. *Child Development,* 1972, **43**, 908-920.

Lesser, G. S., Fifer, G., & Clark, D. H. Mental abilities of children from different social-class and cultural groups. *Monographs of the Society for Research in Child Development,* 1965, **30**, No. 102.

Lethbridge, J. J. Hong Kong under Japanese occupation: Changes in Social Structure. In I. C. Jarvie (Ed.), *Hong Kong: A Society in Transition.* London: Routledge & Kegan Paul, 1969. Pp. 77-127.

Levine, G. N., & Montero, D. M. Socioeconomic mobility among three generations of Japanese-Americans. *Journal of Social Issues,* 1973, **29**, 33-48.

Li, A. K-F. The use of ability tests in Hong Kong. *Scientia Paedagogica Experimentalis,* 1964, **1**, 187-195.

Li, A. K.-F. Parental attitudes, test anxiety, and achievement motivation: A Hong Kong study. *Journal of Social Psychology,* 1974, **93**, 3-11.

Li, A. K.-F. Understanding the new Canadian child. *Teaching Atypical Students in Alberta,* 1976, **6**, 20-26.

Li, W. L., & Liu, S. S. Ethnocentrism among American and Chinese youth. *Journal of Social Psychology,* 1975, **95**, 277-278.

Lin, T-Y. A study of the incidence of mental disorder in Chinese and other cultures. *Psychiatry,* 1953, **16**, 313-336.

Lin, T-Y., Rin, H., Yeh, E-K. *et al.* Mental disorders in Taiwan, fifteen years later: A preliminary report. In W. Caudill & T-Y Lin (Eds.), *Mental Health Research in Asia and the Pacific.* Honolulu, Hawaii: East-West Center Press, 1969. Pp. 66-91.

Lind, A. W. *Hawaii's People.* Honolulu, Hawaii: University of Hawaii Press, 1st ed., 1955, 3rd ed., 1967.

Lindgren, H. C. Measuring need to achieve by N Ach-N Aff scale—A forced-choice questionnaire. *Psychological Reports,* 1976, **39**, 907-910.

Lindgren, H. C., & Yu, R. Cross-cultural insight and empathy among Chinese immigrants to the United States. *Journal of Social Psychology,* 1975, **96**, 305-306.

Lindzey, G. *Projective Techniques and Cross-Cultural Research.* New York: Appleton-Century-Crofts, 1961.

Li-Repac, D. Cultural influences on clinical perception. *Journal of Cross-Cultural Psychology,* 1980, **11**, 327-342.

Liu, P. Y. H., & Meredith, G. M. Personality structure of Chinese college students in Taiwan and Hong Kong. *Journal of Social Psychology,* 1966, **70**, 165-166.

Livesay, T. M. Racial comparison in test-intelligence. *American Journal of Psychology,* 1942, **55**, 90-95.

Lo, C. F. Moral judgments of Chinese students. *Journal of Abnormal & Social Psychology,* 1942, **37**, 264-269.

Loehlin, J. C., Lindzey, G., & Spuhler, J. N. *Race Differences in Intelligence.* San Francisco, California: Freeman, 1975.

Longstreth, L. E. Level I-Level II abilities as they affect performance of two races in the college classroom. *Journal of Educational Psychology,* 1978, **70**, 289-297.

Lorr, M., & Klett, C. J. Cross-cultural comparison of psychotic syndromes. *Journal of Abnormal Psychology,* 1969, **74**, 531-543.

Louttit, C. M. Racial comparisons of ability in immediate recall of logical and nonsense material. *Journal of Social Psychology*, 1931, **2**, 205–215.

Luh, C. W., & Sailer, R. C. The self-estimation of Chinese students. *Journal of Social Psychology*, 1933, **4**, 245–249.

Luh, C. W., & Wu, T. M. A comparative study of the intelligence of Chinese children on the Pintner performance and the Binet tests. *Journal of Social Psychology*, 1931, **2**, 402–408.

Lyman, S. M. *The Asian in the West*. Reno, Nevada: University of Nevada, Western Studies Center, 1970.

Lyman, S. M. Conflict and the web of group affiliation in San Francisco's Chinatown, 1850–1910. In N. Hundley (Ed.), *The Asian American: The Historical Experience*. Santa Barbara, California: Clio Books, 1976. Pp. 26–52.

Lynn, R. *Personality and National Character*. Oxford: Pergamon, 1971.

Lynn, R. The intelligence of the Chinese and Malays in Singapore. *Mankind Quarterly, 1977*, **18**, 125–128. (a)

Lynn, R. The intelligence of the Japanese. *Bulletin of the British Psychological Society*, 1977, **30**, 69–72. (b)

Lynn, R., & Dziobon, J. On the intelligence of the Japanese and other Mongoloid peoples. *Personality & Individual Differences*, 1980, **1**, 95–96.

Lynn, R., & Hampson, S. L. National differences in extraversion and neuroticism. *British Journal of Social & Clinical Psychology*, 1975, **14**, 223–240.

McCarthy, J. L., & Wolfle, D. Doctorates granted to women and minority group members. *Science*, 1975, **189**, 856–859.

McClelland, D. C. *The Achieving Society*. New York: Van Nostrand, 1961.

McGinnies, E., Nordholm, L. A., Ward, C. D., & Bhanthumnavin, L. Sex and cultural differences in perceived locus of control among students in five countries. *Journal of Consulting & Clinical Psychology*, 1974, **42**, 451–455.

MacGregor, G. *Warriors Without Weapons*. Chicago, Illinois: University of Chicago Press, 1946.

MacLean, A. W., & McGhie, A. The AH4 group test of intelligence in a Canadian high school sample. *Canadian Journal of Behavioural Science*, 1980, **12**, 288–291.

McMichael, R. E., & Grinder, R. E. Guilt and resistance to temptation in Japanese- and white-Americans. *Journal of Social Psychology*, 1964, **64**, 217–223.

Macnamara, J. *Bilingualism and Primary Education*. Edinburgh: Edinburgh University Press, 1966.

Magaroh, M. Summary of Tsunoda's seven experimental methods. *Journal of Social & Biological Structures*, 1980, **3**, 267–271.

Mahler, I. A comparative study of locus of control. *Psychologia*, 1974, **17**, 135–139.

Mahler, I. What is the self concept in Japan? *Psychologia*, 1976, **19**, 127–133.

Makita, K. The rarity of reading disability in Japanese children. *American Journal of Orthopsychiatry*, 1968, **38**, 599–614.

Maloney, M. P. The question of achievement in the Japanese American: A comment on cross-cultural research. *Psychologia*, 1968, **11**, 143–158.

Marsella, A. J. Cross-cultural studies of mental disorders. In A. J. Marsella (Ed.), *Perspectives on Cross-Cultural Psychology*. New York: Academic Press, 1979. Pp. 233–262.

Marsella, A. J., & Golden, C. J. The structure of cognitive abilities in Americans of Japanese and of European ancestry. *Journal of Social Psychology*, 1980, **112**, 19–30.

Marsella, A. J., & Higginbotham, H. N. *Sensory types: Toward an interactionist model of human behavior*. Unpublished Report, University of Hawaii, 1976.

Marsella, A. J., Kinzie, D., & Gordon, P. Ethnic variations in the experinece of depression. *Journal of Cross-Cultural Psychology*, 1973, **4**, 435–458.

Marsella, A. J., Murray, M. D., & Golden, C. Ethnic variations in the phenomenology of emotions. I. Shame. *Journal of Cross-Cultural Psychology*, 1974, **5**, 312–328.

Masuda, M., Hasegawa, R. S., & Matsumoto, G. The ethnic identity questionnaire. *Journal of Cross-Cultural Psychology*, 1973, **4**, 229–245.

Masuda, M., Matsumoto, G. H., & Meredith, G. M. Ethnic identity in three generations of Japanese Americans. *Journal of Social Psychology*, 1970, **81**, 199–207.

Matsumoto, G. M., Meredith, G. M., & Masuda, M. Ethnic identification: Honolulu and Seattle Japanese-Americans. *Journal of Cross-Cultural Psychology*, 1970, **1**, 63–76.

Matsumoto, M., & Smith, H. T. Japanese and American children's perception of parents. *Journal of Genetic Psychology*, 1961, **98**, 83–88.

Maykovich, M. K. Changes in racial stereotypes among college students. *Human Relations*, 1971, **24**, 371–386.

Maykovich, M. K. Political activation of Japanese American youth. *Journal of Social Issues*, 1973, **29**, 167–185.

Maykovich, M. K. Attitudes versus behavior in extramarital sexual relations. *Journal of Marriage & the Family*, 1976, **38**, 693–699.

Meade, R. D. Leadership studies of Chinese and Chinese-Americans. *Journal of Cross-Cultural Psychology*, 1970, **1**, 325–332.

Meade, R. D., & Barnard, W. A. Conformity and anticonformity among Americans and Chinese. *Journal of Social Psychology*, 1973, **89**, 15–24.

Meade, R. D., & Barnard, W. A. Group pressure effects on American and Chinese females. *Journal of Social Psychology*, 1975, **96**, 137–138.

Meade, R. D., & Whittaker, J. O. A cross-cultural study of authoritarianism. *Journal of Social Psychology*, 1967, **72**, 3–7.

Meenes, M. A comparison of racial stereotypes of 1935 and 1942. *Journal of Social Psychology*, 1943, **17**, 327–336.

Meredith, G. M. Personality correlates of pidgin English usage among Japanese-American college students in Hawaii. *Japanese Psychological Research*, 1964, **6**, 176–183.

Meredith, G. M. Observations on the acculturation of Sansei Japanese Americans in Hawaii. *Psychologia*, 1965, **8**, 41–49.

Meredith, G. M. Amae and acculturation among Japanese-American college students in Hawaii. *Journal of Social Psychology*, 1966, **70**, 171–180.

Meredith, G. M. Sex temperament among Japanese-American college students in Hawaii. *Journal of Social Psychology*, 1969, **77**, 149–156.

Meredith, G. M. Interpersonal needs of Japanese-American and Caucasian-American college students in Hawaii. *Journal of Social Psychology*, 1976, **99**, 157–161.

Meredith, G. M., & Ching, D. R. Marriage-role attitudes among Japanese-American and Caucasian-American college students. *Psychological Reports*, 1977, **40**, 1285–1286.

Meredith, G. M., & Meredith, C. G. W. Acculturation and personality among Japanese-American college students in Hawaii. *Journal of Social Psychology*, 1966, **68**, 175–182.

Michener, J. A. *Hawaii*. New York: Random House, 1959.

Miller, S. C. *The Unwelcome Immigrant*. Berkeley, California: University of California Press, 1969.

Mitchell, R. E. Some social implications of high density housing. *American Sociological Review*, 1971, **36**, 18–29.

Miyamito, S. F. The forced evacuation of the Japanese minority during World War II. *Journal of Social Issues*, 1973, **29**, 11–31.

Mizushima, K., & DeVos, G. An application of the California Psychological Inventory in a study of Japanese delinquency. *Journal of Social Psychology*, 1967, **71**, 45–51.

Moran, L. J. Comparative growth of Japanese and North American dictionaries. *Child Development*, 1973, **44**, 826–865.

Moran, L. J., & Huang, I-N. Note on cognitive dictionary structure of Chinese children. *Psychological Reports*, 1974, *34*, 154.

Morgan, J. J. B. Attitudes of students toward the Japanese. *Journal of Social Psychology*, 1945, **21**, 219–227.

Morris, C. W. *Variations of Human Value*. Chicago, Illinois: University of Chicago Press, 1956.

Morris, C. W., & Jones, L. V. Value scales and dimensions. *Journal of Abnormal & Social Psychology*, 1955, **51**, 523–535.

Morton, J. *In the Sea of the Sterile Mountains: The Chinese in British Columbia*. Vancouver: Douglas, 1974.

Morton, N. E., Stout, W. T., & Fischer, C. Academic performance in Hawaii. *Social Biology*, 1976, **23**, 13–20.

Murase, T. Mental health problems of Japanese junior high school students. In W. P. Lebra (Ed.), *Youth, Socialization, and Mental Health*. Honolulu, Hawaii: University Press of Hawaii, 1974. Pp. 66–74.

Murdoch, K. A study of differences found between races in intellect and in morality. *School & Society*, 1925, **22**, 628–632, 659–664.

Murphy, H. B. M. Juvenile delinquency iñ Singapore. *Journal of Social Psychology*, 1963, **61**, 201–231.

Murphy, H. B. M. Mass youth protest movements in Asia and the West: Their common characteristics and psychiatric significance. In W. P. Lebra (Ed.), *Youth, Socialization, and Mental Health*. Honolulu, Hawaii: University Press of Hawaii, 1974. Pp. 275–296.

Nachamie, S. Machiavellianism in children: The children's Mach scale and the bluffing game. In R. Christie & F. L. Geis, *Studies in Machiavellianism*. New York: Academic Press, 1970.

Naka, H. Adolescent suicide in Japan: Its socio-cultural background. *Psychologia*, 1965, **8**, 25–40.

Nishiyama, T. Cross-cultural invariance of the California Psychological Inventory. *Psychologia*, 1973, **16**, 75–84.

Nishiyama, T. Validation of the CPI femininity score in Japan. *Journal of Cross-Cultural Psychology*, 1975, **6**, 482–489.

Nobechi, M., & Kimura, T. "Study of Values" applied to Japanese students. *Psychologia*, 1957, **1**, 120–122.

Norbeck, E., & DeVos, G. Japan. In F. L. K. Hsu (Ed.), *Psychological Anthropology: Approaches to Culture and Personality*. Homewood, Illinois: Dorsey Press, 1961. Pp. 19–47.

Norman, W. T. Toward an adequate taxonomy of personality attributes. *Journal of Abnormal & Social Psychology*, 1963, **66**, 574–583.

Ohmura, M., & Sawa, H. Taylor Anxiety Scale in Japan. *Psychologia*, 1957, **1**, 123–126.

Okana, Y., & Spilka, B. Ethnic identity, alienation, and achievement orientation in Japanese-American families. *Journal of Cross-Cultural Psychology*, 1971, **2**, 273–282.

Oksenberg, L. Machiavellianism in traditional and westernized Chinese students. In R. Christie & F. L. Geis, *Studies in Machiavellianism*. New York: Academic Press, 1970.

Onoda, L. Personality characteristics and attitudes toward achievement among mainland high-achieving and underachieving Japanese-American Sansei. *Journal of Educational Psychology*, 1976, **68**, 151–156.

Osaka, R. Intelligence tests in Japan. *Psychologia*, 1961, **4**, 218–234.

Osgood, C. E., May, W. H., & Miron, M. S. *Cross-cultural Universals of Affective Meaning*. Urbana, Illinois: University of Illinois Press, 1975.

Osgood, C. E., Suci, G. J., & Tannenbaum, P. H. *The Measurement of Meaning*. Urbana, Illinois: University of Illinois Press, 1957.

Pai, T., Sung, S. M., & Hsu, E. H. The application of Thurstone's Personality Schedule to Chinese subjects. *Journal of Social Psychology*, 1937, **8**, 47–72.

Palmer, H. *Land of the Second Chance*. Lethbridge, Alberta: Lethbridge Herald, 1972.

Palmer, H. D. Patterns of racism: Attitudes towards Chinese and Japanese in Alberta, 1920–1950. *Social History*, 1980, **13**, 137–160.

Park, R. E. *Race and Culture*. Glencoe, Illinois: Free Press, 1950.

Paschal, B. J., & Kuo, Y-Y. Anxiety and self-concept among American and Chinese college students. *College Student Journal*, 1973, **7**, 7-13.

Peal, E., & Lambert, W. E. The relation of bilingualism to intelligence. *Psychological Monographs*, 1962, **76**, No. 546.

Peters, L., & Ellis, E. N. *An Analysis of WISC Profiles of Chinese-Canadian Children with Specific Reading Disabilities in Chinese, English, or Both Languages*. Vancouver School Board, Unpublished Report, 1970.

Petersen, W. *Japanese Americans: Oppression and Success*. New York: Random House, 1971.

Phua, S. L. *Ability Factors and Familial Psychosocial Circumstances: Chinese and Malays of Singapore*. Ph.D. Thesis, University of Alberta, 1976.

Podmore, D., & Chaney, D. Educational experience as an influence on ''Modern'' and ''Traditional'' attitudes: Some evidence from Hong Kong. *Journal of Social Psychology*, 1974, **94**, 139-140.

Portenier, L. G. Abilities and interests of Japanese-American high school seniors. *Journal of Social Psychology*, 1947, **25**, 53-61.

Porteus, S. D. Racial group differences in mentality. *Tabulae Biologicae Haag*, 1939, **18**, 66-75.

Porteus, S. D., & Babcock, H. *Temperament and Race*. Boston, Massachusetts: Badger, 1926.

Potter, J. M. The structure of rural Chinese society in new territories. In I. C. Jarvie (Ed.), *Hong Kong: A Society in Transition*. London: Routledge & Kegan Paul, 1969. Pp. 3-28.

Preiswerk, R., & Perrot, D. *Ethnocentrism and History*. New York: Nok Publishers International, 1978.

Prichard, A., Bashaw, W. L., & Anderson, H. E. A comparison of the structure of behavioral maturity between Japanese and American primary-grade children. *Journal of Social Psychology*, 1972, **86**, 167-173.

Pusey, H. C. Arithmetic achievement of Japanese-Americans. *Mathematics Teacher*, 1945, **38**, 172-174.

Pyle, W. H. A study of the mental and physical characteristics of the Chinese. *School & Society*, 1918, **8**, 264-269.

Ramcharan, S. Special problems of immigrant children in the Toronto school system. In A. Wolfgang (Ed.), *Education of Immigrant Students*. Toronto: OISE, 1975. Pp. 95-106.

Rashke, V. Premarital sexual permissiveness of college students in Hong Kong. *Journal of Comparative Family Studies*, 1976, **7**, 65-74.

Reitz, H. J., & Groff, G. K. Economic development and belief in locus of control among factory workers in four countries. *Journal of Cross-Cultural Psychology*, 1974, **5**, 344-355.

Richmond, A. H. *Post-War Immigrants in Canada*. Toronto: Toronto University Press, 1967.

Rin, H., Schooler, C., & Caudill, W. A. Culture, social structure, and psychopathology in Taiwan and Japan. *Journal of Nervous & Mental Diseases*, 1973, **157**, 296-312.

Rodd, W. G. A cross-cultural study of Taiwan's schools. *Journal of Social Psychology*, 1959, **50**, 3-36. (a)

Rodd, W. G. Cross-cultural use of ''The Study of Values.'' *Psychologia*, 1959, **2**, 157-164. (b)

Rotter, J. B. Generalized expectancies for internal versus external control of reinforcement. *Psychological Monographs*, 1966, **80**, No. 609.

Rowe, E. *Failure in School: Aspects of the Problem in Hong Kong*. Hong Kong University Press, Educ. Res. Publication No. 3, 1966.

Ryback, D., Sanders, A. L., Lorentz, J., & Koestenblatt, M. Child-rearing practices reported by studies in six cultures. *Journal of Social Psychology*, 1980, **110**, 153-162.

Sagara, M., Yamamoto, K., Nishimura, H., & Akoto, H. A study on the semantic structure of Japanese language by the Semantic Differential method. *Japanese Psychological Research*, 1961, **3**, 146-156.

Saito, H., Inoue, M., & Nomura, Y. Information processing of *Kanji* (Chinese characters) and *Kana* (Japanese characters): The close relationship among graphemic, phonemic, and semantic aspects. *Psychologia*, 1979, **22**, 195–206.

Sakamoto, T., & Makita, K. Reading in Japan. In J. A. Downing (Ed.), *Comparative Reading*. New York: Macmillan, 1973. Pp. 440–465.

Sandiford, P., & Kerr, R. Intelligence of Chinese and Japanese children. *Journal of Educational Psychology*, 1926, **17**, 361–367.

Sangsingkeo, P. Buddhism and some effects on the rearing of children in Thailand. In W. Caudill & T-Y. Lin (Eds.), *Mental Health Research in Asia and the Pacific*. Honolulu, Hawaii: East-West Center Press, 1969. Pp. 286–295.

Sartorius, N., Jablensky, A., & Shapiro, R. Cross-cultural differences in the short-term prognosis of schizophrenic psychoses. *Schizophrenia Bulletin*, 1978, **4**, 102–113.

Sato, K., & Sonohara, T. A proposal for an international study of suicide. *Psychologia*, 1957, **1**, 71–73.

Scanlon, S. N., Dixon, P. W., Roper, R. E. *et al*. A preliminary study of the relationship between personality and cultural values among Japanese nationals. *Psychologia*, 1980, **23**, 87–100.

Schmid, C. F., & Nobbe, C. E. Socioeconomic differentials among nonwhite races. *American Sociological Review*, 1965, **30**, 909–922.

Schutz, W. C. *Firo-B*. Palo Alto, California: Consulting Psychologists Press, 1966.

Schwarting, F. G. A comparison of the WISC and WISC-R. *Psychology in the Schools*, 1976, **13**, 139–141.

Schwartz, A. J. *Traditional Values and Contemporary Achievement of Japanese-American Pupils*. Los Angeles, California: Center for the Study of Evaluation, 1970.

Schwartz, A. J. The culturally advantaged: A study of Japanese-American pupils. *Sociological & Social Research*, 1971, **55**, 341–353.

Scofield, R. W., & Sun, C-W. A comparative study of the differential effect upon personality of Chinese and American child training practices. *Journal of Social Psychology*, 1960, **52**, 221–224.

Scott, S. *The Relation of Divergent Thinking to Bilingualism: Cause or Effect*. Unpublished Report, McGill University, 1973.

Seagoe, M. V., & Murakami, K. A comparative study of children's play in America and Japan. *California Journal of Educational Research*, 1961, **12**, 124–130.

Seifert, J., Draguns, J. G., & Caudill, W. Role orientation, sphere dominance, and social competence as bases of psychiatric diagnosis in Japan. *J. Abnormal Psychology*, 1971, **78**, 101–106.

Shaw, M. E., & Iwawaki, S. Attribution of responsibility by Japanese and Americans as a function of age. *Journal of Cross-Cultural Psychology*, 1972, **3**, 71–81.

Shen, E. Differences between Chinese and American reactions to the Bernreuter Personality Inventory. *Journal of Social Psychology*, 1936, **7**, 471–474.

Shizuru, L., & Marsella, A. J. The sensory processes of Japanese-American and Caucasian-American students. *Journal of Social Psychology*, 1981, **114**, 147–158.

Sibatani, A. Inscrutable epigenetics of the Japanese brain: A book review. *Journal of Social & Biological Structures*, 1980, **3**, 255–266. (a)

Sibatani, A. It may turn out that the language we learn alters the physical operation of our brains. *Science*, 1980, **80**, 24–27. (b)

Singh, P. N., Huang, S. C., & Thompson, G. G. A comparative study of selected attitudes, values, and personality characteristics of American, Chinese, and Indian students. *Journal of Social Psychology*, 1962, **57**, 123–132.

Sloggett, B. B., Gallimore, R., & Kubany, E. S. A comparative analysis of fantasy need achievement among high and low achieving male Hawaiian-Americans. *Journal of Cross-Cultural Psychology*, 1970, **1**, 53–61.

References

& Kitano, H. H. L. Stereotypes as a measure of success. *Journal of Social Issues*, 1973, **29**, -98.

& Sue, D. W. Chinese-American personality and mental health. *Amerasia Journal*, 1971, **1**, -49.

& Sue, D. W. MMPI comparisons between Asian-American and non-Asian students utiliz- ; a student health psychiatric clinic. *Journal of Counseling Psychology*, 1974, **21**, 423–427.

Sue, D. W., & Sue, D. Asian Americans as a minority group. *American Psychologist*, 75, **30**, 906–910.

Zane, N., & Ito, J. Alcohol drinking patterns among Asian and Caucasian Americans. *urnal of Cross-Cultural Psychology*, 1979, **10**, 41–56.

1, M. A. *Federal Policy and the Japanese Canadians: 1942–1950*. M.A. Thesis, University Calgary, 1977.

s, P. M. The intelligence of Chinese in Hawaii. *School & Society*, 1924, **19**, 442.

ni, K. Development of dependency in female adolescents and young adults. *Japanese ychological Research*, 1974, **16**, 179–185.

ni, S. A comparative factorial analysis of semantic structures of Rorschach inkblots in iversity students and juvenile delinquents. *Japanese Psychological Research*, 1965, **7**, –74.

na, S. *A Child in Prison Camp*. Toronto: Tundra Books, 1971.

K. A tentative scale for measuring general intelligence by non-language tests. *Japanese urnal of Psychology*, 1934, **9**, 62–65.

Y. Values in the subjective culture: A social psychological view. *Journal of Cross-Cultural ychology*, 1972, **3**, 57–69.

Y. A cross-cultural psycholinguistic study of attitudes toward nuclear-space development. *panese Psychological Research*, 1973, **15**, 65–81.

Matsumi, J., & Marsella, A. J. Cross-cultural variations in the phenomenological experience depression. *Journal of Cross-Cultural Psychology*, 1976, **7**, 379–396.

J. M. *Growth at Adolescence*. Oxford: Blackwell Scientific Publications, 1962.

na, S. The structure of rejecting attitudes toward the mentally ill in Japan. In W. Caudill & -Y. Lin (Eds.), *Mental Health Research in Asia and the Pacific*. Honolulu, Hawaii: East- 'est Center Press, 1969. Pp. 195–215.

F., Arkoff, A., & Elkind, L. Conceptions of mental health in several Asian and American oups. *Journal of Social Psychology*, 1964, **62**, 21–27.

ke, R. L. *Stanford–Binet Intelligence Scale: 1972 Norms Table*. Boston, Massachusetts: oughton Mifflin, 1973.

J. N. Intermarriage and ethnic boundaries: The Japanese American case. *Journal of Social sues*, 1973, **29**, 49–66.

e, E. P. Lessons about giftedness and creativity from a nation of 115 million overachievers. *ifted Child Quarterly*, 1980, **24**, 10–14.

e, E. P., Wu, J. J., Gowan, J. C., & Aliotti, N. C. Creative functioning of monolingual and lingual children in Singapore. *Journal of Educational Psychology*, 1970, **61**, 72–75.

, H. C., Tanaka, Y., & Shanmugam, A. V. Interpersonal attitudes among American, Indian, d Japanese students. *International Journal of Psychology*, 1966, **1**, 177–206.

V. C., & Pu, A. S. T. Self-ratings of the Chinese. *School & Society*, 1927, **26**, 213–216.

-S. H. Chinese immigration through communist Chinese eyes: An introduction to the his- riography. In N. Hundley (Ed.), *The Asian American: The Historical Experience*. Santa arbara, California: Clio Books, 1976. Pp. 53–66.

M. S. Attitudes toward the disabled: A cross-cultural study. *Journal of Social Psychology*, 972, **87**, 311–312.

W-S., & Hsu, J. Chinese culture, personality formation and mental illness. *International urnal of Social Psychiatry*, 1969, **16**, 5–14.

References

Smith, M. E. The direction of reading and the effect of foreign-l:
learning to read. *Journal of Genetic Psychology*, 1932, *40*, 4:

Smith, M. E. A comparison of the neurotic tendencies of students
Hawaii. *Journal of Social Psychology*, 1938, **9**, 395–417.

Smith, M. E. Some light on the problem of bilingualism as found f
mastery of English among preschool children of non-America
Psychological Monographs, 1939, **21**, 119–284.

Smith, M. E. A comparison of judgment of prejudice toward certain r
since the entry of the United States into World War II. *Journal (
393–400.

Smith, M. E. Have the neurotic tendencies of the students at the Univ
the war began? *Journal of Social Psychology*, 1945, **21**, 179-

Smith, M. E. Measurement of vocabularies of young bilingual childre
Journal of Genetic Psychology, 1949, **74**, 305–310.

Smith, M. E. Progress in the use of English after 22 years by childrer
Journal of Genetic Psychology, 1957, **90**, 255–258.

Smith, S. Language and non-verbal test performance of racial group
fourteen-year interval. *Journal of General Psychology*, 1942,

Smith, W. C. *Americans in Process: A Study of our Citizens of (
Michigan: Edwards Bros., 1937.

Sollenberger, R. T. Chinese-American child-rearing practices and ju
Social Psychology, 1968, **74**, 13–23.

Sowell, T. *Race and Economics*. New York: McKay, 1975.

Sowell, T. (Ed.) *Essay and Data on American Ethnic Groups*.
Institute, 1978.

Statistics Canada. *1971 Census of Canada*. Ottawa: Information C

Stewart, L. H., Dole, A. A., & Harris, Y. Y. Cultural differences
American Educational Research Journal, 1967, **4**, 19–30.

Stodolsky, S. S., & Lesser, G. Learning patterns in the disadvant
view, 1967, **37**, 546–593.

Stoessinger, J. G. China and America: The burden of the past. *Ame
1970, **24**, 579–596.

Stoetzel, J. *Without the Chrysanthemum and the Sword: A Study of t.
Japan*. New York: Columbia University Press, 1955.

Stoller, A. Parameters of mental illness and mental health: A publi
& T-Y. Lin (Eds.), *Mental Health Research in Asia and*
East-West Center Press, 1969. Pp. 3–20.

Stricker, G., Takahashi, S., & Zax, M. Semantic Differential di
Japanese and American students. *Journal of Social Psycholc*

Strong, E. K. *The Second Generation Japanese Problem*. Stanford
Press, 1934. Reprinted, New York: Arno Press, 1970.

Sue, D. W., & Frank, A. C. A typological approach to the psy
Japanese American college males. *Journal of Social Issues*,

Sue, D. W., & Kirk, B. A. Psychological characteristics of Chine:
Counseling Psychology, 1972, **19**, 471–478.

Sue, D. W., & Kirk, B. A. Differential characteristics of Japanese-
college students. *Journal of Counseling Psychology*, 1973,

Sue, D. W., & Sue, S. Counseling Chinese-Americans. *Personne*
637–644.

Sue, D. W., & Sue, D. Understanding Asian-Americans: The r
Guidance Journal, 1973, **51**, 387–389.

Tsujioka, T., & Cattell, R. B. A cross-cultural comparison of second-stratum questionnaire personality factor-structures—Anxiety and Extraversion—in America and Japan. *Journal of Social Psychology*, 1965, **65**, 205–219.

Tsunoda, T. Contralateral shift of cerebral dominance for nonvocal sounds during speech perception. *Journal of Auditory Research*, 1969, **9**, 221–229.

Tsunoda, T. The difference of the cerebral dominance of vowel sounds among different languages. *Journal of Auditory Research*, 1971, **11**, 305–314.

Tsunoda, T. Functional differences between right- and left-cerebral hemispheres detected by the key-tapping method. *Brain & Language*, 1975, **2**, 152–170.

Tsushima, W. T., & Hogan, T. P. Verbal ability and school achievement of bilingual and monolingual children of different ages. *Journal of Educational Research*, 1975, **68**, 349–353.

Tuddenham, R. D. A "Piagetian" test of cognitive development. In W. B. Dockrell (Ed.), *On Intelligence*. Toronto: OISE, 1970. Pp. 49–70.

Tuddenham, R. D., Brooks, J., & Milkovich, L. Mothers' reports of behavior of ten-year-olds and relationships with sex, ethnicity, and mother's education. *Developmental Psychology*, 1974, **10**, 959–995.

Tyler, L. E. *The Psychology of Human Differences* (3rd ed.). New York: Appleton-Century-Crofts, 1965.

U.S. Department of Commerce. *1970 Census of Population*. Washington, D.C.: U.S. Government Printing Office, 1973.

Vandenberg, S. G. The primary mental abilities of Chinese students: A comparative study of the stability of a factor structure. *Annals of the New York Academy of Science*, 1959, **79**, 257–304.

Vandenberg, S. G. The primary mental abilities of South American students. *Multivariate Behavioral Research*, 1967, **2**, 175–198.

Vernon, P. E. *Intelligence and Attainment Tests*. London: University of London Press, 1960.

Vernon, P. E. *The Structure of Human Abilities* (2nd ed.). London: Methuen, 1961.

Vernon, P. E. *Personality Assessment: A Critical Survey*. London: Methuen, 1964.

Vernon, P. E. *Intelligence and Cultural Environment*. London: Methuen, 1969.

Vernon, P. E. *Intelligence: Heredity and Environment*. San Francisco, California: Freeman, 1979.

Vinacke, W. E. Stereotyping among national-racial groups in Hawaii: A study in ethnocentrism. *Journal of Social Psychology*, 1949, **30**, 265–291. (a)

Vinacke, W. E. The judgment of facial expressions by three national-racial groups in Hawaii. I. Caucasian faces. *Journal of Personality*, 1949, **17**, 407–429. (b)

Vinacke, W. E., & Fong, R. W. The judgment of facial expressions by three national–racial groups in Hawaii. II. Oriental faces. *Journal of Social Psychology*, 1955, **41**, 185–195.

Vogel, E. F. A preliminary view of family and mental health in urban Communist China. In W. Caudill & T-Y. Lin (eds.), *Mental Health Research in Asia and the Pacific*. Honolulu, Hawaii: East-West Center Press, 1969. Pp. 393–404.

Vogel, E. F. *Japan as Number One: Lessons for America*. Cambridge, Massachusetts: Harvard University Press, 1979.

Walcott, G. D. The intelligence of Chinese students. *School & Society*, 1920, **11**, 474–480.

Walker, B. M. Ideological underpinnings of education—China and the West. *Australia & New Zealand Journal of Sociology*, 1976, **12**, 101–105.

Walsh, J. Making the multiuniversity more multiethnic. *Science*, 1980, **209**, No. 4455, 473–475.

Wang, S. L. A demonstration of the language difficulty involved in comparing racial groups by means of verbal intelligence tests. *Journal of Applied Psychology*, 1926, **10**, 102–106.

Warden, K. Calgary's Chinese community. Calgary, Alberta: *The Calgary Herald*, March 10, 1979.

Watanabe, C. Self-expression and the Asian-American experience. *Personnel & Guidance Journal*, 1973, **51**, 390–396.

Werner, E. E. Infants around the world: Cross-cultural studies of psychomotor development from birth to two years. *Journal of Cross-Cultural Psychology*, 1972, **3**, 111–134.

Werner, E. E., Bierman, J. M., & French, F. E. *The Children of Kauai*. Honolulu, Hawaii: University Press of Hawaii, 1971.

Werner, E., & Simonian, K. The social maturity of pre-school children in Hawaii: Result of a community survey and a review of two decades of research. *Journal of Social Psychology*, 1966, **69**, 197-207.

Werner, E. E., Simonian, K., & Smith, R. S. Ethnic and socioeconomic status differences in abilities and achievement among preschool and school-age children in Hawaii. *Journal of Social Psychology*, 1968, **75**, 43-59.

Weyl, N. Some comparative performance indexes of American ethnic minorities. *Mankind Quarterly*, 1969, **9**, 106-119.

Wilson, G. D., & Iwawaki, S. Social attitudes in Japan. *Journal of Social Psychology*, 1980, **112**, 175-180.

Wilson, J. R., DeFries, J. C., McClearn, G. E. *et al*. Cognitive abilities: Use of family data as a control to assess sex and age differences in two ethnic groups. *International Journal of Aging & Human Development*, 1975, **6**, 261-276.

Wilson, K. W. *Environmental Relations to Cognitive Abilities Across Three Ethnic Groups*. Unpublished Ph.D. Thesis, University of Hawaii, 1977.

Witkin, H. A., & Berry, J. W. Psychological differentiation in cross-cultural perspective. *Journal of Cross-Cultural Psychology*, 1975, **6**, 4-87.

Witty, P. A., & Lehman, H. C. Racial differences: The dogma of superiority. *Journal of Social Psychology*, 1930, **1**, 394-418.

Wolff, P. H. Ethnic differences in alcohol sensitivity. *Science*, 1972, **175**, 449-450.

Wong, E. K. *Dimensionality of Hawaiian Ethnic Groups*. Unpublished Report, Hawaiian Educational Research Association, 1979.

Wong, L. The Chinese experience. *Civil Rights Digest*, 1976, **9**, 33-35.

World Health Organization. *Schizophrenia: An International Follow-up Study*. New York: Wiley, 1979.

Wright, B. R. Social aspects of change in the Chinese family pattern in Hong Kong. *Journal of Social Psychology*, 1964, **63**, 31-39.

Yang, K-S., & Bond, M. H. Ethnic affirmation by Chinese bilinguals. *Journal of Cross-Cultural Psychology*, 1980, **11**, 411-425.

Yee, A. H. Myopic perceptions and textbooks: Chinese Americans' search for identity. *Journal of Social Issues*, 1973, **29**, 99-113.

Yee, A. H. Spirit and values of the Chinese people. *School Psychology Digest*, 1974, **3**(2), 25-35.

Yee, A. H. Asian Americans in educational research. *Educational Researcher*, 1976, **5**(2), 5-8.

Yee, L. Y., & LaForge, R. Relationship between mental abilities, social class, and exposure to English in Chinese fourth graders. *Journal of Educational Psychology*, 1974, **66**, 826-834.

Yeh, E-K. The Chinese mind and human freedom. *International Journal of Social Psychiatry*, 1972, **18**, 132-136.

Yeh, E-K., & Chu, H-M. The images of Chinese and American character: Cross-cultural adaptation by Chinese students. In W. P. Lebra (Ed.), *Youth, Socialization, and Mental Health*. Honolulu: University Press of Hawaii, 1974. Pp. 200-216.

Yeung, K. T. The intelligence of Chinese children in San Francisco and vicinity. *Journal of Applied Psychology*, 1921, **5**, 267-274.

Yoshioka, J. G. A study of bilingualism. *Journal of Genetic Psychology*, 1929, **36**, 473-479.

Zax, M., & Takahashi, S. Cultural influences on response style: Comparisons of Japanese and American college students. *Journal of Social Psychology*, 1967, **71**, 3-10.

Author Index

Subject Index[1]

[1]Titles of tests of abilities, achievements, attitudes, and personality traits are not listed separately for Canadian, Hawaiian, Hong Kong, or other Orientals, but are grouped together under Chinese (CA and CC) or Japanese (JA and JJ).

PERSONALITY AND PSYCHOPATHOLOGY
A Series of Monographs, Texts, and Treatises

David T. Lykken, Editor

1. The Anatomy of Achievement Motivation, *Heinz Heckhausen.**
2. Cues, Decisions, and Diagnoses: A Systems-Analytic Approach to the Diagnosis of Psychopathology, *Peter E. Nathan.**
3. Human Adaptation and Its Failures, *Leslie Phillips.**
4. Schizophrenia: Research and Theory, *William E. Broen, Jr.**
5. Fears and Phobias, *I. M. Marks.*
6. Language of Emotion, *Joel R. Davitz.*
7. Feelings and Emotions, *Magda Arnold.*
8. Rhythms of Dialogue, *Joseph Jaffe* and *Stanley Feldstein.*
9. Character Structure and Impulsiveness, *David Kipnis.*
10. The Control of Aggression and Violence: Cognitive and Physiological Factors, *Jerome L. Singer* (Ed.).
11. The Attraction Paradigm, *Donn Byrne.*
12. Objective Personality Assessment: Changing Perspectives, *James N. Butcher* (Ed.).
13. Schizophrenia and Genetics. *Irving I. Gottesman* and *James Shields.**
14. Imagery and Daydream Methods in Psychotherapy and Behavior Modification, *Jerome L. Singer.*
15. Experimental Approaches to Psychopathology, *Mitchell L. Kietzman, Samuel Sutton,* and *Joseph Zubin* (Eds.).
16. Coping and Defending: Processes of Self-Environment Organization, *Norma Haan.*
17. The Scientific Analysis of Personality and Motivation, *R. B. Cattell* and *P. Kline.*
18. The Determinants of Free Will: A Psychological Analysis of Responsible, Adjustive Behavior, *James A. Easterbrook.*
19. The Psychopath in Society, *Robert J. Smith.*
20. The Fears of Adolescents, *J. H. Bamber.*
21. Cognitive–Behavioral Interventions: Theory, Research, and Procedures, *Philip C. Kendall* and *Steven D. Hollon* (Eds.).
22. The Psychobiology of the Depressive Disorders: Implications for the Effects of Stress, *Richard A. Depue* (Ed.).
23. The Mental Health of Women, *Marcia Guttenberg, Susan Salasin,* and *Deborah Belle* (Eds.).
24. Assessment Strategies for Cognitive–Behavioral Interventions, *Philip C. Kendall* and *Steven D. Hollon* (Eds.).

*Titles initiated during the series editorship of Brendan Maher.

PERSONALITY AND PSYCHOPATHOLOGY